SQL Server 2012 Integration Services Design Patterns

Andy Leonard
Matt Masson
Tim Mitchell
Jessica M. Moss
Michelle Ufford

Apress·

SQL Server 2012 Integration Services Design Patterns

ISBN-13 (pbk): 978-1-4302-3771-6

ISBN-13 (electronic): 978-1-4302-3772-3

President and Publisher: Paul Manning
Lead Editor: Jonathan Gennick
Developmental Editor: Richard Carey
Technical Reviewers: David Dye, Sergio Filho, Allan Mitchell, and David Stein
Editorial Board: Steve Anglin, Ewan Buckingham, Gary Cornell, Louise Corrigan, Morgan Ertel, Jonathan Gennick,
    Jonathan Hassell, Robert Hutchinson, Michelle Lowman, James Markham, Matthew Moodie, Jeff Olson, Jeffrey
    Pepper, Douglas Pundick, Ben Renow-Clarke, Dominic Shakeshaft, Gwenan Spearing, Matt Wade, Tom Welsh
Coordinating Editor: Adam Heath
Copy Editor: Chandra Clarke
Compositor: SPi Global
Indexer: SPi Global
Artist: SPi Global
Cover Designer: Anna Ishchenko

Distributed to the book trade worldwide by Springer Science+Business Media New York, 233 Spring Street, 6th Floor, New York, NY 10013. Phone 1-800-SPRINGER, fax (201) 348-4505, e-mail orders-ny@springer-sbm.com, or visit www.springeronline.com.

For information on translations, please e-mail rights@apress.com, or visit www.apress.com.

Apress and friends of ED books may be purchased in bulk for academic, corporate, or promotional use. eBook versions and licenses are also available for most titles. For more information, reference our Special Bulk Sales–eBook Licensing web page at www.apress.com/bulk-sales.

Any source code or other supplementary materials referenced by the author in this text is available to readers at www.apress.com/9781430237716. For detailed information about how to locate your book's source code, go to www.apress.com/source-code.

For my loving wife, Christy.
--Andy Leonard

Contents at a Glance

Contents

Foreword

For me, one of the great pleasures of working at Microsoft was shepherding new products from concept to release. However, it was even more fulfilling to witness the birth and growth of new communities of users, for what is a product without a user? Just bits and bytes on a disk. In my role as Group Product Manager of the SQL Server Integration Services team, it was my privilege to watch the evolution of both the SSIS application and the social network of users.

The Integration Services team, under the exceptional leadership of Kamal Hathi, delivered a product in 2005– SQL Server Integration Services– that was intended to be not only a powerful application in its own right, but a platform for customers and partners to extend and expand as their data integration needs changed and grew over time. Over the years (and through several versions of the product) SQL Server Integration Services has grown to become an industry-leading technology.

When we started developing what users now call SSIS, anyone building a data warehouse had only two choices: expensive, highly specialized tools for Extraction Transformation and Loading (ETL), or tedious, difficult-to-maintain, custom coding. With SSIS we wanted to break through those traditional restrictions: to deliver a truly scalable tool, simple enough for the beginner, but with the extensibility and programmability of a platform for the expert.

Little did we anticipate how eagerly the SQL Server user community would embrace this tool! Our user base grew quickly, and, as in any group endeavor, natural leaders emerged. The authors of this splendid book are, quite simply, among the most outstanding contributors to the SSIS social network. They are leaders not only because of their skills, but because of their tireless support and commitment to helping others. This book distills that learning, and that community focus, into a volume to keep by your keyboard for years.

The challenge with a tool such as SSIS is that there are simply so many possibilities facing the user. If I can choose a prebuilt component, which one do I choose? If I can extend the capabilities with script, when should I do that? How do I choose between the many ways to load a slowly-changing-dimension table, or for handling XML?

SQL Server 2012 Integration Services Design Patterns not only provides solutions to such problems; even more usefully, this book channels the authors' extensive experience into *patterns*. In recent years, design patterns have proved their value to software developers as flexible templates for addressing recurring problems that still need specific implementation details. *SQL Server 2012 Integration Services Design Patterns* takes this approach, quite uniquely, into the world of data warehousing and ETL.

The result is a collaborative work by experts, suitable for beginners and advanced users alike.

Even though I moved on from the SSIS team, and from Microsoft, some years ago now, it is a pleasure for me to remain in touch with the user community I admire so much. And it is a honor for me to introduce you to this much-anticipated and valuable book.

Happy integrating!

Donald Farmer
VP Product Management, QlikTech

About the Authors

Andy Leonard is a SSIS trainer and consultant, SQL Server database and Integration Services developer, SQL Server data warehouse developer, community mentor, SQLBlog.com blogger, and engineer. He is co-author of *Professional SQL Server 2005 Integration Services* and *SQL Server MVP Deep Dives*. His background includes web application architecture and development, Visual Basic, ASP, SQL Server Integration Services (SSIS), and data warehouse development using SQL Server 2000, 2005 and 2008.

Matt Masson is a software development engineer working with the SQL Server Integration Services (SSIS) team. Matt has worked on many aspects of the SSIS product, including upgrade, performance, and overall user experience. He is a frequent presenter at Microsoft conferences, and maintains the SSIS Team blog (http://blogs.msdn.com/b/mattm/). Prior to joining Microsoft in 2006, Matt was a developer on a number of business intelligence reporting and analytical products. He lives in Montreal, Quebec, and works remotely with his Redmond-based team.

Tim Mitchell is a business intelligence consultant, database developer, speaker, and trainer. He has been working with SQL Server for more than eight years, primarily in business intelligence, ETL/SSIS, database development, and reporting. He has earned a number of industry certifications, holds a bachelor's degree in computer science from Texas A&M University at Commerce, and is a Microsoft SQL Server "Most Valuable Professional." Tim is a business intelligence consultant for Artis Consulting in the Dallas, Texas area. As an active member of the community, Tim has spoken at venues including numerous SQL Saturday events, Houston Tech Fest, and various user groups and PASS virtual chapters. He is a board member and speaker at the North Texas SQL Server User Group in Dallas, serves as the co-chair of the PASS BI Virtual Chapter, and is an active volunteer for PASS. Tim is an author and forum contributor on SQLServerCentral.com and has published dozens of SQL Server training videos on SQLShare.com. You can visit his website and blog at TimMitchell.net or follow him on Twitter at @Tim_Mitchell.

Jessica M. Moss is a well-known author, and speaker on Microsoft SQL Server business intelligence. She has created numerous data warehouse and business intelligence solutions for companies in different industries, and has delivered training courses on Integration Services, Reporting Services, and Analysis Services. While working for a major clothing retailer, Jessica participated in the SQL Server 2005 TAP program, where she developed best implementation practices for Integration Services. Jessica has authored technical content for multiple magazines, websites, and books, and has spoken internationally at conferences such as the PASS Community Summit, SharePoint Connections, and the SQLTeach International Conference. As a strong proponent of developing user-to-user community relations, Jessica actively participates in local user groups and code camps in central Virginia. In addition, Jessica volunteers her time to help educate people through the PASS organization.

Michelle Ufford is a SQL Server database developer, Integration Services developer, Microsoft SQL Server MVP, and self-proclaimed scripting junkie. She specializes in performance tuning and high-volume VLDB (very large database) development, although her experience also includes database automation, operational predictive analytics, and all stages of the data lifecycle— from OLTP to data warehousing. Michelle is an active member of the SQL Server community and a frequent presenter, most notably at PASS Summit. Michelle has a very popular blog at `SQLFool.com` and can be found on Twitter at `@sqlfool`.

About the Technical Reviewers

David Stein is a Senior Business Intelligence Consultant, specializing in designing, developing, and maintaining data warehouses using Microsoft BI Tools focusing on the health care sector. He enjoys helping others as an active volunteer with his local PASS Chapter, contributor to SQL University, and presenting at the local and regional level. He also blogs regularly at Made2Mentor.com.

Allan Mitchell is the joint owner of Copper Blue Consulting Ltd. Copper Blue Consulting focus on getting the right data to the right people at the right time and in the right format. We are passionate about data integrity and suitability. We have worked all over the world in a variety of industries and on projects both large and small. We specialise in Extract, Transform and Load Complex Event Processing Master Data Management Data Visualisation Operational and Predictive Analytics. We offer training as well as consultancy.

David Dye is a Microsoft SQL Server MVP, instructor, and author specializing in relational database management systems, business intelligence systems, reporting solutions, and Microsoft SharePoint. For the past 9 years David's expertise has been focused on Microsoft SQL Server development and administration. His work has earned him recognition as: a Microsoft MVP in 2009 and 2010, a moderator for the Microsoft Developer Network for SQL Server forums, Innovator of the Year runner-up in 2009 by SQL Server Magazine, and in the Training Associates Technical Trainer Spotlight in April 2011. David currently serves as a technical reviewer and coauthor with APress Publishing in the SQL Server 2012 series, and as an author with Packt Publishing.

Acknowledgments

I would like to thank my coauthors for agreeing to work with me on this project: Matt Masson, Tim Mitchell, Jessica Moss, and Michelle Ufford are awesome people and outstanding technologists, as this book will bear out. Our editorial team at Apress is top-shelf. I sincerely appreciate the leadership of Jonathan Gennick who shepherded this project through many months of writing, editing, and rewriting to deliver this manuscript in its current form. Kudos to Adam Heath and Mark Powers for their help and communications, and to several unnamed - yet vital - people at Apress for making this book possible.

I would like to extend special thanks to Donald Farmer for leading the Microsoft program to develop SSIS, and the many members of the SSIS team - past and present - who have labored to produce and support an outstanding enterprise data integration product. Many thanks to the members of the SSIS Community who selflessly share their expertise with me and others on forums and social media.

Whenever I sign up for a book project, Christy signs up, as well. For her unwavering love and dedication to me and our family, I thank her. I would also like to thank Stevie Ray, Emma, and Riley for as much patience as children their age can muster; and Steve and Tina Smith for their support and help.

–Andy Leonard

I am incredibly grateful to the large group of people who contributed to making this book a reality. To Andy Leonard, who first approached me about this idea some 2 years before its printing, I express my thanks for including me in this project. To Jessica Moss, Matt Masson, and Michelle Ufford, I am honored just to be named in the same publication as all of you. To Jonathan Gennick, Adam Heath, Mark Powers, and rest of the team at Apress, thank you for believing in us, and for keeping us on task and on schedule.

Just as importantly, I'd like to thank a smaller team closer to home. To my wife Rachel, to my kids Ryan, Evan, and Kaylee: thank you for being patient through this whole process. Even though your names aren't on the cover, you had as much invested in this book as I did.

–Tim Michell

The writing of this book has been a great experience with a dedicated team. Thank you to my wonderful coauthors: Andy Leonard, Matt Masson, Tim Mitchell, and Michelle Ufford and the Apress team: Jonathan Gennick, Adam Heath, and Mark Powers. Thank you to my friends and family for their patience as I disappeared to write for hours on end and the SQL community for letting me share my knowledge.

– Jessica M. Moss

First and foremost, I want to extend my deepest thanks to Andy Leonard for his efforts on this book. Andy is one of the smartest and nicest people I know, and I am deeply honored he invited me to be a part of this project. I also want to thank John Hoang and Brian Davis for their time and invaluable contributions to my chapters; the entire SSIS, PDW, and SQLCAT teams for building such incredible products and for sharing their knowledge with me; and Chris Leonard, who encouraged me to get involved in the SQL Server community one afternoon on our way to Starbucks. Little did I know the impact his advice would have on my life and career. I dedicate my writing to my children, Chloe and Ethan, who constantly amaze me and fill my life with such love and joy. To Eliza, whose inquisitive mind inspires me. And most of all, to my husband John, who is the most remarkable father, supportive friend, and loving husband anyone could hope for.

–Michelle Ufford

## CHAPTER 1

Metadata Collection

The first Integration Services design pattern we will cover is metadata collection. What do we mean by "metadata collection"? Good question. This chapter could also be called "Using SSIS to Save Time and Become an Awesome DBA." Many DBAs spend a large portion of time on monitoring activities such as verifying backups, alerting on scheduled job failures, creating schema snapshots ("just in case"), examining space utilization, and logging database growth over time, to name just a very few. Most RDBMS systems provide metadata to help DBAs monitor their systems. If you've been a DBA for a few years, you may even have a "tool bag" of scripts that you use to interrogate metadata. Running these scripts manually is easy when you have just one or two servers; however, this can quickly become unwieldly and consume a large portion of your time as your enterprise grows and as the number of database servers increases.

This chapter examines how to use Integration Services and the metadata that exists within SQL Server to automate some of these routine tasks.

Introducing SQL Server Data Tools

One of the major features of SQL Server 2012 is the introduction of SQL Server Data Tools (SSDT). SSDT replaces Business Intelligence Development Studio (BIDS) and leverages the maturity of the Visual Studio product to provide a unified development platform for SQL Server, Business Intelligence (BI), and .NET applications. This book is written using SSDT, although the appearance of the Integration Services designer interface is largely the same as BIDS 2008. SSDT provides backward compatibility for Integration Services 2008 packages via the SSIS Package Upgrade Wizard.

Tip   Don't have SQL Server Data Tools installed? SSDT is a free component of the SQL Server platform and is available to all SQL Server users. You can install SSDT from your SQL Server installation materials under the "Feature Selection" menu.

A Peek at the Final Product

Let's discuss the Integration Services package we will be creating in this chapter.

In SQL Server, we will do the following:

1. Create a database to act as our central repository for database monitoring.

2. Create a table to store a list of SQL Server instances that we wish to monitor.

3. Create a table for each of the data elements we wish to monitor (unused indexes and database growth).

In Integration Services, we will do the following:

1. Create a new Integration Services package.

2. Retrieve a list of SQL Server instances and store the list in a variable.

3. Create an OLE DB connection with a dynamically populated server name.

4. Iterate through each database and

   a. Retrieve current database and log file sizes for historical monitoring.

   b. Retrieve a list of index candidates for potential redesign or dropping.

   c. Update the Last Monitored value for each SQL Server instance.

This is a very flexible model that can easily be expanded to include many more monitoring tasks. A screenshot of the completed package is displayed in Figure 1-1.

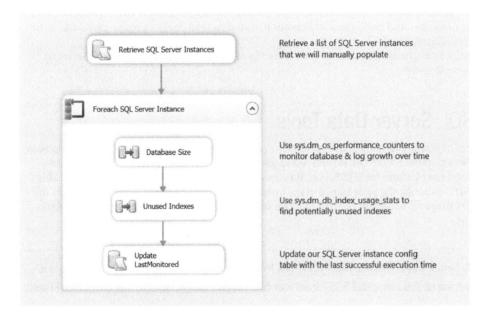

Figure 1-1. *The MetadataCollection package*

If this is not your first Integration Services package, maybe you've noticed that this package is missing a few best practices, such as error handling. In the interest of clarity, the package we create will focus only on core design patterns; however, we will call out best practices when applicable.

Also, please note that the T-SQL examples will only work with SQL Server 2005 or later.

SQL Server Metadata

Although metadata can be collected from any RDBMS that provides an interface for accessing it, this chapter uses SQL Server as its metadata source. The focus of this chapter is not on the actual metadata, but rather the pattern of metadata collection. Still, it is useful for you to have a basic understanding of the type of metadata that is available.

SQL Server exposes a wealth of information through catalog views, system functions, dynamic management views (DMVs), and dynamic management functions (DMFs). Let's briefly examine some of the metadata we will be using in this chapter.

■ **Tip**   SQL Server Books Online is a great resource for learning more about the types of metadata available in SQL Server. Try searching for "metadata functions," "catalog views," and "DMVs" for more information.

---

sys.dm_os_performance_counters

The sys.dm_os_performance_counters DMV returns server performance counters on areas including memory, wait stats, and transactions. This DMV is useful for reporting file sizes, page life expectancy, page reads and writes per second, and transactions per second, to name but a few.

sys.dm_db_index_usage_stats

The sys.dm_db_index_usage_stats DMV contains information on index utilization. Specifically, a counter is incremented every time an index has a seek, scan, lookup, or update performed. These counters are reinitialized whenever the SQL Server service is started. If you do not see a row in this DMV for a particular index, it means that a seek, scan, lookup, or update has not yet been performed since the last server reboot.

sys.dm_os_sys_info

The sys.dm_os_sys_info DMV contains information about server resources. Perhaps the most frequently used piece of information in this DMV is the *sqlserver_start_time* column, which tells you the last time the SQL Server service was started.

sys.tables

The sys.tables catalog view contains information about every table that exists within the database.

sys.indexes

The sys.indexes catalog view contains information about every index in the database. This includes information such as whether an index is clustered or nonclustered and whether the index is unique or nonunique.

sys.partitions

The sys.partitions catalog view gives visibility into the partitioning structure of an index. When an index has more than one partition, the data in the index is split into multiple physical structures that can be accessed using the single logical name. This technique is especially useful for dealing with large tables, such as a transaction history table. If a table is not partitioned, the table will still have a single row in sys.partitions.

sys.allocation_units

The sys.allocation_units catalog view contains information about the number of pages and rows that exist for an object. This information can be joined to the sys.partitions catalog view by joining the *container_id* to the *partition_id*.

Setting Up the Central Repository

Before we can begin development on our Integration Services package, we need to set up some prerequisites in SQL Server. First and foremost, we need to create a database that will act as our central data repository. This is where our list of SQL Server instances will reside and where we will store the metadata we retrieve for each SQL Server instance. Many enterprises also find it convenient to store all error and package logging to this same central database. This is especially beneficial in environments where there are numerous DBAs, developers, and servers, as it makes it easy for everyone to know where to look for information. The T-SQL code in Listing 1-1 creates the database we will use throughout the rest of this chapter.

Listing 1-1. Example of T-SQL Code to Create a SQL Server Database

```
USE [master];
GO

CREATE DATABASE [dbaCentralLogging]
    ON PRIMARY
    (
        NAME = N'dbaCentralLogging'
       ,FILENAME = N'C:\Program Files\Microsoft SQL Server\MSSQL11.MSSQLSERVER\
MSSQL\DATA\dbaCentralLogging.mdf'
       , SIZE = 1024MB
       , MAXSIZE = UNLIMITED
       , FILEGROWTH = 1024MB
    )
    LOG ON
    (
        NAME = N'dbaCentralLogging_log'
      , FILENAME = N'C:\Program Files\Microsoft SQL Server\MSSQL11.MSSQLSERVER\
MSSQL\DATA\dbaCentralLogging_log.ldf'
       , SIZE = 256MB
       , MAXSIZE = UNLIMITED
       , FILEGROWTH = 256MB
    );
GO
```

Please note that your file directory may differ from the one in the preceding example.

This code can be executed from SQL Server Management Studio (SSMS), as demonstrated in Figure 1-2, or from your favorite query tool.

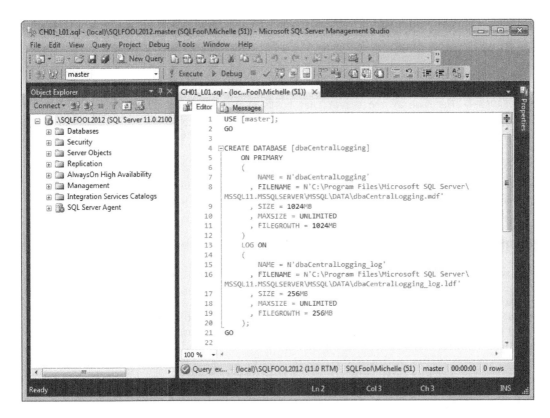

Figure 1-2. *SQL Server Management Studio 2012*

Next, we need a list of SQL Server instances that need to be monitored. The easiest way to accomplish this is to store a list of database instance names in a file or table. We will use the latter method. Using the code in Listing 1-2, create that table now.

Listing 1-2. Example of T-SQL Code to Create a Table for Monitoring SQL Server Instances

```
USE dbaCentralLogging;
GO

CREATE TABLE dbo.dba_monitor_SQLServerInstances
(
SQLServerInstance       NVARCHAR(128)
LastMonitored           SMALLDATETIME           NULL

    CONSTRAINT PK_dba_monitor_SQLServerInstances
        PRIMARY KEY CLUSTERED(SQLServerInstance)
);
```

You will then need to populate the table with the list of SQL Server instances you wish to monitor. The code in Listing 1-3 will walk you through how to do this, although you will need to use real SQL Server instances.

Listing 1-3. Example of T-SQL Code to Insert Data into the dba_monitor_SQLServerInstances Table

```
INSERT INTO dbo.dba_monitor_SQLServerInstances
(
        SQLServerInstance
)
SELECT @@SERVERNAME-- The name of the server that hosts the central repository
UNION ALL
SELECT 'YourSQLServerInstanceHere'-- Example of a SQL Server instance
UNION ALL
SELECT 'YourSQLServerInstance\Here';-- Example of a server with multiple instances
```

We still need to create two tables to store the metadata we collect, but we will create these as we get to the appropriate section in the package. Next, we will create our Integration Services package.

The Iterative Framework

In this section, we lay the foundation for our iterative framework. In other words, we will create a repeatable pattern for populating a variable with a list of SQL Server instances, then iterating through the list and performing an action on each server. Let's do this now.

First, open SSDT. Create a new project by navigating to **File➤New➤Project**. Click **Business Intelligence** under Installed Templates, and then click **Integration Services Project** in the Installed Templates window. Name the project **Meta data Collection**, as illustrated in Figure 1-3.

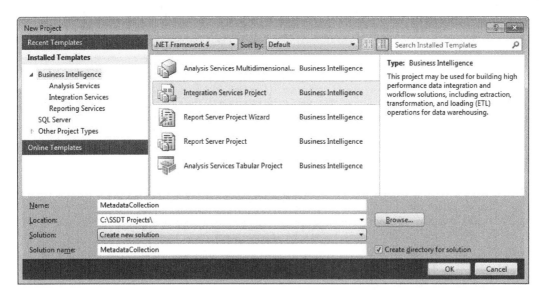

Figure 1-3. *New integration services project*

Please note that your default Location will most likely be different from the directory pictured in Figure 1-3.

We now need to create two variables. The first variable will be used to store the list of SQL Server instances we retrieve. The second variable will store a single instance name as we iterate through our list.

To access the variable menu, select **Variables** under the SSIS menu (Figure 1-4); you can also access the Variables menu by right-clicking the designer surface.

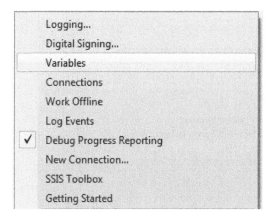

Figure 1-4. Opening the Variables menu

Add the following variables by clicking the **Add Variable** icon on the far left of the Variables menu, as illustrated in Figure 1-5:

- SQLServerList – Object
- SQLServerInstanceName – String

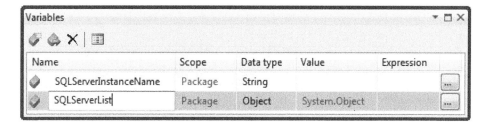

Figure 1-5. Package-scoped variables

Now that we have a place to store our list of instances, we're ready to retrieve them. Drag a new **Execute SQL Task** from the SSIS Toolbox onto the designer surface. Rename the task **Retrieve SQL Server Instances**, and then double-click it to open the Execute SQL Task Editor. Click the drop-down under Connection, and then select < **New connection...**>, as seen in Figure 1-6.

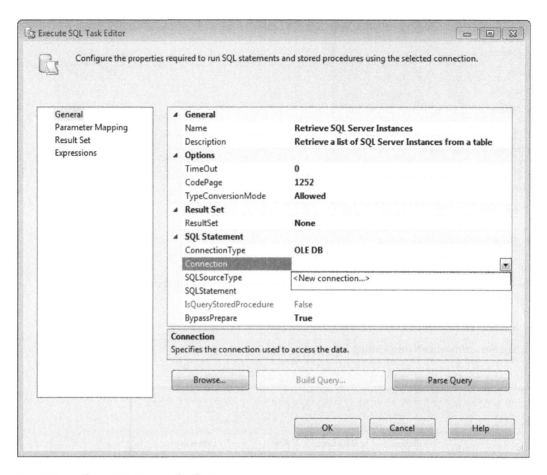

Figure 1-6. *The Execute SQL Task Editor*

In the Configure OLE DB Connection Manager menu, click **New**. In the Server Name field, enter the database server where you created the database in Listing 1-1. Regardless of whether you are using Windows or SQL Server authentication, make sure that the account has sufficient permissions to each of the instances in our *dba_monitor_SQLServerInstances* table. Under "Select or enter a database name," select **dbaCentralLogging** from the drop-down menu, as illustrated in Figure 1-7. Click **OK** to return to the Execute SQL Task Editor.

■ **Note**   Permissions requirements vary depending on the type of metadata you wish to retrieve. For more information on the permissions necessary to access a specific object, please refer to the object page within SQL Server Books Online.

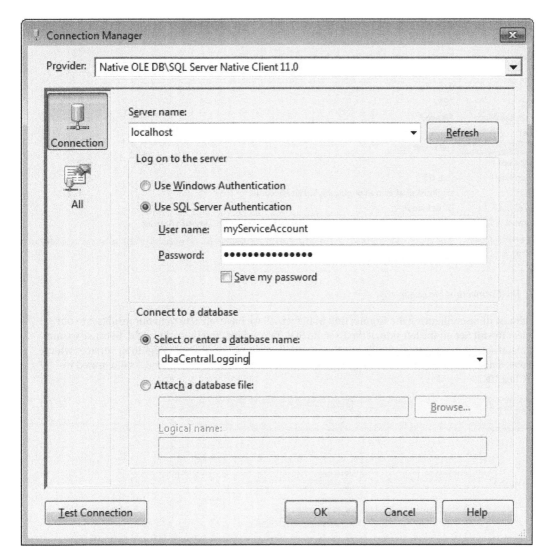

Figure 1-7. *The Connection Manager*

We now need to write the SQL statement that will retrieve the list of SQL Server instances. Click the [...] icon to the right of the SQLStatement field, and then enter the T-SQL code from Listing 1-4.

Listing 1-4. T-SQL Statement to Retrieve SQL Server Instances

```
SELECT SQLServerInstance FROM dbo.dba_monitor_SQLServerInstances;
```

Because we are retrieving an array of values, select **Full result set** from the ResultSet drop-down. Your Execute SQL Task Editor should now resemble Figure 1-8; however, your Connection values will likely be different.

⊿ **General**	
Name	**Retrieve SQL Server Instances**
Description	**Retrieve a list of SQL Server Instances from a table**
⊿ **Options**	
TimeOut	**0**
CodePage	**1252**
TypeConversionMode	**Allowed**
⊿ **Result Set**	
ResultSet	**Full result set**
⊿ **SQL Statement**	
ConnectionType	**OLE DB**
Connection	**localhost.dbaCentralLogging.myServiceAccount**
SQLSourceType	**Direct input**
SQLStatement	**SELECT SQLServerInstance FROM dbo.dba_monitor_SQLServerInstances;**
IsQueryStoredProcedure	False
BypassPrepare	**True**

Figure 1-8. *The Connection Manager*

We're almost done configuring the Connection Manager. All we have left is to map our result set to our variable. Select **Result Set** on the left side of the Execute SQL Task Editor, and then click **Add**. Because we are using a full result set, we must replace the Result Name with **0**. We now need to tell Integration Services which variable to use. Select **User::SQLServerList** from the drop-down under Variable Name, as illustrated in Figure 1-9. Click **OK**.

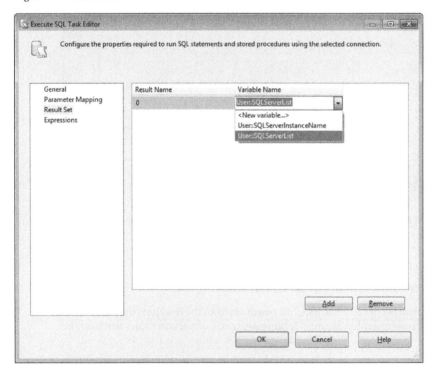

Figure 1-9. *Editing the result set*

Our Execute SQL Task is now complete. Next, we need to iterate through each server to retrieve the metadata we plan to monitor. This process will be encapsulated within a Foreach Loop Container, which will shred the list of SQL Server instances stored in the *SQLServerList* variable.

Add a Foreach Loop Container to the Control Flow and rename it **Foreach SQL Server Instance**. Connect it to the Execute SQL Task with a Success Precedence Constraint—in other words, drag the green arrow from the Execute SQL Task to the Foreach Loop Container, as seen in Figure 1-10.

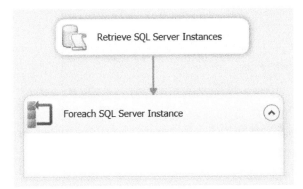

Figure 1-10. *Connecting the Execute SQL Task to the Foreach Loop Container*

Double-click the Foreach Loop Container to edit its properties. Click the **Collection** page, and then select **Foreach ADO Enumerator** in the Enumerator field. Under "ADO object source variable," select **User::SQLServerList**; leave "Enumeration mode" set to **Rows in the first table**. Your Collection properties should match those in Figure 1-11.

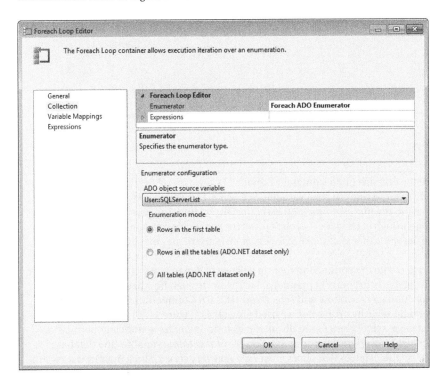

Figure 1-11. *The Foreach Loop Editor*

On the Variable Mappings page, map the *SQLServerInstanceName* variable to Index **0**, as demonstrated in Figure 1-12.

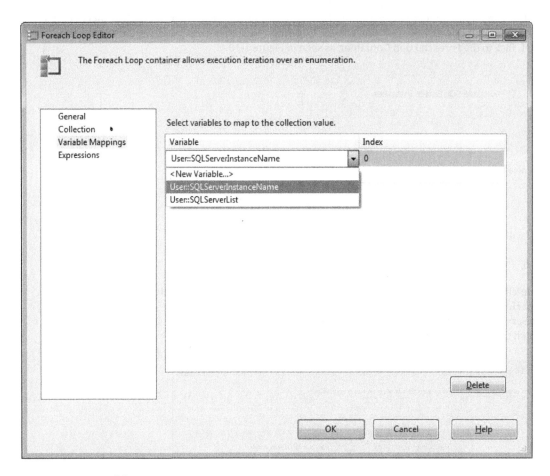

Figure 1-12. *Variable mappings*

Click the **OK** button to close the Foreach Loop Container Editor.

Let's review what we've done so far. We now have a variable, *SQLServerList*, which contains a list of all the SQL Server instances we inserted into the *dba_monitor_SQLServerInstances* table. The Foreach Loop Container then shreds this variable, walking through each value—each SQL Server instance name, in this case—one at a time. At each pass, it pushes the value of one of those SQL Server instance names into another variable, *SQLServerInstanceName*.

Before we proceed, we need to create the connection that we will use to dynamically connect to each server. We can accomplish this through the use of property expressions. Let's walk through how to do this now.

Right-click in the Connection Managers window and select **New OLE DB Connection**.Create a new connection using the same server and security properties we used previously (Figure 1-7), but select **master** as the database this time. The database server does not really matter as long as you have sufficient permissions because whatever value we enter will be overwritten by our *SQLServerInstanceName* variable. The database value does matter, however, because the database we select must exist on every server. Since **master** is a system database, it is a natural choice.

Click **OK** to close the Connection Manager Properties window. But we're not done with this connection just yet. Right-click the newly created connection and select **Properties**. Change the Name property to **DynamicSQLServerInstance**, and then click the [...] icon in the Expressions field. This will bring up the Property Expressions Editor. Select the Property value we wish to dynamically populate—**ServerName**, in this case—and enter **@[User::SQLServerInstanceName]** in the Expression field, as demonstrated in Figure 1-13. Optionally, you can also click the [...] icon in the Expression field to open the Expression Builder, which is helpful if you are not very familiar with Expression syntax.

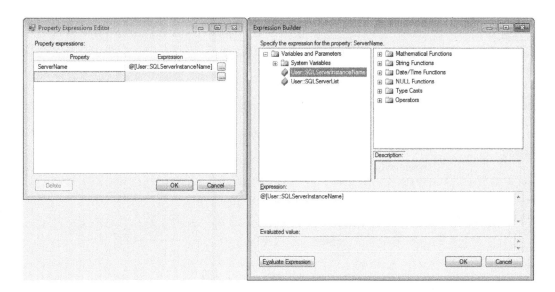

Figure 1-13. *Property Expressions Editor*

The properties of your connection should now resemble those shown in Figure 1-14.

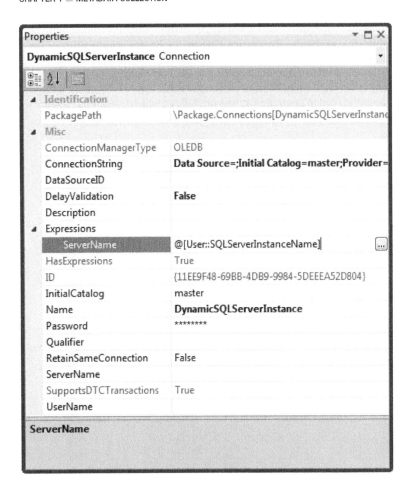

Figure 1-14. *Dynamic connection properties*

At this point, we now have a reusable framework for iterating through a list of SQL Server instances and doing *something* on each server. This in and of itself is a very valuable design pattern. However, because this is a chapter on metadata collection, I would be remiss if I did not actually demonstrate collecting and storing metadata. The next section will walk you through setting up two useful metadata extracts.

Metadata Collection

We're now ready to retrieve metadata from our list of servers. But what should we collect? An incredible wealth of information is available for retrieval, including security information, usage data, table schema snapshots, failed job details, fragmentation levels, and performance counters, to name just a few. For this first example, let's keep it simple and retrieve current database and log file size. This information is useful for historical database growth and capacity planning.

To accomplish this, we will create Data Flows within our Foreach Loop Container to retrieve the metadata from each server and store it in our *dbaCentralLogging* database. The Data Flow task is arguably the most frequently used task in Integration Services. It allows you to easily move data between servers and, if necessary, perform data conversions or cleansing.

Drag a **Data Flow** task from the SSIS Toolbox into the Foreach Loop Container and rename it **Database Size**. Double-clicking the **Data Flow** task will open the Data Flow Designer tab. Notice that the objects available within the Toolbox change once you are inside the Data Flow Designer. Drag the **OLE DB Source** icon into the Designer and rename it **Dynamic SQL Source**. Double-click it to edit its properties.

Select **DynamicSQLServerInstance** in the OLE DB Connection Manager drop-down. Change the Data Access Mode to **SQL Command**, and then copy the code from Listing 1-5 into the SQL Command Text box.

Listing 1-5. Example of T-SQL to Retrieve Current Data and Log File Sizes for All Databases on the Server

```
SELECT GETDATE()        AS [captureDate]
    , @@SERVERNAME      AS [serverName]
    , instance_name     AS [databaseName]
    , SUM(
        CASE
            WHEN counter_name='Data File(s) Size (KB)'
            THEN cntr_value
        END
     )                  AS 'dataSizeInKB'
    , SUM(
        CASE
            WHEN counter_name='Log File(s) Size (KB)'
            THEN cntr_value
        END
     )                  AS 'logSizeInKB'
FROM sys.dm_os_performance_counters
WHERE counter_nameIN ('Data File(s) Size (KB)'
                    , 'Log File(s) Size (KB)')

    /* optional: remove _Total to avoid accidentially
       double-counting in queries */
    AND instance_name<>'_Total'

GROUPBYinstance_name;
```

This query will produce results similar to the following.

captureDate	serverName	databaseName	dataSizeInKB	logSizeInKB
2012-04-29 19:52:21.543	LOCALHOST	_Total	1320896	274288
2012-04-29 19:52:21.543	LOCALHOST	AdventureWorks2012	193536	496
2012-04-29 19:52:21.543	LOCALHOST	dbaCentralLogging	1048576	262136
2012-04-29 19:52:21.543	LOCALHOST	master	4096	760
2012-04-29 19:52:21.543	LOCALHOST	model	2112	760
2012-04-29 19:52:21.543	LOCALHOST	msdb	14080	760
2012-04-29 19:52:21.543	LOCALHOST	mssqlsystemresource	40960	504
2012-04-29 19:52:21.543	LOCALHOST	ReportServer$SQL2012	5184	7032
2012-04-29 19:52:21.543	LOCALHOST	ReportServer$SQL2012TempDB	4160	1080
2012-04-29 19:52:21.543	LOCALHOST	tempdb	8192	760

```
(10 row(s) affected)
```

Your OLE DB Source Editor should now resemble the Editor in Figure 1-15. Click **Parse Query** to ensure the SQL syntax is correct, and then click **Preview** at the bottom of the Editor to see a sample of the results. Click **OK** to exit the OLE DB Source Editor.

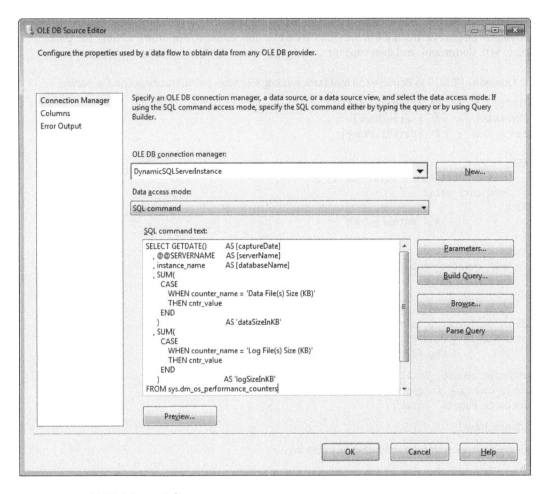

Figure 1-15. *OLE DB Source Editor*

Let's take a moment to discuss this code. We are using the sys.dm_os_performance_counters DMV to retrieve data file and log file sizes. This DMV stores data and log sizes in a separate row for each database, so we are pivoting the data to return one row for each database, with the file size and log size in separate columns. As a reminder, DMVs were introduced in SQL Server 2005, so this example will only work in SQL Server 2005 and newer editions.

It is generally a best practice to create stored procedures for these types of administrative queries and to deploy them to each server, typically into a database like *dbaToolBox*. This introduces some maintenance overhead, but benefits of stored procedures—such as visibility into dependencies, usage, performance tuning, and troubleshooting—typically outweigh the overhead. Also, it allows a DBA or developer to manually execute these same queries on each server without having to search for the code within an Integration Services package. However, in the interests of simplicity, we will just input the code directly into our Data Flow task.

■ **Tip**   The sys.dm_os_performance_counters DMV is very useful for database monitoring and contains much more information than just data and log file sizes. You can easily modify the preceding code to include additional performance counters. However, you should be aware that there are several types of cntr_type values (such as Value/Base, Per Second, and Point-In-Time), and the preceding code only works for the Point-In-Time counter type (cntr_type = 65792). Refer to SQL Server Books Online for more information on the types of information available in this DMV and how to work with each counter type.

Now that we know what our query footprint will look like, we need to create a table to store the results in. From within SSMS, execute the T-SQL statement in Listing 1-6 within the *dbaCentralLogging* database.

Listing 1-6. Example of T-SQL Code to Create a Table to Store Data and Log File Size Information

```
USE dbaCentralLogging;
GO

CREATE TABLE dbo.dba_monitor_databaseGrowth
(
    log_id        INT IDENTITY(1,1)
    ,captureDate  DATETIME
    ,serverName   NVARCHAR(128)
    ,databaseName SYSNAME
    ,fileSizeInKB BIGINT
    ,logSizeInKB  BIGINT

    CONSTRAINT PK_dba_monitor_databaseGrowth
        PRIMARY KEY NONCLUSTERED(log_id)
);

CREATE CLUSTERED INDEX CIX_dba_monitor_databaseGrowth
    ON dbo.dba_monitor_databaseGrowth(captureDate,serverName,databaseName);
```

We can now return to our Integration Services package. We do not need to perform any data cleansing or data transformations in this Data Flow task, so we'll proceed straight to storing our results. Select the **OLE DB Destination** item from the Toolbox and rename it **Central Logging Destination**. Connect it to the OLE DB Source by dragging the blue data flow arrow from the source to the destination. Double-clicking the OLE DB Destination brings up another Editor. This time, select your **dbaCentralLogging** connection from the OLE DB Connection Manager drop-down. Leave **Table or view – fast load** selected in the Data Access Mode drop-down. In the "Name of the table or the view" drop-down, select **[dbo].[dba_monitor_databaseGrowth]**, as seen in Figure 1-16.

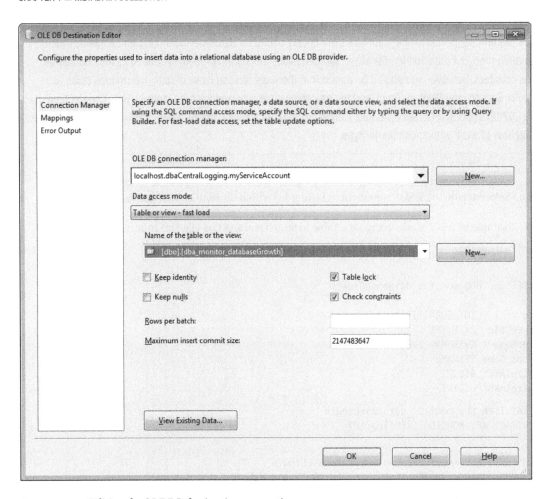

Figure 1-16. *Editing the OLE DB destination connection manager*

When you're done with the Connection Manager, click the **Mappings** menu. You'll notice that Integration Services has taken the liberty to perform an initial mapping based on column names. While this is a nice time-saving feature, be wary in environments where the same column name is used for multiple data elements. Because the *log_id* column is an identity value that is populated during data insertion, we will ignore it in our mappings. Confirm that your mappings resemble those shown in Figure 1-17, and then click **OK** to return to the Data Flow designer.

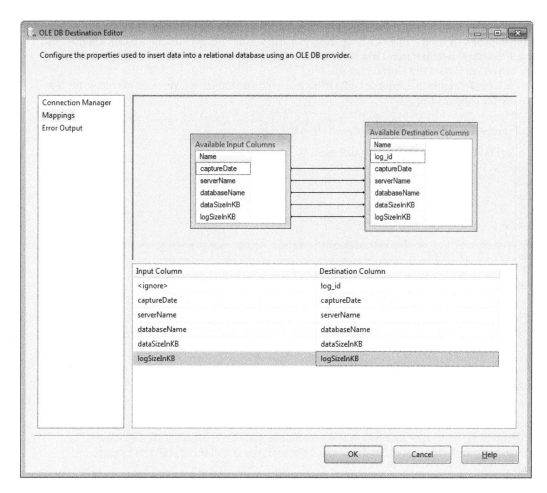

Figure 1-17. *Editing the OLE DB destination mappings*

Our first Data Flow is complete, as seen in Figure 1-18.

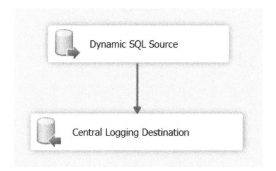

Figure 1-18. *The completed Data Flow task*

We are now ready to create our second Data Flow. From the Control Flow tab, copy and paste the existing Data Flow into the Foreach Loop Container. Drag the green arrow—the Success Precedence Constraint—from the Database Size Data Flow to our new Data Flow. Rename the new Data Flow as **Unused Indexes**, and then double-click it to return to the Data Flow designer.

Double-click the **Dynamic SQL Source** OLE DB Source to edit its properties. We need to change the SQL command to use the code in Listing 1-7.

Listing 1-7. Example of T-SQL Query to Retrieve Unused Indexes

```
/* Create a variable to hold a list of indexes */
DECLARE@Indexes      TABLE
( serverName         NVARCHAR(128)
, schemaName         SYSNAME
, schemaID           INT
, databaseName       SYSNAME
, databaseID         INT
, tableName          SYSNAME
, objectID           INT
, indexName          SYSNAME
, indexID            INT
, indexType          NVARCHAR(60)
, isPrimaryKey       BIT
, isUnique           BIT
, isFiltered         BIT
, isPartitioned      BIT
, numberOfRows       BIGINT
, totalPages         BIGINT);

/* Iterate through all databases */
INSERT INTO@Indexes(serverName,schemaName,schemaID,databaseName,databaseID,tableName,
objectID,indexName,indexID,indexType,isUnique,isPrimaryKey,isFiltered,isPartitioned,
numberOfRows,totalPages)
EXECUTE sys.sp_MSforeachdb
' USE ?;
SELECT @@SERVERNAME
    , SCHEMA_NAME(t.schema_id)
    , t.schema_id
    , DB_NAME()
    , DB_ID()
    , t.name
    , t.object_id
    , i.name
    , i.index_id
    , i.type_desc
    , i.is_primary_key
    , i.is_unique
    , i.has_filter
    , CASE WHEN COUNT(p.partition_id)>1 THEN 1 ELSE 0 END
    , SUM(p.rows)
    , SUM(au.total_pages)
FROM sys.tables          AS t WITH (NOLOCK)
JOIN sys.indexes         AS i WITH (NOLOCK)
```

```
ON i.object_id=t.object_id
JOIN sys.partitions          AS p WITH (NOLOCK)
ON p.object_id=i.object_id
AND p.index_id=i.index_id
JOIN sys.allocation_units     AS au WITH (NOLOCK)
ON au.container_id=p.partition_id
WHERE i.index_id <> 0 /* exclude heaps */
GROUP BY SCHEMA_NAME(t.schema_id)
, t.schema_id
, t.name
, t.object_id
, i.name
, i.index_id
, i.type_desc
, i.has_filter
, i.is_unique
, i.is_primary_key;';

/* Retrieve index stats for return to our central repository */
SELECTGETDATE()               AS [captureDate]
    , i.serverName
    , i.schemaName
    , i.databaseName
    , i.tableName
    , i.indexName
    , i.indexType
    , i.isFiltered
    , i.isPartitioned
    , i.numberOfRows
    , ddius.user_seeks        AS [userSeeksSinceReboot]
    , ddius.user_scans        AS [userScansSinceReboot]
    , ddius.user_lookups      AS [userLookupsSinceReboot]
    , ddius.user_updates      AS [userUpdatesSinceReboot]
    , (i.totalPages * 8) / 1024 AS [indexSizeInMB]/* pages are 8KB */
    , dosi.sqlserver_start_time AS [lastReboot]
FROM @Indexes                 AS i
JOIN sys.dm_db_index_usage_stats    AS ddius
    ON i.databaseID=ddius.database_id
    AND i.objectID=ddius.object_id
    AND i.indexID=ddius.index_id
CROSS APPLY sys.dm_os_sys_info      AS dosi
WHERE /* exclude system databases */
      i.databaseName    NOT IN ('master','msdb','tempdb','model')
    /* exclude unique indexes; assume they are serving a business function */
    AND i.isUnique      =0
    /* exclude primary keys; assume they are serving a business function */
    AND i.isPrimaryKey  =0
    /* no seeks have been performed since the last server reboot */
    AND user_seeks      =0;
```

■ **Tip**   The T-SQL in Listing 1-7 is just a starting point. This query can be easily modified to return information such as which clustered indexes may warrant redesign, which tables have the most updates, and which tables are the most frequently queried.

An example of the output follows.

captureDate	serverName	schemaName	databaseName	tableName
2012-04-29 19:37:36.927	LOCALHOST	Production	AdventureWorks2012	TransactionHistory
2012-04-29 19:37:36.927	LOCALHOST	Production	AdventureWorks2012	TransactionHistory
2012-04-29 19:37:36.927	LOCALHOST	Sales	AdventureWorks2012	SalesOrderDetail

indexName	indexType	isFiltered	isPartitioned	numberOfRows
IX_TransactionHistory_ProductID	NONCLUSTERED	0	0	1134431
IX_TransactionHistory_ReferenceOrderID	NONCLUSTERED	0	0	1134431
IX_SalesOrderDetail_ProductID	NONCLUSTERED	0	1	1213178

userSeeksSinceReboot	userScansSinceReboot	userLookupsSinceReboot	userUpdatesSinceReboot
0	0	0	98
0	8	0	98
0	2	0	124

indexSizeInMB	lastReboot
9 2012-04-28	19:15:28.837
21 2012-04-28	19:15:28.837
28 2012-04-28	19:15:28.837

As you can see, this query is a bit more complex than the last one. Let's discuss what we're doing. Developers are usually very good at identifying performance issues. Why? When a query is slow, someone is usually complaining about it! It's not uncommon for the fix to involve the creation of an index, which can reduce IO and improve query duration. Over time, however, the query may change—resulting in a different indexing being used by the optimizer—or perhaps the query is no longer needed. Unlike the more attention-getting performance issue, these types of changes tend to creep up silently over time. Eventually that same index, which was so beneficial when it was being used, is now consuming unnecessary resources—namely, it slows down inserts, consumes precious disk space, and inflates backups.

One way to stay on top of unused indexes is to search the sys.dm_db_index_usage_stats DMV. This DMV keeps track of index usage information, including how many times an index has been seeked or scanned and how many updates have been performed. This information is refreshed after every reboot, so please note that a server that has been restarted recently may show an inaccurately high number of "unused" indexes. Also, this information is merely a starting point for further research into whether an index should be dropped or redesigned; many organizations may have indexes that are not called frequently but are necessary for important monthly or annual reports.

One other important thing to note is that this script makes use of the undocumented sp_MSforeachdb stored procedure. This stored procedure iterates through every database, executing whatever command is passed to it. For numerous reasons—not the least of which is the fact that it is an undocumented, and therefore unsupported, stored procedure that may occasionally skip databases—I recommend using Aaron Bertrand's sp_foreachdb stored procedure instead. However, once more in the interests of simplicity, we will use the sp_MSforeachdb procedure in our example.

■ **Tip**   Aaron Bertrand's sp_foreachdb stored procedure can be found at www.mssqltips.com/ sqlservertip/2201/making-a-more-reliable-and-flexible-spmsforeachdb/ or by searching for "MSSQLTips sp_foreachdb" in your favorite search engine.

Now that we understand a little more about the metadata we are retrieving, let's return to our package. Click **Parse Query** to ensure you do not have any errors in your syntax, and then click **Preview** to see a sample of the results. Click the **Columns** page to ensure that the column list has been successfully updated. Then, click **OK** to return to the Data Flow designer.

You should now see an error in your Data Flow, as illustrated in Figure 1-19. This is expected because we've changed the columns that our data source is providing, but our destination still expects the old column list.

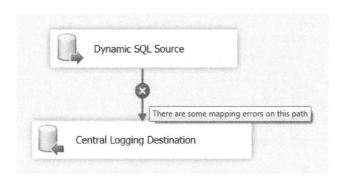

Figure 1-19. *The completed Data Flow task*

Before we can fix this error, we need to return to SSMS to create the table we will use to store our unused index data, *dba_monitor_unusedIndexes*. Do so now, using the code in Listing 1-8.

Listing 1-8. T-SQL Code to Create the dba_monitor_unusedIndexes Table

```
USE dbaCentralLogging;
GO

CREATE TABLE dbo.dba_monitor_unusedIndexes
(log_id                  INT IDENTITY(1,1)
,captureDate             DATETIME
,serverName              NVARCHAR(128)
,schemaName              SYSNAME
```

```
,databaseName                SYSNAME
,tableName                   SYSNAME
,indexName                   SYSNAME
,indexType                   NVARCHAR(60)
,isFiltered                  BIT
,isPartitioned               BIT
,numberOfRows                BIGINT
,userSeeksSinceReboot        BIGINT
,userScansSinceReboot        BIGINT
,userLookupsSinceReboot      BIGINT
,userUpdatesSinceReboot      BIGINT
,indexSizeInMB               BIGINT
,lastReboot                  DATETIME

    CONSTRAINT PK_dba_monitor_unusedIndexes
        PRIMARY KEY NONCLUSTERED(log_id)
);

CREATE CLUSTERED INDEX CIX_dba_monitor_unusedIndexes
    ON dbo.dba_monitor_unusedIndexes(captureDate);
```

Returning to Integration Services, double-click the **Central Logging Database** OLE DB Destination to edit its properties. Change the "Name of the table or the view" value to **[dbo].[dba_monitor_unusedIndexes]**, and then click the **Mappings** page. Because our source and destination are using the same column names, we can easily update the mappings by right-clicking in the space between Available Input Columns and Available Destination Columns and then selecting **Map Items by Matching Names**. Figure 1-20 illustrates this option.

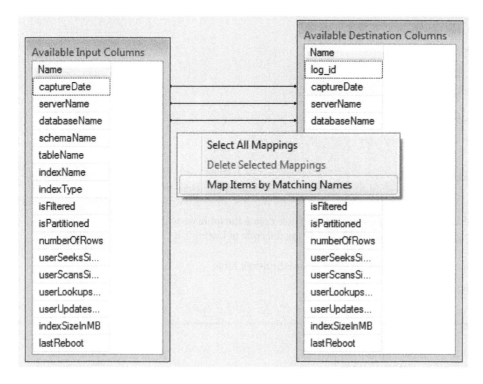

Figure 1-20. *The Map Items by Matching Names option in the Mappings page*

Once more, the *log_id*column will not map to anything because it is an identity column. Click **OK** to return to the Data Flow designer, and then click the Control Flow tab.

See how quickly that second Data Flow went? You can continue to easily add more metadata collection tasks using this same method. All that we have left to do is to update our *Last Monitored* column in the *dba_monitor_ SQLServerInstances* table.

■ **Tip**   It may be tempting to create a one-size-fits-all package. However, it is generally a better idea to separate metadata collections into separate packages organized by frequency requirements. For example, the metadata we have collected in this chapter only requires periodic samples, such as daily or weekly collection. Metadata that requires more frequent collection, such as an hourly check for failed SQL Agent jobs, should be stored in a separate package.

Add an Execute SQL Task to our Foreach Loop Container and rename it **Update LastMonitored**. Connect the **Unused Indexes** Data Flow to the **Update Last Monitored** Execute SQL Task. Double-click the Execute SQL Task to edit its properties. Select the **dbaCentralLogging** connection in the Connection drop-down, and then enter the code from Listing 1-9 in the SQLStatement field.

Listing 1-9. T-SQL Code to Update the LastMonitored Value in dba_monitor_SQLServerInstances

```
UPDATEdbo.dba_monitor_SQLServerInstances
SETLastMonitored = GETDATE()
WHERESQLServerInstance = ?;
```

The question mark (?) tells the Execute SQL Task that we are passing a parameter to this SQL statement. Now we just need to map our variable to our parameter. To do this, click the **Parameter Mapping** page and click **Add**. Edit the properties as follows:

- Variable Name = User::SQLServerInstanceName

- Direction = Input

- Data Type = NVARCHAR

- Parameter Name = 0

- Parameter Size = 128

Confirm that your mappings match those shown in Figure 1-21, and then click **OK**.

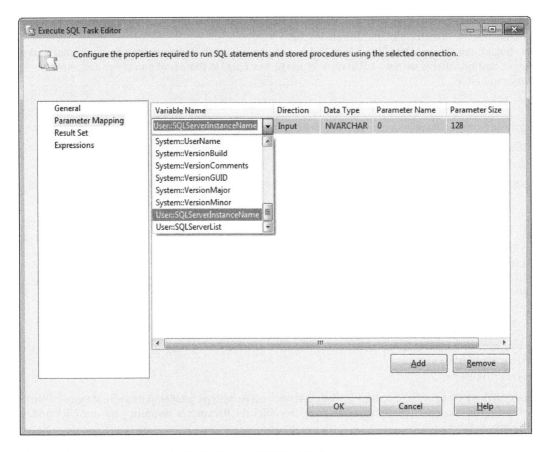

Figure 1-21. *Parameter mapping in the Execute SQL Task Editor*

We are now ready to execute our package! To do this, you can select **Debug►Start Debugging** from the menu, click the green Run icon in the toolbar, or press F5. Your package should resemble Figure 1-22 upon successful execution.

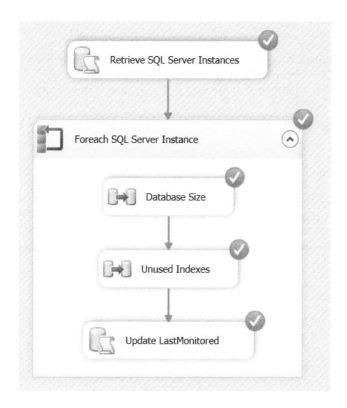

Figure 1-22. Successful execution of the MetadataCollection package

Congratulations! You have now collected metadata from a list of servers and stored the results in your *dbaCentralLogging* database.

This concludes our walk-through on collecting metadata via SSIS. However, there are many more tasks that a diligent developer or DBA may want to consider. First, as we discussed early on in this chapter, this package does not contain any exception handling or logging, which is outside the scope of this chapter. However, a best practice is to include some sort of exception handling and logging on every package. Second, we have only tipped the proverbial iceberg when it comes to collecting metadata. There is much more information to consider, such as security audits, error logs, SQL Server Agent job statuses, and much, much more. If you're not sure where to start, consider ranking metadata tasks by criticality and working in descending order of importance. As a last piece of homework, you may want to consider setting up monitors to alert when unfavorable conditions are met (for example, a SQL Server agent job has failed or available space is getting low).

Summary

In this chapter, we discussed the importance of metadata. We explored some of the metadata that exists within SQL Server and provided two examples of valuable T-SQL metadata queries. We identified a very flexible and reusable pattern for collecting database metadata in an enterprise environment. Lastly, we created an Integration Services package that does the following:

1. Identify a list of SQL Server instances on our network.

2. Iterate through the list of instances and

   a. Connect to each SQL Server Instance.

   b. Retrieve one or more pieces of information.

   c. Log the results to our centralized repository.

Execution Patterns

To have a full understanding of SQL Server 2012 Integration Services execution, you must first understand the different Deployment models. There are two: the Package Deployment Model and the Project Deployment Model. Each exposes and supports a different functionality. The Package Deployment Model primarily supports legacy functionality. It is the model used in SSIS 2005 through SSIS 2008 R2. The new way of doing things involves the Project Deployment Model. Certain execution methods, but not all, are available to both deployment models.

You can build awesome SQL Server Integration Services (SSIS) packages, but they do no good until you execute them! SSIS provides several methods for package execution. In this chapter, we will examine:

- Debug Execution
- Command-line execution
- Execute Package Utility
- The SQL Server 2012 Integration Service service
- Integration Server Catalogs
- Integration Server Catalog Stored Procedures
- Scheduling SSIS Package Execution
- The Execute Package Task
- Metadata-Driven Execution
- Execution from Managed Code

We'll begin by creating a simple SSIS package to use for demonstration purposes.

Building the Demonstration SSIS Package

Create a new SSIS solution named "Chapter2". Rename the SSIS package, changing the name from Package.dtsx to Chapter2.dtsx.

For more information on creating SSIS solutions and packages, see <u>Professional SQL Server 2012 Integration</u> <u>Services</u> *by Michael Coles and Francis Rodrigues (Apress, 2012).*

Drag a Script Component onto the Control Flow canvas and open the editor. Choose your language of choice in the ScriptLanguage property on the Script page. Select the System::PackageName variable in ReadOnlyVariables, and then click the Edit Script button.

If you selected Microsoft Visual Basic 2010 as the ScriptLanguage property setting for the Script Task, replace the code in Public Sub Main with the following:

```
Public Sub Main()

Dim sPackageName As String = Dts.Variables("PackageName").Value.ToString
Dim sMsg As String = "Package Name: "& sPackageName

MsgBox(sMsg, , sPackageName)

Dts.TaskResult=ScriptResults.Success
End Sub
```

If you selected Microsoft Visual C# 2010 as the ScriptLanguage property setting for the Script Task, replace the code in public void Main() with the following:

```
public void Main()
{
    string sPackageName = Dts.Variables["PackageName"].Value.ToString();
    string sMsg = "Package Name: " + sPackageName;

    MessageBox.Show(sMsg, sPackageName);

    Dts.TaskResult = (int)ScriptResults.Success;
}
```

Save the package, project, and solution. You're ready to run!

Debug Execution

Executing the package from within SQL Server Business Intelligence Development Studio (BIDS) is straightforward. It works the same regardless of the Deployment Model selected. However, as with everything in the Visual Studio Integrated Development Environment (VS IDE), you have several ways to accomplish this.

When you execute an SSIS package inside BIDS, you are invoking the SSIS Debugger. The SSIS Debugger file is named DtsDebugHost.exe and it's stored in the <*drive*>:\Program Files\Microsoft SQL Server\110\DTS\Binn folder. It's important to realize you're executing the SSIS package inside a debug host process. Why? There is overhead associated with debugging – those boxes don't change color for free!

To execute the Chapter2.dtsx package in BIDS, press the F5 key. The debug host loads, then loads the package, and executes it. You should see a message box proclaiming the package name. When you press the OK button on the message box, the Script Task in the Chapter2 package Control Flow turns from yellow to green. A link appears beneath the Connections Managers tab to indicate package execution has completed. However, the DtsDebugHost.exe process is still executing. It continues executing until the BIDS Debugger is stopped.

Here are some ways to start the BIDS Debugger:

- Press the F5 key

- Click the "VCR Play button" (green arrow pointing right) on the toolbar

- Click the Debug dropdown menu and select "Start Debugging"

  - Actually, selecting "Step Into" or "Step Over" from the Debug dropdown menu also starts the BIDS Debugger

- In Solution Explorer, right-click the package and select "Execute Package" from the menu

- When the package has completed execution in Debug mode, restart the package:

  - By holding Ctrl+Shift and pressing the F5 key

  - Using the VCR Restart button on the toolbar

  - Clicking the Debug dropdown menu and clicking "Restart"

Here are some ways to stop the Debugger once the package execution completes (or whenever a Debug mode Stop is desired):

- Hold Shift and press the F5 key

- Click the "VCR Stop button" (the square) on the toolbar

- Click the Debug dropdown menu and select "Stop Debugging"

- Click the Debug dropdown menu and select "Terminate All"

- Click the "Package execution completed" link beneath the Connection Managers tab

Command-Line Execution

Command-line SSIS package execution uses the DtExec.exe utility. DtExec supports Project and Package Deployment Models. You can manually invoke DtExec from inside BIDS by clicking the Debug dropdown menu and selecting "Start Without Debugging" (or by holding the Ctrl key and pressing F5). You can also manually start DtExec from a command prompt.

DtExec isn't often invoked manually. Instead it's common to see DtExec command-lines used with scheduling software to execute SSIS packages in Production environments. For example, when you schedule an SSIS package using SQL Server Agent (covered later in this chapter), DtExec is instantiated.

To execute the Chapter2.dtsx SSIS package using DtExec, open a command prompt and enter the following command:

```
dtexec /FILE "G:\Projects\SSIS Design Patterns\SSIS Design Patterns\Chapter2.dtsx"
```

This command executes the Chapter2.dtsx SSIS package located in the G:\Projects\SSIS Design Patterns\ SSIS Design Patterns folder. Edit the command line to reflect the location of your SSIS package if you're playing along at home.

When you execute the package from the command line, the message box displays the package name – as when the package is executed from inside the BIDS debugger.

If the SSIS package is deployed to the new SSIS catalog, you can still execute it from the command line using a command similar to:

```
dtexec.exe /ISSERVER "\"\SSISDB\Chapter2\Chapter2\Chapter2.dtsx\"" /SERVER "\"SSISMVP-RC0\""
/Par "\"$ServerOption::SYNCHRONIZED(Boolean)\"";True /REPORTING E /CALLERINFO Andy
```

Execute Package Utility

The Execute Package Utility (DtExecUI) runs in its own process and executes SSIS packages. I like using the Execute Package Utility to build DtExec command lines, but it only supports the Package Deployment Model. You can invoke the Execute Package Utility in at least three ways:

- Click Start→All Programs→Microsoft SQL Server→Integration Services→Execute Package Utility

- Click Start→Run and type "dtexecui" (without the double-quotes) in the Open textbox

- Double-click on a dtsx file (if you haven't re-mapped the default application settings for dtsx files)

My favorite option is double-clicking the dtsx file. This not only opens the Execute Package Utility, but it sets the General page settings to indicate that the Package Source is the File System and configures the Package path textbox with the full path of the dtsx file I double-clicked. Neat.

If I execute Package2.dtsx using the Execute Package Utility, the Package Execution Progress form displays, informing me of the package's execution progress (how appropriate) and the message box appears as it had when I executed using the BIDS debugger and the command line.

See Professional SQL Server 11 Integration Services by Michael Coles and Francis Rodrigues (Apress, 2012) for more information about the Execute Package Utility.

The SQL Server 2012 Integration Services Service

The SQL Server Integration Services 11.0 service installs with SQL Server. To connect, open SQL Server Management Studio (SSMS). If prompted to connect with the Connect To Server window at SSMS startup, make sure Server Type is set to Integration Services. Enter the name of the server in the Server Name dropdown. Please note there aren't named instances of SSIS: there's one per server (for now, anyway). You can also enter "localhost" (without the double-quotes) to connect to the local server's default instance of SSIS.

Once the connection is configured, click the Connect button. Navigate to the package you desire to execute. SSIS packages stored in the File System or the MSDB database can be executed from the SSIS 2012 Service.

SQL Server 2012 provides a new way to manage and execute Integration Services packages: Integration Server Catalogs. We explore this method next.

Integration Server Catalogs

You can only manage SSIS projects that use the Project Deployment Model in Integration Services Catalogs. To execute a package in the catalog, use SSMS to connect to the instance of SQL Server hosting the SSISDB database. Expand the Integration Services Catalogs node, and then expand the SSISDB node. Drill into the folder containing the SSIS project and package(s). Right-click the package you wish to execute and click Execute, as shown in Figure 2-1.

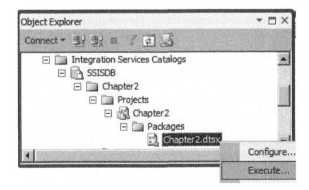

Figure 2-1. *Executing an SSIS Package deployed to the SSIS Catalog*

The Execute Package Window displays, as shown in Figure 2-2. It allows you to override Parameter values, ConnectionString properties of Connection Managers built at design-time, or any other externalize-able property accessible from a Package Path (via the Advanced tab) for this execution instance of the SSIS package stored in the SSIS Catalog.

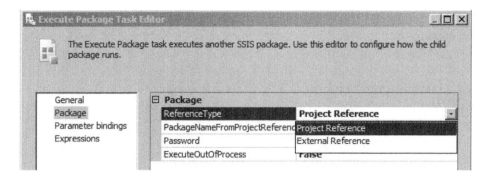

Figure 2-2. *Execute Package Window*

Integration Server Catalog Stored Procedures

Please note the Script button above the Parameters tab in Figure 2-2. This button allows you to generate Transact-SQL statements that will execute the SSIS package. For the Chapter2.dtsx package stored in the SSIS Catalog, the scripts will appear similar to that in Listing 2–1.

Listing 2–1. *Transact-SQL Script Generated From the Execute Package Window*

```
Declare @execution_id bigint
EXEC [SSISDB].[catalog].[create_execution]
   @package_name=N'Chapter2.dtsx'
  ,@execution_id=@execution_id OUTPUT
  ,@folder_name=N'Chapter2'
  ,@project_name=N'Chapter 2'
  ,@use32bitruntime=False
  ,@reference_id=Null
Select @execution_id
DECLARE @var0 smallint=1
EXEC [SSISDB].[catalog].[set_execution_parameter_value]
   @execution_id
  ,@object_type=50
  ,@parameter_name=N'LOGGING_LEVEL'
  ,@parameter_value=@var0
EXEC [SSISDB].[catalog].[start_execution] @execution_id
GO
```

You can use these same stored procedures to execute SSIS Packages in the SSIS Catalog! In fact, I designed a script to create a wrapper stored procedure that will call the Transact-SQL statements executed when an SSIS Package is executed in the SSIS Catalog. You can see that script in Listing 2–2.

Listing 2-2. Script to Build a Wrapper Stored Procedure for Executing SSIS Packages in the SSIS Catalog

```
/* Select the SSISDB database */
Use SSISDB
Go

/* Create a parameter (variable) named @Sql */
Declare @Sql varchar(2000)

/* Create the Custom schema if it does not already exist */
print 'Custom Schema'
If Not Exists(Select name
              From sys.schemas
                Where name='custom')
 begin
  /* Create Schema statements must occur first in a batch */
  print ' - Creating custom schema'
  Set @Sql = 'Create Schema custom'
  Exec(@Sql)
  print ' - Custom schema created'
 end
Else
 print ' - Custom Schema already exists.'
print ''

/* Drop the Custom.execute_catalog_package Stored Procedure if it already exists */
print 'Custom.execute_catalog_package Stored Procedure'
  If Exists(Select s.name+'.' + p.name
            From sys.procedures p
            Join sys.schemas s
              On s.schema_id=p.schema_id
          Where s.name='custom'
            And p.name='execute_catalog_package')
   begin
    print ' - Dropping custom.execute_catalog_package'
    Drop Procedure custom.execute_catalog_package
    print ' - Custom.execute_catalog_package dropped'
   end
  /* Create the Custom.execute_catalog_package Stored Procedure */
  print ' - Creating custom.execute_catalog_package'
go

/*

    Stored Procedure: custom.execute_catalog_package
    Author: Andy Leonard
    Date: 4 Mar 2012
    Description: Creates a wrapper around the SSISDB Catalog procedures
                 used to start executing an SSIS Package. Packages in the
                 SSIS Catalog are referenced by a multi-part identifier
                 - or path - that consists of the following hierarchy:
        Catalog Name: Implied by the database name in Integration Server 2012
        |-Folder Name: A folder created before or at Deployment to contain the SSIS project
        |-Project Name: The name of the SSIS Project deployed
        |-Package Name: The name(s) of the SSIS Package(s) deployed
```

```
          Parameters:
          @FolderName [nvarchar(128)] {No default} -
           contains the name of the Folder that holds the SSIS Project
          @ProjectName [nvarchar(128)] {No default} -
           contains the name of the SSIS Project that holds the SSIS Package
          @PackageName [nvarchar(260)] {No default} -
           contains the name of the SSIS Package to be executed
          @ExecutionID [bigint] {Output} -
           Output parameter (variable) passed back to the caller
          @LoggingLevel [varchar(16)] {Default} -
           contains the (case-insensitive) name of the logging level
           to apply to this execution instance
          @Use32BitRunTime [bit] {Default} -
           1 == Use 64-bit run-time
           0 == Use 32-bit run-time
          @ReferenceID [bigint] {Default} -            contains a reference to an Execution
Environment
          @ObjectType [smallint] -            contains an identifier that appears to be related to
the        SSIS PackageType property
          Guessing: @ObjectType == PackageType.ordinal (1-based-array) * 10
           Must be 20, 30, or 50 for catalog.set_execution_parameter_value
           stored procedure


          Test:
          1. Create and deploy an SSIS Package to the SSIS Catalog.
          2. Exec custom.execute_catalog_package and pass it the
            following parameters: @FolderName, @ProjectName, @PackageName, @ExecutionID Output
          @LoggingLevel, @Use32BitRunTime, @ReferenceID, and @ObjectType are optional and
          defaulted parameters.


           Example:
             Declare @ExecId bigint
             Exec custom.execute_catalog_package
            'Chapter2'
          ,'Chapter 2'
          ,'Chapter2.dtsx'
          ,@ExecId Output
          3. When execution completes, an Execution_Id value should be returned.
          View the SSIS Catalog Reports to determine the status of the execution
          instance and the test.
*/
Create Procedure custom.execute_catalog_package
  @FolderName nvarchar(128)
```

```
  ,@ProjectName nvarchar(128)
  ,@PackageName nvarchar(260)
  ,@ExecutionID bigint Output
  ,@LoggingLevel varchar(16) = 'Basic'
  ,@Use32BitRunTime bit = 0
  ,@ReferenceID bigint = NULL
  ,@ObjectType smallint = 50
As

  begin

   Set NoCount ON

    /* Call the catalog.create_execution stored procedure
       to initialize execution location and parameters */
   Exec catalog.create_execution
    @package_name = @PackageName
   ,@execution_id = @ExecutionID Output
   ,@folder_name = @FolderName
   ,@project_name = @ProjectName
   ,@use32bitruntime = @Use32BitRunTime
   ,@reference_id = @ReferenceID

    /* Populate the @ExecutionID parameter for OUTPUT */
   Select @ExecutionID As Execution_Id

    /* Create a parameter (variable) named @Sql */
   Declare @logging_level smallint
    /* Decode the Logging Level */
   Select @logging_level = Case
                            When Upper(@LoggingLevel) = 'BASIC'
                            Then 1
                            When Upper(@LoggingLevel) = 'PERFORMANCE'
                            Then 2
                             When Upper(@LoggingLevel) = 'VERBOSE'
                            Then 3
                            Else 0 /* 'None' */
                            End
   /* Call the catalog.set_execution_parameter_value stored
      procedure to update the LOGGING_LEVEL parameter */
   Exec catalog.set_execution_parameter_value
    @ExecutionID
   ,@object_type = @ObjectType
   ,@parameter_name = N'LOGGING_LEVEL'
   ,@parameter_value = @logging_level

    /* Call the catalog.start_execution (self-explanatory) */
   Exec catalog.start_execution
    @ExecutionID

  end
GO
```

If you execute this script to create the custom schema and stored procedure in your instance of the SSISDB database, you can test it using the statement in Listing 2-3.

Listing 2-3. Testing the SSISDB.custom.execute_catalog_package Stored Procedure

```
Declare @ExecId bigint
Exec SSISDB.custom.execute_catalog_package 'Chapter2','Chapter 2','Chapter2.dtsx',
@ExecId Output
```

Adding a Data Tap

The SSISDB.custom.execute_catalog_package stored procedure can be modified slightly to create a data tap – a new feature for packages executed from the SSISDB Catalog in SSIS 2012. Adding a few parameters and some T-SQL to the stored procedure allows it to execute an SSIS package and export a comma-separated values (CSV) file filled with some or all of the rows that flowed through a point in a Data Flow Task. Data taps provide a much-needed window on the state of data as they move through an SSIS Data Flow, facilitating root-cause analysis and troubleshooting in Production environments without altering the package code. Data taps are one of the most important enhancements to Integration Services 2012. Listing 2-4 contains the script to build SSISDB.custom.execute_catalog_package_with_data_tap:

Listing 2-4. Script to Build a Wrapper Stored Procedure for Executing SSIS Packages in the SSIS Catalog

```
/* Select the SSISDB database */
Use SSISDB
Go

 /* Create a parameter (variable) named @Sql */
Declare @Sql varchar(2000)

 /* Create the Custom schema if it does not already exist */
print 'Custom Schema'
If Not Exists(Select name
               From sys.schemas
Where name='custom')
 begin
   /* Create Schema statements must occur first in a batch */
  print ' - Creating custom schema'
  Set @Sql='Create Schema custom'
  Exec(@Sql)
  print ' - Custom schema created'
 end
Else
 print ' - Custom Schema already exists.'
print ''

 /* Drop the Custom.execute_catalog_package_with_data_tap
 Stored Procedure if it already exists */
print 'Custom.execute_catalog_package_with_data_tap Stored Procedure'
  If Exists(Select s.name+'.' +  p.name
            From sys.procedures p
            Join sys.schemas s
                On s.schema_id=p.schema_id
       Where s.name='custom'
          And p.name='execute_catalog_package_with_data_tap')
   begin
```

```
    print ' - Dropping custom.execute_catalog_package_with_data_tap'
    Drop Procedure custom.execute_catalog_package_with_data_tap
    print ' - Custom.execute_catalog_package_with_data_tap dropped'
  end

  /* Create the Custom.execute_catalog_package_with_data_tap Stored Procedure */
  print ' - Creating custom.execute_catalog_package_with_data_tap'
go

/*


  Stored Procedure: custom.execute_catalog_package_with_data_tap
  Author: Andy Leonard
  Date: 4 Apr 2012
  Description: Creates a wrapper around the SSISDB Catalog procedures
               used to start executing an SSIS Package and create a
               data tap. Packages in the
               SSIS Catalog are referenced by a multi-part identifier
               - or path - that consists of the following hierarchy:
   Catalog Name: Implied by the database name in Integration Server 2012
   |-Folder Name: A folder created before or at Deployment to contain the SSIS project
     |-Project Name: The name of the SSIS Project deployed
       |-Package Name: The name(s) of the SSIS Package(s) deployed
Parameters:
   @FolderName [nvarchar(128)] {No default} - contains the name of the
     Folder that holds the SSIS Project
   @ProjectName [nvarchar(128)] {No default} - contains the name of the
    SSIS Project that holds the SSIS Package
   @PackageName [nvarchar(260)] {No default} - contains the name of the
    SSIS Package to be executed
   @ExecutionID [bigint] {Output} - Output parameter (variable) passed back
    to the caller
   @LoggingLevel [varchar(16)] {Default} - contains the (case-insensitive)
    name of the logging level to apply to this execution instance
   @Use32BitRunTime [bit] {Default} - 1 == Use 64-bit run-time
                                      0 == Use 32-bit run-time
   @ReferenceID [bigint] {Default} - contains a reference to an Execution Environment
   @ObjectType [smallint] - contains an identifier that appears to be related
    to the SSIS PackageType property

   Guessing: @ObjectType == PackageType.ordinal (1-based-array) * 10
    Must be 20, 30, or 50 for catalog.set_execution_parameter_value
      stored procedure
```

@DataFlowTaskName [nvarchar(255)] - contains the name of the Data Flow Task in which to
   to apply the data tap.
@IdentificationString [nvarchar(255)] - contains the Data Flow Path Identification string
   in which to apply the data tap.
@DataTapFileName [nvarchar(4000)] - contains the name of the file to create to contain
   the rows captured from the data tap.
   Saved in the <drive>:\Program Files\Microsoft SQL Server\110\DTS\DataDumps folder.
@DataTapMaxRows [int] - contains the maximum number of rows to send to the data tap file.

Test:
  1. Create and deploy an SSIS Package to the SSIS Catalog.
  2. Exec custom.execute_catalog_package_with_data_tap and pass it the
     following parameters: @FolderName, @ProjectName, @PackageName,
     @DataFlowTaskName, @IdentificationString, @DataTapFileName,
     @ExecutionID Output
  @LoggingLevel, @Use32BitRunTime, @ReferenceID, @ObjectType,
   and @DataTapMaxRows are optional and defaulted parameters.

Example:
 Declare @ExecId bigint
 Exec custom.execute_catalog_package_with_data_tap
  'SSISConfig2012','SSISConfig2012','Child1.dtsx',
  'Data Flow Task', 'OLESRC Temperature.OLE DB Source Output',
  'Child1_DataFlowTask_OLESRCTemperature_OLEDBSourceOutput.csv',@ExecId Output

  3. When execution completes, an Execution_Id value should be returned.
     View the SSIS Catalog Reports to determine the status of the
     execution instance and the test.

*/
Create Procedure [custom].[execute_catalog_package_with_data_tap]
  @FolderName nvarchar(128)
 ,@ProjectName nvarchar(128)
 ,@PackageName nvarchar(260)
 ,@DataFlowTaskName nvarchar(255)
 ,@IdentificationString nvarchar(255)
 ,@DataTapFileName nvarchar(4000)
 ,@ExecutionID bigint Output
 ,@LoggingLevel varchar(16) = 'Basic'
 ,@Use32BitRunTime bit = 0
 ,@ReferenceID bigint = NULL
 ,@ObjectType smallint = 50
 ,@DataTapMaxRows int = NULL
As

 begin

  Set NoCount ON

```
    /* Call the catalog.create_execution stored procedure
       to initialize execution location and parameters */
  Exec catalog.create_execution
   @package_name=@PackageName
  ,@execution_id=@ExecutionID Output
  ,@folder_name=@FolderName
  ,@project_name=@ProjectName
  ,@use32bitruntime=@Use32BitRunTime
  ,@reference_id=@ReferenceID

   /* Populate the @ExecutionID parameter for OUTPUT */
  Select @ExecutionID As Execution_Id

  /* Configure Data Tap parameters */
  If (Left(@DataFlowTaskName, 9) <> '\Package\')
   Set @DataFlowTaskName='\Package\'+@DataFlowTaskName

  If Left(@IdentificationString,6) <> 'Paths['
   Set @IdentificationString='Paths['+@IdentificationString+']'

  /* Create the Data Tap */
  EXEC [SSISDB].[catalog].add_data_tap  @ExecutionID, @DataFlowTaskName,
   @IdentificationString, @DataTapFileName, @DataTapMaxRows

   /* Create a parameter (variable) named @Sql */
  Declare @logging_level smallint
   /* Decode the Logging Level */
  Select @logging_level=Case
                            When Upper(@LoggingLevel)='BASIC'
                                     Then 1
                                     When Upper(@LoggingLevel)='PERFORMANCE'
                                     Then 2
                                      When Upper(@LoggingLevel)='VERBOSE'
                                     Then 3
                                     Else 0 /* 'None' */
                                     End
   /* Call the catalog.set_execution_parameter_value stored
      procedure to update the LOGGING_LEVEL parameter */
  Exec catalog.set_execution_parameter_value
    @ExecutionID
   ,@object_type=@ObjectType
   ,@parameter_name=N'LOGGING_LEVEL'
   ,@parameter_value=@logging_level

   /* Call the catalog.start_execution (self-explanatory) */
  Exec catalog.start_execution
    @ExecutionID

  end
```

Creating a Custom Execution Framework

SSIS Execution Frameworks support repeatable and reliable SSIS package execution. The SSISDB.custom. execute_catalog_package stored procedure can be used as the centerpiece for an SSIS Execution Framework. To create the tables to support this framework, execute the statements in Listing 2–5.

Listing 2–5. Tables to Support a Custom SSIS Execution Framework

```
/* Switch to SSISDB database */
Use SSISDB
Go

/* Build custom Schema */
print 'Custom Schema'
/* Check for existence of custom Schema */
If Not Exists(Select name
              From sys.schemas
                        Where name = 'custom')
 begin
  /* Build and execute custom Schema SQL
     if it does not exist */
  print ' - Creating custom schema'
  declare @CustomSchemaSql varchar(32) = 'Create Schema custom'
  exec(@CustomSchemaSql)
  print ' - Custom schema created'
 end
Else
 /* If the custom schema exists, tell us */
 print ' - Custom schema already exists.'
 print ''
Go

/* Build custom.Application table */
print 'Custom.Application Table'
/* Check for existence of custom.Application table */
If Not Exists(Select s.name + '.' + t.name
              From sys.tables t
                        Join sys.schemas s
                          On s.schema_id = t.schema_id
                        Where s.name = 'custom'
                          And t.name = 'Application')
 begin
  /* Create custom.Application table
     if it does not exist */
  print ' - Creating custom.Application Table'
  Create Table custom.Application
  (
    ApplicationID int identity(1,1)
        Constraint PK_custom_Application Primary Key Clustered
```

```
   ,ApplicationName nvarchar(256) Not Null
     Constraint U_custom_ApplicationName Unique
   ,ApplicationDescription nvarchar(512) Null
  )
  print ' - Custom.Application Table created'
 end
Else
  /* If the custom.Application table exists, tell us */
 print ' - Custom.Application Table already exists.'
print ''

/* Build custom.Package table */
print 'Custom.Package Table'
/* Check for existence of custom.Package table */
If Not Exists(Select s.name+'.'+t.name
              From sys.tables t
                        Join sys.schemas s
                          On s.schema_id=t.schema_id
                        Where s.name='custom'
                          And t.name='Package')
 begin
  /* Create custom.Package table
     if it does not exist */
  print ' - Creating custom.Package Table'
  Create Table custom.Package
  (
    PackageID int identity(1,1)
        Constraint PK_custom_Package Primary Key Clustered
   ,FolderName nvarchar(128) Not Null
   ,ProjectName nvarchar(128) Not Null
   ,PackageName nvarchar(256) Not Null
   ,PackageDescription nvarchar(512) Null
  )
  print ' - Custom.Package Table created'
 end
Else
  /* If the custom.Package table exists, tell us */
 print ' - Custom.Package Table already exists.'
print ''

/* Build custom.ApplicationPackage table */
print 'Custom.ApplicationPackage Table'
/* Check for existence of custom.ApplicationPackage table */
If Not Exists(Select s.name+'.'+t.name
              From sys.tables t
                        Join sys.schemas s
                          On s.schema_id=t.schema_id
                        Where s.name='custom'
                          And t.name='ApplicationPackage')
```

```
begin
 /* Create custom.ApplicationPackage table
    if it does not exist */
 print ' - Creating custom.ApplicationPackage Table'
 Create Table custom.ApplicationPackage
 (
   ApplicationPackageID int identity(1,1)
        Constraint PK_custom_ApplicationPackage Primary Key Clustered
  ,ApplicationID int Not Null
    Constraint FK_custom_ApplicationPackage_Application
         Foreign Key References custom.Application(ApplicationID)
  ,PakcageID int Not Null
    Constraint FK_custom_ApplicationPackage_Package
         Foreign Key References custom.Package(PackageID)
  ,ExecutionOrder int Not Null
    Constraint DF_custom_ApplicationPackage_ExecutionOrder
         Default(10)
  ,ApplicationPackageEnabled bit Not Null
    Constraint DF_custom_ApplicationPackage_ApplicationPackageEnabled
         Default(1)
 )
 print ' - Custom.ApplicationPackage Table created'
 end
Else
  /* If the custom.ApplicationPackage table exists, tell us */
 print ' - Custom.ApplicationPackage Table already exists.'
print ''
/* Build custom.GetApplicationPackages stored procedure */
print 'Custom.GetApplicationPackages'
/* Check for existence of custom.GetApplicationPackages stored procedure */
If Exists(Select s.name+'.'+p.name
          From sys.procedures p
                Join sys.schemas s
                  On s.schema_id=p.schema_id
                Where s.name='custom'
                  And p.name='GetApplicationPackages')
 begin
  /* If custom.GetApplicationPackages stored procedure
     exists, drop it */
  print ' - Dropping custom.GetApplicationPackages Stored Procedure'
  Drop Procedure custom.GetApplicationPackages
  print ' - custom.GetApplicationPackages Stored Procedure dropped'
 end
print ' - Creating custom.GetApplicationPackages Stored Procedure'
go

/*

        Procedure: custom.GetApplicationPackages
           Author: Andy Leonard
 Parameter(s): ApplicationName [nvarchar(256)]
               - contains the name of the SSIS Application
                          for which to retrieve SSIS Packages.
```

43

```
       Description: Executes against the custom.ApplicationPackages
                 table joined to the custom.Application
                              and custom.Packages tables. Returns a
                              list of enabled Packages related to the
                              Application ordered by ExecutionOrder.
           Example: exec custom.GetApplicationPackages 'TestSSISApp'
*/
Create Procedure custom.GetApplicationPackages
 @ApplicationName nvarchar(256)
As
 begin

  Set NoCount On

       Select p.FolderName, p.ProjectName, p.PackageName, ap.ExecutionOrder
       From custom.ApplicationPackage ap
       Join custom.Package p
         On p.PackageID = ap.PackageID
       Join custom.Application a
         On a.ApplicationID = ap.ApplicationID
       Where a.ApplicationName = @ApplicationName
         And ap.ApplicationPackageEnabled = 1
       Order By ap.ExecutionOrder
 end
go
print ' - Custom.GetApplicationPackages Stored Procedure created.'
print ''

/* Build custom.AddApplication stored procedure */
print 'Custom.AddApplication'
If Exists(Select s.name + '.' + p.name
          From sys.procedures p
                  Join sys.schemas s
                    On s.schema_id = p.schema_id
                  Where s.name = 'custom'
                    And p.name = 'AddApplication')
 begin
  /* If custom.AddApplication stored procedure
     exists, drop it */
  print ' - Dropping custom.AddApplication Stored Procedure'
  Drop Procedure custom.AddApplication
  print ' - custom.AddApplication Stored Procedure dropped'
 end
print ' - Creating custom.AddApplication Stored Procedure'
go

/*
```

```
            Procedure: custom.AddApplication
            Author: Andy Leonard
             Parameter(s): ApplicationName [nvarchar(256)]
                     - contains the name of the SSIS Application
                              to add to the Framework database.
                         ApplicationDescription [nvarchar(512)]
                         - contains a description of the SSIS Application.
            Description: Stores an SSIS Application.
             Example: exec custom.AddApplication 'TestSSISApp', 'A test SSIS Application.'
*/
Create Procedure custom.AddApplication
  @ApplicationName nvarchar(256)
 ,@ApplicationDescription nvarchar(512)=NULL
As
 begin

   Set NoCount On

        Insert Into custom.Application
        (ApplicationName
        ,ApplicationDescription)
        Output inserted.ApplicationID
        Values
        (@ApplicationName
        ,@ApplicationDescription)

 end
go
print ' - Custom.AddApplication Stored Procedure created.'
print ''

/* Build custom.AddPackage stored procedure */
print 'Custom.AddPackage'
If Exists(Select s.name+'.' + p.name
          From sys.procedures p
                  Join sys.schemas s
                    On s.schema_id=p.schema_id
                  Where s.name='custom'
                    And p.name='AddPackage')
 begin
  /* If custom.AddPackage stored procedure
     exists, drop it */
  print ' - Dropping custom.AddPackage Stored Procedure'
  Drop Procedure custom.AddPackage
  print ' - custom.AddPackage Stored Procedure dropped'
 end
print ' - Creating custom.AddPackage Stored Procedure'
go

/*
```

```
            Procedure: custom.AddPackage
            Author: Andy Leonard
            Parameter(s): FolderName [nvarchar(128)]
                    - contains the name of the SSISDB Catalog
                            folder containing the SSIS Package.
                        ProjectName [nvarchar(128)]
                    - contains the name of the SSISDB Catalog
                            project containing the SSIS Package.
                        PackageName [nvarchar(128)]
                    - contains the name of the SSISDB Catalog
                            SSIS Package.
                        PackageDescription [nvarchar(512)]
                    - contains a description of the SSIS Package.
        Description: Stores an SSIS Package.
          Example: exec custom.AddPackage 'Chapter2', 'Chapter 2'
                                    , 'Chapter2.dtsx', 'A test SSIS Package.'
*/
Create Procedure custom.AddPackage
  @FolderName nvarchar(128)
 ,@ProjectName nvarchar(128)
 ,@PackageName nvarchar(256)
 ,@PackageDescription nvarchar(512)=NULL
As
 begin

  Set NoCount On

        Insert Into custom.Package
        (FolderName
        ,ProjectName
        ,PackageName
        ,PackageDescription)
        Output inserted.PackageID
        Values
        (@FolderName
        ,@ProjectName
        ,@PackageName
        ,@PackageDescription)

 end
go
print ' - Custom.AddPackage Stored Procedure created.'
print ''

/* Build custom.AddApplicationPackage stored procedure */
print 'Custom.AddApplicationPackage'
If Exists(Select s.name+'.'+p.name
        From sys.procedures p
                Join sys.schemas s
```

```
                On s.schema_id=p.schema_id
            Where s.name='custom'
                And p.name='AddApplicationPackage')
 begin
  /* If custom.AddApplicationPackage stored procedure
     exists, drop it */
  print ' - Dropping custom.AddApplicationPackage Stored Procedure'
  Drop Procedure custom.AddApplicationPackage
  print ' - custom.AddApplicationPackage Stored Procedure dropped'
 end
print ' - Creating custom.AddApplicationPackage Stored Procedure'
go

/*


        Procedure: custom.AddApplicationPackage
        Author: Andy Leonard
        Parameter(s): ApplicationID [int]
              - contains the ID returned from the execution
                        of custom.AddApplication.
                    PackageID [int]
              - contains the ID returned from the execution
                        of custom.AddPackage.
                    ExecutionOrder [int]
              - contains the order the package will execute
                        within the SSIS Application.
                    ApplicationPackageEnabled [bit]
                    - 1 == Enabled and will run as part of the SSIS Application.
                    0 == Disabled and will not run as part of the SSIS Application.
        Description: Links an SSIS Package to an SSIS Application
          Example: exec custom.AddApplicationPackage 1, 1, 10, 1

*/
Create Procedure custom.AddApplicationPackage
  @ApplicationID int
 ,@PackageID int
 ,@ExecutionOrder int = 10
 ,@ApplicationPackageEnabled bit = 1
As
 begin

  Set NoCount On

        Insert Into custom.ApplicationPackage
        (ApplicationID
        ,PackageID
        ,ExecutionOrder
        ,ApplicationPackageEnabled)
        Values
        (@ApplicationID
```

```
            ,@PackageID
            ,@ExecutionOrder
            ,@ApplicationPackageEnabled)

 end
go
print ' - Custom.AddApplicationPackage Stored Procedure created.'
print ''
```

Create a new SSIS Package in the Chapter2 project and rename it Parent.dtsx. Click the Parameters tab on the Package – it's the third tab from the left (Control Flow, Data Flow, Parameters). Click the Add Parameter button and create a parameter named ApplicationName, String data type, with a default value of "testSSISApp" (without the double-quotes). Set the Required property to True.

Add an Execute SQL Task to the Control Flow and rename it "Get Packages". Open the editor and set the ConnectionType property to ADO.NET. In the Connection property dropdown, select (or create a connection to) the SSISDB database. In the SQLStatement property, enter "custom.GetApplicationPackages" without the double-quotes. Set the IsQueryStoredProcedure property to True. Change the ResultSet property to "Full result set".

Navigate to the Parameter Mapping page and click the Add button. Click the Variable Name dropdown and select "$Package::ApplicationName" at the very top of the list. Change the Data Type to String and the Parameter Name to "ApplicationName" (without the double-quotes). This maps the value in the Parent package Parameters into the ApplicationName parameter sent to the custom.GetApplicationPackages stored procedure when it is called by the Execute SQL Task.

Navigate to the Result Set page and click the Add button. If the Add button is disabled, you did not change the ResultSet property on the General page from the default setting ("None"). If ResultSet is set to any other setting, the Add button is enabled. Enter "0" (without the double-quotes)for the Result Name. In the Variable Name dropdown, create a Variable named Packages. For this variable, set the Value Type property to Object.

■ **Note:** Object is an interesting data type. Akin to a variant, Object can contain a scalar like a date or integer. It can also hold a collection or string array. In this example, Object will contain an ADO.Net Dataset value. If we had set the ConnectionType property to OLEDB (the default), this result set variable would be populated with an ADO Recordset. Yes, that is a COM object – in 2012. COM (and COBOL) will never die…

Let's review. First, the task will use an ADO.Net connection to the SSISDB database to execute the custom. GetApplicationPackages stored procedure we created earlier. Because we set the IsQueryStoredProcedure to True, we do not need to add placeholders for parameters or the "exec" command. Since we used ADO.Net, we can address parameters by name instead of ordinal ("ApplicationName" instead of "0") on the Parameter Mapping page. Finally, we configured the Execute SQL Task to push the results of the stored procedure execution into an object variable named Packages.

Click the Ok button to close the Execute SQL Task editor. Drag a Foreach Loop Container onto the Control Flow surface and open its editor. On the General page, change the Name property to "Foreach Package in Packages". On the Collection page, select the Foreach ADO Enumerator. In the ADO Object Source Variable dropdown, select the Packages variable. Leave the Enumeration Mode default option "Rows in the first table" selected.

I can hear you thinking, "So what would I need to do if I had an ADO Recordset in the Packages object variable?" That is an excellent question. The answer is, "Nothing different." Even though object variables can hold ADO Recordsets and ADO.Net datasets (and other collections and scalars), the Foreach ADO Enumerator is smart enough to *detect* the type of object inside the SSIS object variable – and then read it. Isn't that cool? I thought so too.

Navigate to the Variable Mappings page. Create four variables at Package scope. These variables match the fields returned from the `custom.GetApplicationPackages` stored procedure; and subsequently loaded into the first table in an ADO.Net dataset now housed inside the Packages SSIS variable. If you didn't get that sentence, reread it (I'll wait). That's a lot to take in, but it is vital to understanding what we're doing here. Got it? Good.

I will walk you through creating the first variable listed as follows using the method I prefer for variable creation. Click the Variable dropdown and select "<New variable . . .>" at the very top of the list. When the Add Variable window displays, make sure the Container property is set to Parent (the name of the package). This ensures the variable has package scope. Enter "FolderName" (without the double-quotes) in the Name textbox. Click the Ok button and change the Index property to "0" (without the double-quotes). I almost always create SSIS Variables in this fashion. I have more control over scope, and I am creating and configuring the Variable where it will be used. This functionality saves time and simply rocks.

Create the variables in the following order:

Container: Parent
Name: FolderName
Namespace: User
Value Type: String
Value:

Container: Parent
Name: ProjectName
Namespace: User
Value Type: String
Value:

Container: Parent
Name: ChildPackageName
Namespace: User
Value Type: String
Value:

Container: Parent
Name: ExecutionOrder
Namespace: User
Value Type: Int32
Value: 0

Make sure the Index values align as shown here:

FolderName: 0
ProjectName: 1
PackageName: 2
ExecutionOrder: 3

The fields do not *have* to be listed in this order, but the Index values have to align with the (zero-based) ordinal value of the fields returned by the custom.GetApplicationPackages.

Click the Ok button to close the Foreach Loop Container editor. Drag an Execute SQL Task into the Foreach Loop Container and rename it "Execute Package". Set the ConnectionType to ADO.NET and select the SSISDB connection you created earlier. Set the IsQueryStoredProcedure property to True and SQL Statement property to custom.execute_catalog_package. On the Parameter Mapping page, add and create a new variable named ExecutionID, Int32 data type, package scope, default value: 0. Change the Direction of the parameter to Output and couple the SSIS variable you just created to the ExecutionID parameter by supplying the Parameter Name: ExecutionID. Add three more parameter mappings; one each for FolderName, ProjectName, and ChildPackageName. Map them to the stored procedure parameters FolderName, ProjectName, and PackageName; respectively. The custom.execute_catalog_package stored procedure accepts other parameters: LoggingLevel, Use32BitRunTime, ReferenceID, and ObjectType; but these parameters all contain default values that will serve our purposes. Click the Ok button to close the Execute SQL Task editor.

Your Parent.dtsx SSIS package should appear as shown in Figure 2-3.

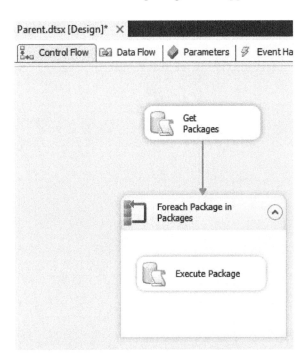

Figure 2-3. *Parent Package Control Flow*

Return to SQL Server Management Studio (SSMS). Let's provide our simple execution framework with metadata to execute. Execute the T-SQL statements in Listing 2–6.

Listing 2-6. Building the Metadata for an SSIS Application

```
Use SSISDB
Go
Set NoCount On

Declare @ApplicationName nvarchar(256)
Declare @ApplicationDescription nvarchar(512)
Declare @ApplicationID int
Declare @FolderName nvarchar(256)
Declare @ProjectName nvarchar(256)
Declare @PackageName nvarchar(256)
Declare @PackageDescription nvarchar(512)
Declare @PackageID int
Declare @ExecutionOrder int
Declare @ApplicationPackageEnabled bit
Declare @ApplicationTbl table(ApplicationID int)
Declare @PackageTbl table(PackageID int)

begin tran

  -- Build Application --
Select @ApplicationName = 'TestSSISApp'
      ,@ApplicationDescription = 'A test SSIS application'

Insert Into @ApplicationTbl
Exec custom.AddApplication
  @ApplicationName
 ,@ApplicationDescription

 Select @ApplicationID = ApplicationID
 From @ApplicationTbl

  -- Build Package --
Select @FolderName = 'Chapter2'
      ,@ProjectName = 'Chapter 2'
      ,@PackageName = 'Chapter2.dtsx'
      ,@PackageDescription = 'A test SSIS package'

Insert Into @PackageTbl
Exec custom.AddPackage
  @FolderName
 ,@ProjectName
 ,@PackageName
 ,@PackageDescription

 Select @PackageID = PackageID
 From @PackageTbl

  -- Build ApplicationPackage --
Select @ExecutionOrder = 10
      ,@ApplicationPackageEnabled = 1
```

```
Exec custom.AddApplicationPackage
  @ApplicationID
 ,@PackageID
 ,@ExecutionOrder
 ,@ApplicationPackageEnabled

Delete @PackageTbl


-- Build Package --
Select @FolderName = 'Chapter2'
      ,@ProjectName = 'Chapter 2'
      ,@PackageName = 'Chapter2.dtsx'
      ,@PackageDescription = 'Another test SSIS package'

Insert Into @PackageTbl
Exec custom.AddPackage
 @FolderName
,@ProjectName
,@PackageName
,@PackageDescription

 Select @PackageID = PackageID
 From @PackageTbl


 -- Build ApplicationPackage --
Select @ExecutionOrder = 20
      ,@ApplicationPackageEnabled = 1

 Exec custom.AddApplicationPackage
   @ApplicationID
  ,@PackageID
  ,@ExecutionOrder
  ,@ApplicationPackageEnabled

 Delete @PackageTbl

Commit
```

The T-SQL in Listing 2–6 builds a simple SSIS Application in the execution framework. It calls our Chapter2. dtsx SSIS package twice. If you return to SQL Server Data Tools (SSDT) and execute the Parent package, you will note the Chapter2.dtsx SSIS package executes twice in quick succession. You can see that execution in Figure 2-4.

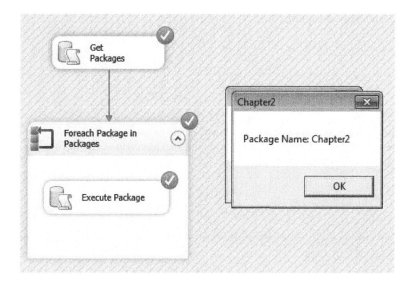

Figure 2-4. Chapter2.dtsx executing twice without waiting

It is important to understand that the framework is a "fire and forget" design. The screenshot in Figure 2-4 shows both instances of Chapter2.dtsx showing their respective message boxes, yet the tasks in the background have completed. This approach works well if your SSIS packages can be executed in parallel. But what if there are dependencies between packages? This framework does not facilitate dependent package execution, but I will show you a way to couple the framework with the SQL Agent Job scheduler in the next section. Coupling will allow you to execute the parent package for each "step" of a process, calling an SSIS Application each step, and in turn calling one or more SSIS Packages in parallel.

■ **Note** Appendix A contains information on building a serial SSIS framework that was originally built for SSIS 2005. It works in SSIS 2012 if you use the Package Deployment Model.

Scheduling SSIS Package Execution

There are many commercially available software execution schedulers on the market. They range from relatively simple to highly complex, allowing time- or event-based execution. Many include metadata collection capabilities that track metrics such as execution time. SQL Server Agent is a fairly robust job scheduling application included with SQL Server. We will use SQL Server Agent to schedule the execution of our demo package.

■ **Caution** Before proceeding, deploy the Chapter2 project to the SSIS Catalog. Doing so will deploy Chapter2. dtsx and Parent.dtsx.

Scheduling an SSIS Package

Open SQL Server Management Studio (SSMS) and connect to an instance of SQL Server 2012. Open Object Explorer and expand the SQL Server Agent node. Right-click the Jobs virtual folder and click New→Job. When the New Job window displays, name the job "Ch2" and select "SQL Server Integration Services Package" from the Type dropdown. Click on the Steps page and click the New button. Name the new step "Execute Chapter 2 Package".

Select a Package Source from the dropdown. The options are:

- SQL Server
- File system
- SSIS Package Store
- SSIS Catalog

Let's schedule an SSIS package from the catalog to start. Type "localhost", or the name of the SSIS server that contains the SSIS Catalog, into the Server dropdown. Click the ellipsis beside the Package textbox and navigate to the demonstration package, Chapter2.dtsx, as shown in Figure 2-5.

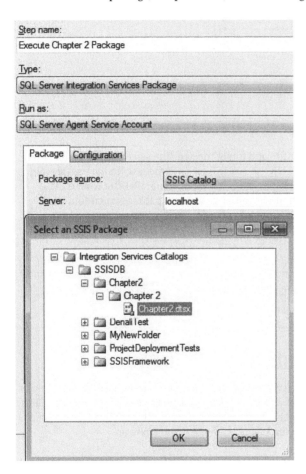

Figure 2-5. *Configuring a SQL Server Agent Job to execute an SSIS package in the SSIS Catalog*

Clicking the Ok button will complete the scheduling procedure.

Scheduling a File System Package

To schedule a package stored in the file system, select "File system" in the Package Source dropdown. Click the ellipsis beside the Package textbox and navigate to the desired SSIS package file. Once configured, the step will appear as shown in Figure 2-6.

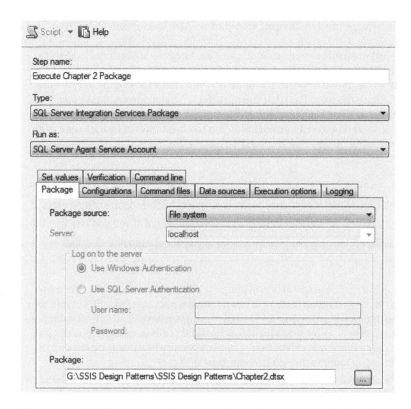

Figure 2-6. SQL Server Agent job step configured to execute an SSIS Package from the file system

You can test the job by right-clicking the job name in SSMS and then clicking "Start job at step."

Running SQLAgent Jobs with the Custom Execution Framework

We can run a SQL Agent Job with our Custom Execution Framework. To demonstrate, create a new SQL Agent job named "Framework Execution". On the Steps page, add a new step named "TestSSISApp Framework Execution". Select the SSIS Package Step Type and accept the default Package Source property of "SSIS Catalog." Enter or select the name of your server in the Server dropdown and click the ellipsis beside the Package textbox to open the "Select an SSIS Package" window. Navigate to the Parent.dtsx SSIS Package, and then click the Ok button.

Click the Configuration tab on the New Job Step window. The package parameter ApplicationName should appear in the Parameters list. To enter a value for this parameter, click the ellipsis beside the Value textbox, and then enter "TestSSISApp" without the double-quotes. Click the Ok button to close and save the New Job Step window, and then click the Ok button again to close and save the New Job window.

To test, right click the Framework Execution SQL Agent Job and click "Start Job at Step..." The SQL Agent job will execute and succeed, but I have bad news: the package executions will fail. I can hear you thinking, "Wait, what?" I kid you not. Remember that note previously about this being a "fire and forget" execution framework? That fact haunts us here – and elsewhere in SSIS execution. It's better for you to become aware of this now – trust me on this. The other way to gain this knowledge involves arguing with your boss (or worse, your client) that "the job succeeded!" and being wrong.

How do you know the package execution failed? Let's go look. Expand the Integration Services Catalogs virtual folder in SQL Server Management Studio (SSMS) Object Explorer. Right-click SSISDB and hover over Reports, then Standard Reports, and click Integration Services Dashboard. If you have followed my instructions, you will see a large, reddish-colored "2" above the word Failed. If you click the "2," the reports will take you to a page containing a list of failed executions. If you then click the All Messages link, you will see an error message informing you that the Script Task experienced an error (Exception has been thrown by the target of an invocation). That message means (among other things) that you used a message box in a script task. No, I am not making this up.

■ **Note:** "Are message boxes bad?" Absolutely not! In fact, they're the only way to troubleshoot a certain class of errors in SSIS. I use them all the time, but I qualify the MsgBox calls in an If/Then statement. If you don't do this, the message box calls will execute and cause SQL Agent Jobs to either fail or lie to you about execution success.

All is not lost. The problem here is that a service account is providing the security context for the execution. The account used to start the SQL Agent service is the account used to execute the packages from SQL Agent jobs. That account typically does not have the InteractWithDesktop role assigned, and you have to admit- a desktop is handy for displaying message boxes. The caveat is: You cannot include unqualified calls to message box displays in SSIS packages. Use a parameter or variable (I use one called Debug) and make sure its value is external to the package so you can turn it on and off when you *want* to display message boxes.

You can also execute the Parent.dtsx package from the SSIS Catalog. In SSMS Object Explorer, continue drilling into the Chapter2 folder. Open Projects, then Chapter 2, then Packages, and right-click the Parent.dtsx package. Click Execute and supply "TestSSISApp" for the ApplicationName parameter. When you click the Ok button, the package executes and the two message boxes appear. Why? Because you are no longer running the security context of the service account that starts the SQL Agent service; you are running in the security context with which you connected to SSMS Object Explorer. This is most likely a domain or machine account that uses Windows Authentication and *your* personal credentials. If you've been watching a desktop all this time, you (and all the other users in your domain or machine) have the InteractWithDesktop role assigned.

Running the Custom Execution Framework with SQL Agent

You can run SQL Agent jobs with the custom execution framework. You just cannot pop up message boxes. For example, you can create an SSIS Application for each "step" in your process. The SSIS Application can contain SSIS Packages that can execute in parallel. You then build a SQL Agent job with several Job Steps – one for each SSIS Application. A SQL Agent job executes its steps serially, waiting for one to succeed (by default) before starting the next step.

Most data warehouses require an extraction step that stages all data – from dimension and fact sources – to a staging database. Next, dimension data are loaded into the data warehouse. Finally, fact data are loaded from the staging database into the data warehouse.

The precedence of operations is as follows: Extract Fact and Extract Dimensions can run concurrently (in parallel). You can design one package for each dimension and fact source table extract operation, add them to the Extract SSIS Application, and execute that SSIS Application as Step 1 of your DW ETL Job. Once that completes, Step 2 can load the dimension data from the stage database to the data warehouse. Once that completes, Step 3 can load the fact data from the staging database to the data warehouse. So while relatively simple and somewhat limited, our custom execution framework can facilitate configurable parallel and serial ETL operations. Execute Package Task.

The Execute Package Task is best understood in action. To demonstrate, create a new SSIS package and rename it "Parent.dtsx". Add an Execute Package Task to the Control Flow. Open the editor and observe the selections for the ReferenceType property as shown in Figure 2-7.

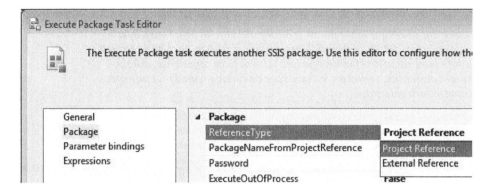

Figure 2-7. *The Execute Package Task Reference Property*

If the ReferenceType property is set to Project Reference, the Execute Package Task can be used to start packages in the SSIS project, supporting the Project Deployment Model. Setting this property to External Reference allows executing SSIS packages stored in either the MSDB database or file system, supporting the Package Deployment Model. Figure 2-8 shows the Execute Package Task configured to execute the Chapter2.dtsx package.

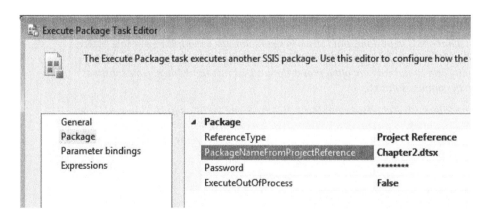

Figure 2-8. *Selecting the Project Reference Package*

You can close the editor after selecting the package. Test it by executing Parent.dtsx in the SSIS debugger.

Metadata-Driven Execution

I have used all of the methods for SSIS package execution listed in this chapter. They each have advantages and disadvantages. How then, do you select which method to use? I'm glad you asked! That is an excellent question. I consider the following:

- *Troubleshooting – At some time in the future, someone will have to figure out why a package failed execution. Facilitating troubleshooting is not something to be tacked onto the end of a data integration development project; it needs to be considered up front. It is as important as security. I select an SSIS package execution method that supports troubleshooting in each enterprise.*

- *Code maintenance – The SSIS project will possibly be modified in the future. This means the packages, projects, and execution methodology need to be documented. It also means I need to consider the skills and comfort -levels of the individuals or team maintaining this code. If the individuals or team are skilled .Net developers, I lean towards using the Script Task and Component for complex operations. I also attempt to develop in the .Net language of choice, if this is the case. If they found their way to SSIS via a role as a database administrator, I use more Transact-SQL in developing the solution. If they have DTS, SSIS, or other ETL development platform experience, I develop packages slightly differently to match their comfort zones. Again, this is different for different enterprises.*

- *Enterprise requirements – I often encounter "best practices" at enterprises. I enclose the terms in quotations because, well, some of them aren't actually best. They exist because something bad happened and someone reacted. Sometimes the reactions make sense from an SSIS point-of-view, sometimes they are security matters that vex the SSIS developers, and sometimes they just do not make good sense for anyone.*

- *Complexity – I do not like complex solutions. I tolerate them if they are the only way to accomplish what needs to be done, but I strive to keep solutions as simple as possible. Fewer moving parts means there is less to break, less to troubleshoot, and less to maintain. That said, flexibility and complexity are often proportional. That means highly flexible solutions are likely to be complex solutions.*

I write this here, especially the bullet about complexity, to introduce Execution from Managed Code. Complexity is the only disadvantage of executing SSIS from .Net. Executing SSIS from managed code offers maximum flexibility: If you can think it, you can find a way to build it in .Net. In my opinion, knowing .Net is no longer optional for the data integration developer in the Microsoft space.

Execution from Managed Code

There is a ton (or tonne, if you prefer) of benefit from executing SSIS packages from .Net managed code. There are various limitations to executing SSIS in other ways. Without exception, they can all be overcome by controlling execution from .Net. In this section, we will demonstrate the basics of using VB.Net to execute SSIS packages.

The Demo Application

For this demonstration, I used Visual Basic 2010 and the .Net Framework 4. Unless otherwise specified, I accepted the default settings for VB applications in the Visual Studio 2010 Integrated Development Environment (IDE).

To begin, create a new VB Windows Forms project in Visual Studio 2010. Add references for the following assemblies:

- Microsoft.SqlServer.ConnectionInfo

- Microsoft.SqlServer.DTSRuntimeWrap

- Microsoft.SqlServer.Management.IntegrationServices

- Microsoft.SqlServer.Management.Sdk.Sfc

- Microsoft.SqlServer.Smo

The frmMain Form

Rename Form1 to frmMain. Add two GroupBox controls to the form, arranged with one over the other as shown in Figure 2-9. Change the Text property of the top groupbox to "SSIS Package in the File System" and the Text property of the lower groupbox to "SSIS Package in the Catalog". In the upper groupbox, add a label, textbox, and two buttons. Change the Text property of the label to "Package Path:". Name one of the buttons "btnOpenSSISPkg" and change its Text property to " …". Name the other button "btnStartFile" and set its Text property to "Start".

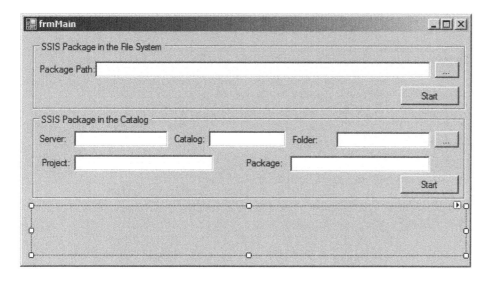

Figure 2-9. *The frmMain controls layout*

In the "SSIS Package in the Catalog" groupbox, add five labels, five textboxes, and two buttons. Change the Text properties of the labels to "Server:", "Catalog:", "Folder:", "Project:", and "Package:". Position each textbox to the right of each labels and name them "txtSSISCatalogServer", "txtCatalog", "txtFolder", "txtCatalogProject", and "txtCatalogPackage", respectively. Name one of the buttons "btnOpenSSISPkgInCatalog" and set its Text property to " …". Name the other button "btnStartCatalog" and set its Text property to "Start".

Add a textbox beneath the "SSIS Package in the Catalog" groupbox. Name it "txtStatus", set the MultiLine property to True, BackColor to "ButtonFace", and the BorderStyle to "None". Position the controls similar to the way shown in Figure 2-9. Finally, add a FileOpenDialog control to the form, leaving it configured to defaults.

It will likely surprise no one to learn that I was first exposed to design patterns while a software developer. The pattern I use in this application puts a minimum amount of code behind the form. The code that is in the form calls code in a form-specific module. You can view the code for frmMain by right-clicking frmMain in Solution Explorer and selecting View Code. Replace the code displayed with the following:

```
'
' frmMain code
'
' I use a Helper Pattern when developing interfaces.
' Each form is named frm_____ and there is a corresponding module named
' frm_____Helper.vb.
' Each event method calls a subroutine in the Helper module.
'

Public Class frmMain

    Private Sub frmMain_Load(ByVal sender As System.Object, ByVal e As System.EventArgs) _
Handles MyBase.Load
        InitFrmMain()
    End Sub

    Private Sub btnStartFile_Click(ByVal sender As System.Object, _
                                   ByVal e As System.EventArgs) Handles btnStartFile.Click
        btnStartFileClick()
    End Sub

    Private Sub btnOpenSSISPkg_Click(ByVal sender As System.Object, _
                                     ByVal e As System.EventArgs) Handles _
btnOpenSSISPkg.Click
        btnOpenSSISPkgClick()
    End Sub

    Private Sub btnStartCatalog_Click(ByVal sender As System.Object, _
                                      ByVal e As System.EventArgs) Handles _
btnStartCatalog.Click
        btnStartCatalogClick()
    End Sub

    Private Sub btnOpenSSISPkgInCatalog_Click(ByVal sender As System.Object, _
                                              ByVal e As System.EventArgs) Handles _
btnOpenSSISPkgInCatalog.Click
        btnOpenSSISPkgInCatalogClick()
    End Sub
End Class
```

Again, the code behind the form is sparse. Most of the real work is done elsewhere. Let's build that part now.

Add a module to the solution and name it frmMainHelper. Add the following code to the new module:

```
'
' frmMainHelper module
'
' I use a Helper Pattern when developing interfaces.
' Each form is named frm_____ and there is a corresponding module named frm_____Helper.vb.
' Each event method calls a subroutine in the Helper module.
'
' This module supports frmMain.
'

Imports System
Imports System.Windows
```

```
Imports System.Windows.Forms
Imports Microsoft.SqlServer.Dts.Runtime.Wrapper
Imports Microsoft.SqlServer.Management.IntegrationServices
Imports Microsoft.SqlServer.Management.Smo

Module frmMainHelper

    Public Sub InitFrmMain()

        ' initialize and load frmISTree

        ' define the version
        Dim sVer As String = System.Windows.Forms.Application.ProductName & "  v" & _
System.Windows.Forms.Application.ProductVersion

        ' display the version and startup status
        With frmMain
            .Text = sVer
            .txtStatus.Text = sVer & ControlChars.CrLf & "Ready"
        End With

    End Sub

    Public Sub btnStartFileClick()

        ' configure an SSIS application and execute the selected SSIS package file

        With frmMain
            .Cursor = Cursors.WaitCursor
            .txtStatus.Text = "Executing " & .txtSSISPkgPath.Text
            .Refresh()
            Dim ssisApp As New Microsoft.SqlServer.Dts.Runtime.Wrapper.Application
            Dim ssisPkg As Package = ssisApp.LoadPackage(.txtSSISPkgPath.Text, _
AcceptRejectRule.None, Nothing)
            ssisPkg.Execute()
            .Cursor = Cursors.Default
            .txtStatus.Text = .txtSSISPkgPath.Text & " executed."
        End With

    End Sub

    Public Sub btnOpenSSISPkgClick()

        ' allow the user to navigate to an SSIS package file

        With frmMain
            .OpenFileDialog1.DefaultExt = "dtsx"
            .OpenFileDialog1.ShowDialog()
            .txtSSISPkgPath.Text = .OpenFileDialog1.FileName
            .txtStatus.Text = .txtSSISPkgPath.Text & " package path loaded."
        End With

    End Sub

    Sub btnOpenSSISPkgInCatalogClick()

        ' allow the user to navigate to an SSIS package stored in a catalog

        frmISTreeInit()
```

```vb
        Dim sTmp As String = sFullSSISPkgPath
        Dim sServerName As String = Strings.Left(sTmp, Strings.InStr(sTmp, ".") - 1)
        Dim iStart As Integer = Strings.InStr(sTmp, ".") + 1
        Dim iEnd As Integer = Strings.InStr(sTmp, "\")
        Dim iLen As Integer
        Dim sCatalogName As String
        Dim sFolderName As String
        Dim sProjectName As String
        Dim sPackageName As String

    If iEnd > iStart Then
        iLen = iEnd - iStart
        sCatalogName = Strings.Mid(sTmp, iStart, iLen)
        sTmp = Strings.Right(sTmp, Strings.Len(sTmp) - iEnd)

        iStart = 1
        iEnd = Strings.InStr(sTmp, "\")
        If iEnd > iStart Then
            iLen = iEnd - iStart
            sFolderName = Strings.Mid(sTmp, iStart, iLen)
            sTmp = Strings.Right(sTmp, Strings.Len(sTmp) - iEnd)

            iStart = 1
            iEnd = Strings.InStr(sTmp, "\")
            If iEnd > iStart Then
                iLen = iEnd - iStart
                sProjectName = Strings.Mid(sTmp, iStart, iLen)
                sTmp = Strings.Right(sTmp, Strings.Len(sTmp) - iEnd)
                sPackageName = sTmp
            End If
        End If
    End If

    With frmMain
        .txtSSISCatalogServer.Text = sServerName
        .txtCatalog.Text = sCatalogName
        .txtFolder.Text = sFolderName
        .txtCatalogProject.Text = sProjectName
        .txtCatalogPackage.Text = sPackageName
        .txtStatus.Text = sFullSSISPkgPath & " metadata loaded and parsed."
    End With

End Sub

Sub btnStartCatalogClick()

    ' configure an SSIS application and execute the selected SSIS package from the
    ' catalog

    With frmMain
        .Cursor = Cursors.WaitCursor
        .txtStatus.Text = "Loading " & sFullSSISPkgPath
        .Refresh()
        Dim oServer As New Server(.txtSSISCatalogServer.Text)
        Dim oIS As New IntegrationServices(oServer)
```

```
            Dim cat As Catalog=oIS.Catalogs(.txtCatalog.Text)
            Dim fldr As CatalogFolder=cat.Folders(.txtFolder.Text)
            Dim prj As ProjectInfo=fldr.Projects(.txtCatalogProject.Text)
            Dim pkg As PackageInfo=prj.Packages(.txtCatalogPackage.Text)
            .txtStatus.Text = sFullSSISPkgPath & " loaded. Starting validation..."
            .Refresh()
pkg.Validate(False, PackageInfo.ReferenceUsage.UseAllReferences, Nothing)
            .txtStatus.Text = sFullSSISPkgPath & " validated. Starting execution..."
            .Refresh()
pkg.Execute(False, Nothing)
            .txtStatus.Text = sFullSSISPkgPath & " execution started."
            .Cursor = Cursors.Default
        End With

    End Sub

End Module
```

Let's walk through the portion of this code that executes an SSIS package in the file system. In Figure 2–9, we are looking at the functionality represented in the upper groupbox.

The application works when the user either enters the full path to an SSIS package in the file system or clicks the ellipsis to browse to a SSIS package (dtsx) file. After selecting a file, the full path will display in the Package Path textbox. To execute the package, click the Start button in the "SSIS Package in the File System" groupbox. When the Start button is pressed, the form code in the btnStartFile_Click subroutine is executed, and it executes a single line of code that calls the btnStartFileClick subroutine in the frmMainHelper module.

The btnStartFileClick subroutine first changes the form cursor to a WaitCursor. Next it updates the txtStatus textbox to display the text "Executing" followed by the full path of the SSIS package in the Package Path textbox. The Refresh statement causes the form to update, displaying the WaitCursor and the message in txtStatus. The code then creates an instance of an SSIS Application (Microsoft.SqlServer.Dts.Runtime.Wrapper.Application) in the form of the ssisApp variable. ssisPkg is an instance of an SSIS Package object. It is created by calling the LoadPackage method of the SSIS Application object (ssisApp). We use the Package object's Execute method to start the SSIS Package. The remainder of the subroutine resets the form cursor and updates the txtStatus message to indicate the package executed.

Were I to harden this code for Production, I would wrap much of the code in this subroutine in a large Try-Catch block. In the Catch section, I would reset the cursor and update txtStatus with the error message. I like logging – a lot. In a Production-hardened version, I would log my intention to execute the package and include the full path displayed in the Package Path textbox. I would also log the result of the attempted execution, whether it succeeded or failed.

The code that executes an SSIS package stored in the SSIS Catalog is found in the frmMainHelper module's btnStartCatalogClick subroutine. The code that manages the cursor and messaging to the txtStatus textbox is comparable to that found in the btnStartFileClick subroutine.

There are a few more moving parts to an SSIS package stored in the SSIS Catalog, shown in Figure 2-10.

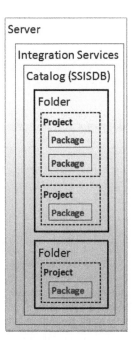

Figure 2-10. *A representation of the SSIS Catalog*

Integration Services is contained by a Server and, in turn, contains a Catalog. In SQL Server 2012, Integration Services contains a single catalog named "SSISDB". SSISDB is also the name of the database used to manage SSIS metadata in the catalog. A catalog contains one or more Folders. Folders contain one or more Projects, which contain one or more Packages.

In the btnStartCatalogClick subroutine, the code declares variables for the objects in this hierarchy (using Dim statements) and sets their value based on the names supplied in the five textboxes: txtSSISCatalogServer, txtCatalog, txtFolder, txtCatalogProject, and txtCatalogPackage. As you can see by comparing the names of the textboxes to Figure 2-10, an SSIS package stored in the catalog can be uniquely identified using this hierarchy. How are the textboxes populated? The user can enter the information manually if desired. But the application contains a second form, launched by the ellipsis in the "SSIS Package in the Catalog" groupbox, to facilitate SSIS catalog navigation.

To build it, add a second form to the application and name it frmISTree. Add a groupbox control to the form and position it near the top. Change the Text property of the groupbox to "Connection". Add a label, textbox, and button to the groupbox. Change the Text property of the label to "Server:". Name the textbox "txtServer". Name the button "btnConnect" and change its Text property to "Connect". Add a TreeView control to the lower portion of the form and name it "tvCatalog". Add a button just below the treeview, name it "btnSelect" and change its Text property to "Select". Add an ImageList control and name it "ilSSDB". You will either have to rustle up your own images or download the demo project containing the four images I used for treeview node levels. Set the treeview's ImageList property to "ilSSDB". The form should appear as shown in Figure 2-11.

Figure 2-11. *ISTree Form*

Replace the code behind the form with the following code:

```
'
' frmISTree code
'
' I use a Helper Pattern when developing interfaces.
' Each form is named frm_____ and there is a corresponding module named frm_____Helper.vb.
' Each event method calls a subroutine in the Helper module.
'
Public Class frmISTree

    Private Sub btnConnect_Click(ByVal sender As System.Object, _
                            ByVal e As System.EventArgs) Handles btnConnect.Click
        btnConnectClick()
    End Sub

    Private Sub btnSelect_Click(ByVal sender As System.Object, _
                            ByVal e As System.EventArgs) Handles btnSelect.Click
        btnSelectClick()
    End Sub

    Private Sub tvCatalog_AfterSelect(ByVal sender As System.Object, _
                                ByVal e As System.Windows.Forms.TreeViewEventArgs) _
Handles tvCatalog.AfterSelect

    End Sub

    Private Sub tvCatalog_DoubleClick(ByVal sender As Object, _
                                ByVal e As System.EventArgs) _
Handles tvCatalog.DoubleClick
        tvCatalogDoubleClick()
    End Sub
End Class
```

Again, this code merely points to the Helper module, in this case frmISTreeHelper. Add a new module, so named, and replace it with the following code:

```
'
' frmISTreeHelper module
'
' I use a Helper Pattern when developing interfaces.
' Each form is named frm_____ and there is a corresponding module named frm_____Helper.vb.
' Each event method calls a subroutine in the Helper module.
'
' This module supports frmISTree.
'

Imports Microsoft.SqlServer.Management.IntegrationServices
Imports Microsoft.SqlServer.Management.Smo

Module frmISTreeHelper
    ' variables
    Public sFullSSISPkgPath As String

    Sub frmISTreeInit()

        ' initialize and load frmISTree

        With frmISTree
            .Text="Integration Services"
            .txtServer.Text = "localhost"
            .ShowDialog()
        End With

    End Sub

    Sub btnConnectClick()

        ' connect to the server indicated in the txtServer textbox
        ' hook into the SSISDB catalog
        ' build out the SSISDB node by iterating the objects stored therein
        ' load the node and display it

        With frmISTree
            Dim oServer As New Server(.txtServer.Text)
            Dim oIS As New IntegrationServices(oServer)
            Dim cat As Catalog = oIS.Catalogs("SSISDB")
            Dim L1Node As New TreeNode("SSISDB")
            L1Node.ImageIndex = 0
            Dim L2Node As TreeNode
            Dim L3Node As TreeNode
            Dim L4Node As TreeNode

            For Each f As CatalogFolder In cat.Folders
                L2Node = New TreeNode(f.Name)
                L2Node.ImageIndex = 1
                L1Node.Nodes.Add(L2Node)
                '.tvCatalog.Nodes.Add(L2Node)
                For Each pr As ProjectInfo In f.Projects
                    L3Node = New TreeNode(pr.Name)
                    L3Node.ImageIndex = 2
```

```
                L2Node.Nodes.Add(L3Node)
                '.tvCatalog.Nodes.Add(L3Node)
                For Each pkg As PackageInfo In pr.Packages
                    L4Node = New TreeNode(pkg.Name)
                    L4Node.ImageIndex = 3
                    L3Node.Nodes.Add(L4Node)
                    '.tvCatalog.Nodes.Add(L4Node)
                Next
            Next
        Next

        .tvCatalog.Nodes.Add(L1Node)
    End With

End Sub

Sub btnSelectClick()

    ' if the image index level indicates a package,
    ' select this node, populate the sFullSSISPkgPath variable,
    ' and close the form

    With frmISTree
        If Not .tvCatalog.SelectedNode Is Nothing Then
            If .tvCatalog.SelectedNode.ImageIndex = 3 Then
sFullSSISPkgPath = .txtServer.Text& "." &_
.tvCatalog.SelectedNode.FullPath
                    .Close()
            End If
        End If
    End With

End Sub

Sub tvCatalogDoubleClick()

    ' run the Select Click logic

    With frmISTree
        btnSelectClick()
    End With

End Sub

End Module
```

All the action in this module happens in the subroutines that populate the treeview control (btnConnectClick) and select the node (btnSelectClick). The code defaults the name of the server to "localhost". The user can change it before clicking the Connect button. Once the button is clicked, the code calls btnConnectClick.

The btnConnectClick subroutine creates objects for the Server, Integration Services, and Catalog objects in the model. Next, it builds a hierarchy of four levels of nodes starting with the catalog. The variables – L1Node, L2Node, L3Node, and L4Node – represent the Catalog, Folder, Project, and Package levels of the hierarchy. The code uses a series of nested For Each loops to iterate the SSIS Catalog and populate the sub-nodes under L1Node (Catalog), and then the L1Node is added to the tvCatalogtreeview.

The btnSelectClick subroutine builds a string the represents the unique path to the SSIS package in the Catalog hierarchy. The code checks to see if a node is selected, and then checks to see if the selected node is at the package level. If all is right with the treeview, the variable sFullSSISPkgPath is populated with the path to the

SSIS package in the catalog. Immediately thereafter, the frmISTree form closes. Users can also double-click on a package node in the treeview and invoke the btnSelectClick subroutine.

Execute the application to test it! You should see results as in Figure 2-12.

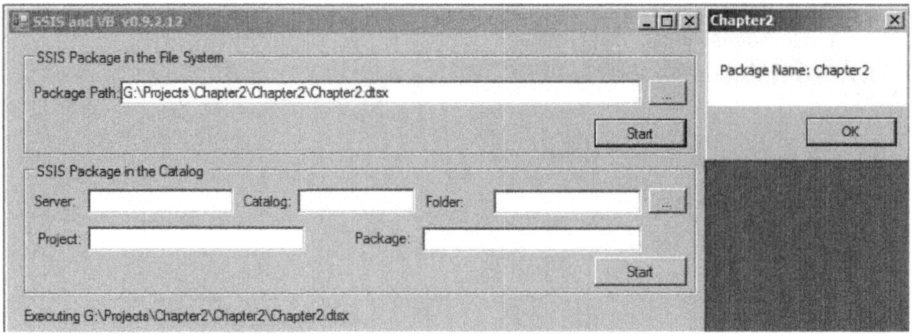

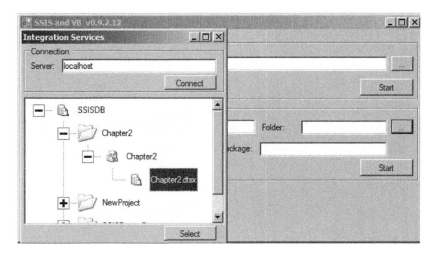

Figure 2-12. *Executing a package from the file system*

Selection of a package in the SSIS Catalog appears as shown in Figure 2-13.

Figure 2-13. *Selecting a package in the SSIS Catalog*

Execute a package selected from the SSIS Catalog as illustrated in Figure 2-14.

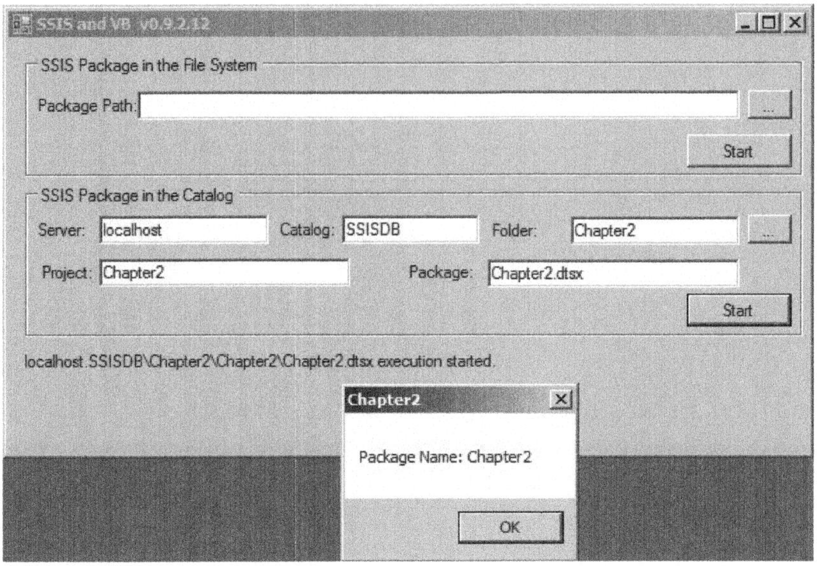

Figure 2-14. *Executing an SSIS Package stored in the SSIS Catalog*

Summary

In this chapter, we surveyed many ways to execute an SSIS package. We examined the many built-in ways for convenient execution of SSIS packages. Then we kicked things up a notch by extending the SSISDB functionality. In the end, we produced a simple, yet functional, custom execution framework and demonstrated how to couple it to the scheduling capabilities of SQL Agent jobs to produce a custom parallel-/serial-capable execution engine. We built a .Net application to demonstrate the flexibility (and complexity) of executing SSIS packages from managed code.

## CHAPTER 3

Scripting Patterns

As I have shown throughout this book, SQL Server Integration Services is a multifaceted product, with many native capabilities that can handle even the most difficult of data challenges. With highly flexible transformations, such as the Lookup, Conditional Split, Derived Column, and Merge Join, the data flow is well-equipped to perform a limitless number of transformations to in-flight data. On the control flow side, tools including the File System Task, For Each Loop (and its cousin, the For Loop), File System Task, and Data Profiling Task provide critical services to support fundamental ETL operations. Right out of the box, you get a toolbox that's full of flexible and powerful objects.

However, even the most casual ETL developer will eventually encounter scenarios that requiremore flexibility than what is afforded in the native components. Dealing with data movement and transformation is often ugly and unpredicListing, and requires a level of extensibility that would be difficult to build into general-purpose tools. Fortunately, there is a solution for these uncommon ETL needs: custom .NET scripting.

The Toolset

SQL Server Integration Services has the capability to build very powerful ETL logic directly into your SSIS packages. Through Visual Studio and its various niceties (familiar development environment, Intellisense, and project-based development, among many others), the burden of embedding custom logic in your ETL processes is made significantly easier.

Unlike its predecessor Data Transformation Services (DTS), SQL Server Integration Services exposes the entire .NET runtime within its scripting tools. Gone is the requirement to use only ActiveX scripts within ETL packages (although this capability does still in SSIS, for those loyal to VBScript). With the introduction of the rich scripting environments in SSIS, you now have the ability to access the same framework features used in "real" software development. True object-oriented development, events, proper error handling, and other capabilities are now fully accessible within custom scripts in SSIS.

SQL Server Integration Services includes two different vehicles for leveraging .NET code into your packages, each designed to allow different types of custom behaviors. The Script Task, which resides in the control flow toolbox, is a broad general-purpose tool intended to perform support and administrative tasks. Within the data flow toolbox, you'll find the Script Component, a versatile yet precise data movement and manipulation tool.

If you're new to scripting in SSIS, you might wonder why there are two different script tools in SSIS. Beyond that, the critical design pattern will include a decision on which of these tools to use in a given scenario. The short answer: it depends. As mentioned, the Script Task is typically the better choice for operational behavior, and is most commonly used for operations affecting overall package flow (as opposed to data movement). On the other hand, if your ETL needs require generating, consuming, or manipulating rows of data, then the Script Component is normally the better tool.

Although they have nearly identical interfaces, the Script Task and Script Component differ greatly in their default design. As you explore each of these tools, you'll find that there is a significant amount of code automatically added to the script project when you introduce it to your work surface. As a tool designed for direct data interaction, the script component will include preconfigured code defining inputs and/or outputs to allow data to flow through the component. In contrast, the behaviors built into the script task have no facilities for either inputs or puts, further illustrating that this tool was built for purposes other than data flow.

The Script Task and Script Component share many similarities. Both tools feature a script designer that resembles the familiar Visual Studio development environment used for mainstream software development. In both of these, you'll find the workspace organized into a virtual solution (displayed very similarly to the solution container found in Visual Studio development) that may include multiple files and folders. Also common to both script tools is the ability to include external code or services within the virtual solution. This capability allows you to leverage code that has already been written and compiled elsewhere, whether it's a DLL file you include with the project or some external resource such as a web service. The language behaviors in both tools will be identical; functionality such as error handling, compiler directives, and core framework functionality is shared between these two scripting tools.

Should I Use Script?

Before we get started exploring the inner workings of the script tools in SSIS, a fundamental question should be answered: should I be using the scripting tools at all?

As much as I believe in using the script tools in SSIS to solve difficult problems, there's one piece of advice I almost always dish out when talking or writing about this topic: only use the Script Task or Script Component in situations where existing tools can't easily address the problem you're trying to solve. Although you gain a great deal in terms of flexibility, you also lose a few things— design-time validation, easy reusability, and a GUI settings editor, among others— when you deploy an instance of script into your packages.

Now don't take any of this to mean that scripting is bad, or that is reflective of poor package design (after all, this is a chapter describing recommended practices for using script!). Quite the opposite, in fact—I've found many situations where the only tool that could satisfy the ETL requirement was a well-designed script instance. The point is that the Script Task and Script Component are complex tools. Native components are much simpler to use and maintain. In situations where one or more native elements of SSIS can easily dispatch any ETL issues, don't complicate the issue by reinventing the wheel with a script.

The Script Editor

Though their purposes differ greatly, you can expect a similar experience in the script editor for both the Script Task and the Script Component tools. Features of both tools include

- The ubiquitous code window
- Project Explorer
- Full .NET runtime
- Compiler

I'll cover the semantics of writing code in each of these tools later in the chapter. Now, I'll explore some of the other features shared by the Script Task and the Script Component.

Project Explorer

Software development elements in Visual Studio are stored in logical groups called projects. The Visual Studio environment in SQL Server Data Tools (SSDT) in SQL Server 2012 or Business Intelligence Development Studio (BIDS) in SQL Server 2008 and earlier will behave in much the same way; as shown in Figure 3-1, the file(s) for a given script are represented in the Project Explorer window. In the same figure, you can see that the project has a rather lengthy and arbitrary name. This is a system-generated identifier used to identify the project and the namespace in which it resides, but it can be changed if you prefer to have a more standardized naming convention in your script.

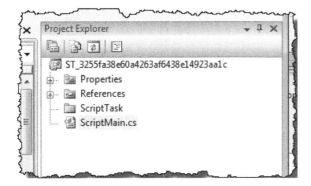

Figure 3-1. Script Task Project Explorer

It's worth pointing out that the C# and VB.NET files that you create in Project Explorer are not physically materialized in your project. Rather, the filenames exist only to logically separate the code files within the project—the code itself is embedded inline within the XML of the package (the .dtsx file).

Also included in the Project Explorer is a virtual folder named References. In this folder, you will find the assembly references for core functionality required by the script. In addition, you can add your own references to this list to further extend the capability of the Script Task or Script Component.

Because each instance of the Script Task or Script Component in your package is surfaced as a Visual Studio project, you have a significant amount of control over the properties of that project. Much like a full-featured software development project, an instance of the Script Task or Script Component allows the ETL developer the ability to control various parameters of behavior, including the version of the .NET framework, the compilation warning level, and the assembly name. The project properties window is shown in Figure 3-2, and can be accessed by right-clicking the project name in Project Explorer and choosing Properties. Do keep in mind, however, that the scope of any changes you make is limited to the single instance of the script task or script component with which you're currently working.

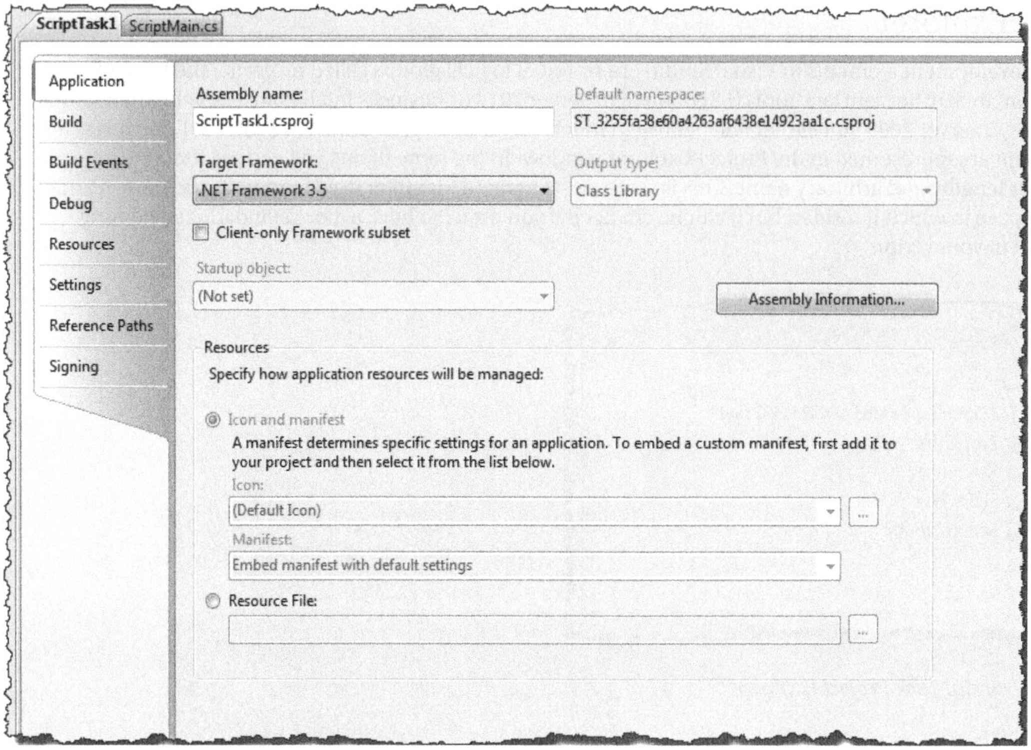

Figure 3-2. *Script Task Project Properties*

In practice, it's quite rare to have to modify the project-level properties of instances of the Script Task or Script Component. In the majority of cases, the default project settings will suffice.

Full .NET Runtime

Both scripting tools in SSIS have full access to the objects, methods, and events within the .NET framework runtime. This level of accessibility allows the ETL developer to leverage exiting assemblies—including network libraries, filesystem tools, advanced mathematical operations, and structured error handling, among many others—as part of their scripts. Need to create a complex multidimensional array? Looking for an easier way to perform tricks with string manipulation? All this and more is easily accessible, just below the covers of the .NET runtime environment.

Compiler

Finding errors in code is critical, and is generally easier to do early in the development process. To understand how this works in SSIS scripting, it's useful to understand the life cycle of script development.

When SSIS first surfaced with SQL Server 2005, the ETL developer could choose to store the code text in a Script Task or Script Component without actually building (compiling) the script project. By opting not to precompile the script, a trivial amount of processing resources would be saved (or more specifically, delayed) by forcing the SSIS design environment to accept the code as written. Two problems arose from this behavior: first, there was a performance penalty, however slight, caused by compiling the script on the fly during the execution of the package. Second, the risk of runtime errors increased, due to the minimized up-front validation in the designer.

Starting with SQL Server 2008, script precompilation is required. Now when you write a script, it is compiled in the background and the resulting binary output is serialized and stored inline within the package XML. As soon as you modify your script and close the editor, the .NET compiler is invoked and creates the serialized binary data. If you've made an error in your code that prevents compilation, you'll be presented with a validation error on the Script Task or Script Component indicating that the binary code cannot be found (see Figure 3-3).

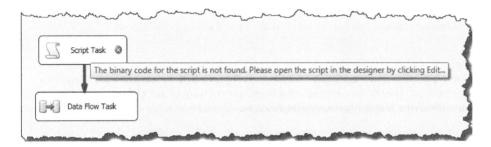

Figure 3-3. *Compilation error with a script task*

This validation step is a safety mechanism to make sure your packages don't make it to deployment with uncompilable code. However, it's also possible to build the script project from within the script editor, so you can periodically check your code for compilation errors before closing the editing window. In the menu bar of the script editor, you'll find the option to Build ->Build [script project name] (or my favorite, the shortcut method of Control + Shift + B) to compile all of the code in your script project. When you build the project in this manner, any errors found during compilation will be reported in the Error List window (Figure 3-4).

	Description	File	Line	Column	Project
⊗ 1	; expected	ScriptMain.cs	50	17	scriptcomponent101
⊗ 2	Identifier expected	ScriptMain.cs	50	17	scriptcomponent101

Error List — ⊗ 2 Errors ⚠ 0 Warnings ⓘ 0 Messages

Figure 3-4. *Error List*

Also present in the Error List windows are any warnings generated by the compiler; although they don't prevent the code from being compiled, it's always a wise idea to perform a thorough review of any warnings that appear in this list before sending the code any further down the development process.

The Script Task

Within the control flow pane, the workspace for writing custom code is the Script Task. The Script Task can be used for many jobs that are not typically associated directly with ETL operations; although it technically can be used for direct data manipulation, this tool is best suited for supporting operations that can't easily be accomplished using data flow components. Think of the Script Task as a helper object to be used to tie together other data-centric operations within the package.

The following are a few requirements frequently served by the script task:

- Checking for the existence and accessibility of source or destination files

- Using a file archive utility API to zip or unzip files

- Generating custom event messages (such as HTML-formatted e-mail messages)

- Setting variable values

- Performing cleanup operations upon package completion or if an error occurs

- Inspecting environmental data, such as available disk space, the status of Windows services, etc.

Because it's not designed for manipulating data, there is no need to define input or output metadata, which makes the Script Task relatively easy to configure. As shown in Figure 3-5, there are just a few required configuration elements for this task: specify the programming language you want to use, choose the variables you want to make visible within the script, and you're ready to write code!

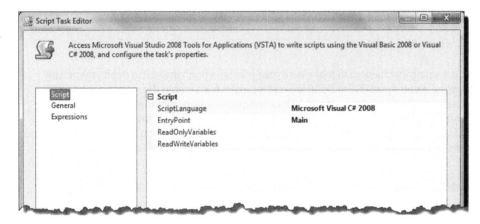

Figure 3-5. *Script Task Editor*

■ **Note:**   For both the Script Task and the Script Component, the decision to use either C# or VB.NET should be considered permanent. Once you've selected a language and opened the script editor, the language selector is disabled. This behavior is by design; although both languages compile to the same intermediate language (MSIL) code, it would be difficult for any tool to convert source code from one language to another. The default language for both tools is C#, so those who prefer VB.NET will have to change the ScriptLanguage property.

Once the language and variables are set, you're ready to open up the code editor. When you click the Edit Script . . . button, you'll be presented with the familiar Visual Studio development environment. If you have written code using this IDE in the past (to develop Windows applications, web apps, etc.), you'll recognize many entities—the Solution Explorer, the code window, the properties window, and many other common components. Although the behaviors will be a bit different in this minimized version of Visual Studio, the concepts remain the same.

The Script Component

Although both SSIS scripting tools have similar properties, they serve very different roles. Unlike the Script Task, which is intended mostly for administrative and operational programmability, the Script Component is designed for the more traditional moving parts of ETL: retrieving data from a source, performing some manner of transformation or validation on said data, and loading data to destination.

Common uses of the Script Component include:

- Connecting to sources of data for which there is no suiListing native source component

- Sending data to destinations that do not offer a native destination, or are structured differently than the typical columnar layout

- Performing advanced data manipulation that requires functionality not offered with the built-in SSIS transformations

- Complex splitting, filtering, or aggregating of the in-pipeline data

The Script Component is built with the versatility to behave in one of three modes: transformation, source, or destination. When you introduce an instance of the Script Component into your data flow workspace, you'll be prompted to select a configuration, as shown in Figure 3-6. This is an important choice, as the selection you make will determine which code template is used to initially configure the component. I'll dig more into each of these roles momentarily.

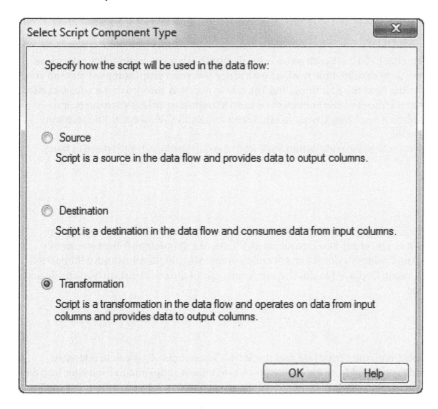

Figure 3-6. *Script Component Configuration*

▒ **Note:**   You should consider the selection of the script component role (transformation, source, or destination) to be permanent. If you mistakenly select the wrong configuration role, it's usually easier to delete and recreate the script instance rather than trying to reconfigure it.

Chances are good that you'll use the script component in each of these roles (source, transformation, and destination) from time to time. However, my experience has been that transformation is the most frequently used role for the Script Component.

Script Maintenance Patterns

Designing custom logic in your ETL processes is a hard but rewarding task. However, the job is not done once the code is promoted from development to testing or even to production. The effective ETL developer maintains a long-term vision when designing script solutions, as the packages often survive well beyond the tenures of the ETL developers who create those solutions.

To that end, an integral part of the solution design process should be evaluating the flexibility, maintainability, and reusability of the project as a whole, making specific allowances for the project-within-a-project instances of script.

Code Reuse

Laziness is a good thing. (Pause for effect.) To clarify: all great technologists find ways to avoid solving the same problems repeatedly. Let's say you've spent some time working with script tasks and script components, and you come up with a whiz-bang idea for The Next Big ETL Thing. The Thing is so narrowly focused that it adds behavior not present in native SSIS tools, but it's also versatile enough to be used in multiple packages across several domains. Since you worked so hard on it once, you'll want to avoid reinventing The Thing again. The solution: find a way to make The Thing reusable.

To that end, there are several ways to reuse code within SSIS, from the old-fashioned copy/paste to fancy modularization.

Copy/Paste

No further definition is needed here: code reuse via copy/paste is exactly as it sounds. Although copying and pasting code as a reuse mechanism is a bit crude and unstructured, it's also the simplest and most commonly used means to do so within SSIS. The upside is a quick and easy deployment with few administrative limitations. However, this simplicity comes at a cost. Deployed in this manner, each copy of the code exists in its own silo and must be independently maintained.

External Assemblies

As I mentioned earlier in the chapter, both the Script Task and the Script Component allow you to reference external assemblies (compiled code generated from a separate project) to import supplemental behavior into the instance of the script task/component. The details of creating an external assembly are beyond the scope of this chapter, but in a nutshell, you would use a separate development environment to code and compile the classes, methods, and events to be used in your ETL processes. The resulting binary file, known as an assembly, would be deployed to the development machine and any server machine(s) that would execute the package. The assembly would then be added to the list of script references, and the result would be that the behaviors defined in the assembly would be accessible from within the instance of the script task or script component.

There are several upsides to this approach. First of all, it's a more modular way of handling code reuse within your package. Rather than relying on rudimentary copy/paste operations, this method permits a single point of administration and development for the shared custom functions of your ETL processes. Since all references to the custom behavior would point to a single assembly on each development machine or server, any updates to the code would be addressed at the machine level rather than having to touch every script in every package. In addition, the behaviors built into the external assemblies could be used by other processes or applications; because these standalone assemblies are built using the Common Language Runtime, their use could be leveraged beyond the borders of SSIS.

There are a few limitations to this approach. First, you cannot use SSDT or BIDS to create custom assemblies. Although both tools use the Visual Studio shell, they are only installed with the templates to create business intelligence projects and do not natively support other project types. To create an assembly containing custom code, you'd need to use a version of Visual Studio that was configured to generate Class Library projects (the Standard and Professional versions, or even the language-specific free Express versions)—or, for highly experienced developers, plain old Notepad and the .NET compiler. Another limitation is that any assemblies referenced in your script must be deployed to and registered in the GAC on the machine(s) that will execute the package. This deployment and registration process is not complex, but it does add to the total of moving parts in your ETL infrastructure.

Custom Tasks/Components

At the top of the SSIS reusability food chain you will find the custom task and custom component. As with a custom assembly, the ability to add your own tasks and components to SSIS allows you create highly customized behaviors within SSIS. In addition, custom tasks and components enable you to create a more customized user interface for these behaviors, allowing for relatively simple drag-and-drop use in your SSIS packages. In the interest of brevity, we won't detail the use of custom tasks or custom components in this chapter, but it is worth mentioning that if there is script behavior that is often repeated in many of your packages, it's worth considering converting the script task or script component into a custom tool that can easily integrate into SSDT or BIDS.

Source Control

Ask any good developer for their short list of required project elements, and source control will almost always be near the top of the list. Because any SSIS project really is software development – albeit in a mostly graphical environment – the same consideration must be made by ETL developers as well. Being that the storage for an SSIS package is simply an XML file, it's not difficult to add SSIS packages to most any existing source control system.

To some, the Script Task and Script Component have the appearance of residing outside the SSIS package – after all, both of these are managed through what appears to be a separate Visual Studio project. This thinking sometimes brings up the question of how integrate SSIS script logic into source control. The easy answer is that there is no requirement above and beyond source controlling the package itself. Because all of the code is stored inline within the package XML, there is no need to separately track in source control the code within instances of the script task or script component.

Scripting Design Patterns

As a born-and-raised Southerner, I was always taught that there's more than one way to skin a cat. Although I've never attempted this particular exercise, I can confirm that for any given problem (in life, as well as in SSIS) there may be dozens or perhaps even hundreds of correct solutions.

Because of the highly flexible nature of scripting solutions, it's not possible to predict every possible permutation of logic that could find its way into SSIS code. However, as Integration Services has evolved, some commonly used design patterns have emerged. In this section, I'll look at some of these patterns.

Connection Managers and Scripting

Connection Managers are built into SQL Server Integration Services as a modular way to reuse connections to databases, data files, and other sources of information. Most everyone with even a little experience using SSIS is aware of connection managers and how they relate to conventional components such as OleDB Source/Destination and Flat File Source/Destination, as well as tasks such as the FTP Task and the Execute SQL Task. You can instantiate a connection object once as a package-level entity (as shown in Figure 3-7) and use it throughout the remainder of the package.

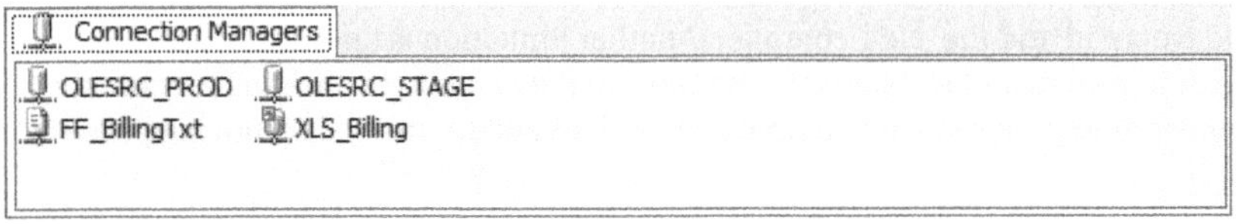

```
  Connection Managers
  OLESRC_PROD    OLESRC_STAGE
  FF_BillingTxt    XLS_Billing
```

Figure 3-7. *Connection Manager objects*

Not as widely known is the fact that you can access most connection manager objects within instances of the Script Task and the Script Component as well. Connecting to a data source is a very common task in SSIS scripting, particularly within instances of the Script Component used as a source or destination. However, it's quite common for the ETL developer to create a new instance of a connection within the script, even if the package already has a connection manager.

If a connection manager object already exists in your SSIS package for for a particular connection, it's preferable to use that existing connection manager object when connecting to a data store from within a script. If the connection manager does not yet exist, consider creating one: there are numerous benefits to abstracting the connection from the script, including ease of change and the ability for the connection to engage in transactions within SSIS.

■ **Note:** For an in-depth analysis on why to use connection manager objects as opposed to connections created entirely in script, you can review an excellent blog post on this topic by Todd McDermid here: `http://toddmcdermid.blogspot.com/2011/05/use-connections-properly-in-ssis-script.html`. In this post, the author specifically discusses the use of connection managers in the Script Task, but most of the same principles would apply to the use of connection managers within the Script Component as well.

Although it's possible to reuse connection managers for most any connection type within a script, to keep things simple I'll limit my discussion to SQL Server database connections. With some modification, many of these principles would apply to other connection types as well.

Using Connection Managers in the Script Task

Although not entirely intuitive, the coding syntax to reference an existing connection manager in the Script Task is relatively easy to understand. I'll look at examples for the two most common ways to connect to SQL Server—through the OleDB connection, and the ADO.NET connection.

Connecting to an ADO.NET connection manager through the Script Task is a two-step process, as shown in Listing 3-1. First, create a reference to your existing ConnectionManager object (using the name you gave it in the SSIS package), and acquire a connection from that object in code.

Listing 3-1. Use an existing ADO.NET connection in the Script Task

```
// Create the ADO.NET database connection
ConnectionManager connMgr = Dts.Connections["ADONET_PROD"];
System.Data.SqlClient.SqlConnection theConnection
        = (System.Data.SqlClient.SqlConnection)connMgr.AcquireConnection(Dts.Transaction);
```

Using an OLE DB connection manager in the script task requires a little more effort, but is a similar exercise to its ADO.NET counterpart. As shown in Listing 3-2, we have to add an intermediate object to make the appropriate data type cast when using the OLE DB provider:

Listing 3-2. Using an existing OLE DB connection in the Script Task

```
// Create the OLEDB database connection
ConnectionManager cm=Dts.Connections["OLEDB_PROD"];
Microsoft.SqlServer.Dts.Runtime.Wrapper.IDTSConnectionManagerDatabaseParameters100 cmparams
    = cm.InnerObject AS
Microsoft.SqlServer.Dts.Runtime.Wrapper.IDTSConnectionManagerDatabaseParameters100;
System.Data.OleDb.OleDbConnection conn =
(System.Data.OleDb.OleDbConnection)cmParams.GetConnectionForSchema();
```

■ **Note:** It's worth mentioning that it is technically possible to reference a connection by number rather than by name (e.g., using `Dts.Connections[3]` rather than `Dts.Connections["Conn_Name"]`). I strongly recommend against this practice! It makes for rather ambiguous connection references, and since the order of connection managers cannot be guaranteed, you might end up with a runtime error at best—and at worst, wildly unexpected behavior in your package.

Using Connection Managers in the Script Component

As I mentioned in the previous section, many of the same concepts apply to the reuse of connection managers, whether you're working in the Script Task or the Script Component. For the same reasons, it's almost always a best practice to reuse an existing connection manager object (or create a new one if necessary) rather than building a connection object from scratch within code.

Logistically, connection managers are a little easier to use in the Script Component. Because the purpose of this tool is to move data (which is not always the case with the Script Task), some additional functionality comes baked in to make the job of reusing connection managers less cumbersome. In the Script Component, you can declare the use of one or more connections within the script's graphical editor (much like you declare the use of read-only or read-write variables, to be discussed shortly). As shown in Figure 3-8, this interface allows you easily reference an existing connection.

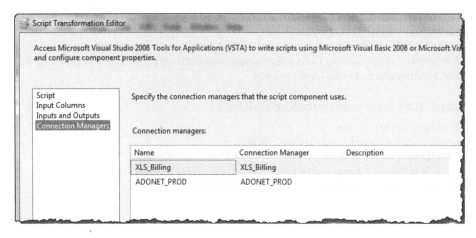

Figure 3-8. *Declaring connection managers in the Script Component*

Once they are referenced here, the syntax to use the connection within your code is much simpler as well. Rather than using the connection name as an indexer, you can access any of these connections through the UserComponent.Connections collection. For example:

Listing 3.3. Using a previously declared connection manager in Script Component

```
// Create the OLEDB database connection
SqlConnection conn = Connections.ADONET_PROD.AcquireConnection(null);
```

Variables

In many—if not most—instances of the Script Task and Script Component, you'll need to inspect or manipulate values stored in SSIS variables. Because they are so prevalent in these implementations, it's important to understand how best to address SSIS variables within the scripting tools.

■ **Note:** It is important to draw a distinction between variables in SSIS and variables declared within the script task and script component. Although there's some commonality in their usage, they are separate and distinct entities with very different properties. SSIS variables are defined as part of the SSIS package, and may be used across many different tasks and components. Script variables, on the other hand, are declared within individual instances of the Script Task or Script Component and are only valid within the instance in which they are defined.

Variable Visibility

In both the Script Task and Script Component, you can explicitly expose one or more variables using the GUI editor for each. In Figure 3-9, you can see that we have the option of including SSIS variables in the script, and can specify whether those variables will be surfaced as read-only or read-write.

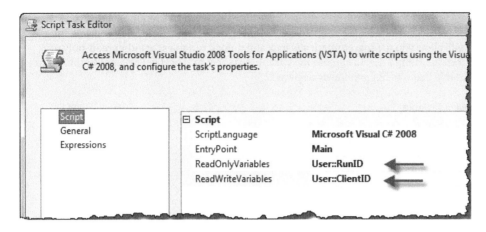

Figure 3-9. *Including Variables in Script*

It is possible to read or modify SSIS variables with a script even if you don't explicitly include them. However, it's usually preferable to declare any required variables as shown, as the syntax within the script is much simpler when references to the SSIS variables are declared ahead of time in this manner.

Variable Syntax in Code

Declaring read-only or read-write variables is a similar experience whether you're using the Script Task or the Script Component. However, the syntax to address these variables in code is different depending on the tool you're using. As shown in Listing 3-4, SSIS variables within a script task instance are addressed by using a string indexer to specify the name of the variable.

Listing 3-4. Script Task Variable Syntax

```
public void main()
{
        // Get the current RunID
        int runID = int.Parse(Dts.Variables["RunID"].Value.ToString());

        // Set the ClientID
        Dts.Variables["ClientID"].Value = ETL.GetClientID(runID);

        Dts.TaskResult = (int)ScriptResults.Success;
}
```

When using an instance of the script component, the syntax is noticeably different. Rather than using an indexer to read from or write to the referenced SSIS variables, you can use the Variables.<Variable Name> syntax as shown in Listing 3-5:

Listing 3-5. Script Component Variable Syntax

```
public override void Input0_ProcessInputRow(Input0Buffer Row)
{
        // Push the SSIS variable ClientName to the value in the current row
        Row.ClientName = Variables.ClientName;
}
```

83

It is possible to access variables within instances of the Script Task or the Script Component even if you do not explicitly declare their use in the graphical settings editor. Within the SSIS scripting toolset, you will find a couple of functions that will allow you to programmatically lock and unlock variables for either read-only or read-write access. As shown in Listing 3-6, you can use the `VariableDispenser.LockOneForRead()` function to capture the value of a variable that was not previously declared.

Listing 3-6. Manually lock a variable

```
// Programmatically lock the variable we need
Variable vars=null;
Dts.VariableDispenser.LockOneForRead("RunID", ref vars);

// Assign to script variable
runID=int.Parse(vars["RunID"].Value.ToString());

// Unlock the variable object
vars.Unlock();
```

Using a method similar to the one shown above, you can manipulate variable values by using the function `VariableDispenser.LockOneForWrite()`, which would allow you to write to as well as read from the variable value.

Variable Data Types

As you may have derived from Listing 3-4 and Listing 3-5 above, the interpreted data type for variable values will differ between the Script Task and the Script Component. With the latter, any variable that you declare in the graphical settings editor will surface as the .NET data type equivalent of the SSIS variable type, and there is no need to perform a type cast. When using the Script Task (and the Script Component, if you opt to use either the `LockOneForRead()` or `LockOneForWrite()` method), variables are presented as the generic Object type, and most of the time you'll have to cast to an appropriate type any variable used in script code. As shown in Figure 3-10, you'll get a compiler error if you forget to cast a variable value to the appropriate type.

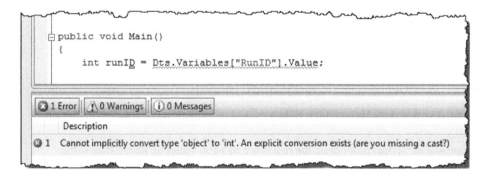

Figure 3-10. *Script Task variables must be cast*

Naming Patterns

If you have worked as a software developer in the past, the following section will be nothing more than a review. If you haven't, I'll share an important tidbit of information: naming conventions are important.

I've known many a developer in my time, and I've never found one who wasn't loyal to some type of naming convention. Why? It's familiar. It's predicListing. When patterns emerge in the way you develop software, it becomes easier to maintain—by others as well as yourself. Technically, there's no difference between code written in camel case, Hungarian notation, mnemonic notation, or Pascal Style. This is purely a matter of clarity, readability, and maintainability. By finding and sticking with a style (even if it's a hybrid of other styles), you'll have more navigable code, and will likely find that your fellow developers appreciate the approach.

A few suggestions regarding naming conventions:

- Be consistent. This is the number-one rule and should be followed above all others. Whatever style you develop, stick with it. You can change or modify your naming convention style later, but at least be consistent within each project.

- Be clear. I can't tell you how many times I've had to debug code (and yes, sometimes it was my own) littered with single-character object names, ambiguous function names, and other pull-your-hair-out kinds of practices. Now, don't go overboard here. Most object names don't need to read like `bool database_write_failed_and_could_not_display_interactive_error`, but there's probably some happy medium between that and `bool f`.

- Be a follower. If you don't have your own style, do as those around you do. Some organizations, especially larger ones, may dictate the naming convention style you'll use.

Summary

The scripting tools in SQL Server Integration Services are both capable and complex. When scripting for ETL first surfaced with DTS many years ago, it was a quick-and-dirty way to solve some data movement and manipulation problems. With SSIS, the latest generation of scripting tools is robust and enterprise-ready. With a few recommended practices, it can be a great addition to any ETL developer's toolkit.

## CHAPTER 4

SQL Server Source Patterns

In the first section of this book, we looked at patterns focused on the Control Flow area of SQL Server Integration Services, including metadata, workflow execution, and scripting. The second section focuses on the Data Flow area of SQL Server Integration Services. This and the following chapters will discuss source, transformation, and logging patterns in the pipeline area of an Integration Services package.

Integration Services supports a wide variety of sources, including SQL Server, Oracle, and SAP. In addition, developers and third-party vendors have the ability to create custom sources for providers not included out-of-the-box. This technology-agnostic approach creates a very flexible system for loading all sorts of data. Even with all of the potential sources, loading data into or out of a SQL Server database is a very common occurrence, as a company that owns Integration Services typically uses all Microsoft products.

This chapter discusses different patterns associated with using SQL Server as a source. Due to the common occurrence of SQL Server databases in shops using Integration Services, we have a defined set of patterns for extracting data from SQL Server. Specifically, we will look at the best way to connect to a SQL Server database, how to choose the data you will use, and how to more easily use the rest of the Data Flow's objects. Finally, we will look at a new component in SQL Server 2012 that helps jump start your development when connecting to any source.

Setting up a Source

When connecting to external data, Integration Services uses a few objects to help make the connection, retrieve the correct data, and start any necessary data manipulations. Every time an Integration Services developer creates a package, the developer will need to select the correct objects and ensure they have all been created. The objects that will need to be set up are as follows:

- *Connection Manager:* The object that tells Integration Services where to get data. Can be used in the Control Flow, Data Flow, and Event Handlers.

- *Provider:* The object that the connection manager uses to talk to the data source.

- *Source Component:* The object that sets the properties to tell Integration Services what data to get. The matching Connection Manager object is set in this object.

- *Source Component Query:* The information the external data source needs to give Integration Services data. The query is stored in the Source Component object.

Let's take a look at the important factors associated with each of these items. We'll begin in the next section by looking at connection managers.

Selecting a SQL Server Connection Manager and Provider

Between ADO.NET, ODBC, and OLE DB, there are enough connection managers to make you want to pull your hair out! All of these connection managers will connect to SQL Server, so how do we know when we should use which one? To answer that question, let's talk about what the connection manager is actually doing, and then look at each connection manager type that can be used to connect to SQL Server.

A connection manager is the object that holds connection information for an external source, akin to an application data source or a Reporting Services shared data source. The connection manager provides an abstraction layer between Integration Services and the rest of the components, so that information about the external source can be modified in one place to affect all tasks and components. To see all of the connection manager types available, see Figure 4-1.

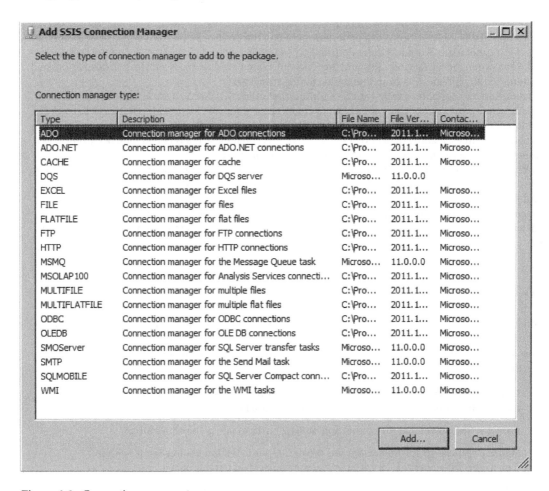

Figure 4-1. *Connection manager types*

The three connection manager types that can be used to connect to a SQL Server database are:

- ADO.NET
- ODBC
- OLE DB

Let's take a look at each connection manager type individually.

ADO.NET

The ADO.NET connection manager type is used to make a connection through the .NET framework. Not only can this type be used for SQL Server, but it also provides access to other applications and other databases. The ADO.NET layer quickly retrieves data from the source using a DataReader object in the .NET framework.

The ADO.NET connection manager for SQL Server is best used as a source when you are using it elsewhere in the package. For example, the Lookup component uses an ADO.NET connection manager to connect, so then use it as a source. On the other hand, if a component uses another connection manager type, stick with that connection manager type. Consistency is really the key here. For a sample connection manager property window set to connect to the AdventuresWorks2008R2 database on the same server, see Figure 4-2.

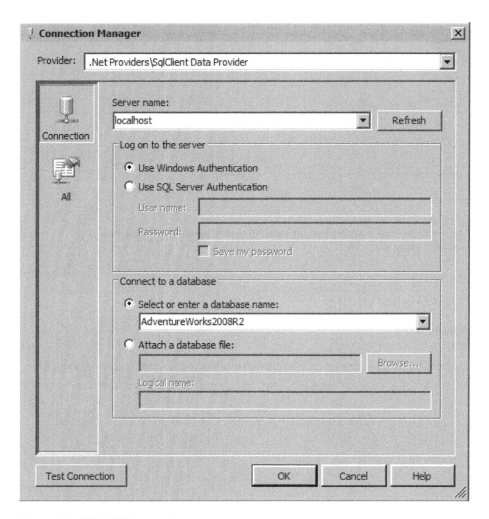

Figure 4-2. *ADO.NET connection manager property screen*

ODBC

ODBC is the open database connectivity standard. Its purpose is to allow connections from any application to any database, regardless of the vendor. Often, an organization will use DSNs (data source names), to create an abstraction layer between the application and the connection string the ODBC provider uses. If you have an organization that really wants to use DSNs with SQL Server, ODBC is the option for you. Otherwise, stick with an ADO.NET or OLE DB connection manager.

If you decide that ODBC is the way to go, don't be fooled into using the ODBC connection manager. No Integration Services source uses this connection manager. Instead, use the ADO.NET connection manager with a few tweaks. After creating the ADO.NET connection manager, change the provider at the top of the window to **Odbc Data Provider**, as shown in Figure 4-3.

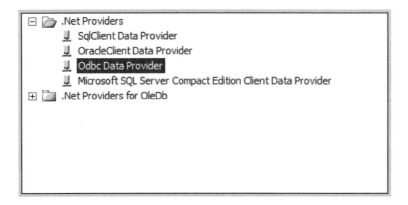

Figure 4-3. *ADO.NET providers*

Then add the DSN name or connection string. For our local AdventureWorks2008R2 database, the connection string will look like Listing 4-1.

Listing 4-1. ODBC Connection String

```
Driver={SQL Server Native Client 11.0};
Server=localhost;
Database=AdventureWorks2008R2;
Trusted_Connection=yes
```

Our completed connection manager screen for an ADO.NET connection with an ODBC provider looks like Figure 4-4.

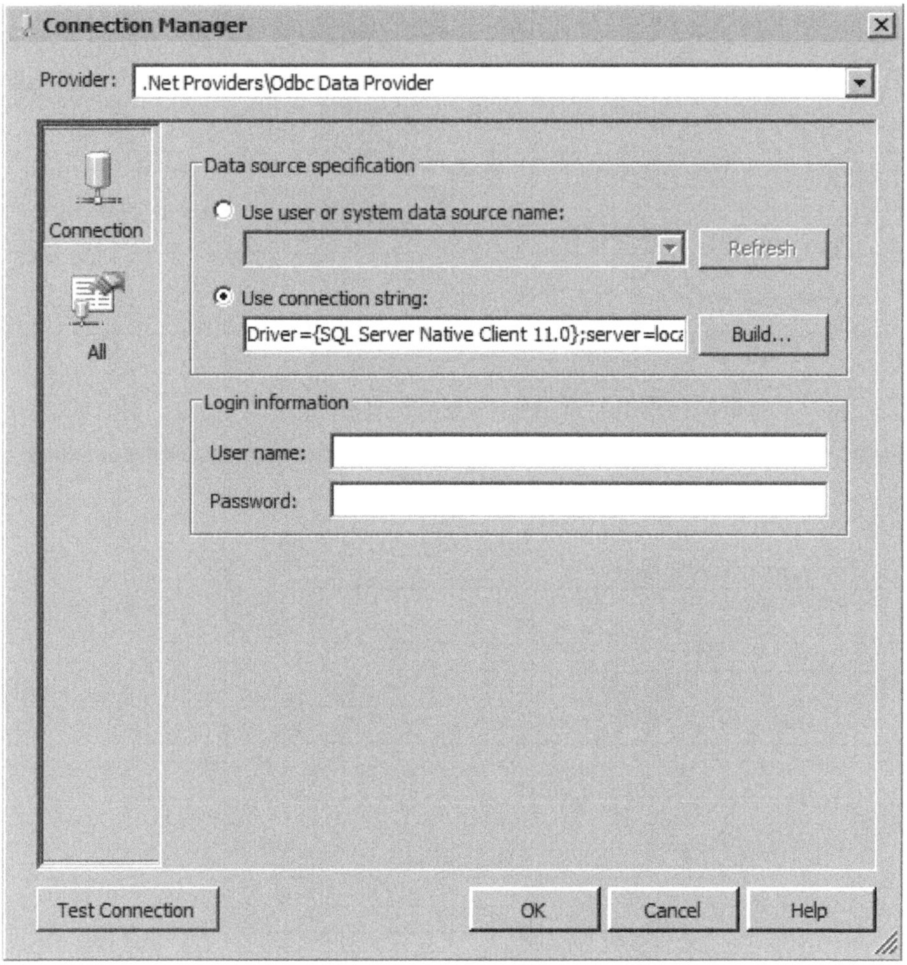

Figure 4-4. *ODBC ADO.NET connection manager property screen*

OLE DB

Finally, we move on to what is arguably the most common connection manager used to connect to SQL Server: OLE DB. The OLE DB protocol was written by Microsoft as the next version of the ODBC provider. In addition to SQL Server databases, it can be used to connect to file-based databases or Excel spreadsheets.

OLE DB tends to be my default when connecting to a SQL Server database. If you did not fall into the category of using mostly components that use an ADO.NET connection manager, and you did not fall into the category of having an organization that wants to use a DSN, you will want to use an OLE DB connection manager.

You can fill out the property screen of the OLE DB connection manager as shown in Figure 4-5.

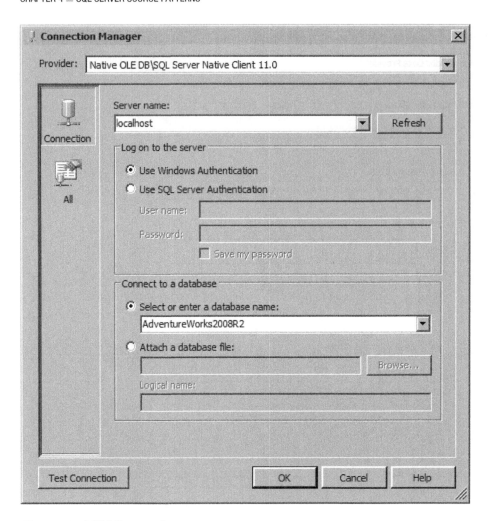

Figure 4-5. *OLE DB connection manager property screen*

Creating a SQL Server Source Component

Once we've picked the correct connection manager and provider, we need to use them in a Source Component for our data pull. We begin by looking at the SSIS Toolbox when on the Data Flow tab. If you have not rearranged the SSIS Toolbox, you will see all possible sources under the Other Sources grouping, as seen in Figure 4-6.

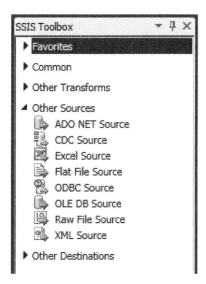

Figure 4-6. *Other Sources grouping in SSIS Toolbox*

Figure 4-6 shows all the possible sources. Now it's time to choose one.

Most of the hard decision-making was already completed when we set up the connection manager. If we used an OLE DB connection manager, then we must use the OLE DB source. If we decided to use an ADO.NET connection manager with either an ADO.NET or ODBC provider, we must use the ADO NET source.

Once we drag the desired source onto the Data Flow design window, the data flow contains one component, as shown in Figure 4-7. Integration Services lets the developer know that there is an issue with the source through the red circle with the white X in it. In this case, the issue is that we have not yet set any of the source's properties, starting with the destination table, as shown in the tooltip.

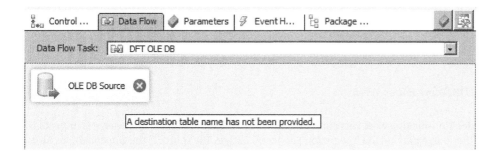

Figure 4-7. *Data flow task with new source*

To open the source component, either double-click the component or right-click and select **Edit**. Inside the source component, we can fill in the connection manager property. The first connection manager of the appropriate type will automatically be populated, but selecting the drop-down list arrow will let you select any of the other connection managers that match. The source component property screen up to this point can be seen in Figure 4-8.

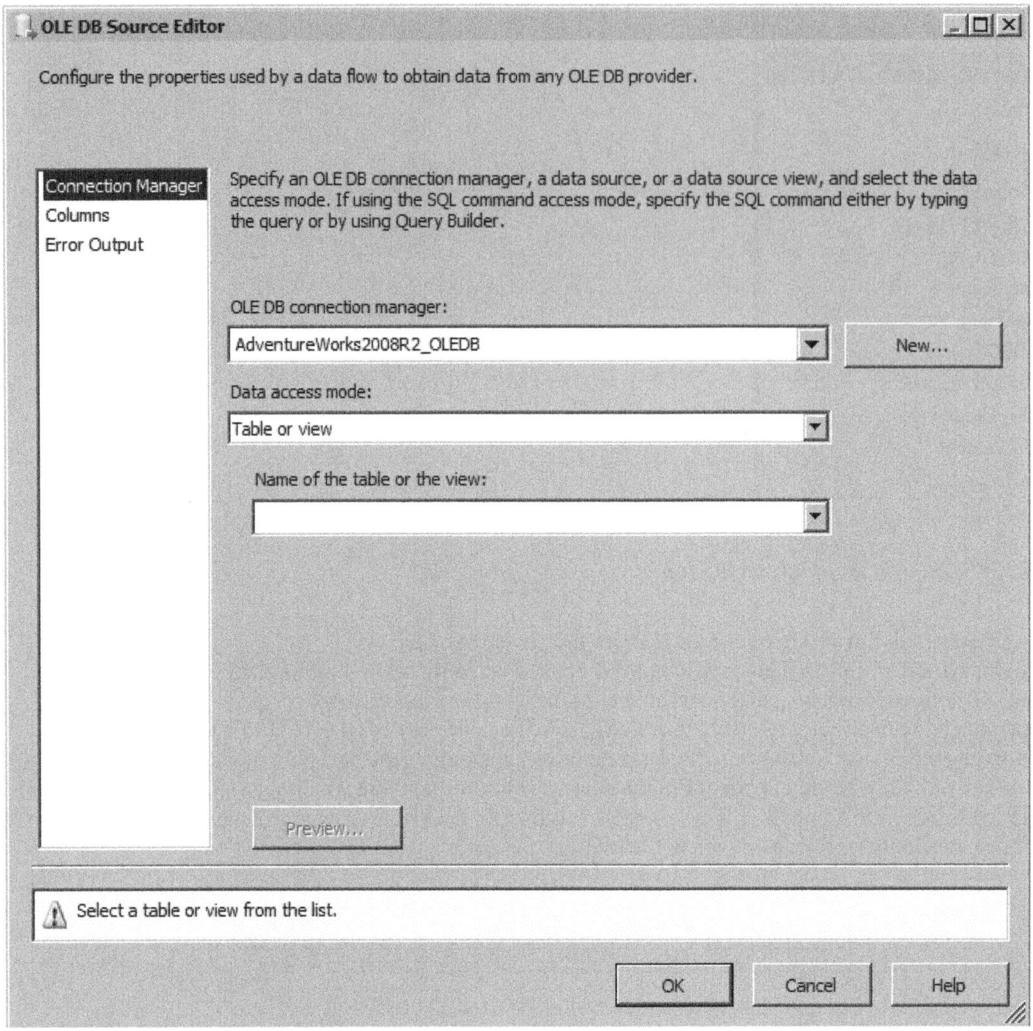

Figure 4-8. Initial OLE DB Source Editor screen

While most of the decision-making work was done when we created the connection manager, it is important to understand the part the source plays in the Integration Services package. The source is the glue that holds all of the other pieces together and ensures that we have one place to go to for future maintenance issues or changes. Setting up the SQL Server source was an easy step before we move on to the creating and optimization of the query that the source uses.

Writing a SQL Server Source Component Query

After walking through the creation of the connection manager and provider and deciding which source component to use, we need to set up the metadata for pulling the data. We do this by selecting what type of access we want to make and then adding the query information to the source component. In addition, there are a few patterns that we will want to review when setting up the query and column metadata. Let's get started.

ADO.NET Data Access

If we decided to use the ADO.NET source component, either with the ADO.NET or ODBC provider, we have two options to select what data we want to see:

- *Table or view:* Select which table or view from which you want to receive data. The list of tables and views should be prepopulated and listed based on your access. We do not recommend this option because it includes unnecessary columns, even if you restrict the column list in the component.

- *SQL Command:* Enter text that will be executed on the SQL Server database.

Because the *Table or view* option is not our recommended option, let's dig into the *SQL Command* option a little deeper. You can enter either a direct SQL query that returns a dataset or a stored procedure using the EXEC statement.

Whether you are using a SQL query or executing a stored procedure, you will need to be aware that the ADO. NET source does not allow you to use parameters in your query. If you need to modify the query that gets used, you will need to use an expression. Expressions are only set at the Control Flow level, so we will need to take a look there to set up our expression. Follow these steps to set a new SQL command at design time:

1. When in Data Flow Task, click the background to ensure no components are selected and look in the Properties menu for the Expressions property.

2. Once the Expression Property window is open, select the [ADO NET Source]. [SqlCommand] option in the Property field and click the ellipses button next to the Expression field.

3. In the Expression Editor, create your command using variables. For example, if you were to run a stored procedure where you wanted to pass in an end date, you could use the following expression: "EXEC GetCustomerData '" + (DT_STR, 29, 1252)@ [System::ContainerStartTime]+" '".

4. Once the expression has been validated, select the OK button. The final Expression screen should look like Figure 4-9.

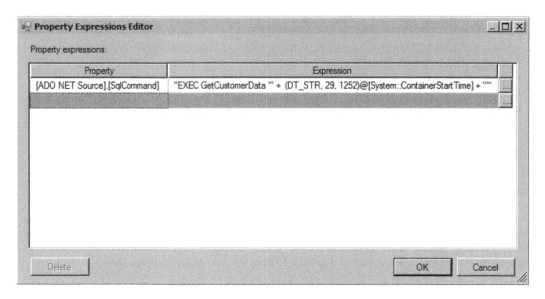

Figure 4-9. *Property Expressions Editor with SQLCommand property*

When the package runs, it will now use the expression you just created.

OLE DB Data Access

If we've selected the OLE DB source component, we have four options for how to retrieve data:

- *Table or view:* Similar to access in the ADO.NET source, this option allows you to select a table or view to pull all columns of data into the package. This option is not recommended for the same reason explained in the ADO.NET source.

- *Table name or view name variable:* Instead of hardcoding the name of the table or view, you can instead point to a user-created variable that contains that information. This option is not recommended.

- *SQL Command:* Similar to access in the ADO.NET source, you can enter the SQL query or execution of a stored procedure once you've selected this option.

- *SQL Command from variable:* If you want to create a query to change at runtime or to pass a variable to a stored procedure, this is the option you will want to use. Instead of creating an expression to modify the SQL Command, as we did with ADO.NET, we will create a variable that creates our expression. We can then select the variable we created after selecting this option.

Picking one of these options will determine how the data is returned from SQL Server. After you select the type of data retrieval, you'll want to add the appropriate properties. For example, if you select the *Table or view* option, you'll need to select the object that contains the data. If you select the *SQL Command* option, you'll need to enter the SQL query or stored procedure execution that returns the data. Once that is set, you can move on to designing the rest of your data flow.

Waste Not, Want Not

As data professionals, we often think that the more data we can get, the better. This isn't always the best scenario when we are dealing with sources. When we are talking about the amount of data to pull, you will want to follow a different pattern.

No matter which query option you selected, it is important to only ask for the columns that are needed in your data load process. Requesting all columns is similar to running a `select * from table` query against a database. Not only are you asking the database and network to do more work, but you are also asking Integration Services to do more work. All of that unnecessary data will get stored in memory or even cause paging if there isn't enough memory, using up space that could be used to grab more data for the important columns and slowing down the overall package execution.

All source components give you the option to pick a subset of columns on the Columns menu. Be sure to make the column reduction in the query itself rather than in the Columns menu to reap the full benefit of a faster package.

Data Translations

Another Integration Services source trap that is easy to fall into is to perform the majority of the data transformations in the source query itself. Because Integration Services developers often have a SQL background, we tend to want to use a familiar tool to accomplish our task.

The types of data transformations that can be undertaken in either the source query or the rest of the data flow include merging of datasets, case statements, string concatenation, and more. Remember that SQL Server is very good at set-based actions, while Integration Services is very good at computationally expensive tasks that use a lot of memory. While you should test your individual situation, these are good rules of thumb to follow.

Follow the pattern listed in Table 4-1 when deciding where to put your data translation logic.

Table 4-1. *Data Translation Locations*

Data Translation	Concern	Location
Merge datasets	Set-based	Source Component
Case statements	Memory intensive	Data Flow
String concatenation	Procedural	Data Flow
Sorting data	Set-based	Source Component

Source Assistant

Once we have retrieved data from SQL Server the hard way, we're going to learn the easy way to do the same thing. The Source Assistant is a new wizard introduced in SQL Server 2012 that takes a developer through the steps of setting up their Source objects without having to make many of the same decisions that we just had to go through. This is a great way for people who are just getting started with Integration Services to get up and running quickly.

To begin, create a new Data Flow task. As seen in Figure 4-10, the Source Assistant appears in the SSIS Toolbox. Initially it will be in the Favorites grouping, unless someone has moved the items around.

Figure 4-10. Source Assistant in Favorites grouping in SSIS Toolbox

Dragging the Source Assistant component onto the Data Flow design area will start the wizard. The first screen can be seen in Figure 4-11.

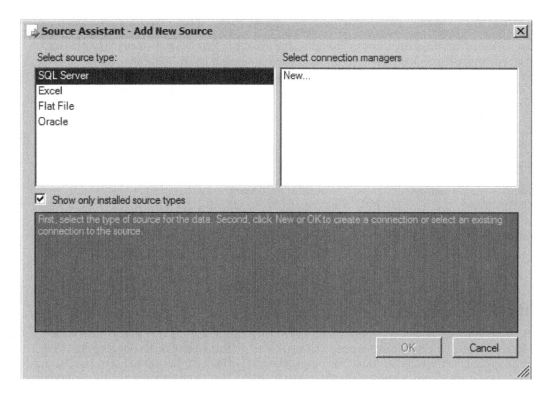

Figure 4-11. Add New Source screen in Source Assistant

To begin, we can see that there are only a few types listed for us to use: SQL Server, Excel, Flat File, and Oracle. If we want to see a list of components available if we install the providers, we can uncheck the *Show installed only* option. By only offering the one SQL Server choice, Integration Services is making our life easier by directing us to the correct provider immediately. Selecting the Source Assistant's SQL Server type will use the OLE DB connection manager, which is also our go-to connection manager!

Once we select the SQL Server type, we have the option of selecting an existing connection manager from the pane on the right or creating a new one. Creating a new connection manager will take us through the exact steps we looked at previously for setting up an OLE DB connection manager.

Finally, we will pick our new or existing connection manager and select the OK button. This will create the connection manager and add the SQL Server source to the Data Flow task. We can then immediately pick up our development with creating and optimizing the SQL query. The Source Assistant is a great way to get started with developing your Integration Services package, especially if you are new to Integration Services. If you know that you want to use one of the other types of connections, you can just create the connection manager and source directly, without having to use the Source Assistant. Either way, you have a few ways to start your development as quickly as possible.

Summary

At this point, we described why we would want to use certain SQL Server sources over others, how to set up the source, and how to clean up the source query to get the best performance out of our package. We also covered sources in general to set up the rest of the source chapters.

While all of the principles described in this chapter are patterns for SQL Server, many of them can be applied to other source types as well. Be sure to review the rest of the source chapters for patterns that can be used for SQL Server in addition to what we have already discussed.

■ ■ ■

## CHAPTER 5

Data Cleansing with Data Quality Services

Data Quality Services (DQS) is a new product in SQL Server 2012 that provides data cleansing functionality – a key component for most ETL processes. This chapter describes how DQS integrates with SSIS, and provides patterns that enable you to achieve reliable, low effort data cleansing within your ETL packages.

■ **Note**   The Data Quality Services product requires some manual steps post-installation to create the DQS databases, and set default permissions. See the "Installing Data Quality Services" page in books online for more information: http://msdn.microsoft.com/en-us/library/gg492277(v=SQL.110).aspx

---

Overview of Data Quality Services

The data cleansing and matching operations you perform with DQS revolve around the use of a Knowledge Base. A Knowledge Base (or KB) is made up of one or more Domains. An example Domain for doing address cleansing would be City, State, or Country. Each of these fields would be a separate Domain. Two or more related domains can be grouped together to form a Composite Domain (or CD). Composite Domains allow you to validate multiple fields as a single unit. For example, a Company composite domain could be made up of Name, Address, City, State, and Country domains. Using a Composite Domain would allow you to validate that "Microsoft Corporation" (Name) exists at "One Redmond Way" (Address), "Redmond" (City), "WA" (State), "USA" (Country). If the DQS KB has all of the relevant knowledge, it would be able to flag the entry as incorrect if you had "Las Vegas" as the City – even though "Las Vegas" is a valid city name, the knowledge base has defined that the Microsoft office is located in "Redmond".

Data Quality Services has three main components: the client utility (shown in Figure 5-1), which allows you to build and manage your knowledge bases; an SSIS Data Flow transform for bulk data cleansing; and a server component where the actual cleansing and matching takes place. The DQS server is not a standalone instance – is it essentially a set of user databases (DQS_MAIN, DQS_PROJECTS, DQS_STAGING_DATA) with a stored procedure based API - much like the SSIS Catalog in SQL Server 2012.

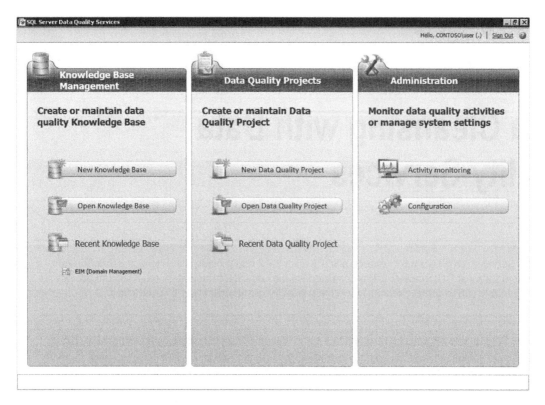

Figure 5-1. *The Data Quality Client application*

Using the Data Quality Client

The Data Quality Client application is used to build and manage your knowledge bases. It can also be used as a standalone tool for cleansing data. The tool is targeted towards Data Stewards and IT Professionals who own and manage data within your organization. Users of the tool will fall into three different roles (shown in Table 5-1), which map to roles within the main DQS database. The functionality you can access through the tool will depend on what role you are currently assigned to.

Table 5-1. *Data Quality Services Roles*

Name	SQL Role	Description
DQS KB Operator	dqs_kb_operator	User can edit and execute an existing data quality project.
DQS KB Editor	dqs_kb_editor	User can perform project functions, and create and edit knowledge bases.
DQS Administrator	dqs_administrator	User can perform project and knowledge functions, as well as administer the system.

■ **Note**   Members of the sysadmin role on the SQL Server instance on which DQS is hosted have the same level of permissions as a DQS Administrator by default. It is recommended that you still associate users with one of the three DQS roles.

Knowledge Base Management

The options under the Knowledge Base Management section allow you to create and maintain your knowledge bases. When creating a new knowledge base, you have the option to create an empty knowledge base, or to base it on an existing knowledge base, which will prepopulate the new knowledge base with the domains from the original. Knowledge bases can also be created from a DQS file (.dqs extension), allowing you to back up or share knowledge bases across systems.

You'll perform three main activities when interacting with your knowledge bases through this UI (shown in Figure 5-2). These activities are available after you've created a new knowledge base, or have opened an existing one.

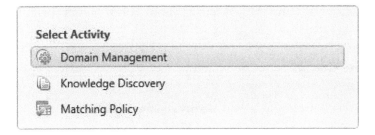

Figure 5-2. Knowledge base management activities

When doing Domain Management, you can verify and modify the domains within the knowledge base. This includes changing domain properties (shown in Figure 5-3), configuring online reference data, as well as viewing and modifying rules and values. You also have the option to export the knowledge base or individual domains to a DQS file, as well as import new domains from a DQS file.

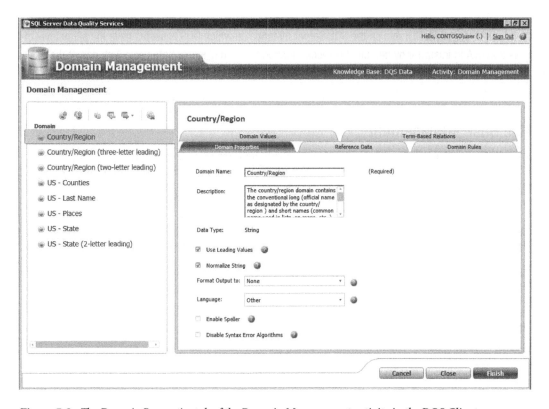

Figure 5-3. *The Domain Properties tab of the Domain Management activity in the DQS Client*

The Matching Policy activity is used to prepare DQS for the data de-duplication process. From this UI, a data steward can create a policy that contains one or more matching rules that DQS will use to determine how rows of data should be compared. DQS Matching functionality is not currently available through SSIS. You can perform this type of work using the DQS Client, and it is also available through the Excel add-in for noun phrases Services.

Knowledge Discovery is a computer-assisted process to build knowledge base information. You supply source data (from a SQL Server table or view, or Excel file), and map the input columns to knowledge base domains. This data will be imported into DQS, and stored as a set of known Domain Values.

Data Quality Projects

A data quality project is one where you interactively cleanse or match your data. You'll select the source of your data (SQL Server or an Excel file, which you can upload through the client), and then map source columns to domains within your knowledge base. Figure 5-4 shows a data quality project that will attempt to cleanse the EnglishCountryRegionName and CountryRegionCode columns against domains from the default DQS knowledge base.

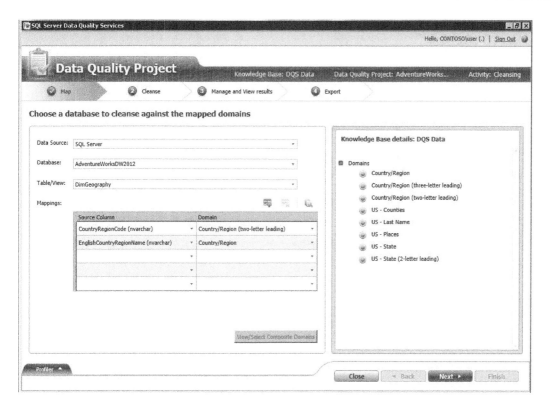

Figure 5-4. *Creating a new data cleansing project*

After you've mapped your columns to domains, DQS will process your data and provide you with the results of the cleansing operation. When you review the results, you have the option to approve or reject certain corrections, add new values to the list of known domain values, and specify correction rules. For example, as the data steward for your organization, you know that "Jack Ryan" and "John Ryan" is the same person. After approving the corrections, you can export the results to a SQL Server table, Excel file, or CSV file. DQS does not give you the option to correct the value in-place – you will need a separate process to update the original source data you examined.

At various times during the process you can save your data quality project. The project status is saved to the DQS server, allowing you to resume at a later point. This is especially useful when working with large sets of data that can take a while to scan. It also allows you to come back to the correction results in case you need to do some research on what the correct values should be for a particular domain.

To manage your active data quality projects, click on the Open Data Quality Project button on the home page of the client. From here, you can see all projects that are currently in progress. Right clicking on a project gives you management options, such as renaming the project or deleting it if it is no longer needed.

Administration

The Administration section is available to users in the DQS Administrator's role. From here, you can monitor all activity on the DQS server (such as Domain Management, and Cleansing projects), and set system wide configuration options. From these pages, you can set logging levels for various operations, as well as set the minimum confidence scores for suggestions, and automatic corrections. If you are using online reference data from the Azure DataMarket, you'd configure your account information and service subscriptions from this page as well (as shown in Figure 5-5). More information about online reference data providers can be found later in this chapter.

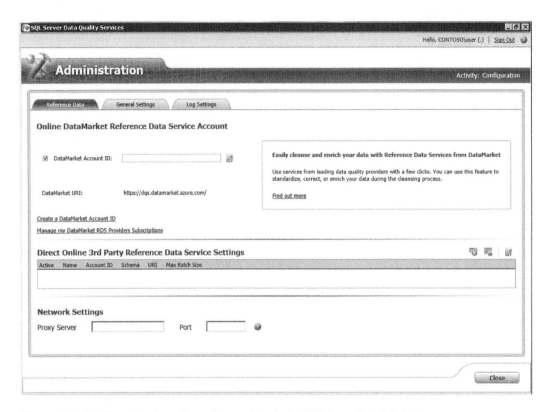

Figure 5-5. *Configuration for online reference data in the SQL Azure DataMarket*

Using the Default Knowledge Base

DQS comes with a default knowledge base containing domains related to cleansing and validation of Countries and locations within the United States. Figure 5-6 shows the Domain Values for the "US – State" domain. In this figure, you can see that "*Alabama*" has synonyms defined for it – it will automatically correct "*AL*" to "*Alabama,*" and mark "*Ala.*" as an error.

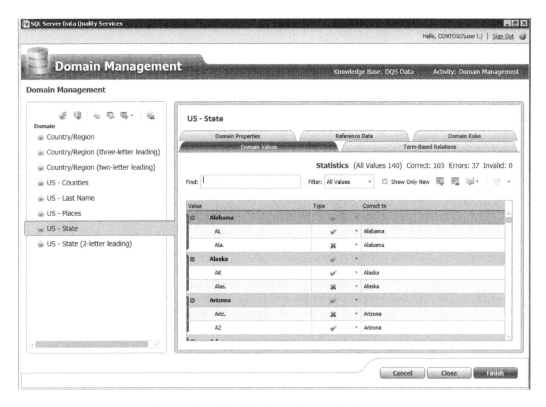

Figure 5-6. *The US – State domain from the default DQS knowledge base*

Online Reference Data Services

DQS has two types of data it will use to perform cleansing and matching operations; *local data*, and *reference data*. Local data make up the values shown on the Domain Values page in the DQS Client – these are known values that are imported into DQS as part of the Knowledge Discovery process. The values are stored along with the knowledge base in the DQS_MAIN database. If these values change, you must update your domain with the new values. Reference data is not stored in the knowledge base – it is queried from an Online Reference Data Service. Using online reference data may impact performance, as your cleansing process will need to call out to an external system, but it requires less maintenance as you don't need to worry about keeping values in sync.

The Online Reference Data Services (RDS) that can be linked to your domains are configured on the Administration page in the DQS Client. There are two types of data providers: DataMarket providers, and Direct Online 3rd Party providers. DataMarket providers require that you have a DataMarket Account ID and subscription to the data set you wish to use. The Direct Online provider option allows you to point to other 3rd party web services that support the DQS provider interface.

Using DQS with SSIS

While you can't use SSIS for DQS Matching, you are able to take advantage of its data correction capabilities through the new DQS Cleansing transform. The DQS Cleansing transform can be found in the Data Flow Toolbox (shown in Figure 5-7). It will appear under the Other Transforms section by default.

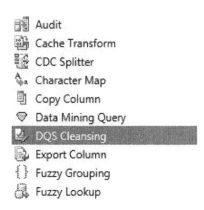

Figure 5-7. The DQS Cleansing transform.

After dragging the DQS Cleansing transform onto the designer, you can double click the component to bring up its editor UI.

The first thing you need to set in the DQS Cleansing Transformation Editor is the Data Quality Connection Manager (as shown in Figure 5-8). This will point to a DQS installation residing on a SQL Server instance. Once the connection manager has been created, you select the Knowledge Base you want to use. Selecting the Knowledge Base you want to use will bring up its list of domains.

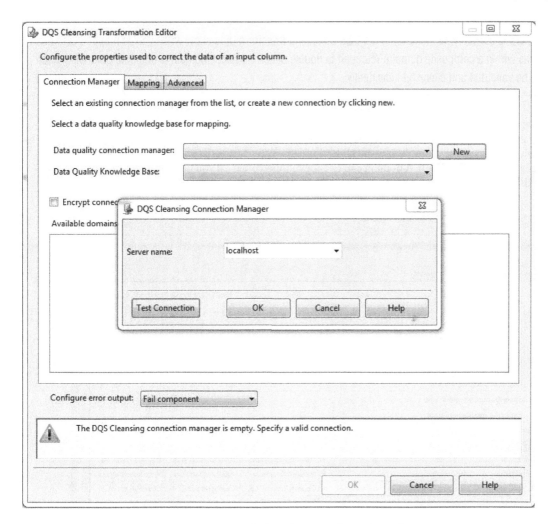

Figure 5-8. The DQS Connection Manager and Cleansing Transformation Editor

As mentioned earlier in the chapter, there are two types of domains in this list; regular Domains (ex. City, State, Zip), and Composite Domains, which are made up of two or more regular domains. When using the DQS Cleansing transform, you can map columns from your data flow to domains in the knowledge base. You can also make use of Composite Domains in two ways:

1. **A single (string) column** – for this to work, all values must appear in the same order as the domains do. So using the "Company" example above, your column values would need to look like this: Microsoft Corporation, One Redmond Way, Redmond, WA, USA.

2. **Multiple columns** – Individual columns are always cleansed by the knowledge and rules stored within the DQS knowledge base. If you map a column to each domain of a composite domain, the row will also be cleansed using the composite domain logic.

■ **Note**   There is currently no indicator in the DQS Cleansing transform UI to show when you've mapped columns to all domains within a composite domain. You need to double check that each domain is mapped; otherwise, each column will be validated and cleansed individually.

The Mapping tab (Figure 5-9) allows you to select the columns you want to cleanse, and map them to domains in your knowledge base. Note that the Domain dropdown will automatically filter out columns with incompatible data types. For example, it won't show domains with a String data type if you are using a DT_I4 (four-byte signed integer) column. A domain can only be mapped once – if you have multiple columns for the same domain, you'll need to use two separate DQS Cleansing transforms in your data flow.

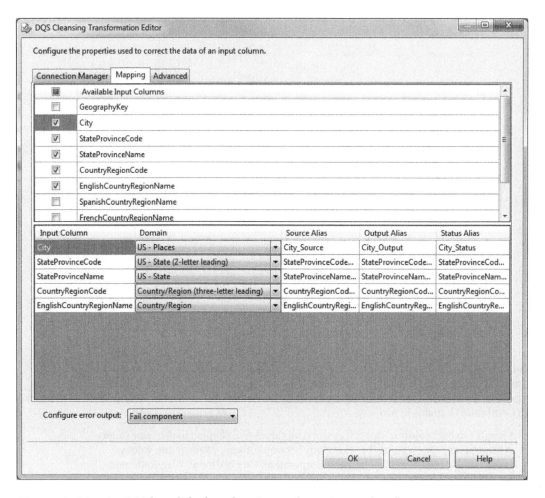

Figure 5-9. *Mapping DQS knowledge base domains to columns in your data flow*

■ **Note**   If your data contains multiple columns with values from the same domain, consider using the Linked Domain feature when creating your knowledge base. For more information, see the "Create a Linked Domain" page in books online: `http://msdn.microsoft.com/en-us/library/hh479582(v=SQL.110).aspx`

Each column you map causes at least three additional columns to be added to your data flow – `Source`, `Output`, and `Status`. More columns may be added, depending on the advanced options you select (more on that to follow). The list of columns created by the DQS Cleansing transform can be found in Table 5-2. Each additional column will be prefixed with the name of the original column by default, and can be renamed on the Mapping tab. In addition to the columns that are prefixed with the name of the original, a `Record Status` column is added to record the overall status of the row. Details on how to handle the columns added by the DQS Cleansing transform are covered later in this chapter.

Table 5-2. *Additional Columns Created by the DQS Cleansing Transform*

Column	Default	Description
Record Status	Yes	The overall status of the record, based on the status of each mapped column. The overall status is based on the following algorithm:
		If one or more columns is:
		• `Invalid`, the record status is `Invalid`
		• `Auto suggest`, the record status is `Auto suggest`
		• `Corrected`, the record status is `Corrected`
		If all columns are `Correct` or `New`, then the record status will be `Correct`.
		If all columns are `New`, then the record status will be `New`.
		See Table 5-3 for possible Status values.
_Source	Yes	This column contains the original value passed to the transform.
_Output	Yes	If the original value was modified during the cleansing process, this column contains the corrected value. If the value was not modified, this column contains the original value. When doing bulk cleansing through SSIS, downstream components will typically make use of this column.
_Status	Yes	The validation or cleansing status of the value.
		See Table 5-3 for possible values of the Status column.
_Confidence	No	This column contains a score that is given to any correction or suggestion. The score reflects to what extent the DQS server (or the relevant Reference Data Source) has confidence in the correction/suggestion. Most ETL packages will want to include this field, and use a conditional split to redirect values that do not meet the minimum confidence threshold so they can be manually inspected.
_Reason	No	This column explains the reason for the column's cleansing status. For example, if a column was `Corrected`, the reason might be due to the DQS Cleansing algorithm, knowledge base rules, or a change due to standardization.

(continued)

Table 5-2. (*continued*)

Column	Default	Description
_Appended Data	No	This column is populated when there are domains attached to a Reference Data Provider. Certain reference data providers will return additional information as part of the cleansing– not only values associated with the mapped domains. For example, when cleansing an address, the reference data provider might also return Latitude and Longitude values.
_Appended Data Schema	No	This column is related to the Appended Data setting (above). If the RDS returned additional information in the Appended Data field, this column contains a simple schema which can be used to interpret that data.

The Advanced tab (as shown in Figure 5-10) has number of different options, most of which add new columns to the data flow when selected. The `Standardize output` option is an exception to this. When enabled, DQS will modify the output values according to the domain settings defined in the DQS client application. You can see how the standardization settings are defined in the DQS Client on the Domain Management | Domain Properties tab (shown earlier in Figure 5-3).

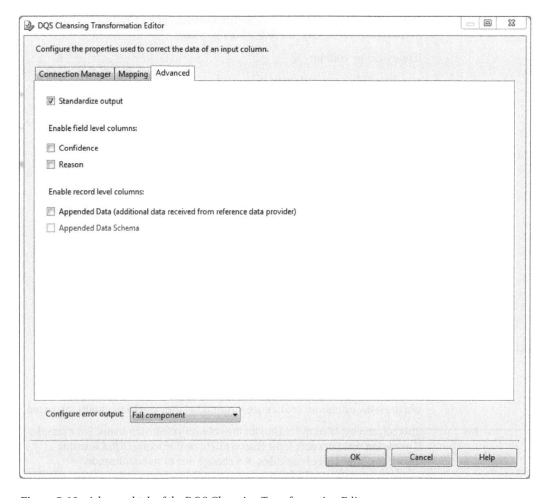

Figure 5-10. *Advanced tab of the DQS Cleansing Transformation Editor*

There are two kinds of standardization:

> **Reformatting operations.** These include operations such as conversion to uppercase, to lowercase, and to capitalized words in a string.

> **Correction to a leading value.** For example, if multiple values (or synonyms) are defined for a term, the current value will be replaced with the leading term (as defined in the KB).

The DQS Cleansing transformation logs Information events that indicate when it sends rows to the DQS server. There will be one event for each batch, and one event at the end, with a summary for all records. The messages contain details about how long the cleansing process took to process the batch, and the counts for each status. Listing 5-1 shows an example of what these messages look like. The transform processes data in 1000 row chunks. The chunk size is currently hardcoded – there is no way to configure the size of the batch sent to the DQS server.

■ **Note** The default chunk size for data sent from the DQS Cleansing transform to the DQS server was changed from 1,000 rows to 10,000 rows in SQL Server 2012 CU1.

Listing 5-1. DQS Cleansing Transform Log Messages

```
[DQS Cleansing] Information: The DQS Cleansing component received 1000 records from the DQS
server. The data cleansing process took 7 seconds.
[DQS Cleansing] Information: DQS Cleansing component records chunk status count -  Invalid:
0, Autosuggest: 21, Corrected: 979, Unknown: 0, Correct: 0.
[DQS Cleansing] Information: DQS Cleansing component records total status count -  Invalid:
0, Autosuggest: 115, Corrected: 4885, Unknown: 0, Correct: 0.
```

Cleansing Data in the Data Flow

The following section contains design patterns for cleansing data in the SSIS data flow using the DQS Cleansing transform. There are two key issues to keep in mind when cleansing data:

- The cleansing process is based on the rules within your knowledge base. The better the cleansing rules are, the more accurate your cleansing process will be. You may want to reprocess your data as the rules in your knowledge base improve.

- Cleansing large amounts of data can take a long time. See the Performance Considerations section below for patterns which can be used to reduce overall processing time.

Handling the Output of the DQS Cleansing Transform

The DQS Cleansing transform adds a number of new columns to the data flow (as described earlier in this chapter). The way you'll handle the processed rows will usually depend on the status of the row, which is set in the Record Status column. A Conditional Split transformation can be used to redirect rows down the appropriate data flow path. Figure 5-11 shows what the Conditional Split transformation would look like with a separate output for each Record Status value. Table 5-3 contains a list of possible status values.

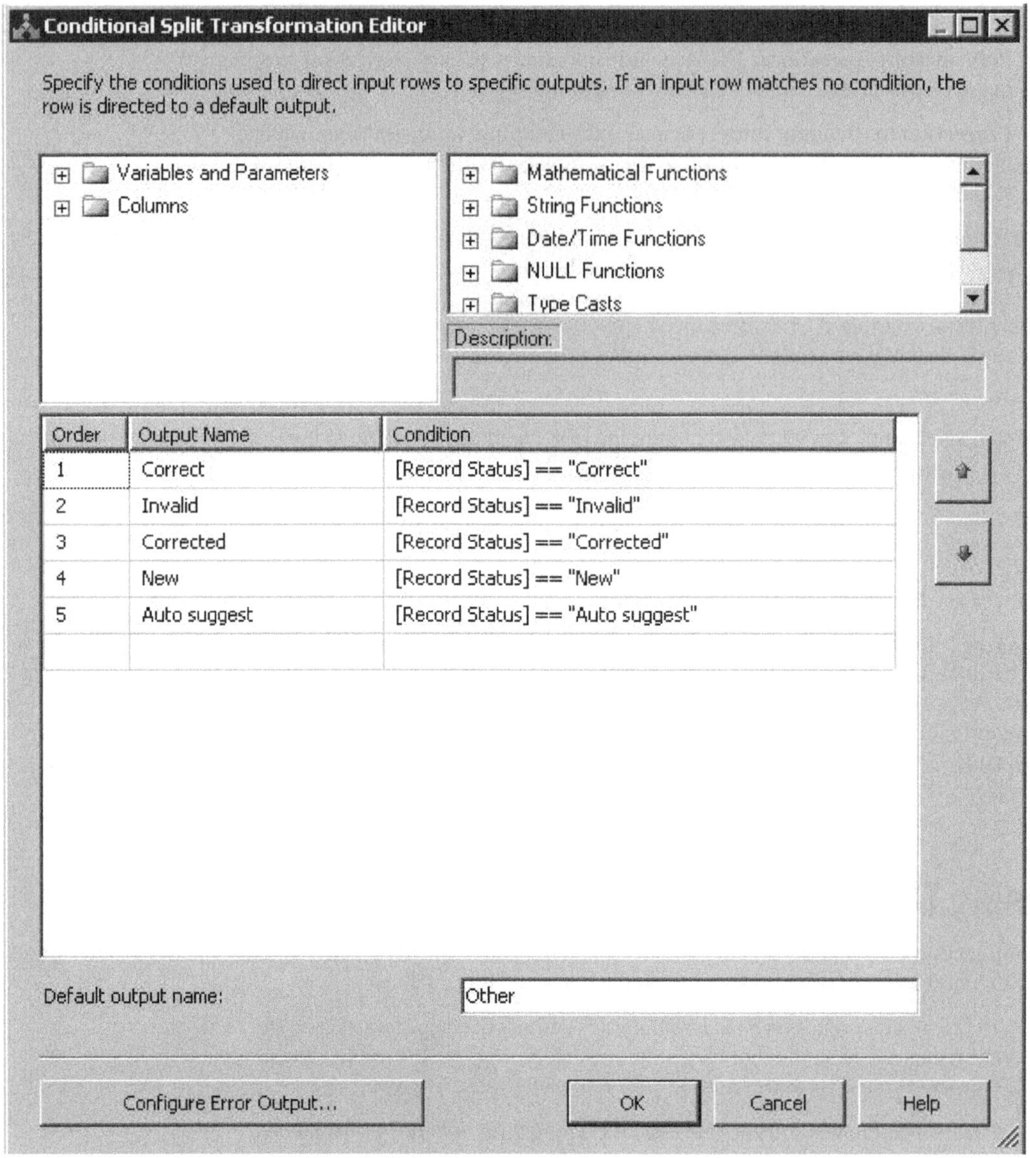

Figure 5-11. *Conditional Split transformation configured to process the DQS Record Status*

Table 5-3. *Column Status Values*

Option	Description
Correct	The value was already correct, and needs no further modification. The Corrected column will contain the original value.
Invalid	The domain contained validation rules that marked this value as invalid.
Corrected	The value was incorrect, but DQS was able to correct it. The Corrected column will contain the modified value.
New	The value wasn't in the current domain, and did not match any domain rules. DQS is unsure whether or not it is valid. The value should be redirected, and manually inspected.
Auto suggest	The value wasn't an exact match, but DQS has provided a suggestion. If you include the Confidence field, you could automatically accept rows above a certain confidence level, and redirect others to a separate table for later review.

■ **Note** The column status values are localized - they actual string will change depending on the language of your SQL Server installation. This might require you to add additional processing logic to your Conditional Split expressions if you expect your packages to run under different system locales. For more information about the status values, see the Data Cleansing (DQS) page in books online: `http://msdn.microsoft.com/en-us/library/gg524800(v=SQL.110).aspx`

The status values you handle and downstream data flow logic you use will depend on the goals of your data cleansing process. Typically, you will want to split your rows into two paths. Correct, Corrected, and Auto suggest rows will go down a path that will update your destination table with the cleansed data values (found in the < column_name > _Output column). New and Invalid rows will usually go into a separate table so someone can examine them later on, and either correct the data (in the case of Invalid rows), or update the Knowledge Base (in the case of New rows) so that these values can be handled automatically in the future. You may wish to include a check against the confidence level (<column_name> _Confidence) of the Auto suggest rows to make sure it meets a minimum threshold. Figure 5-12 shows an SSIS data flow with logic to process rows from the DQS Cleansing transform.

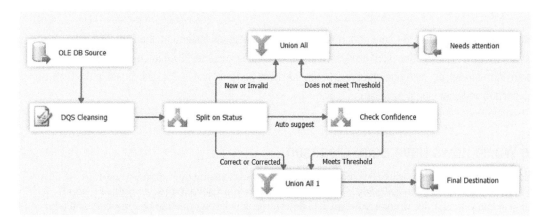

Figure 5-12. *Data Flow processing logic following a DQS Cleansing transform*

■ **Note**   Although the Confidence columns output by the DQS Cleansing transforms are numeric, they are output as `DT_WSTR(100)` columns (strings). To check the confidence level against a minimum threshold, you'll need to cast the value to a `DT_R4` (float) or `DT_R8` (double).

Performance Considerations

Data cleansing can be a CPU and memory intensive operation, and may take some time to complete. Domains that rely on online reference data services may round trip incoming data to the Azure Data Marketplace, which will have a further impact on the time it takes to cleanse your data. As a result, when processing large amounts of data, you will typically want to reduce your dataset before passing it through the DQS Cleansing transform.

The DQS Cleansing transform sends incoming data to the DQS server (running within a SQL Server instance), where the actual cleansing operations are performed. While this may offload a lot of the work being done by the SSIS machine, there may be some overhead in sending the data across the network to another server. Another thing to note is that the DQS Cleansing transform is an Asynchronous component, which means it makes copies of data flow buffers at runtime. This can further impact the performance of your data flow, and is another reason for only passing through the rows that need to be cleansed.

The following sections describe some package design tips that can be used to improve overall performance when cleansing data with the DQS Cleansing transform.

Parallel Processing

The DQS Cleansing transform sends its rows to the DQS server one batch at a time. This single threaded approach isn't ideal if you have a lot of spare CPU power on your system, so designing your packages in a way that allows DQS to send multiple batches to the server in parallel will give you a performance boost. You have two main options for parallel processing. First, you can split the incoming rows down multiple paths, and have a separate DQS Cleansing transform on each path, performing the same set of work. If your data set has a key or row that can be easily split using SSIS Expressions, you can use a Conditional Split transform. Otherwise, you can consider using a third party component like the Balanced Data Distributor. The second approach is to design your data flow in such a way that multiple instances of your package can be run in parallel. For this approach to work, you will need to partition your source query so that it pulls back a certain key range, and each instance of the package will work on a different range. This approach gives you a bit more flexibility, as you can dynamically control how many package instances you run in parallel by playing with the key ranges.

■ **Note**   You might find that the DQS Client performs its cleansing operations faster than the DQS Cleansing transform in SSIS. This is because the client processes multiple batches in parallel by default, while the DQS Cleansing transform processes them one at a time. To get the same performance in SSIS as you do in the DQS Client, you'll need to add your own parallelism.

Tracking Which Rows Have Been Cleansed

You can track which rows have already been cleansed, and when the cleansing operation was performed. This allows you to filter-out rows that have already been cleansed, so you don't need to process them a second time. By using a date value for this marker, you can also determine which rows need to be reprocessed if your knowledge base gets updated. Remember, as your knowledge base changes and your cleansing rules improve, you will get more accurate results each time data is processed by the DQS Cleansing transform.

To track when a row has been cleansed, add a new datetime column to your destination table (DateLastCleansed). A NULL or very early date value can be used to indicate that a row has never been processed. Alternatively, you can track dates in a separate table, linked to the original row with a foreign key constraint. Your SSIS package will contain the following logic:

1. Retrieve the date the DQS knowledge base was last updated using an Execute SQL Task. This value should be stored in a package variable (@[User::DQS_KB_Date]).

2. Inside of a Data Flow task, retrieve the data to be cleansed with the appropriate source component. The source data should contain a DateLastCleansed column to track when the row was last processed with the DQS Cleansing transform.

3. Use a Conditional Split transform to compare the DQS knowledge base date against the date the row was last processed. The expression might look like this: [DateLastCleansed] < @[User::DQS_KB_Date]. Rows matching this expression will be directed to a DQS Cleansing transformation.

4. Handle the cleansed rows according to their status.

5. Use a Derived Column transform to set a new DateLastCleansed value.

6. Update the destination table with any corrected values and the new DateLastCleansed value.

Figure 5-13 shows the data flow for the package logic described in the steps above.

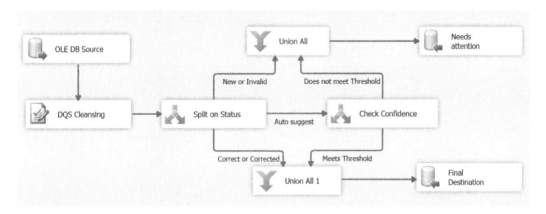

Figure 5-13. *Example Data Flow when pre-filtering rows that have already been cleansed*

Filtering Rows with the Lookup Transform

You can reduce the number of rows you need to cleanse by validating the data with a faster data flow component, such as the Lookup Transform. Using one or more Lookup Transforms, you can check if values exist in a reference table using quick, in-memory comparisons. Rows that match existing values can be filtered out. Rows with values that aren't found in the reference table can then be sent to Data Quality Services for cleansing. Pre-filtering rows this way means you won't be able to take advantage of the standardized formatting that DQS provides, and this makes it difficult to do complex validation that involves relationships between multiple fields. This approach works best when you are working with a small number of unrelated fields that don't require any special formatting as part of the cleansing process.

To use this pattern, your data flow will use the following logic:

1. Retrieve the data containing the fields to be cleansed using a source component.

2. Set the component to Ignore failure when there are no matching entries.

3. Add a Lookup Transform for each field you are going to cleanse. Each Lookup Transform will use a SQL query that pulls in a unique set of values for that field, and a static Boolean (bit) value. This static value will be used as a flag to determine whether the value was found. Since you are ignoring lookup failures, the flag value will be NULL if the lookup failed to find a match. Listing 5-2 shows what the query would look like for the CountryRegionCode field, coming from the DimGeography table.

Listing 5-2. Sample Lookup Query for the CountryRegionCode Field

```
SELECT DISTINCT CountryRegionCode, 1 as [RegionCodeFlag]
FROM DimGeography
```

4. On the Columns tab, map the field to the related lookup column, and add the static flag value as a new column in your data flow (as shown in Figure 5-14).

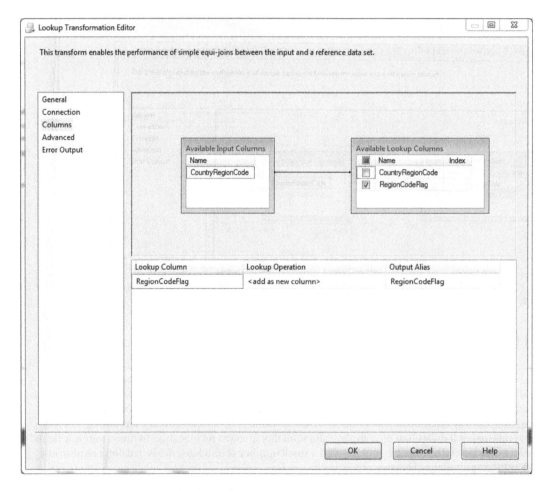

Figure 5-14. *Column mapping for the Lookup Transform.*

5.   Repeat steps 2-4 for each field you will be cleansing. The Lookup transforms should be connected using the Lookup Match Outputs.

6.   Add a Conditional Split transform with a single expression that checks each of the flag fields. If any of the flag fields are NULL, the row should be sent to DQS for proper cleansing. For example, the expression to check the RegionCodeFlag for a NULL value would be: ISNULL([RegionCodeFlag]).

7.   Connect the Conditional Split output you created to the DQS Cleansing transform. Rows going to the Conditional Split's default output can be ignored (as their values were successfully validated using the Lookup transforms).

8.   Complete the rest of the data flow based on the appropriate logic for handling the output of the DQS Cleansing transform.

Figure 5-15 shows a screenshot of a data flow to cleanse a single field using the logic described above.

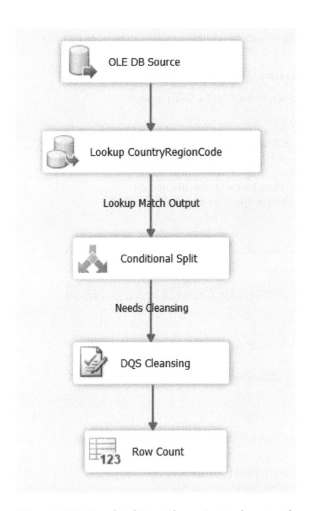

Figure 5-15. *Completed Data Flow using Lookup transforms to pre-filter rows*

■ **Note**   This approach works especially well when looking up key fields that are part of an entity in Master Data Services (MDS), another product that ships with SQL Server 2012. Using an MDS Subscription View, you can expose your dimension as a view that can be queried by a Lookup Transform. For more information about Master Data Services, see the books online entry: `http://msdn.microsoft.com/en-us/library/ee633763.aspx`

Approving and Importing Cleansing Rules

When a data flow with a DQS Cleansing transform is run, a cleansing project is created on the DQS Server. This allows the KB editor to view the corrections performed by the transform, and approve or reject rules. A new project is created automatically each time the package is run, and can be viewed using the DQS Client. When performing parallel cleansing with multiple DQS Cleansing transforms in a single data flow, a project will be created for each transform you are using.

Once correction rules have been approved by the KB editor, they can be imported into the knowledge base so they can be automatically applied the next time cleansing is performed. This process can be done with the following steps:

1. Run the SSIS package containing the DQS Cleansing transform.

2. Open the DQS Client, and connect to the DQS server used by the SSIS package.

3. Click on the Open Data Quality Project button.

4. The newly created project will be listed on the left hand pane (as shown in Figure 5-16). The project's name will be generated using the name of the package, the name of the DQS Cleansing transform, a timestamp of when the package was executed, the unique identifier of the Data Flow Task which contained the transformation, and another unique identifier for the specific execution of the package.

Figure 5-16. Running the DQS Cleansing transform will create a project on the DQS server

5. Selecting the project name will display details in the right hand pane (shown in Figure 5-17), such as the domains that were used in this cleansing activity.

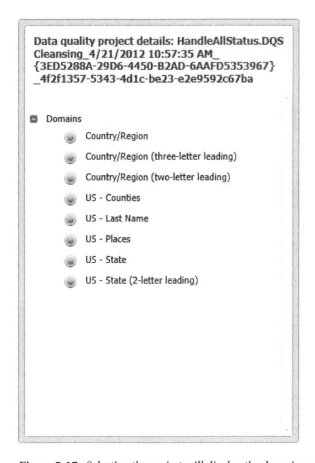

Figure 5-17. *Selecting the project will display the domains used in this activity*

6. Click Next to open the project.

7. Select the domains you would like to review the corrections for.

8. Click the Approve or Reject radio buttons for each correction, or change the "Correct to" value for the entry.

9. Click the Next button when you have finished with the rules.

10. (Optional) Export the corrected data to SQL Server, CSV or Excel. You will be able to skip this step in most scenarios, as your SSIS package will be responsible for handling the corrected data.

11. Click the Finish button to close the project.

12. From the home screen, select your knowledge base, and choose the Domain Management activity.

13. Select the domain you have defined new rules for.

14. Click the Domain Values tab.

15. Click the Import Values button, and select Import project values (as shown in Figure 5-18).

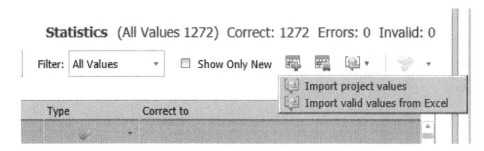

Statistics (All Values 1272) Correct: 1272 Errors: 0 Invalid: 0

Filter: All Values ▼ ☐ Show Only New

Import project values
Import valid values from Excel

Type   Correct to

Figure 5-18. Importing domain values from an existing project

16. Repeat steps 13-15 for each domain you wish to update.

17. Click the Finish button to publish your knowledge base changes.

18. If you have modified any of the correction rules, you may want to re-run your SSIS package to pick up the new values.

Summary

This chapter described the new DQS Cleansing transform, and how you can use it to take advantage of the advanced data cleansing functionality provided by Data Quality Services in SQL Server 2012. The design patterns detailed in this chapter will help you get the best possible performance while doing data cleansing with SSIS.

■ ■ ■

## CHAPTER 6

DB2 Source Patterns

In the previous chapters in this section, you learned about patterns that relate to SQL Server and Oracle Sources. In this chapter, I will move on to patterns that relate to sourcing data from the IBM DB2 database. DB2 describes a variety of databases, so it is essential to learn about the different databases I will discuss, as well as how to use each database as an Integration Services source.

As I described in Chapter 4, setting up a source entails four different objects: connection manager, provider, source component, and a source component query. While this remains true for the DB2 database, you need the additional first step of determining what type of database you own. DB2 has a number of types, providers, and ways to query data. As we look at the different patterns associated with each of these components, picture how they will work with other sources as well. Combining these steps will put you on the right path to pulling data from your DB2 database.

This chapter highlights patterns that may be of use while connecting to a DB2 database, but does not cover every possible scenario that you may run into in your environment.

DB2 Database Family

There are several different types of DB2 databases available on the market today. How you connect to the database depends on the DB2 version. DB2 separates its products into three groups:

- **DB2 for i**: This version has gone through multiple names over the years, including DB2 for AS/400, iSeries, System I, and Power Systems. DB2 is included in this server, so people commonly refer to this version when they think of DB2.

- **DB2 for z/OS**: This DB2 version is the main database available for the z/OS platform and is only available in 64-bit mode.

- **DB2 for LUW**: This version of DB2 is a later addition to the DB2 family. The Linux, UNIX, and Windows (LUW) version comes in multiple editions, depending on the purpose of your database instance. More information on these editions can be found on IBM's website.

The different product types affect how you query data from Integration Services. As I walk you through setting up your connection, I will point out some of the differences you need to be aware of based on the product type. The first thing you need to do is pick a provider to use in your connection manager.

Selecting a DB2 Provider

The first step in pulling data from DB2 is to select a provider that can be used in your environment. There are two steps to accomplishing this:

1. Find Database Version

2. Pick Provider Vendor

Find Database Version

The first step in selecting your DB2 provider is to learn what version you own. Combining the version information with the product type will help you choose what provider to use. If you're not sure what type of server you're working with, you have a couple of options. The first option is to use a DB2 administration tool to check the properties of your instance. For example, if you use Control Center, you can right-click on the instance name, and click the **About** menu option. This will show something similar to Figure 6-1.

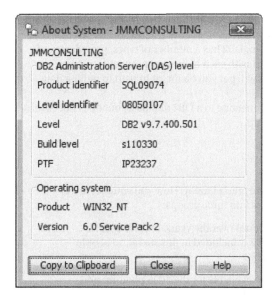

Figure 6-1. *Control Center About window showing database version and information*

If you don't have access to connect directly to the instance, you can run a query against the database instead to pull the same information. A sample query that shows this information can be seen in Listing 6-1, with the results shown in Figure 6-2.

Listing 6-1. Sample query to show database version and information

```
SELECT inst_name
       , release_num
       , service_level
       , bld_level
       , ptf
       , fixpack_num
FROM TABLE (sysproc.env_get_inst_info())
```

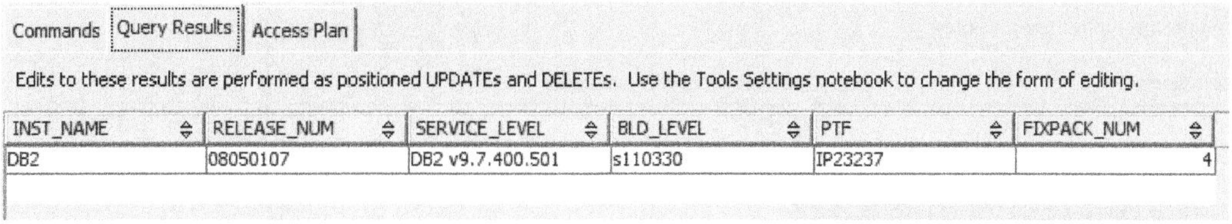

| Commands | Query Results | Access Plan | | | | | | | | |

Edits to these results are performed as positioned UPDATEs and DELETEs. Use the Tools Settings notebook to change the form of editing.

INST_NAME	⇕	RELEASE_NUM	⇕	SERVICE_LEVEL	⇕	BLD_LEVEL	⇕	PTF	⇕	FIXPACK_NUM	⇕
DB2		08050107		DB2 v9.7.400.501		s110330		IP23237			4

Figure 6-2. *Query results showing database version and information*

Pick Provider Vendor

While it is possible to use ODBC or ADO.NET to connect to a DB2 database, we will focus on OLE DB providers in this chapter to ensure that we can use the connection for all transformations. Here are two of the more common providers and when you would use each one.

- **IBM OLE DB Provider for DB2**: IBM produces their own OLE DB provider, which can be used in applications such as Integration Services. You can download this provider from IBM's website, www.ibm.com. This provider can be used for all versions and the latest products.

- **Microsoft OLE DB Provider for DB2 Version 4.0**: Microsoft created a provider that uses OLE DB to connect to DB2. You can download this provider separately, or as part of the Microsoft SQL Server Denali CTP 3 Feature Pack, found here: http://www.microsoft.com/download/en/details.aspx?id=26726. This provider can be used for all versions of DB2. See the latest documentation for which product numbers it supports.

Don't forget to make sure you've selected either the 32-bit or 64-bit version, based on the database server. Also ensure that the database version matches the supported version and product for the provider you want to use. I recommend using the provider most often used in your organization to facilitate ease of development and maintenance. If you are trying a provider for the first time, try the different versions to see what works best for you, as the performance and security discrepancies may vary per environment.

Connecting to a DB2 Database

For this chapter, we'll use the Microsoft OLE DB Provider for DB2. No matter what provider you choose, the next step is to make a connection to the DB2 database. To do this, you need to create a connection manager, select the correct provider, and fill out the appropriate server information.

Once you download your desired provider, you will install it on the server where you will develop and execute your Integration Services packages. If the provider has installed correctly, you can see it by opening up the Source Assistant. A correctly installed provider can be seen in Figure 6-3.

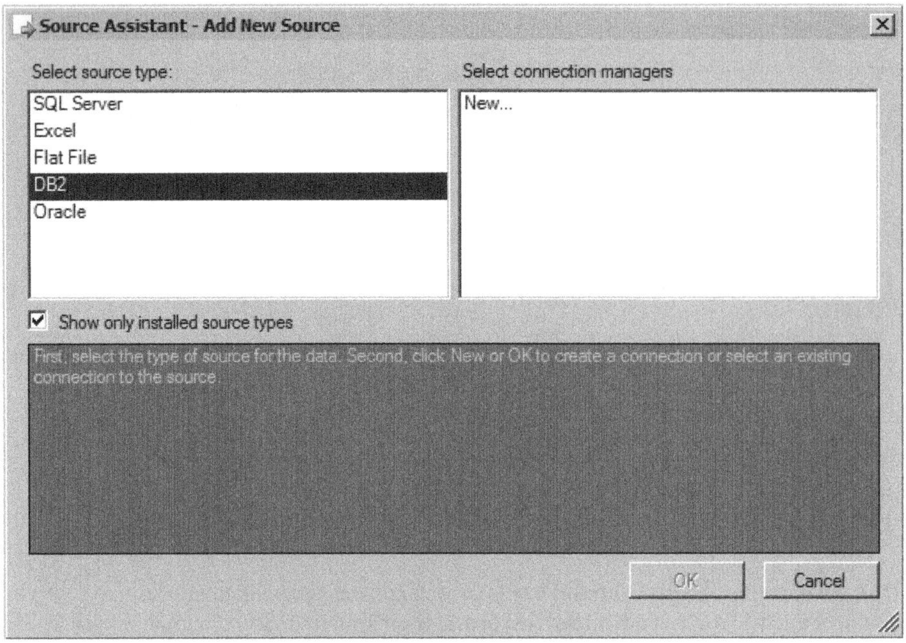

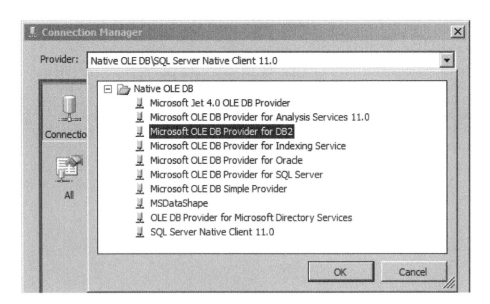

Figure 6-3. Source Assistant's Add New Source window

Begin by creating a shared OLE DB connection manager in the Solution Explorer of your package. In the provider dropdown list at the top of the Connection Manager window, change the provider to Microsoft OLE DB Provider for DB2, as seen in Figure 6-4.

Figure 6-4. Connection Manager window Provider List

Next, you can add the name of the database instance, the correct authentication method, and the database you want to connect to. If you prefer, you can directly enter a connection string in the Connection property of the Source.

■ **Note**   If you ever have a question on the correct connection string to use, `http://www.connectionstrings.com` is a great resource to answer your question.

In additional to telling Integration Services how to connect to the DB2 database, you also need to tell Integration Services how to view the data. To store data, databases use an encoding scheme and character codeset. The two encoding schemes that you need to understand are:

- **ASCII**: The **American Standard Code for Information Interchange** is a 7-bit encoding scheme that contains 128 printable and non-printable characters.

- **EBCDIC**: The **Extended Binary Coded Decimal Interchange Code** was created by IBM and is an 8-bit encoding scheme used in their mainframe servers.

Both DB2 for i and DB2 for z/OS use the EBCDIC encoding scheme, and DB2 for LUW uses the ASCII encoding scheme. Typically, the EBCDIC schemes use the codeset number 37, and the DB2 for LUW uses the ANSI-1252 codeset. Using the Microsoft OLE DB Provider for DB2, the next step is to modify the codeset for whichever version you are using.

Begin by clicking on the **Data Links...** button next to the Provider name in the Connection Manager, seen in Figure 6-5.

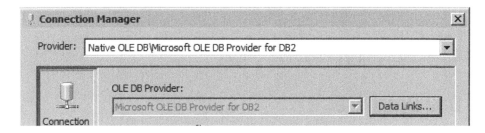

Figure 6-5. *Data Links button on the Connection Manager window*

The Data Link Properties window should open. Under the **Advanced** tab > **Host CCSID** property, you can use the default value of **EBCDIC – U.S./Canada [37]** or change it to **ANSI – Latin I [1252]**, as shown in Figure 6-6. In addition, you may find it necessary to check the **Process binary as character** option if you are seeing output that looks like data type names rather than your data.

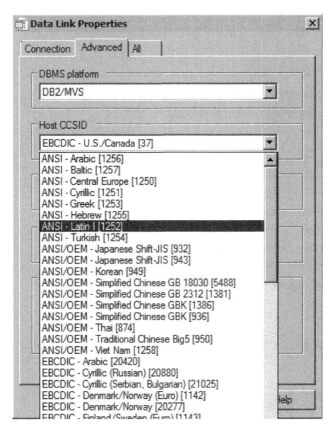

Figure 6-6. *Data Link Properties window with Host CCSID List*

Querying the DB2 Database

The final set of DB2 Source patterns covers querying the DB2 database. Because the Integration Services package uses an OLE DB provider, it will also need an OLE DB source component. As with any other database, the source component should point to the DB2 connection manager already created. Once the package successfully connects to the database, it is time to query the database.

■ **Note**   A number of companies provide alternatives to the Integration Services connection managers and source components. They provide a different interface and different functionality than the OLE DB source component. If you need additional functionality, such as EBCDIC to ASCII conversion, see aminoSoftware's Lysine EBCDIC source.

All source component queries are written in whatever brand of SQL the database uses. DB2's RDBMS-specific language is called **SQL PL**, and **PL/SQL** can also be used for later versions. If you receive an error message about syntax, be sure that your syntax matches the guidelines found on IBM's website: http://publib. boulder.ibm.com/infocenter/db2luw/v9r7/index.jsp?topic=/com.ibm.db2.luw.apdv.plsql.doc/doc/ c0053607.html.

In certain cases, you may want to use parameters to limit the data returned from the database. Let's take a look at parameterizing your queries now.

DB2 Source Component Parameters

An important part of writing source queries is the ability to filter the data that enters the pipeline. There are a number of reasons why you would want to do this, including loading data incrementally, reusing the same package for different departments, or reducing the amount of data that is run at one time. When using the Microsoft OLE DB Provider for DB2, you need to set the Derive Parameters property to True. This property is found in the connection manager, under the **Data Links...** button, and the **All** tab, as shown in Figure 6-7.

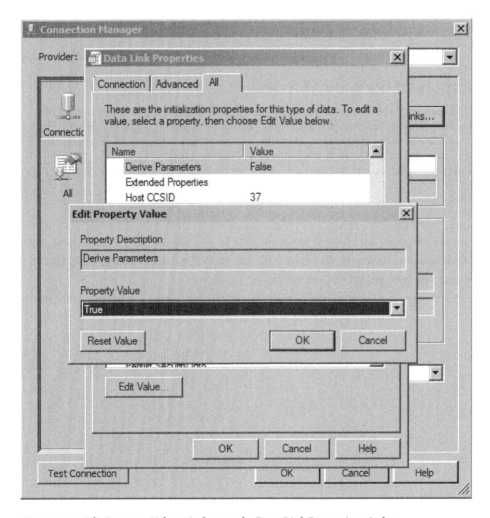

Figure 6-7. *Edit Property Value window on the Data Link Properties window*

Once the Derive Parameters property is set, you will write your query using question marks, similar to Listing 6-2. Put the query in the SQL command in the source component.

Listing 6-2. Sample query to illustrate DB2 parameters

```
SELECT col1
     , col2
     , col3
FROM tab1
WHERE col4 = ?
```

Be sure to click the **Parameters** button next to the query in the source to assign variables to each parameter that you set. It is important that the list of variables in the Parameters window matched the correct order in the query.

There are some scenarios where using query parameters won't work. Let's look at when you can't use query parameters, and what to do instead.

DB2 Source Component Dynamic Queries

Parameterized queries will not work if the content of the source query needs to be changed for any reason. The table, schema, or column names could change as part of the query content. A typical example of this in DB2 is when you have different schemas in each environment. To fix this, we set an expression on a variable and use the variable in the SQLStatement property. Let's walk through the steps of setting this up.

Begin by creating two string variables: environment and query. Set the following properties on the query variable:

EvaluateAsExpression: `True`
Value: `"select col1, col2 from" + @environment + ".tab1"`

■ **Note**   In Integration Services's editions prior to SQL Server 2012, expressions had a limit of 4000 characters. This restriction is now removed, allowing you to create strings as long as needed.

In the OLE DB source component, change the query type to SQL Statement as Variable, and pick the query variable that you just selected, as shown in Figure 6-8.

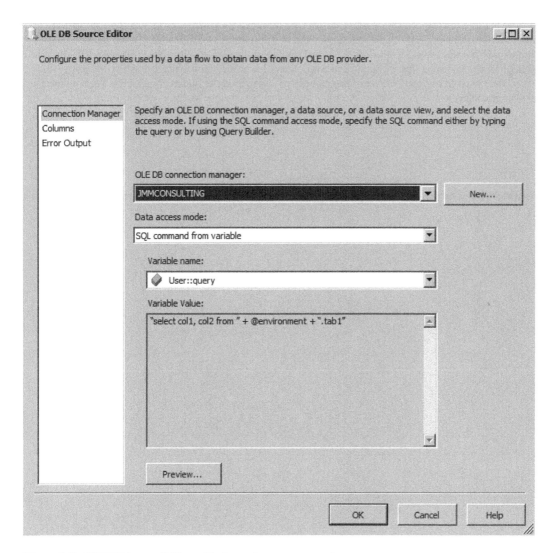

Figure 6-8. *OLE DB Source Editor with dynamic query properties*

When this package runs, use a package parameter to pass in the correct environment schema name. The expression on the query variable will be set to the new query and execute correctly. Make sure to set the ValidateExternalMetadata property on the OLE DB Source to False to ensure that the package will validate successfully.

Summary

This chapter has covered many of the patterns necessary to connect to the different types of the IBM DB2 database. You've learned how to determine what type of DB2 database you own, how to pick the appropriate provider, and different ways of querying the database. Note that sometimes organizations go a different route when dealing with DB2: exporting the data into a file and then loading the file using SSIS. This is a perfectly valid option, and might make sense for you if you have network latencies or problems with connectivity to your DB2 database. If you decide to go this route instead, you can learn how to load the data using Flat File Source Patterns, which I will discuss in Chapter 7.

CHAPTER 7

Flat File Source Patterns

A common way to transfer data between systems is to export the source data to a flat file and then import the contents of this file into the destination database. Flat files come in all shapes, sizes, and types. There are no row-length limitations. File size is limited by the maximum size allowed by the operating system. When examining flat file types, there are two initial considerations: file format and schema. Common file formats of flat file sources include:

- Comma-Separated Values (CSV)
- Tab-Delimited File (TDF)
- Fixed Width

In a flat file, as in a database, schema includes columns and data types. Schema options also allow for more exotic file format options such as "ragged right" and "variable-length rows" flat files.

In this chapter, we'll examine a common pattern for loading a vanilla flat file source into SQL Server, then we'll expand that pattern to load a variable-length row flat file source. We will next examine creating and consuming flat file header rows, which are found in some flat file formats. Finally, we will construct an extremely useful SSIS design pattern: Archive File.

Flat File Sources

Let's begin with a simple flat file source. You can copy and paste the data below into a text editor such as Notepad and save it as MyFlatFile.csv:

```
RecordType,Name,Value
A,Simple One,11
B,Simple Two,22
C,Simple Three,33
A,Simple Four,44
C,Simple Five,55
B,Simple Six,66
```

The column names are in the first row. This is convenient but you don't always get column names in the first row - or anywhere inside a source flat file.

Before leaving the setup phase of our demo project, let's create a database named StagingDB that we can use as a destination. I use the following re-executable T-SQL script to create the StagingDB database:

```
use master
go
```

```
If Not Exists(Select name
              From sys.databases
              Where name='StagingDB')
 begin
  print 'Creating StagingDB database'
  Create Database StagingDB
  print 'StagingDB database created'
 end
Else
 print 'StagingDb database already exists.'
```

Execute this script on a server you can use for testing and development. Now we're all set to begin building the demo!

Moving To SSIS!

Open SQL Server Data Tools and create a new SSIS project named "Chapter 7", and rename the initial package to Chapter7.dtsx. Drag a Data Flow Task onto the Control Flow canvas and double-click it to open the editing tab.

There are a couple ways to create a Flat File Source for the Data Flow. You can use the Source Assistant or you can you can expand Other Sources in the Data Flow SSIS Toolbox and configure a Flat File Source adapter. Let's utilize the latter method: Drag a Flat File Source adapter from the Data Flow toolbox onto the Data Flow canvas and open the editor. Figure 7-1 shows the Connection Manager page for the Flat File Source Editor:

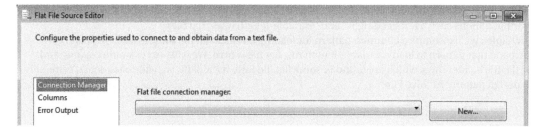

Figure 7-1. *Flat File Source Editor Connection Manager configuration*

Since there are no connection managers defined in this new SSIS project, click the New button beside the Flat File Connection Manager dropdown to open the Flat File Source Editor. On the General page, name the connection manager "My Flat File." Click the Browse button beside the File Name textbox and navigate to the location you saved MyFlatFile.csv. As shown in Figure 7-2, check the "Column names in the first data row" checkbox:

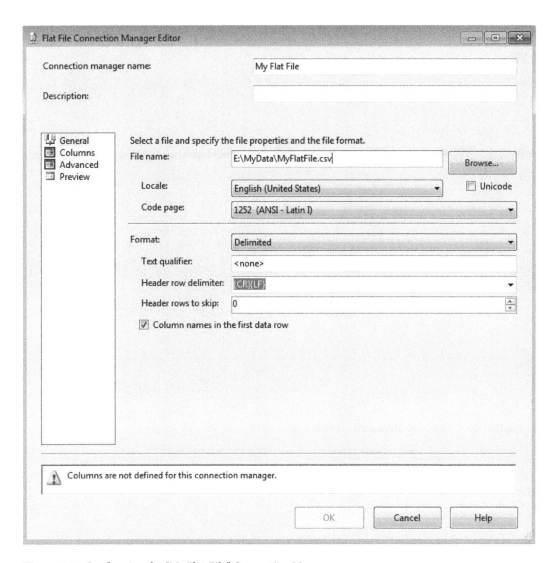

Figure 7-2. *Configuring the "My Flat File" Connection Manager*

Note the warning near the bottom of the window: Columns are not defined for this connection manager. For a properly formatted simple CSV file, SSIS now has enough information to read the schema of the flat file and complete the mapping for the connection manager. Figure 7-3 shows the Columns page used to define the column and row delimiters:

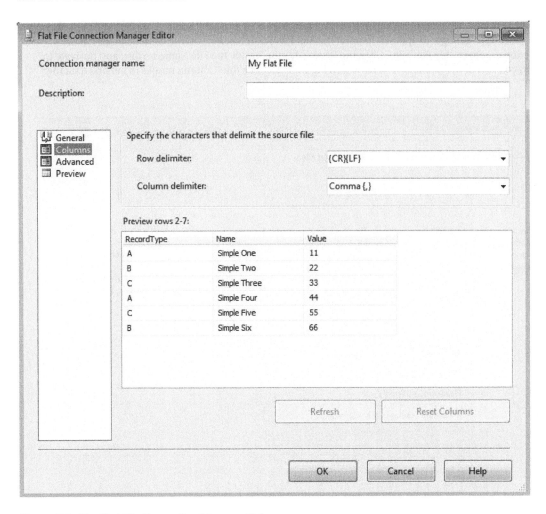

Figure 7-3. The Flat File Connection Manager Columns page

All data in a flat file are text by default.

Click the OK button to close the Flat File Connection Manager Editor, and then click the OK button to close the Flat File Source Editor.

Strong-Typing the Data

Why would you want to use strongly typed data? Consider the Value column in our example. Right now, Value is a DT_WSTR data type but the column contains numeric data. In fact, the numeric data is integers. In Sql Server, the INT data type consumes 4 bytes and covers the range from -2^31 (-2,147,483,648) through 2^31 - 1 (2,147,483,647) according to Books Online. If we wanted to store the integer value -2,147,483,600 as text, this would consume at least one byte per character. In this case, that's a minimum of 11 bytes (not counting the commas), and it could be more bytes depending on the data type chosen. Converting these data to the DT_I4 data type allows me to store that value in 4 bytes. As an added bonus, the data are numeric, so sorts on this field will outperform sorts on a string data type.

Let's manipulate the data types provided by the Flat File connection manager and source adapter. Drag a Derived Column Transformation onto the Data Flow canvas and connect a data flow path from the Flat File Source to the new Derived Column Transformation. Double-click it to open the editor.

Expand the Type Casts virtual folder in the SSIS Expression Language functions provided in the listbox in the upper right section of the Derived Column Editor. Drag a DT_STR type cast into the Expression cell of the first row of the Derived Column grid in the lower section of the Editor. The Derived Column column of the grid defaults to "<add as new column>" but allows you to choose to replace the value in any of the rows flowing through the transformation. You can make changes to the values as rows flow through the Derived Column transformation, but you cannot change the data type (which is precisely what we're going to do here), so we need to add a new column to the Data Flow. The default Derived Column Name is Derived Column *n*, where *n* is a 1-based array of columns configured in the transformation. Change the default derived column name to strRecordType. Return to the Expression column and complete the DT_STR cast function by replacing the "«length»" placeholder text with the desired length of the field: 1. Next, replace the "«code_page»" placeholder with the number that matches your Window Code Page identifier. For US English, this number is 1252. To complete the configuration, expand the Columns virtual folder in the Available Inputs listbox located in the upper left section of the Derived Column Transformation Editor, and drag the RecordType column into the Expression cell to the right of the DT_STR cast function that you just configured.

When you click anywhere else in the editor, the logic of the transformation validates the expression. This has been happening all along, changing the text color in the Expression to red when an issuewas encountered with the state of the expression. When you navigate off the Expression cell now, the expression (DT_STR, 1, 1252) [RecordType] should pass muster. The text should return to black to indicate a valid expression.

You can similarly create additional columns with casting expressions to manipulate the data types of the other fields moving through the Data Flow. Figure 7-4 shows how my example looks when I've completed editing the Derived Column Transformation:

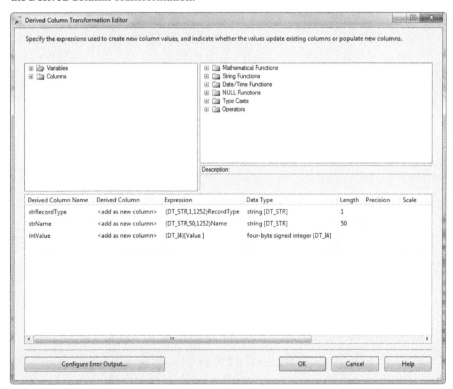

Figure 7-4. Derived Column Transformation, Configured

Introducing a Data-Staging Pattern

Data staging is an important concept. Every ETL developer has thoughts and opinions about the best way to stage data, and each thinks their way is best! (This is as it should be... we want and need confident ETL developers.) In my opinion, the data integration requirements drive the amount and type of staging.

For flat files, copying all the data into staging tables represents one pattern. Once the data are captured in a query-able format (a relational database), they can be manipulated and shaped by numerous transformations before they are loaded into the destination data warehouse or data mart.

Beyond flat files, staging supports a key tenet of the Extraction phase of any ETL solution: Impact the source system-of-record as little as possible. Often, an important business driver for building an ETL solution in the first place is the difficulty of querying data in the system-of-record for reporting purposes. ETL's first goal is similar to that of the Hippocratic Oath: "*Primum non nocere*" (First, do no harm).

Staging requirements for some ETL lend themselves to storing a copy of all source data, whether from flat files or not. Other requirements allow for applying some transformative logic prior to staging. Which is the correct answer? "It depends." In my opinion, the very act of copying data from a text source and landing it in a relational database represents a transformation.

This, then, becomes a pattern of staging data: copying data straight from a flat file into a database. To that end, let's complete the example we've started.

Drag an OLE DB Destination adapter onto the Data Flow canvas and connect a Data Flow Path from the Derived Column Transformation to the OLE DB Destination. Before we proceed, double-click on the Data Flow Path to open its editor, and then click on the Metadata page. You'll see something that looks like Figure 7-5:

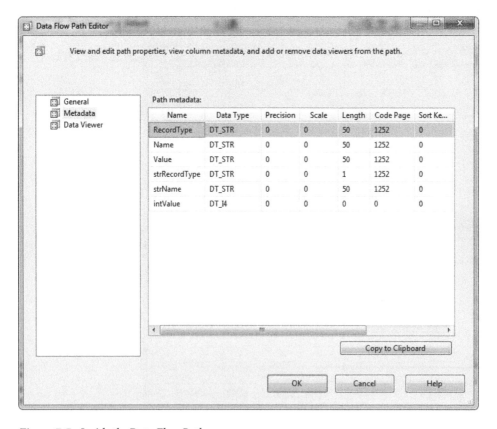

Figure 7-5. *Inside the Data Flow Path*

I often describe the buffers inside the Data Flow as "table-ish." It's an adjective I made up, but it fits. This peek under the hood of a data flow path is evidence. We'll come back to this diversion shortly. Click OK to close the Data Flow Path editor.

Rename the OLE DB Destination adapter "FlatFileDest" without the double-quotes. Open the OLE DB Destination editor and click the New button beside the OLE DB Connection Manager dropdown to configure an OLE DB Connection Manager. When the Configure OLE DB Connection Manager window displays, click the New button to create a new OLE DB Connection Manager. Add the name of your testing and development server/instance (the same server/instance you used earlier to create the StagingDB database) in the Server Name dropdown. In the "Select or enter a database name" dropdown, select StagingDB. Click the Ok button to complete the OLE DB Connection Manager configuration, and click the next Ok button to select this new connection manager for use with the OLE DB Destination adapter. Set the Data Access Mode property to "Table or view – fast load" and accept the default properties configured. Click the New button beside the "Name of the table or the view" dropdown. The Create Table window displays containing the following T-SQL Data Definition Language (DDL) statement:

```
CREATE TABLE [FlatFileDest] (
    [RecordType] varchar(50),
    [Name] varchar(50),
    [Value ] varchar(50),
    [strRecordType] varchar(1),
    [strName] varchar(50),
    [intValue] int
)
```

The name of the table the OLE DB Destination is going to create is "FlatFileDest" – the name we gave the OLE DB Destination adapter. Where did the column names come from? That's right! From the Data Flow Path metadata we viewed earlier. This functionality is pretty cool, when you think about it.

We don't need all these columns to store our data in our StagingDB. Since we are using this table to stage data from the flat file, let's use the same column names found in the source file. However, let's also use the strong data types we created in our Derived Column Transformation. Fortunately for us, our naming convention makes these changes relatively painless. Simply delete the DDL for the first three columns (RecordType, Name, and Value); and then remove the first three letters of the remaining columns, which will rename them to RecordType, Name, and Value:

```
CREATE TABLE [FlatFileDest] (
    [RecordType] varchar(1),
    [Name] varchar(50),
    [Value] int
)
```

When you click the OK button, the DDL statement is executed against StagingDB – creating the FlatFileDest table. That's a good thing, because our OLE DB Dastination adapter is warning us we need to complete Input-to-Output mappings, shown in Figure 7-6:

 Map the columns on the Mappings page.

Figure 7-6. The Columns have not been mapped

As shown in Figure 7-7, when we click on the Mappings page to begin this mapping, auto-mapping kicks in and finds it can auto-complete some of the mappings:

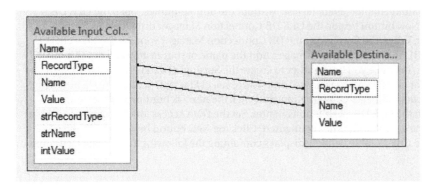

Figure 7-7. *OLE DB Destination Auto-Mapping*

One issue is that these fields don't contain the data we want to load. We want to load the Derived Columns instead. There a couple ways to correct the mapping, but I like dragging and dropping the fields I *want* mapped to the columns where I wish them mapped. Since mapping is, by definition, field-to-field, the existing (auto-) mappings will be overwritten by the new. Try it! Drag the strRecordType field from Available Input Columns to the RecordType cell in Available Output Columns. See? The old mapping is updated. Now map strName to Name and itnValue to Value, as shown in Figure 7-8:

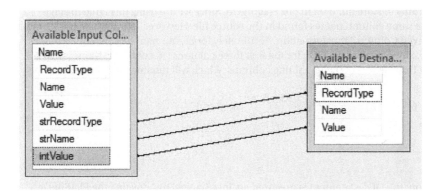

Figure 7-8. *Overwriting the auto-mappings*

Click the OK button, we're finished configuring the OLE DB Destination adapter. Press the F5 key to execute the SSIS package in the SSDT debugger. Hopefully, your Data Flow Task succeeds and appears as in Figure 7-9:

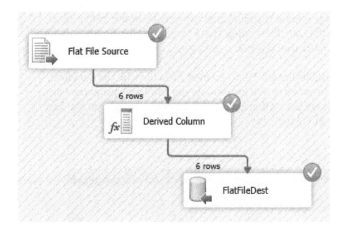

Figure 7-9. *A successful Data Flow!*

In this introductory section, I've introduced concepts of staging and we built a pattern to stage data from a flat file into a database table. Along the way, we delved into some data warehousing thinking and peeked under the hood of the Data Flow Task. Next up: loading another format of flat file – one with variable-length rows.

Variable-Length-Rows

A variable-length row flat file is a text source file. It can be a comma-separated values (CSV) file or a tab-delimited file (TDF). It can be a fixed-length file where columns are identified positionally or by ordinal. The major difference between a "normal" flat file and a variable-length row flat file is that the number of text positions is fixed in a normal flat file, and that number can change with each row in a variable-length flat file.

Let's look at an example of a variable-length flat file:

```
RecordType,Name1,Value1,Name2,Value2,Name3,Value3
A,Multi One,11
B,Multi Two,22,Multi Two A,23
C,Multi Three,33,Multi Three A,34,Multi Three B,345
A,Multi Four,44
C,Multi Five,55,Multi Five A,56,Multi Five B,567
B,Multi Six,66,Multi Six A,67
```

There are seven potential columns: RecordType, Name1, Value1, Name2, Value2, Name3, and Value3. Not all rows contain seven values. In fact, the first row contains only 3 values:

```
A,Multi One,11
```

In this format, the RecordType is in the first column and this indicates how many columns of data to expect in the row. Rows of RecordType A contain three values, rows of RecordType B contain five values, and those of RecordType C contain seven values.

Reading into a Data Flow

It's typical to load data from a flat file into an SSIS data flow using a Flat File connection manager. Let's walk through configuring a flat file connection manager for this file.

If you want to sing along, add a new SSIS package named VariableLengthRows.dtsx to your SSIS project. Add a Data Flow Task to the Control Flow and open the Data Flow editor (tab). Drag a Flat File Source adapter onto the Data Flow Task canvas and open its editor. Click the New button to create a new Flat File Connection Manager.

I named my Flat File Connection Manager "Variable-Length File." I created a text file with the data from above and named it VarLenRows.csv. I saved it and browsed to that location for the File Name property. I also checked the "Column names in the first data row" checkbox. When I click on the Columns page, the Flat File Connection manager Editor appears as shown here in Figure 7-10:

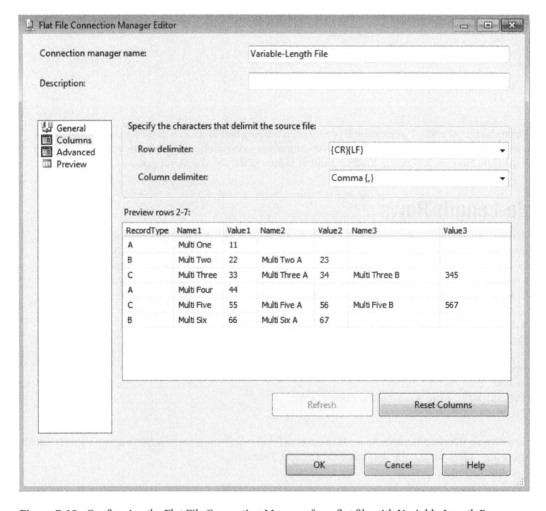

Figure 7-10. *Configuring the Flat File Connection Manager for a flat file with Variable-Length Rows*

This behavior is different from earlier editions of SSIS. In previous versions, the Flat File Connection Manager would raise an error. I blogged about this in a post entitled SSIS Design Pattern: Loading Variable-Length Rows (`http://sqlblog.com/blogs/andy_leonard/archive/2010/05/18/ssis-design-pattern-loading-variable-length-rows.aspx`). That post inspired this chapter in this book.

Splitting Record Types

Thanks to the new functionality in the SSIS 2012 Flat File Connection Manager, we have all the data coming in as separate rows. But the data rows contain information of different types. The rows need to be filtered based on Record Type. I can hear you thinking "Great, Andy. Now what?" I'm glad you asked! Now we need to parse the data as it flows through the Data Flow Task. There are a couple ways to approach this, but I like the Conditional Split.

Drag a Conditional Split Transformation onto the Data Flow Task canvas and connect a data flow path from the Flat File Source adapter to the Conditional Split.Open the editor for the transformation. In the Output Name column of the grid, enter "TypeA". Into the corresponding Condition, drag (or type) the RecordType column, appending the text ' == "A" ' (note that the "A" is in double-quotes. Do not type the single-quotes). Repeat this for each RecordType; "B" and "C," as shown in Figure 7-11:

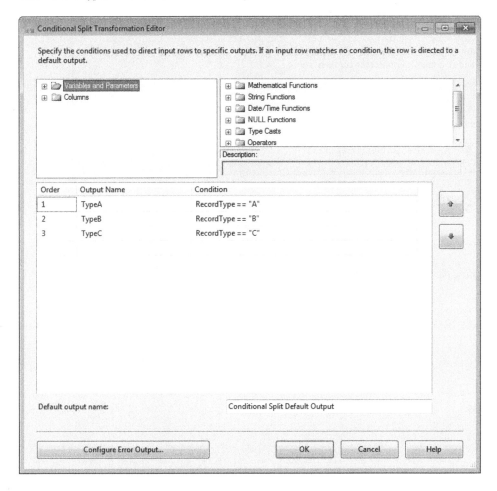

Figure 7-11. *Configuring the Script Component Inputs*

Click the OK button to close the Conditional Split transformation Editor. It is important to note that this would have required a Script Component in earlier versions of SSIS because the Flat File Connection Manager in previous versions couldn't parse files containing rows with a varying number of columns.

Terminating the Streams

You can use several Data Flow components to terminate a data flow path. In a Production environment, this would likely be an OLE DB Destination adapter. In a development or test environment, you may want to terminate with a component that doesn't require database connectivity or database object creation.

You can use the Trash Destination (www.sqlis.com/post/Trash-Destination-Adapter.aspx) adapter. You can also use any component that doesn't require configuration to execute and succeed in the Data Flow Task, such as a Derived Column or Multicast Transformation. Here, I will use multicast transformations to terminate the data flow path streams.

Drag three Multicast Transformations onto the Data Flow Task canvas. Connection an output from the Script Component to the TypeA multicast. When prompted, select the TypeA output buffer for the Script Component, as shown in Figure 7-12:

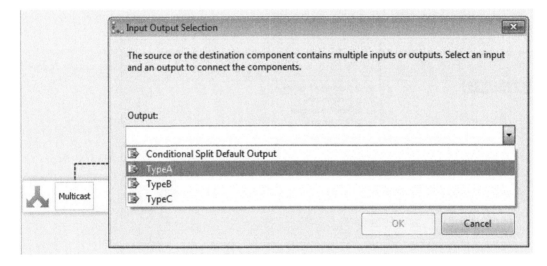

Figure 7-12. *Terminating the "Record Type A" Output from the Script Component*

Repeat this process for TypeB and TypeC connections. When complete, your Data Flow could appear as shown in Figure 7-13:

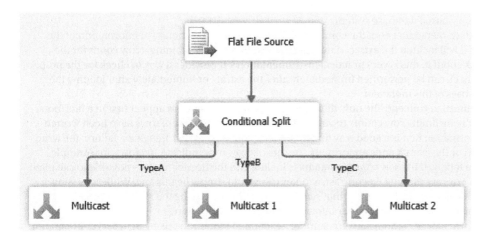

Figure 7-13. *The Script Component's Outputs, Terminated*

Let's run it! Execution should succeed, and when it does, the results will be the green checkmarks that you see in Figure 7-14.

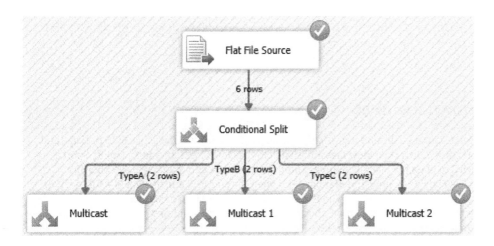

Figure 7-14. *Happiness is Green Checks*

This isn't the only way to address loading files of this format. It is one way, and it has the advantage of offering a lot of flexibility.

Header and Footer Rows

Header and footer rows are included in extract files from many sources. I regularly see these rows in flat files delivered from mainframe-based database systems.

A header row contains metadata about the contents of the extract file – a summary of information of the extract. At a minimum, it will include the extract date. There is usually a field containing a row count for the extract. When you think about it, this is very practical instrumentation – it provides a way to check for the proper number of rows. This check can be performed immediately after the extract or immediately after loading the extract – both are valid uses of this metadata.

A footer row is identical in concept. The only difference is location: header rows appear first in a file; footer rows appear last. If you're including row counts to validate that the correct number of rows have been written or read, writing this information first is a good way toincrease fault-tolerance. Why? Imagine a failure: the write operation is interrupted or the extract ends abnormally. The header row may indicate 100 rows, for example, but only 70 rows of data follow. If the row count metadata is included in the header row, it's possible to calculate exactly how many data rows are missing. In contrast, a footer row would simply be missing. While a missing footer would indicate that the extract had failed, that's *all* it would indicate. Having the rowcount metadata present would allow you to glean more and better information regarding the failure.

In this section, we will look at creating and consuming header and footer rows using SQL Server Integration Services 2012.

Consuming a Footer Row

We begin by looking at how to consume a footer row. To start, create a file containing a footer row. My file looks like this:

```
ID,Name,Value
11,Andy,12
22,Christy,13
33,Stevie Ray,14
44,Emma Grace,15
55,Riley Cooper,16
5 rows, extracted 10/5/2011 10:22:12 AM
```

To demonstrate, create your own file and name it MyFileFooterSource.csv. Create a new SSIS package and rename it ParseFileFooter.dtsx. Add a Data Flow task and switch to the Data Flow tab. Add a Flat File Source adapter and double-click it to open the Flat File Source Editor. On the Connectin Manager page, click the New button to create a new Flat File Connection Manager and open the editor. Name the Flat File Connection Manager "My File Footer Source File" and set the File Path property to the location of MyFileFooterSource. csv. Check the "Column names in the first data row" checkbox. Navigate to the Columns page to verify your configuration matches that shown here in Figure 7-15:

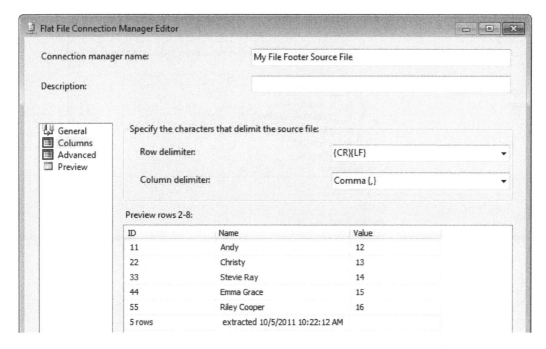

Figure 7-15. *Flat File Connection Manager Columns page for a File Containing a Footer Row*

You can see the footer row contents in the preview show above. You may or may not be able to view the footer row on the Columns page of the Flat File Connection Manager Editor.

The next step is to separate the footer row from the data rows. To accomplish this, we will use a Condition Split Transformation to isolate the footer row. There are a *lot* of different ways to detect the footer row, but the trick is to pick something unique about that row. In the SSIS Expression Language expression I define in Figure 7-16, I search for the term "rows" in the ID column. This condition will work as long as there's *never a chance* that the term "rows" will legitimately show up in the ID column of the data rows. Never is a very long time.

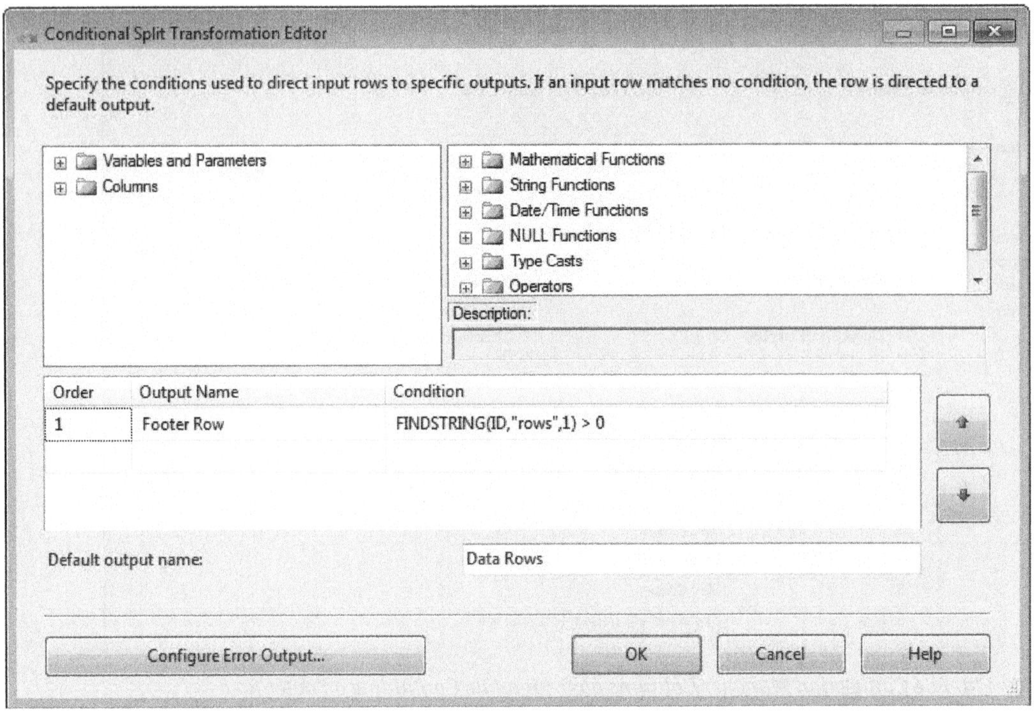

Figure 7-16. Configuring the Conditional Split Transformation

To terminate the data rows pipeline – which flows from the Conditional Split Transformation's Default output – I use a Derived Column Transformation.

The Footer Row output requires more parsing. We send it to another Derived Column Transformation named "der Parse Footer."

■ **Note:** Jamie Thomson wrote a great post entitled "SSIS: Suggested Best Practices and Naming Conventions" (http://sqlblog.com/blogs/jamie_thomson/archive/2012/01/29/suggested-best-practises-and-naming-conventions.aspx). I often use Jamie's naming conventions.

We want the number of rows and the datetime of the extraction. I use the expressions in Figure 7-17 to parse the Footer Row Count and Footer Extract DateTime:

Derived Column Name	Derived Column	Expression	Data Type
FooterRowCount	\<add as new column\>	(DT_I4)TRIM(LEFT(ID,FINDSTRING(ID," ",1)))	four-byte signed integer [DT_I4]
FooterExtractDateTime	\<add as new column\>	(DT_DBTIMESTAMP)TRIM(RIGHT(Name,LEN(Name) - FINDSTRING(Name," ",2)))	database timestamp [DT_DBTIMESTAMP]

Figure 7-17. Parsing the Row Count and Extract Date

Now we have the footer row metadata in the Data Flow pipeline. We can terminate this branch of the pipeline using another Derived Column transformation: "der Trash Destination Footer." Connect "der Parse Footer" to "der Trash Destination Footer." Right-click the data flow path and click Enable Data Viewer. Execute the package in the Debugger to view the contents of the footer row, as shown in Figure 7-18:

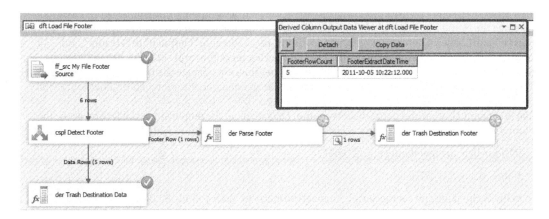

Figure 7-18. *Footer Row, Parsed*

You can see from the figure above that five (5) data rows exited the Conditional Split transformation named "cspl Detect Footer." We can observe the contents of the footer row after parsing in the Data Viewer.

Consuming a Header Row

Header rows are even easier to read. Let's start with a look at the source file named MyFileHeaderSource.csv:

```
5 rows, extracted 10/5/2011 10:22:12 AM
---------------
ID,Name,Value
11,Andy,12
22,Christy,13
33,Stevie Ray,14
44,Emma Grace,15
55,Riley Cooper,16
```

You can read header rows a few different ways. In this solution, we utilize one Flat File Connection Manager and one Data Flow to parse the header row the data. We rely heavily on Script Component logic for parsing and buffering operations.

Begin by creating a new SSIS package. I named mine ParseFileHeader2.dtsx.

■ **Note:** In the demo code, there is a messy solution for loading file headers and data – a package named ParseFileHeader.dtsx. It avoids the Script Component at the expense of loading the file contents twice. Yuck! It's suitable for very small files, but even then it's not optimal. I left this package in the solution to demonstrate that some patterns function but don't scale. In my career, I have written many SSIS packages that do not scale. It is how I learned to write packages that do scale!

Add a Data Flow Task and open the Data Flow Task editor. Add a Flat File Source adapter and open its editor. Use the New button to create a new Flat File Connection Manager aimed at MyFileHeaderSource.csv. Uncheck the "Column names in the first data row" checkbox. Be sure to click the Advanced page of the Connection Manager Editor and change the names of Column 0 and Column 1 to ID and Name, respectively.

Close the Connection Manager and Source adapter editors and drag a Script Component onto the Data Flow canvas. When prompted, select Transformation as the use of this Script Component. Open the Script Component editor and change the Name property to "scr Parse Header and Data." Click the Input Columns page and select both columns (ID and Name). Click on the Inputs and Outputs page. Rename "Output 0" to "Header" and change the SynchronousInputID property to None. Expand the Header output and click the Output Columns virtual folder. Click the Add Column button, name it ExtractDateTime, and change the Data Type to "database timestamp [DT_DBTIMESTAMP]." Click the Add Column button again, name this new column RowCount, and leave the Data Type set to the default ("four-byte unsigned integer [DT_UI4]").

Click the Add Output button and name this new output Data. Expand the output virtual folder and select the Output Columns virtual folder. As you did for the Header output, create two columns with the following properties:

- ID, four-byte unsigned integer [DT_UI4]
- Name, string [DT_STR]

Return to the Script page and set the ScriptLanguage property to Microsoft Visual Basic 2010. Click the Edit Script button. When the editor opens, add a variable declaration at the top of the class:

```
Public Class ScriptMain
    Inherits UserComponent

Dim iRowNum As Integer = 0
```

Replace the code in the Input0_ProcessInputRow subroutine with the following code:

```
Public Overrides Sub Input0_ProcessInputRow(ByVal Row As Input0Buffer)

' increment rownum
        iRowNum += 1

        Select Case iRowNum
            Case 1
                ' parse
                Dim sTmpCount As String = Row.ID
                sTmpCount = Strings.Trim(Strings.Left(Row.ID, Strings.InStr(Row.ID, " ")))
                Dim sTmpDate As String = Row.Name
                sTmpDate = Strings.Replace(Row.Name, " extracted ", " ")

                ' header row
                With HeaderBuffer
                    .AddRow()
                    .RowCount = Convert.ToInt32(sTmpCount)
                    .ExtractDateTime = Convert.ToDateTime(sTmpDate)
                End With
            Case 2
                ' ignore
            Case 3
                'column names
            Case Else
                ' data rows
```

```
            With DataBuffer
                .AddRow()
                .ID = Convert.ToInt32(Row.ID)
                .Name = Row.Name
            End With
      End Select
End Sub
```

This script counts the rows flowing through the Script Component and uses the number of the row to decide the disposition of the output row. A Select Case statement is driven by row number detection, and each row increments the row number incrementor (iRowNum). The first row is the header row and contains the extract metadata. The next two rows contain a scratch row of dashes and the Column Names, respectively. The remainder of the file contains data rows, and is addressed in the Select Case Else condition of the Select Case statement.

Close the VSTA Projects script editor and click the OK button on the Script Component editor. Terminate the Header and Data pipelines with the Data Flow component of your choice (I use Derived Column transformations named "der Header" and "der Data").

Test the package by executing it in the Debugger. Your results should be similar to those shown in Figure 7-19:

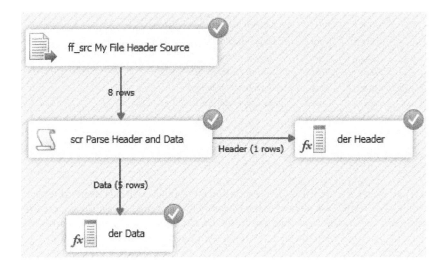

Figure 7-19. *Green checks rock!*

Producing a Footer Row

Let's look at producing a footer row and adding it to the data file. For this pattern, we will leverage project and package parameters. We will also leverage the Parent-Child pattern, which will be discussed in detail in another chapter. We are not going to build the package that creates a flat file containing data. We will start with the assumptions that an extract file exists and we know the number of rows and the extract date. We will use parameters to transmit metadata from the parent package to the child package. Let's get started!

Create a new SSIS package and name it WriteFileFooter.dtsx. Click on the Parameters tab and add the following parameters:

Name	Data Type	Value	Required
AmountSum	Decimal	0	False
DateFormat	String		True
Debug	Boolean	True	False
Delimiter	String	,	True
ExtractFilePath	String		True
LastUpdateDateTime	DateTime	1/1/1900	True
RecordCount	Int32	0	True

The parameters, when entered, appear as shown in Figure 7-20:

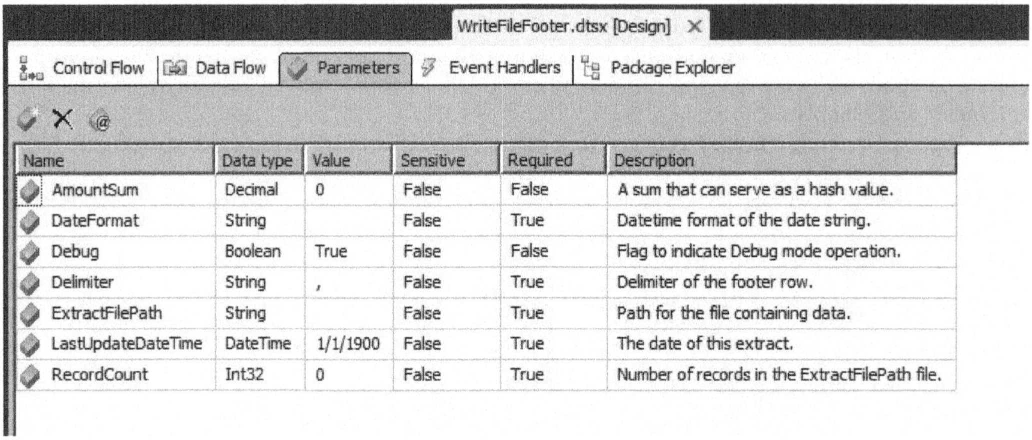

Name	Data type	Value	Sensitive	Required	Description
AmountSum	Decimal	0	False	False	A sum that can serve as a hash value.
DateFormat	String		False	True	Datetime format of the date string.
Debug	Boolean	True	False	False	Flag to indicate Debug mode operation.
Delimiter	String	,	False	True	Delimiter of the footer row.
ExtractFilePath	String		False	True	Path for the file containing data.
LastUpdateDateTime	DateTime	1/1/1900	False	True	The date of this extract.
RecordCount	Int32	0	False	True	Number of records in the ExtractFilePath file.

Figure 7-20. *Parameters for the WriteFileFooter.dtsx Package*

The Sensitive property for each parameter is set to False. The Description is optional and available in the image.

We're going to do the heavy lifting in a Script Task. Return to the Control Flow and drag a Script Task onto the canvas. Change the name to "scr Append File Footer" and open the editor. On the Script page, click the ellipsis in the ReadOnlyVariables property's value textbox. When the Select Variables window displays, select the following variables:

- System::PackageName
- System::TaskName
- $Package::AmountSum
- $Package::DateFormat
- $Package::Debug
- $Package::Delimiter
- $Package::ExtractFilePath
- $Package::LastUpdateDateTime
- $Package::RecordCount

The Select Variables window will not appear exactly as shown in Figure 7-21, but these are the variables you need to select for use inside the "scr Append File Footer" Script Task:

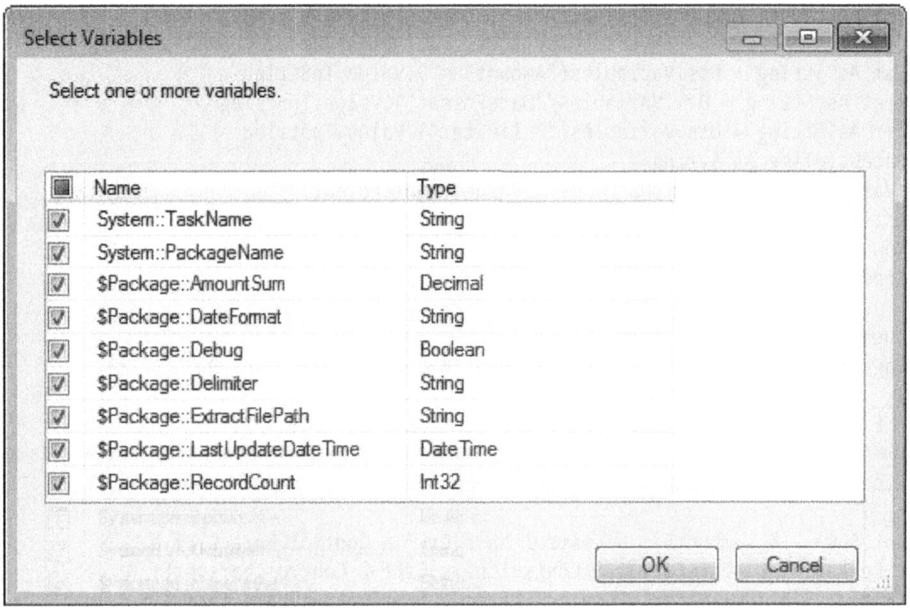

Figure 7-21. *Selecing Variables for the Footer File*

Click the OK button to close the Select Variables window. Set the ScriptLanguage property to Microsoft Visual Basic 2010. Click the Edit Script button to open the VstaProjects window. At the top of the ScriptMain.vb code window, you will find an "Import" region. Add the following lines to that region:

```
Imports System.IO
Imports System.Text
```

Just after the Partial Class declaration, add the variable declaration for the bDebug variable (the Dim statement below):

```
Partial Public Class ScriptMain
    Inherits Microsoft.SqlServer.Dts.Tasks.ScriptTask.VSTARTScriptObjectModelBase

Dim bDebug As Boolean
```

Replace the code in Public Sub Main with the following:

```
Public Sub Main()

    ' 1: detect Debug setting...
    bDebug = Convert.ToBoolean(Dts.Variables("Debug").Value)

    ' 2: declare and initialize variables...
    ' 2a: generic variables...
    Dim sPackageName As String = Dts.Variables("PackageName").Value.ToString
    Dim sTaskName As String = Dts.Variables("TaskName").Value.ToString
    Dim sSubComponent As String = sPackageName & "." & sTaskName
    Dim sMsg As String
    ' 2b: task-specific variables...
```

153

```vb
        Dim sExtractFilePath As String = Dts.Variables("ExtractFilePath").Value.ToString
        Dim iRecordCount As Integer = Convert.ToInt32(Dts.Variables("RecordCount").Value)
        Dim sAmountSum As String = Dts.Variables("AmountSum").Value.ToString
        Dim sDateFormat As String = Dts.Variables("DateFormat").Value.ToString
        Dim sDelimiter As String = Dts.Variables("Delimiter").Value.ToString
        Dim sLastUpdateDateTime As String= _
 Strings.Format(Dts.Variables("LastUpdateDateTime").Value, sDateFormat) _
'"yyyy/MM/dd hh:mm:ss.fff")
        Dim sFooterRow As String
        Dim s As Integer = 0

        ' 3: log values...
        sMsg = "Package Name.Task Name: " & sSubComponent & ControlChars.CrLf & _
 ControlChars.CrLf & _
            "Extract File Path: " & sExtractFilePath & ControlChars.CrLf & _
ControlChars.CrLf & _
            "Record Count: " & iRecordCount.ToString & ControlChars.CrLf & _
ControlChars.CrLf & _
                "Amount Sum: " & sAmountSum & ControlChars.CrLf & ControlChars.CrLf & _
                "Date Format: " & sDateFormat & ControlChars.CrLf & ControlChars.CrLf & _
                "Delimiter: " & sDelimiter & ControlChars.CrLf & ControlChars.CrLf & _
            "LastUpdateDateTime: " & sLastUpdateDateTime & ControlChars.CrLf & _
ControlChars.CrLf & _
                "Debug: " & bDebug.ToString
        Dts.Events.FireInformation(0, sSubComponent, sMsg, "", 0, True)
        If bDebug Then MsgBox(sMsg)

        ' 4: create footer row...
        sFooterRow = iRecordCount.ToString & sDelimiter & sAmountSum & sDelimiter & _
sLastUpdateDateTime

        ' 5: log...
        sMsg = "Footer Row: " & sFooterRow
        Dts.Events.FireInformation(0, sSubComponent, sMsg, "", 0, True)
        If bDebug Then MsgBox(sMsg)

        ' 6: check if the file is in use...
        While FileInUse(sExtractFilePath)
            ' 6a: if file is in use, sleep for a second...
            System.Threading.Thread.Sleep(1000)
            ' 6b: incrementor...
            s += 1
            ' 6c: if incrementor reaches 10 (10 seconds),
            If s > 10 Then
                ' exit the loop...
                Exit While
            End If 's > 10
        End While 'FileInUse(sExtractFilePath)
```

```vbnet
    ' 7: log...
    If s = 1 Then
        sMsg = "File was in use " & s.ToString & " time."
    Else ' s = 1
        sMsg = "File was in use " & s.ToString & " times."
    End If ' s = 1
    Dts.Events.FireInformation(0, sSubComponent, sMsg, "", 0, True)
    If bDebug Then MsgBox(sMsg)

    ' 8: if the file exists...
    If File.Exists(sExtractFilePath) Then
        Try
            ' 8a: open it for append, encoded as built, using a streamwriter...
            Dim writer As StreamWriter = New StreamWriter(sExtractFilePath, True, _
Encoding.Default)
            ' 8b: add the footer row...
            writer.WriteLine(sFooterRow)
            ' 8c: clean up...
            writer.Flush()
            ' 8d: get out...
            writer.Close()
            ' 8e: log...
            sMsg = "File " & sExtractFilePath & " exists and the footer row has " & _
"been appended."
            Dts.Events.FireInformation(0, sSubComponent, sMsg, "", 0, True)
            If bDebug Then MsgBox(sMsg)
        Catch ex As Exception
            ' 8f: log...
            sMsg = "Issue with appending footer row to " & sExtractFilePath & _
" file: " & ControlChars.CrLf & ex.Message
            Dts.Events.FireInformation(0, sSubComponent, sMsg, "", 0, True)
            If bDebug Then MsgBox(sMsg)
        End Try
    Else
        ' 8g: log...
        sMsg = "Cannot find file: " & sExtractFilePath
        Dts.Events.FireInformation(0, sSubComponent, sMsg, "", 0, True)
        If bDebug Then MsgBox(sMsg)
    End If ' File.Exists(sExtractFilePath)

    ' 9: return success...
    Dts.TaskResult = ScriptResults.Success

End Sub
```

Add the following function after Public Sub Main():

```vbnet
Function FileInUse(ByVal sFile As String) As Boolean

    If File.Exists(sFile) Then
        Try
```

```
              Dim f As Integer = FreeFile()
              FileOpen(f, sFile, OpenMode.Binary, OpenAccess.ReadWrite, _
OpenShare.LockReadWrite)
              FileClose(f)
          Catch ex As Exception
              Return True
          End Try
      End If
  End Function
```

This script builds the footer row and appends it to the Extract file. The first thing we do – at the comment labeled 1 – is assign a value to the Debug variable. I use the Debug variable to control message boxes displaying variable values and other pertinent information. I describe why in the chapter on Execution Patterns.

At comment 2, we declare and initialize variables. I break variables into two categories: generic and task-specific variables. At comment 3, we build a message in the variable sMsg. This message contains the values of each variable used in the Script thus far. If we are running in Debug mode (if bDebug is True), the code displays a message box (via the MsgBox function) containing the contents of sMsg. Whether we're running in Debug Mode or not, I use the Dts.Events.FireInformation method to raise an OnInformation event, passing it the contents of sMsg. This means the information is always logged and is optionally displayed by a message box. I like options (a lot).

Comment 4 has us constructing the actual footer row and placing its text in the String variable sFooterRow. Note the delimiter is also dynamic. The String variable sDelimiter contains the value passed to the WriteFileFooter into the Package Parameter named $Package::Delimiter. At comment 5, we log the contents of the footer row.

At comment 6, we initiate a check to make sure the Extract File is not marked as "in use" by the operating system. There are many ways to detect the state of the file in the file system, so I created a Boolean function named FileInUse to encapsulate this test. If the function I created doesn't work for you, you can construct your own. If the file is in use, the code initiates a While loop that sleeps the thread for one second. Each iteration through the loop causes the variable s (the incrementor in this example) to increment at comment 6b. If s exceeds ten, the loop exits. We will only wait 10 seconds for the file to be usable. Note that if the file remains in use at this juncture, we *still* move on. We'll deal with the file in use matter later, but we will not hang ourselves in a potentially endless loop waiting for the file's availability. We will instead fail. Whether the file is in use or not in use, the script logs its state at comment 7.

At comment 8, we check for the existence of the file and begin a Try-Catch. If the file doesn't exist, I opt to log a status message (via Dts.Events.FireInformation) and continue (see comment 8g). The Try-Catch enforces the final test of the file's usability. If the file remains in use here, the Catch fires and logs the status message at comment 8f. At 8f and / or 8g, you may very well decide to raise an error using the Dts.Events.FireError method. Raising an error causes the Script Task to fail, and you may want this to happen. At comments 8a through 8d, we open the file, append the footer row, close the file, and clean up. At comment 8e, the code logs a status message. If anything fails when executing 8a through 8e, code execution jumps to the Catch block.

If all goes well, the code returns Success to the SSIS Control Flow via the Dts.TaskResult function (comment 9). The Script Task does all the work in this pattern.

I created a test package called TestParent.dtsx to test this package. The package has variables that align with the parameters of the WriteFileFooter.dtsx package, as shown in Figure 7-22:

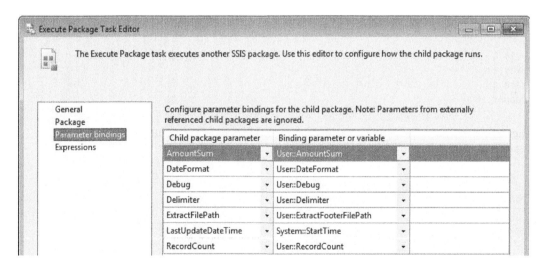

Name	Scope	Data type	Value
AmountSum	TestParent	Decimal	123.45
DateFormat	TestParent	String	yyyy/MM/dd HH:mm:ss.fff
Debug	TestParent	Boolean	False
Delimiter	TestParent	String	,
ExtractFooterFilePath	TestParent	String	G:\Data\SourceFiles\FileFooters\MyFileFooterSource.csv
RecordCount	TestParent	Int32	42

Figure 7-22. *Variables in the TestParent.dtsx Package*

If you're playing along at home, you should adjust the path of the ExtractFooterFilePath variable.

I added a Sequence Container named "seq Test WriteFileFooter" and included an Execute Package Task named "ept Execute WriteFileFooter Package." On the Package page of the Execute Package Task Editor, set the ReferenceType property to "Project Reference" and select WriteFileFooter.dtsx from the PackageNameFromProjectReference property dropdown. Map the TestParent package variables to the WriteFileFooter package parameters as shown in Figure 7-23:

Figure 7-23. *Mapping Package Parameters*

Execute TestParent.dtsx to test the functionality. The package executes successfully and the footer row is appended to the file as shown in Figure 7-24:

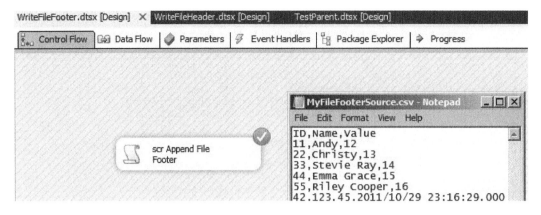

Figure 7-24. *Mission Accomplished*

Producing a Header Row

Producing a header row is a very simple operation in SSIS 2012, provided you know the number of rows to be loaded in advance. You simply load the destination flat file with the header row in one Data Flow Task, and then load the data rows to the same flat file in a subsequent Data Flow Task. As we say in Farmville, Virginia: "dog simple." There are some subtle complexities in this design, though.

We'll start with a simple file named MyFileHeaderExtract.csv that contains the following data:

```
ID,Name,Value
11,Andy,12
22,Christy,13
33,Stevie Ray,14
44,Emma Grace,15
55,Riley Cooper,16
```

Add a new SSIS package named WriteFileHeader.dtsx to your SSIS project. Add the package parameters shown in Figure 7-25:

Name	Data type	Value	Sensitive	Required	Description
AmountSum	Decimal	0	False	False	A sum that can serve as a has value.
DateFormat	String		False	True	Datetime format of the date string.
Debug	Boolean	False	False	False	Flag to indicate Debug mode operation.
Delimiter	String	,	False	True	Delimiter for the footer row.
ExtractFilePath	String		False	True	Path for the file containing data.
LastUpdateDateTime	DateTime	1/1/1900	False	True	The date of this extract.
OutputFilePath	String		False	True	the path of the output file.
RecordCount	Int32	0	False	True	Number of records in the ExtractFilePath file.

Figure 7-25. *WriteFileHeader.dtsx Parameters*

Add two Data Flow Tasks to the Control Flow. Name the first "dft Write Header Row" and the second "dft Write Data Rows." Open the editor for "dft Write Header Row" and add a Script Component named "scrc Build Header Row" to the Data Flow Task. When prompted, configure the Script Component to act as a Source. Open the editor and set the ScriptLanguage property to Microsoft Visual Basic 2010. Set the ReadOnlyVariables property to reference:

- $Package::AmountSum

- $Package::Delimiter

- $Package::LastUpdateDateTime

- $Package::RecordCount

On the Inputs and Outputs page, change the SynchronousInputID property of Output 0 to None and add an output column named HeaderRow (String datatype, 500 length) to Output 0. Click the Script page and the Edit Script button. Replace the code in the CreateNewOutputRows() subroutine:

```
Public Overrides Sub CreateNewOutputRows()

        ' create header row...          ' Get variable values...
        Dim iRecordCount As Integer = Me.Variables.RecordCount
        Dim sDelimiter As String = Me.Variables.Delimiter
        Dim dAmountSum As Decimal = Convert.ToDecimal(Me.Variables.AmountSum)
        Dim dtLastUpdateDateTime As DateTime = _
Convert.ToDateTime(Me.Variables.LastUpdateDateTime)

        Dim sHeaderRow As String = iRecordCount.ToString & sDelimiter & _
                              dAmountSum.ToString & sDelimiter & _
dtLastUpdateDateTime.ToString

        With Output0Buffer
            .AddRow()
            .HeaderRow = sHeaderRow
        End With
    End Sub
```

Add a Flat File Destination adapter and connect a Data Flow Path from the Script Component to it. Open the Flat File Destination Editor and click the New button beside the Flat File Connection Manager dropdown. When the Flat File Format window displays, select Delimited and click the OK button. Name the Flat File Connection Manager "Flat File Header Output" and supply (or select) a file path. On the Columns page, configure a landing column for the HeaderRow column from the "scrc Build Header Row" Script Component. Click the OK button to return to the Flat File Destination Editor. Make sure the "Overwrite data in the file" checkbox (in the Connection Manager page) is checked. It should be; this is the default. Click on the Mappings page and complete the Destination configuration. This Data Flow Task will construct and load the Header Row.

On the Control Flow, add a Success Precedence Constraint from "dft Write Header Row" to the "dft Write Data Rows" Data Flow Task. Open the editor for "dft Write Data Rows" and add a Flat File Source adapter. Open the Flat File Source Editor and click the New button to create a new Flat File Connection Manager. When prompted, select Delimited. Name it "Extract File Input" and navigate to the MyFileHeaderExtract.csv file you created earlier. On the Columns page, delete the value in the Column Delimiter dropdown. To refresh the view, click the Refresh button. On the Advanced page, rename the column from "ID,Name,Value" to "Row" and set the OutputColumnWidth property to 500. Click the Ok buttons to close the Flat File Connection Manager Editor and the Flat File Source Editor.

Add a Flat File Destanation adapter and connect a Data Flow Path from the Flat File Source adapter to the Flat File Destination adapter. Open the Flat File Destination adapter and set its Connection Manager to the Flat File Header Output. Be sure to uncheck the "Overwrite the data in the file" checkbox on the Connection Manager page. On the Mappings page, map the Row column from the Available input Columns to the HeaderRow in the Available Destination Columns. Close the Flat File Destination Editor.

Let's make these Connection Managers dynamic! Click the Extract File Input Flat File Connection Manager, and then press the F4 key to display Properties. Click the Expressions property and click the ellipsis in the value textbox. Click the dropdown in the Property column of the first row and click ConnectionString. In the corresponding Expression value textbox, click the ellipsis to display the Expression Builder. Expand the Variables and Parameters virtual folder in Expression Builder and drag $Package::ExtractFilePath into the Expression textbox. Click the Ok button to close the Expression Builder. The Property Expressions Editor window will appear as shown in Figure 7-26:

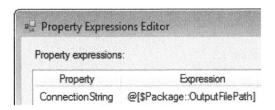

Figure 7-26. *Dynamic ConnectionString Property*

Close the Property Expressions Editor. You have now assigned the ConnectionString property to the value passed to the ExtractFilePath package parameter passed to this package when it is called from another package. Repeat this process to dynamically assign the value of the $Package::OutputFilePath package parameter to the ConnectionString property of the Flat File Header Output Flat File Connection Manager.

To test this package, return to TestParent.dtsx. Let's add a couple of variables to use with the parameters we just mapped to Connection Manager expressions: ExtractHeaderFilePath and OutputPath. Supply a value for the OutputPath variable that represents the location of the file you want to create. (Note: this file may not exist!) Also, supply the path to the MyFileHeaderExtract.csv as the default value for the ExatrctHeaderFilePath cariable. On the Control Flow, add a Sequence Container and rename it "seq Test WriteHeader.. Add an Execute Package Task to the Sequence Container and rename it "ept Execute WriteFileHeader Package." Open the Execute Package Task Editor and configure a Project Reference to execute the WriteFileHeader.dtsx package. Configure the Parameter Bindings page as shown in Figure 7-27:

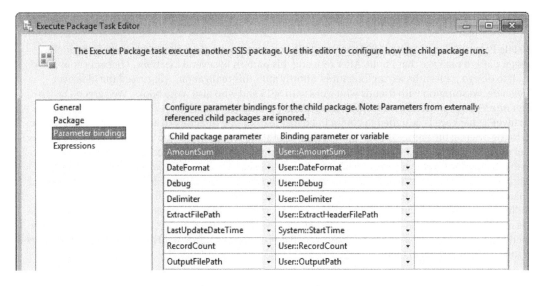

Figure 7-27. Parameter Mapping in the Execute Package Task

Close the Execute Package Task Editor and disable the "seq Test WriteFileFooter" Sequence Container. Execute the package and observe the results. You should results like those shown in Figure 7-28:

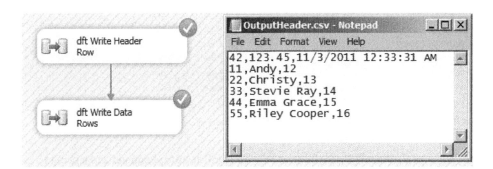

Figure 7-28. Success!

I like this pattern because it utilizes SSIS components without resorting to too much scripting. I don't like everything about this pattern, though. I need to know the number of rows before calling this package, which isn't hard to acquire – I can simply add a Row Count Transformation to a Data Flow and count the rows as they are loaded into the extract file. But then I must *reload* the extract file, after the fact. For large files and scalability, I would attempt to ascertain the number of rows before loading the file and then integrate the functionality demonstrated in this package into the loader package. For smaller loads of data that will not scale, this package is acceptable.

The Archive File Pattern

The Archive File Pattern is largely responsible for the book you are now reading. How? It was the first widely adopted design pattern package that I built. After re-using this pattern in several locations, I became convinced SSIS lent itself to design pattern-based architectures. Shortly after this realization, I discussed the idea over dinner in Bellevue, Washington with friends who work with SSIS and who also write books. We agreed Design Patterns offer interesting solutions to many data integration problems.

The ArchiveFile package is designed to copy a flat data file from one directory to another, appending a date-time stamp to the original file name. The full path of the original file is supplied in the SourceFilePath parameter, the format of the date-time stamp in the DateStampFormat parameter. The destination, or Archive, directory is supplied to the ArchiveDirectory parameter. Should the target file already exist, you can control overwrites of the destination file via the OverwriteDestination parameter. The package usually deletes the original file, but the CopyOnly parameter controls this function. If the SourceFilePath is not found, you can raise an error or simply log this condition. The ExceptionOnFileNotFound parameter controls whether the package raises an error if the source file is not found. Finally, the Debug parameter controls whether the package is being executed in Debug mode (something I cover in more detail in the Execution Patterns chapter). The ArchiveFile package parameters, when configured, will appear as in Figure 7-29:

Name	Data type	Value	Sensitive	Required
ArchiveDirectory	String	C:\Users\A. Ray Leonard\Documents\Archive	False	True
CopyOnly	Boolean	True	False	False
DateStampFormat	String	_yyyyMMdd_hhmmss	False	False
Debug	Boolean	True	False	False
ExceptionOnFileNotFound	Boolean	True	False	False
OverwriteDestination	Boolean	True	False	False
SourceFilePath	String	C:\Users\A. Ray Leonard\Documents\randomdata.csv	False	False

Figure 7-29. ArchiveFile Package Parameters

Be sure you include default values for an existing folder for the ArchiveDirectory parameter and a path to a valid file for the SourceFilePath parameter. For all other parameter default values, use what I have supplied in Figure 7-29.

There are a couple ways to design this package. You can rely heavily on scripting or utilize the File System Task. Which should you choose? When consulting, I ask questions to determine the comfort-level of those charged with maintaining the packages. Some data integration developers are comfortable with .Net coding; others are not. Since SSIS gives me a choice, I build packages so they are easily maintained by the team charged with maintenance.

In this package, I am choosing a hybrid of scripting and the File System Task, leaning away from scripting. Add the following variables to the package:

- User::FormattedFileName [String]

- User::OkToProceed [Boolean]

- User::SourceFileDirectory [String]

- User::WorkingCopyFileName [String]

Add a Script Task to the Control Flow and name it "scr Apply Format." Open the editor and change the ScriptLanguage property to Microsoft Visual Basic 2010. Add the following variables and parameters to the ReadOnlyVariables property:

- System::TaskName
- System::PackageName
- $Package::CopyOnly
- $Package::DateStampFormat
- $Package::Debug
- $Package::ExceptionOnFileNotFound
- $Package::SourceFilePath

Add the following variables and parameters to the ReadWriteVariables property:

- User::FormattedFileName
- User::OkToProceed
- User::SourceFileDirectory
- User::WorkingCopyFileName

Click the Edit Script button to open the VSTAProjects script editor. At the top of the ScriptMain.vb file, add the following statement to the Imports region:

```
Imports System.IO
```

Replace the code in Public Sub Main() with the following:

```
' 1: declare bDebug
Dim bDebug As Boolean

Public Sub Main()

    ' 2: detect Debug mode...
    bDebug = Convert.ToBoolean(Dts.Variables("Debug").Value)

    ' 3:variables declaration...
    Dim sPackageName As String = Dts.Variables("System::PackageName").Value.ToString
    Dim sTaskName As String = Dts.Variables("System::TaskName").Value.ToString
    Dim sSubComponent As String = sPackageName & "." & sTaskName
    Dim sDateStampFormat As String = _
Dts.Variables("$Package::DateStampFormat").Value.ToString
    Dim sSourceFilePath As String = _
Dts.Variables("$Package::SourceFilePath").Value.ToString
    Dim bExceptionOnFileNotFound As Boolean = _
Convert.ToBoolean(Dts.Variables("ExceptionOnFileNotFound").Value)
    Dim bCopyOnly As Boolean = Convert.ToBoolean(Dts.Variables("CopyOnly").Value)
    Dim sFileName As String
    Dim sBaseFileName As String
    Dim sExtension As String
    Dim sSourceFileDirectory As String
```

```vbnet
            Dim sWorkingCopyFileName As String
            Dim sFormattedFileName As String
            Dim sMsg As String


            ' 4: work with the file
            Try
                ' 4a: parse the source file directory...
                sSourceFileDirectory = Strings.Trim(Strings.Left(sSourceFilePath, _
    Strings.InStrRev(sSourceFilePath, "\")))
                ' 4b: parse the filename...
                sFileName = Strings.Trim(Strings.Right(sSourceFilePath, _
    Strings.Len(sSourceFilePath) - Strings.InStrRev(sSourceFilePath, "\")))
                ' 4c: parse the filepath minus the extension...
    sBaseFileName = Strings.Left(sSourceFilePath, Strings.InStrRev(sSourceFilePath, _
    ".") - 1)
                ' 4d: build working copy file name...
                sWorkingCopyFileName = sSourceFileDirectory & "_" & sFileName

                ' 4e: parse extension...
                sExtension = Strings.Trim(Strings.Right(sSourceFilePath, _
    Strings.Len(sSourceFilePath) - Strings.InStrRev(sSourceFilePath, ".")))
                ' 4f: apply formatting to filename and set the output value of FormattedFileName
                sFormattedFileName = sBaseFileName & _
    Strings.Format(Date.Now, sDateStampFormat) & "." & sExtension
                ' 4g: assign external varables...
                Dts.Variables("User::FormattedFileName").Value = sFormattedFileName
                Dts.Variables("SourceFileDirectory").Value = sSourceFileDirectory
                Dts.Variables("WorkingCopyFileName").Value = sWorkingCopyFileName

                ' 4h: check for valid file...
                If File.Exists(sSourceFilePath) Then
                    ' 4i: set OkToProceed flag...
                    Dts.Variables("OkToProceed").Value = True
                Else
                    ' 4j: if raising an exception on file not found...
                    If bExceptionOnFileNotFound Then
                        ' 4k: fire an error...
                        Dts.Events.FireError(1001, sSubComponent, "cannot locate file " & _
    sSourceFilePath, "", 0)
                    End If
                    ' 4l: set OkToProceed flag...
                    Dts.Variables("OkToProceed").Value = False
                    sMsg = "file " & sSourceFilePath & " not found."
                    If bDebug Then MsgBox(sMsg, MsgBoxStyle.OkOnly, sSubComponent)
                    ' 4m: log file not found, exception or not...
                    Dts.Events.FireInformation(2001, sSubComponent, sMsg, "", 0, True)
                End If

            Catch ex As Exception
                ' 4n: log error message...
                Dts.Events.FireError(1001, sSubComponent, ex.Message, "", 0)
            End Try
```

```
        ' 5: log information
        sMsg = "DateStampFormat: " & sDateStampFormat & ControlChars.CrLf & _
ControlChars.CrLf & _
                "ExceptionOnFileNotFound: " & bExceptionOnFileNotFound.ToString & _
ControlChars.CrLf & ControlChars.CrLf & _
                "CopyOnly: " & bCopyOnly.ToString & ControlChars.CrLf & ControlChars.CrLf & _
                "OkToProceed: " & Dts.Variables("OkToProceed").Value.ToString & _
ControlChars.CrLf & ControlChars.CrLf & _
                "SourceFileDirectory: " & sSourceFileDirectory & ControlChars.CrLf & _
ControlChars.CrLf & _
                "FileName: " & sFileName & ControlChars.CrLf & ControlChars.CrLf & _
                "Extension: " & sExtension & ControlChars.CrLf & ControlChars.CrLf & _
                "BaseFileName: " & sBaseFileName & ControlChars.CrLf & ControlChars.CrLf & _
                "FormattedFileName: " & sFormattedFileName & ControlChars.CrLf & _
ControlChars.CrLf & _
                "WorkingCopyFileName: " & sWorkingCopyFileName & ControlChars.CrLf & _
ControlChars.CrLf

        If bDebug Then MsgBox(sMsg, MsgBoxStyle.OkOnly, sSubComponent)
        Dts.Events.FireInformation(2001, sSubComponent, sMsg, "", 0, True)
        ' 6: output
        Dts.TaskResult = ScriptResults.Success
    End Sub
```

As in other scripts, we declare (Dim) a variable named bDebug to detect whether the package is executing in Debug Mode at comments 1 and 2. At comment 3, the script declares the remainder of the variables used, assigning some values passed in from SSIS package variables and parameters. At comments 4a through 4c, the code picks the Source File Path variable apart, parsing the source directory, filename with extension, and filename without extension. At comments 4d through 4f, the filename extension is parsed and a filename for a "working copy" is created and formatted with the date time-stamp supplied from the SSIS package parameters. At comment 4g, the script assigns variable values to SSIS package variables. The code between comments 4h and 4m tests and responds to the existence of the source file. If an exception is encountered in any of the steps between comments 4a and 4m, the Catch block at comment 4n is executed and logs the exception as an error, which halts the execution of the Script Task. The code at comment 5 builds, displays (if running in Debug Mode), and logs a message containing the variable values inside the Script Task. This is extremely useful information when troubleshooting. At comment 6, the Script returns a Success result to the Dts.TaskResult object.

The remaining steps in the file archive process are as follows:

1. Create a working copy of the source file

2. Rename the working copy to the Formatted File Name (including the date time-stamp)

3. Move the newly-renamed file to the archive directory

4. Delete the orginal file (unless this is a CopyOnly operation)

If the OkToProceed (Boolean) package variable is set to True (this is accomplished in the Script code at comment 4i), the remaining steps in the process are managed by File System Tasks.

Drag four File System Tasks onto the Control Flow canvas. Rename the first "fsys Copy Working File" and open its editor. Change the Operation property to "Copy File." Set the IsSourcePathVariable property to True and the SourceVariable property to "$Package::SourceFilePath." Set the IsDestinationPathVariable to True and set the DestinationVariable property to "User::WorkingCopyFileName." Set the OverwriteDestination property to True. Close the File System Task Editor.

Rename the second File System Task "fsys Rename File" and open its editor. Set the Operation property to "Rename File". Set the IsSourcePathVariable property to True and the SourceVariable property to

"User::WorkingCopyFileName." Set the IsDestinationPathVariable to True and set the DestinationVariable property to "User::FormattedFileName." Set the OverwriteDestination property to True. Close the File System Task Editor.

Rename the third File System Task "fsys Move File" and open its editor. Set the Operation property to "Move File." Set the IsSourcePathVariable property to True and the SourceVariable property to "User::FormattedFileName." Set the IsDestinationPathVariable to True and set the DestinationVariable property to "$Package::ArchiveDirectory." Set the OverwriteDestination property to True. Close the File System Task Editor.

Rename the fourth File System Task "fsys Delete Original File" and open its editor. Set the Operation property to "Delete File." Set the IsSourcePathVariable property to True and the SourceVariable property to "$Package::SourceFilePath." Close the File System Task Editor.

Use a Success Precedence Constraint to connect the "scr Apply Format" Script Task to the "fsys Copy Working File" File System Task. Double-click the precedence constraint to open the editor and set the Evaluation Option property to "Expression and Constraint." Set the Value property to "Success" and the Expression property to "@[User::OkToProceed]." This constraint will only fire if the "scr Apply Format" Script Task completes execution successfully and sets the OkToProceed (Boolean) variable to True. Connect Success Precedence Constraints between the "fsys Copy Working File" File System Task and the "fsys Rename File" File System Task, the "fsys Rename File" File System Task and the "fsys Move File" File System Task, and the "fsys Move File" File System Task and the "fsys Delete Original File" File System Task. Double-click the Precedence Constraint between the "fsys Move File" File System Task and the "fsys Delete Original File" File System Task to open the editor. Set the Evaluation Option property to "Expression and Constraint." Set the Value property to "Success" and the Expression property to "!@[$Package::CopyOnly]" (this equates to NOT [!] $Package::CopyOnly, or when $Package::CopyOnly is False). For the "fsys Delete Original File" File System Task to fire, the "fsys Move File" File System Task must succeed and the $Package::CopyOnly package parameter must be False. This makes sense, if you only want to copy the file to the archive directory; you don't want to delete the original.

In many versions of this design pattern, I also "variable-ize" the OverwriteDestination properties of the various File System Tasks, managing these values on the Expressions pages by setting the OverwriteDestinationFile dynamic property expressions with Boolean package parameters. I do this because some enterprises have requirements regarding keeping or discarding data files regardless of whether they are temporary or not.

Your File System tasks may be marked with error indicators (red circles containing white "X"'s). Hovering over a task so marked will display the error. For example, I see the error show in Figure 7-30: "Variable 'WorkingCopyFileName' is used as a source or destination and is empty."

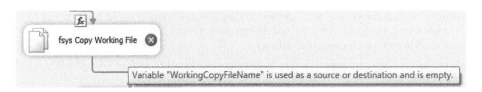

Figure 7-30. *The WorkingCopyFileName Variable is Empty*

At issue is the content of the WorkingCopyFileName variable. The error is correct; the variable value is currently empty. However, since we wrote the code, we know that, in section 4d of the code listing, the script will populate the content of an internal string variable named sWorkingCopyFile. In section 4g of the code, the content of this interal variable will be assigned to the value of the SSIS package variable named WorkingCopyFileName. We know that, but the SSIS Package does not. It is doing its level best to inform us of this issue. In fact, we cannot execute the package in its current state without raising an error message, as shown in Figure 7-31:

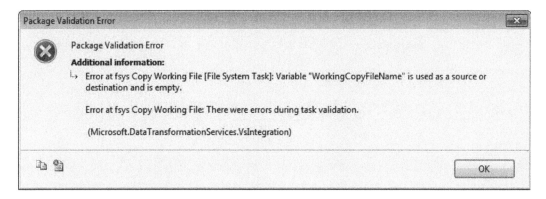

Figure 7-31. *Package Validation Error*

The validation is accurate. Now what? There's a clue in the error, near the very top. This is a "Package Validation Error." To address this, click on the "fsys Copy Working File" File System Task and press the F4 key to display Properties. In the Execution group of properties, at the top of the list, we find the DelayValidation property. This property's default setting is False and that makes sense. There is a lot of design-time validation in SSIS and it is mostly a good thing. Change this property value to True. Change DelayValidation to True for the "fsys Rename File" and "fsys Move File" File System Tasks as well.

Now, try executing the ArchiveFile.dtsx SSIS package. My results are shown in Figure 7-32:

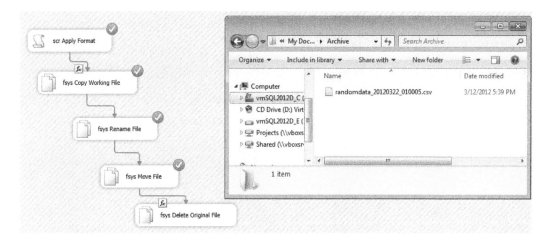

Figure 7-32. *Successful Execution of the ArchiveFile.dtsx SSIS Package*

Summary

In this chapter, we examined a common pattern for loading a basic flat source file into SQL Server, a pattern to load a variable-length rows, patterns for creating and consuming flat file header and footer rows, and an extremely useful SSIS design pattern for archiving flat files.

CHAPTER 8

■ ■ ■

Parallel Data Warehouse Patterns

Microsoft's SQL Server Parallel Data Warehouse (PDW) appliance was introduced with SQL Server 2008 R2 and is Microsoft's first *massively parallel processing* (MPP) offering. Although PDW is built upon the SQL Server platform, it is a completely different product. As the name suggests, MPP uses multiple servers working as one system, called an appliance, to achieve much greater performance and scan rates than in traditional SMP systems. SMP refers to *symmetric multi-processing*; most database systems, such as all other versions of SQL Server, are SMP.

To obtain a better understanding of the difference between SMP and MPP systems, let's examine a common analogy. Imagine you are handed a shuffled deck of 52 playing cards and asked to retrieve all of the Queens. Even at your fastest, it would take you several seconds to retrieve the requested cards. Let's now take that same deck of 52 cards and divide it across ten people. No matter how fast you are, these ten people working together can retrieve all of the Queens much faster than you can by yourself.

As you may have inferred, you represent the SMP system, and the ten people represent the MPP system. This divide-and-conquer strategy is why MPP appliances are particularly well suited for high-volume, scan-intensive data warehousing environments, especially ones that need to scale to hundreds of terabytes of storage. There are other MPP appliance vendors available besides Microsoft; however, close integration with the Microsoft business intelligence stack (SQL Server, Integration Services, Analysis Services, and Reporting Services) and a compelling cost-per-terabyte make PDW a natural progression for organizations needing to take their SQL Server data warehouse to the next level. In this chapter, we will walk through how to load data into the PDW appliance using Integration Services. But first we will need to discuss some of the differences between PDW and SMP SQL Server.

PDW is built upon the SQL Server platform but has an architecture entirely its own. While the details of this architecture could easily consume a book in its own right, we will only cover the most pertinent parts to ensure you have the foundation necessary for loading data.

■ **Tip**   Learn more about Microsoft's Parallel Data Warehouse at `http://microsoft.com/pdw` and `http://sqlpdw.com`.

Before we proceed, it is important to note that only SQL Server 2008 R2 Business Intelligence Studio (BIDS) was supported at the time of writing for the creation of Integration Services packages to load data into PDW. Thus, this chapter will depart from the rest of the book in that it uses BIDS for its screenshots. Also, an actual PDW appliance is required to execute the samples in this chapter. For those who do not have a PDW appliance, there is still much information that can be gathered from this chapter regarding PDW architecture and loading best practices.

PDW Architecture Overview

Each PDW appliance has one control rack and one or more data racks. The control rack contains the following nodes:

- Control Node – Perhaps the most critical node in the appliance, the Control Node is responsible for managing the workload, creating distributed query plans, orchestrating data loads, and monitoring system operations.

- Management Node – Among other administrative functions, the management node is responsible for authentication, software updates, and system monitoring.

- Backup Node – As the name suggests, this is where backups are stored.

- Landing Zone Node – This is the node that is most relevant to this chapter. The Landing Zone node is the only node in the entire appliance that is accessible for loading data.

■ **Tip** Microsoft recommends running Integration Services packages from an external server. This best practice reduces memory contention on the Landing Zone. If this type of server is not within your budget, you can purchase and install SQL Server Integration Services on the Landing Zone to facilitate package execution and job scheduling through SQL Agent Jobs.

Figure 8-1 depicts a single data-rack PDW configuration. Each PDW appliance is comprised of one or more data racks but only a single control rack. In every data rack are ten Compute Nodes, plus one hot-spare standby Compute Node for high availability.

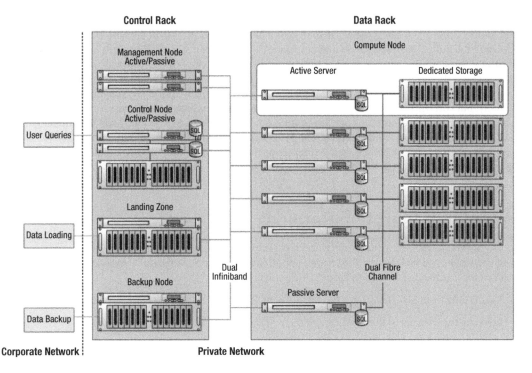

Figure 8-1. *A single data-rack PDW configuration*

At the core of PDW is the concept of "shared-nothing" architecture, where a single logical table is broken up into numerous smaller pieces. The exact number of pieces depends on the number of data racks you have. Each of these smaller pieces is then stored on a separate Compute Node. Within a single Compute Node, each data piece is then split across 8 distributions. Furthermore, each of these 8 distributions has its own dedicated CPU, memory, and LUNs (hence the term "shared-nothing"). There are numerous benefits that a shared-nothing architecture enables, such as more linear scalability. But perhaps PDW's greatest power is its ability to scan data at incredible speeds.

Let's do some math. Assume we have a PDW appliance with one data rack, and we need to store a table with one billion rows. Each Compute Node will store 1/10th of the rows, and each Compute Node will split its data across 8 distributions. Thus, the one billion row table will be split into 80 pieces (10 Compute Nodes x 8 distributions each). That means each distribution will store 12,500,000 rows.

But what does this mean from the end-user's standpoint? Let's look at a hypothetical situation. You are a user who needs to submit a query that joins two tables together: a Sales table with one billion rows, and a Customer table with 50 million rows. And, as luck would have it, there are no indexes available that will cover your query. This means you will need to *scan*, or read, every row in each table.

In an SMP system – where memory, storage, and CPU are shared – this query could take hours or days to run. On some systems, it might not even be feasible to attempt this query, depending on factors such as the server hardware and the amount of activity on the server. Suffice it to say, the query will take a considerable amount of time to return and will most likely have a negative impact on other activity on the server.

In PDW, these kinds of queries often return in minutes – and a well-designed schema can even execute this query in seconds. This is because the hardware is *optimized* for scans; PDW *expects* to scan every row in the table. Remember how we said that every distribution has its own dedicated CPU, memory, and storage? Well, when you submit the query to join one billion rows to 50 million rows, each distribution is performing a scan on its own Sales table of 12,500,000 rows and Customer table with 625,000 rows. Not nearly as intimidating, is it? The data is then sent back to the Control Node across an ultra-fast Dual-Infiniband channel to consolidate the results and return the data to the end user. It is this divide-and-conquer strategy that results in PDW significantly outperforming SMP systems.

PDW is also able to load data very efficiently. As previously mentioned, data is brought into the appliance through the Landing Zone. Each Compute Node then uses a hashing algorithm to determine where to store the data – down to the individual distribution and associated LUNs. A relatively small amount of overhead is associated with this process. Because this overhead is incurred on every single load, transactional load patterns (i.e., singleton inserts) should be avoided. PDW performs at its best when data is loaded in large, incremental batches – you will see much better performance loading 10 files with 100,000 rows each than loading 1,000,000 rows individually, but you will see the best performance loading one file with 1,000,000 rows.

Data can be imported from numerous platforms, including from Oracle, SQL Server, MySQL, and flat files. There are two primary methods of loading data into the PDW appliance: DWLoader and Integration Services. We will briefly discuss when to use DWLoader versus Integration Services. After that, we will actually walk through an example of loading data from SQL Server using Integration Services.

DWLoader vs. Integration Services

DWLoader is a command-line utility that ships with PDW. Those familiar with SQL Server BCP (bulk copy program) will have an easy time learning DWLoader, as both utilities share a very similar syntax. One very common pattern for loading data into PDW from SQL Server is to:

1. Export data from SQL Server to a flat file using BCP

2. Relocate the data file to the Landing Zone

3. Import the data file to PDW using DWLoader

This is a very efficient method for loading data, and it is very easy to generate scripts for table DDL, BCP commands, and DWLoader commands. For this reason, you may want to consider DWLoader for performing initial and incremental loading of the large quantity of small dimensional tables that often exist in data warehouses. Doing so can greatly speed up data warehouse migration. This same load pattern can also be used with flat files generated from any system, not just SQL Server.

For your larger tables, you may instead want to consider Integration Services. Integration Services offers greater functionality and arguably more end-to-end convenience. This is because Integration Services is able to connect directly to the data source and load the data into the PDW appliance without having to stop at a file share. Integration Services can also perform transformations in flight, which DWLoader does not support.

It's important to note that each Data Flow within Integration Services is single-threaded and can bottleneck on IO. Typically, a single-threaded Integration Services package will perform up to ten times slower than DWLoader. However, a multi-threaded Integration Services package – similar to the one we will create shortly – can mitigate that limitation. For large tables requiring data type conversions, an Integration Services package with 10 parallel Data Flows provides the best of both worlds: similar performance to DWLoader and all the advanced functionality that Integration Services offers.

A number of variables should be considered when deciding whether to use DWLoader or Integration Services. In addition to table size, the network speed and table design can have an impact. At the end of the day, most PDW implementations will use a combination of both tools. The best idea is to test the performance of each method in your environment and use the tool that makes the most sense for each table.

ETL vs. ELT

Many Integration Services packages are designed using an Extract, Transform, and Load (ETL) process. This is a practical model that strives to lessen the impact of moving data on the source and destination servers – which are traditionally more resource-constrained – by placing the burden of data filtering, cleansing, and other such activities on the (arguably more easy-to-scale) ETL server. Extract, Load, and Transform (ELT) processes, in contrast, place the burden on the destination server.

While both models have their place and while PDW can support both models, ELT clearly performs better with PDW from both a technical and business perspective. On the technical side, PDW is able to utilize its massively parallel processing power to more efficiently load and transform large volumes of data. From the business aspect, having more data co-located allows more meaningful data to be gleaned during the transformation process. Organizations with MPP systems often find that the ability to co-locate and transform large quantities of disparate data allows them to make the leap from reactive data marts (*How much of this product did we sell?*) to predictive data modeling (*How can we sell **more** of this product?*).

Deciding on an ELT strategy does not necessarily mean your Integration Services package will not have to perform any transformations, however. In fact, many Integration Services packages may require transformations of some sort to convert data types. Table 8-1 illustrates the data types supported in PDW and the equivalent Integration Services data types.

Table 8-1. *Data Type Mappings for PDW and Integration Services*

SQL Server PDW Data Type	Integration Services Data Type(s) That Map to the SQL Server PDW Data Type
BIT	DT_BOOL
BIGINT	DT_I1, DT_I2, DT_I4, DT_I8, DT_UI1, DT_UI2, DT_UI4
CHAR	DT_STR
DATE	DT_DBDATE
DATETIME	DT_DATE, DT_DBDATE, DT_DBTIMESTAMP, DT_DBTIMESTAMP2
DATETIME2	DT_DATE, DT_DBDATE, DT_DBTIMESTAMP, DT_DBTIMESTAMP2
DATETIMEOFFSET	DT_WSTR
DECIMAL	DT_DECIMAL, DT_I1, DT_I2, DT_I4, DT_I4, DT_I8, DT_NUMERIC, DT_UI1, DT_UI2, DT_UI4, DT_UI8
FLOAT	DT_R4, DT_R8
INT	DT_I1, DTI2, DT_I4, DT_UI1, DT_UI2
MONEY	DT_CY
NCHAR	DT_WSTR
NUMERIC	DT_DECIMAL, DT_I1, DT_I2, DT_I4, DT_I8, DT_NUMERIC, DT_UI1, DT_UI2, DT_UI4, DT_UI8
NVARCHAR	DT_WSTR, DT_STR
REAL	DT_R4
SMALLDATETIME	DT_DBTIMESTAMP2
SMALLINT	DT_I1, DT_I2, DT_UI1
SMALLMONEY	DT_R4
TIME	DT_WSTR
TINYINT	DT_I1
VARBINARY	DT_BYTES
VARCHAR	DT_STR

Also, it is worth noting that PDW does not currently support the following data types at the time of this writing:

- DT_DBTIMESTAMPOFFSET
- DT_DBTIME2
- DT_GUID
- DT_IMAGE
- DT_NTEXT
- DT_TEXT

Any of these unsupported data types will need to be converted to a compatible data type using the Data Conversion transformation. We will walk through how to perform such a transformation in just a moment.

Installing the PDW Destination Adapter

As we have previously discussed, data is loaded into the PDW through the Landing Zone. All Integration Services packages will either be run from the Landing Zone node or, preferably, from a non-appliance server with access to the Landing Zone. The 32-bit destination adapter is required for Integration Services and should be installed on the server running the packages. If you are using a 64-bit machine, you will need to install both the 32-bit and 64-bit adapters. The Windows Installer packages are accessible from C:\PDWINST\media\msi on both the Management node and the Landing Zone node, or from the network share at \\<Landing Zone IP Address>\redistr.

Once the PDW destination adapter has been installed, you will need to add it to the Integration Services Toolbox. Let's walk through how to do this now. Start a new **Integration Services Project** and name it *PDW_Example*. After the project loads, select **Tools** from the main menu, and then navigate to **Choose Toolbox Items**, as illustrated in Figure 8-2.

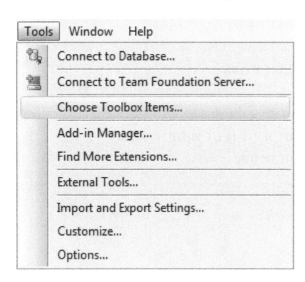

Figure 8-2. *Select "Choose Toolbox Items…" to add the PDW adapter to Integration Services*

Once the **Choose Toolbox Items** modal appears, click on the **SSIS Data Flow Items** tab. Navigate down to **SQL Server PDW Destination** and check the box to the left of the adapter, as illustrated in Figure 8-3. Click **OK**.

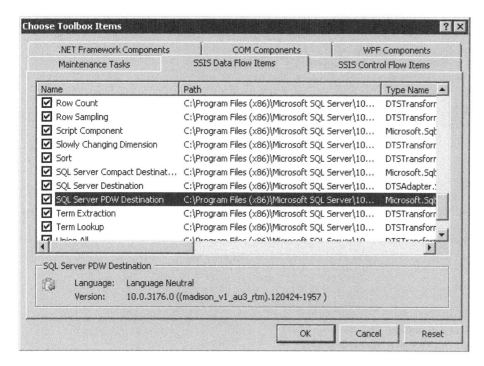

Figure 8-3. The "SSIS Data Flow Items" toolbox

The PDW Destination Adapter is now installed. Let's move on to setting up our data source.

The Data Source

In preparation for moving data from SQL Server to PDW, we need to create a database in SQL Server and populate it with some test data. Execute the T-SQL code in Listing 8-1 from SQL Server Management Studio (SSMS) to create a new database called *PDW_Source_Example*.

Listing 8-1. Example of T-SQL Code to Create a SQL Server Database

```
USE [master];
GO

/* Create a database to experiment with */
CREATE DATABASE [PDW_Source_Example]
    ON PRIMARY
    (
        NAME = N'PDW_Source_Example'
        , FILENAME = N'C:\Program Files\Microsoft SQL Server\
MSSQL11.MSSQLSERVER\MSSQL\DATA\PDW_Source_Example.mdf'
        , SIZE = 1024MB
        , MAXSIZE = UNLIMITED
        , FILEGROWTH = 1024MB
    )
```

```
    LOG ON
    (
        NAME = N'PDW_Source_Example_log'
      , FILENAME = N'C:\Program Files\Microsoft SQL Server\
MSSQL11.MSSQLSERVER\MSSQL\DATA\PDW_Source_Example_log.ldf'
      , SIZE = 256MB
      , MAXSIZE = UNLIMITED
      , FILEGROWTH = 256MB
    );
GO
```

Please note that your database file path may vary depending on the details of your particular installation.

Now let's create a table and populate it with some data. As we discussed before, Integration Services works best with large tables that can be multi-threaded. One good example of this is a Sales Fact table that is partitioned by year. Listing 8-2 will provide the T-SQL code to create the table and partitioning dependencies.

Listing 8-2. Example of T-SQL Code to Create a Partitioned Table in SQL Server

```
USE PDW_Source_Example;
GO


/* Create your partition function */
CREATE PARTITION FUNCTION example_yearlyDateRange_pf
(DATETIME) AS RANGE RIGHT
FOR VALUES('2010-01-01', '2011-01-01', '2012-01-01');
GO


/* Associate your partition function with a partition scheme */
CREATE PARTITION SCHEME example_yearlyDateRange_ps
AS PARTITION example_yearlyDateRange_pf ALL TO([Primary]);
GO


/* Create a partitioned fact table to experiment with */
CREATE TABLE PDW_Source_Example.dbo.FactSales (
    orderID             INT IDENTITY(1,1)
  , orderDate           DATETIME
  , customerID          INT
  , webID               UNIQUEIDENTIFIER DEFAULT (NEWID())

  CONSTRAINT PK_FactSales
      PRIMARY KEY CLUSTERED
      (
            orderDate
          , orderID
      )
) ON example_yearlyDateRange_ps(orderDate);
```

> ■ **Note** Getting an error on the above syntax? Partitioning is a feature only available in SQL Server Enterprise and Developer editions. You can comment out the partitioning in the last line:
>
> ON example_yearlyDateRange_ps(orderDate);
>
> and replace it with:
>
> ON [Primary];

Next, we need to generate data using the T-SQL in Listing 8-3. This is the data we will be loading into PDW.

Listing 8-3. Example of T-SQL Code to Populate a Table with Sample Data

```
/* Declare variables and initialize with an arbitrary date */
DECLARE @startDate DATETIME = '2010-01-01';

/* Perform an iterative insert into the FactSales table */
WHILE @startDate < GETDATE()
BEGIN

    INSERT INTO PDW_Source_Example.dbo.FactSales
    (orderDate, customerID)
    SELECT @startDate
        , DATEPART(WEEK, @startDate) + DATEPART(HOUR, @startDate);

    /* Increment the date value by hour; for more test data,
        replace HOUR with MINUTE or SECOND */
    SET  @startDate = DATEADD(HOUR, 1, @startDate);

END;
```

This script will generate roughly twenty thousand rows in the *FactSales* table, although you can easily increase the number of rows generated by replacing HOUR in the DATEADD statement with MINUTE or even SECOND.

Now that we have a data source to work with, we are ready to start working on our Integration Services package.

The Data Flow

We are now going to configure the Data Flow that will move data from SQL Server to PDW. We will first create a connection to our data source via an OLE DB Source. We will transform the UNIQUEIDENTIFIER to a Unicode string (DT_WSTR) using a Data Conversion. We will then configure our PDW Destination Adapter to load data into the PDW appliance. Lastly, we will multi-thread the package to improve load performance.

One easy way to multi-thread is to create multiple Data Flows that execute in parallel for the same table. You can have up to 10 simultaneous loads – 10 Data Flows – for a table. However, you want to be careful not to cause too much contention. You can limit contention by querying on the clustered index or, if you have SQL Server Enterprise Edition, separating the loads by partition. This latter method is preferable and is the approach our example will use.

The Data Source

If you have not already done so, create a new **Integration Services Project** named *PDW_Example* (File ➤ New ➤ Project ➤ Integration Services Project).

Add a **Data Flow Task** to the Control Flow designer surface. Name it *PDW Import*.

Add an **OLE DB Source** to the designer surface from the **SSIS Toolbox**. Edit the properties of the **OLE DB Source** by double-clicking on the icon. You should see the source editor shown in Figure 8-4.

You will need to create an **OLE DB Connection Manager** that points to the *PDW_Source_Example* database. Once this is done, change the **Data Access Mode** to *SQL Command*, then enter the code in Listing 8-4. You should see results similar to those in Figure 8-4. Click **OK** when finished entering the code.

Listing 8-4. Example SQL Command

```
/* Retrieve sales for 2010 */

SELECT
     orderID
   , orderDate
   , customerID
   , webID
FROM PDW_Source_Example.dbo.FactSales
WHERE orderDate >= '2010-01-01'
    AND orderDate < '2011-01-01';
```

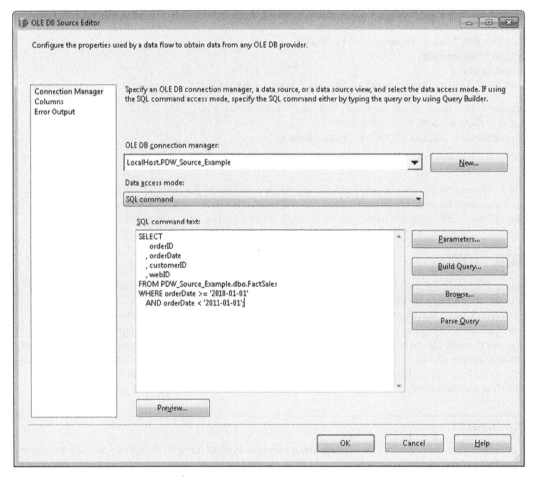

Figure 8-4. *The OLE DB Source Editor*

Let's take a minute to discuss what we're doing. By searching our *FactSales* table on *orderDate* – the column we specified as our partitioning key in Listing 8-2 – we are able to achieve partition elimination. This gives us a clean way to divide the multiple Data Flows while also minimizing resource contention. We can achieve a similar result even without partitioning *FactSales*, because we would still be performing the search on our clustered index. But what if *FactSales* was clustered on just *orderID* instead? We can apply the same principles and achieve good performance by searching for an evenly distributed number of rows in each Data Flow. For example, if *FactSales* has one million rows and we are using 10 Data Flows, each OLE DB Source should search for 100,000 rows (i.e. `orderID >= 1` and `orderID < 100000; orderID >= 100000` and `orderID < 200000;` and so on). These types of design considerations can have a significant impact on the overall performance of your Integration Services package.

▓ **Tip**   Not familiar with partitioning? Table partitioning is particularly well suited for large data warehouse environments and offers more than just the benefits briefly mentioned here. More information is available in the whitepaper, "Partitioned Table and Index Strategies Using SQL Server 2008," at `http://msdn.microsoft.com/en-us/library/dd578580.aspx`.

The Data Transformation

Remember how PDW does not currently support DT_GUID? Our source table has a UNIQUEIDENTIFIER column that is stored as a CHAR(38) column in PDW. In order to load this data, we will need to transform our UNIQUEIDENTIFER to a Unicode string. To do this, drag the **Data Conversion** icon from the **SSIS Toolbox** to the designer surface. Next, connect the green line from **OLE DB Source** to **Data Conversion**, as shown in Figure 8-5.

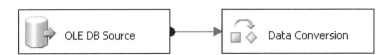

Figure 8-5. *Connecting the OLE DB Source to the Data Conversion*

Double-click on the **Data Conversion** icon to open the **Data Conversion Transformation Editor**. Click on the box to the left of *webID*, then edit its properties to reflect the following values:

> **Input Column:** webID
> **Output Alias:** converted_webID
> **Data Type:** string [DT_WSTR]
> **Length:** 38

Confirm that the settings match those in Figure 8-6, then click **OK**.

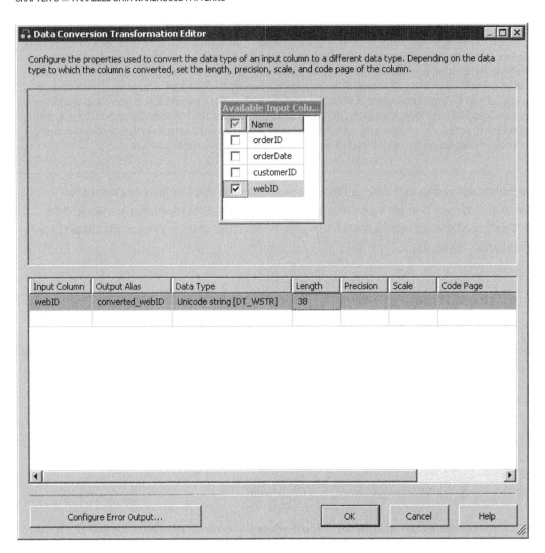

Figure 8-6. The Data Conversion Transformation Editor

■ **Tip** Wonder why we use a string length of 38 when converting a UNIQUEIDENTIFIER to a CHAR? This is because the global representation of a GUID is **{00000000-0000-0000-0000-000000000000}**. The curly brackets are stored implicitly in SQL Server for UNIQUEIDENTIFIER columns. Thus, during conversion, Integration Services materializes the curly brackets for export to the destination system. That is why, while a UNIQUEIDENTIFIER may *look* like it would only consume 36 bytes, it actually requires 38 bytes to store in PDW.

The Data Destination

The next few tasks, which prepare the PDW appliance for receiving *FactSales* data, will take place in the Nexus Query Chameleon – or just Nexus, for short. Nexus, illustrated in Figure 8-7, is a 3rd party tool used for connecting to the PDW appliance. This is currently the recommended graphical query editor for working with PDW, although SQL Server Management Studio (SSMS) will support PDW in future releases.

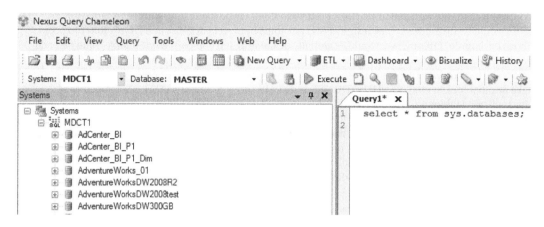

Figure 8-7. *The Nexus Query Tool*

Please refer to the section "Connect With Nexus Query Chameleon" in the PDW Books Online for more information on installing and configuring Nexus.

Before we go any further, we should discuss the use of a staging database. While it is not required, Microsoft recommends the use of a staging database during incremental loads to reduce table fragmentation. When a staging database is used, the data is first loaded into a temporary table in the staging database before insertion into the permanent table in the destination database.

■ **Tip**   Using a staging database? Make sure your staging database has enough space available to accommodate all tables being loaded concurrently. If you do not allocate enough space initially, don't worry; you'll still be okay – the staging database will autogrow. Your loads may just slow down while the autogrow is occurring. Also, your staging database will likely need to be larger when you perform the initial table loads during system deployment and migration. However, once your system becomes more mature and the initial ramp-up is complete, you can recover some space by dropping and recreating a smaller staging database.

From within Nexus, execute the code in Listing 8-5 on your PDW appliance to create a staging database.

Listing 8-5. PDW Code to Run from Nexus to Create a Staging Database

```
CREATE DATABASE StageDB_Example
WITH
(
      AUTOGROW              = ON
    , REPLICATED_SIZE       = 1 GB
```

```
    , DISTRIBUTED_SIZE      = 5 GB
    , LOG_SIZE              = 1 GB
);
```

PDW introduces the concept of *replicated* and *distributed* tables. In a distributed table, the data is split across all nodes using a distribution hash specified during table creation. In a replicated table, the full table data exist on every Compute Node. This is done to improve join performance. As a hypothetical example, consider a small *DimCountry* dimension table with 200 rows. *DimCountry* would likely be replicated, whereas a much larger *FactSales* table would be distributed. This design allows any joins between *FactSales* and *DimCountry* to take place locally on each node. Although we would essentially be creating ten copies of *DimCountry* – one on each Compute Node – because the dimension table is small, the benefit of performing the join locally outweighs the minimal cost of storing duplicate copies of the data.

Let's take another look at our CREATE DATABASE code in Listing 8-5. REPLICATED_SIZE specifies space allocation for replicated tables *on each Compute Node*, whereas DISTRIBUTED_SIZE specifies space allocation for distributed tables *across the appliance*. That means *StageDB_Example* actually has 16 GB of space allocated: 10 GB for replicated tables (10 Compute Nodes with 1 GB each), 5 GB for distributed tables, and 1 GB for the log.

All data is automatically compressed using page-level compression during the PDW load process. This is not optional, and the amount of compression will vary greatly from customer-to-customer and table-to-table. If you have SQL Server Enterprise or Developer Editions, you can execute the command in Listing 8-6 to estimate compression results.

Listing 8-6. Code to Create the Destination Database and Table Inside of PDW

```
/* Estimate compression ratio */
EXECUTE sp_estimate_data_compression_savings
'dbo','FactSales',NULL, NULL,'PAGE';
```

You can generally use 2:1 as a rough estimate. With a 2:1 compression ratio, the 5 GB of distributed data we specified in Listing 8-5 actually stores 10 GB of uncompressed SQL Server data.

We still need a place to store our data. Execute the code in Listing 8-7 in Nexus to create the destination database and table for FactSales.

Listing 8-7. PDW Code to Create the Destination Database and Table

```
CREATE DATABASE PDW_Destination_Example
WITH
(
      REPLICATED_SIZE       = 1 GB
    , DISTRIBUTED_SIZE      = 5 GB
    , LOG_SIZE              = 1 GB
);
CREATE TABLE PDW_Destination_Example.dbo.FactSales
(
      orderID          INT
    , orderDate        DATETIME
    , customerID       INT
    , webID            CHAR(38)
)
```

```
WITH
(
      CLUSTERED INDEX (orderDate)
    , DISTRIBUTION = HASH (orderID)
);
```

Now that we have our destination objects created, we can return to our Integration Services package. From within BIDS, drag the **SQL Server PDW Destination** from the **Toolbox** to the Data Flow pane. Double-click on the **PDW Destination**, illustrated in Figure 8-8, to edit its configuration.

Figure 8-8. *The SQL Server PDW Destination*

Next, click on the down arrow next to **Connection Manager** and select *Create a New Connection*, as shown in Figure 8-9.

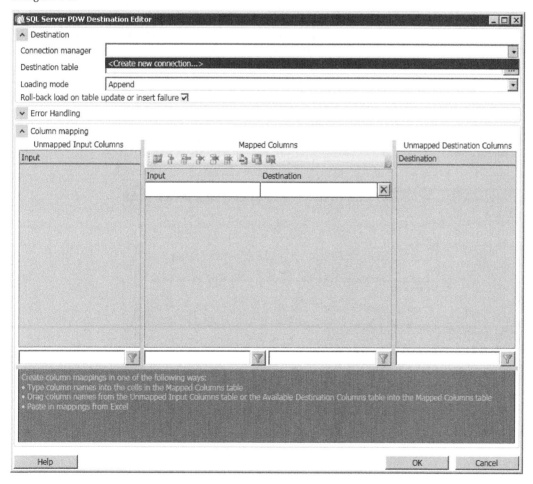

Figure 8-9. *The SQL Server PDW Destination Editor*

Enter your connection information in the **SQL Server PDW Connection Manager Editor** using the items described in Table 8-2.

Table 8-2. *PDW Connection Information*

Server	The IP address of the *Control Node* on your appliance (Best practice is to use the clustered IP address to support Control Node failover)
User	Your login name for authenticating to the appliance
Password	Your login password
Destination Database	PDW_Destination_Example
Staging Database	StageDB_Example

Let's discuss a few best practices relating to this connection information. First, you should specify the IP address of the Control Node cluster instead of the IP address of the active Control Node server. Using the clustered IP address will allow your connection to still resolve without manual intervention in the event of a Control Node failover.

Secondly, although Figure 8-10 shows the *sa* account being used for authentication, best practice is to use an account other than *sa*. Doing so will improve the security of your PDW appliance.

Lastly, as we previously discussed, Microsoft recommends the use of a staging database for data loads. The staging database is selected in the **Staging Database Name** drop-down. This tells PDW to first load the data to a temporary table in the specified staging database before loading the data into the final destination database. This is optional, but loading directly into the destination database will increase fragmentation.

When you are done, your **SQL Server PDW Connection Manager Editor** should resemble Figure 8-10. Click on **Test Connection** to confirm your information was entered correctly, then click **OK** to return to the **SQL Server PDW Destination Editor**.

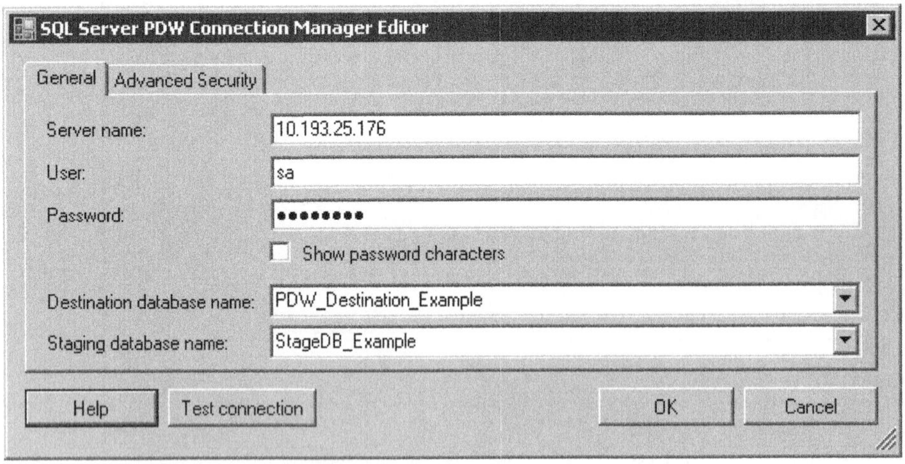

Figure 8-10. *The SQL Server PDW Connection Manager Editor*

■ **Note** If the Staging Database is not specified, SQL Server PDW will perform the load operation directly within the destination database, causing high levels of table fragmentation.

Clicking on the **Destination Table** field will bring up a modal for **Select Destination Table**. Click on *FactSales*, as depicted in Figure 8-11.

Figure 8-11. *The Select Destination Table modal*

There are four loading modes available, as listed in Table 8-3.

Table 8-3. *The four loading modes*

Append	Inserts the rows at the end of existing data in the destination table. This is the mode you are probably most used to.
Reload	Truncates the table before load.
Upsert	Performs a MERGE on the destination table, where new data is inserted and existing data is updated. You will need to specify the one or more columns that will be used to join the data on.
FastAppend	As its name implies, FastAppend is the fastest way to load data into a destination table. The trade-off is that it does not support rollback; in the case of a failure, you are responsible for removing any partially-inserted rows. FastAppend will also bypass the staging database, causing high levels of fragmentation.

Let's take a moment to discuss how to use the modes from Table 8-3 with two common load patterns. If you are performing regular, incremental loads on a large table (say, updating a transactional sales table with the previous day's orders), you should load the data directly using Append, since no transformations are required. Now let's say you're loading the same data, but you plan to instead transform the data and load into a mart before deleting the temporary data. This second example would be better suited to the FastAppend mode. Or, to say it more concisely, use FastAppend any time you are loading into an empty, intermediate working table.

There is one last option we need to discuss. Underneath the **Loading Mode** is a checkbox for "Roll-back load on table update or insert failure." In order to understand this option, you need to understand a little about how data is loaded into PDW. When data is loaded using the Append, Reload, or Upsert modes, PDW performs a 2-phase load. In Phase 1, the data is loaded into the staging database. In Phase 2, PDW performs an INSERT/SELECT of the sorted data into the final destination table. By default, data is loaded in parallel on all Compute Nodes, but loaded serially within a Compute Node to each distribution. This is necessary in order to support rollback. Roughly 85-95% of the load process is spent in Phase 1. When "Roll-back load on table update or insert failure" is de-selected, each distribution is loaded in parallel instead of serially during Phase 2. So, in other words, deselecting this option will improve performance but only affects 5-15% of the overall process. Also, deselecting this option removes PDW's ability to roll back; in the event of a failure during Phase 2, you would be responsible for cleaning up any partially-inserted data.

Because of the potential risk and minimal gain, it is best practice to deselect this option only when loading to an empty table. FastAppend is unaffected by this option because it always skips Phase 2 and loads directly into the final table, which is why FastAppend also does not support rollback.

■ **Tip** "Roll-back load on table update or insert failure" is also available in dwloader using the –m option.

Let's return to our PDW Destination Editor and select *Append* in the **Loading Mode** field. Because our destination table is currently empty, deselect the "Roll-back load on table update or insert failure" option to get a small, risk-free performance boost. Your **PDW Destination Editor** should now look similar to Figure 8-12.

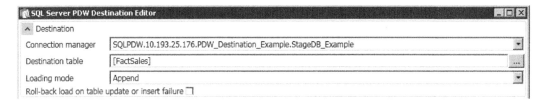

Figure 8-12. *The SQL Server PDW Destination Editor*

We are almost done with our first Data Flow. All we have left to do is to map our data. Drag the green arrow from the **Data Conversion** box to the **SQL Server PDW Destination** box, and then double-click on **SQL Server PDW Destination**. You should see results like those in Figure 8-13.

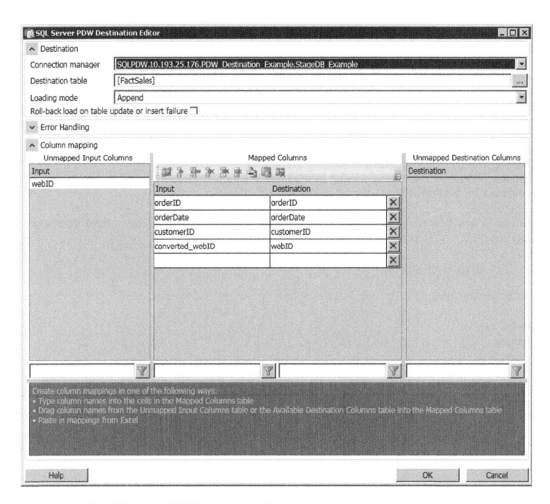

Figure 8-13. *The SQL Server PDW Destination Editor*

Map your input and destination columns. Make sure to map *webID* to our transformed *converted_webID* column. Click **OK**.

We have now successfully completed our first Data Flow connecting SQL Server to PDW. All we have left is to multi-thread our package.

Multi-Threading

We have completed our Data Flow for 2010, but we still need to create identical Data Flows for 2011 and 2012. We can do this easily by using copy and paste.

First, click on the **Control Flow** tab and rename the first Data Flow "SalesMart 2010." Then, copy and paste "SalesMart 2010" and rename it "SalesMart 2011."

Double-click on "SalesMart 2011" to return to the Data Flow designer, then double-click on the **OLE DB Source**. Replace the **SQL Command** with the code in Listing 8-8.

Listing 8-8. SQL Command for 2011 data

```
/* Retrieve sales for 2011 */
SELECT
      orderID
    , orderDate
    , customerID
    , webID
FROM PDW_Source_Example.dbo.FactSales
WHERE orderDate >= '2011-01-01'
    AND orderDate < '2012-01-01';
```

Return to the Control Flow tab and copy the "SalesMart 2010" Data Flow again. Rename it "Sales Mart 2012." Using the code in Listing 8-9, replace the **SQL Command** in the **OLE DB Source**.

Listing 8-9. SQL Command for 2012 Data

```
/* Retrieve sales for 2012 */
SELECT
      orderID
    , orderDate
    , customerID
    , webID
FROM PDW_Source_Example.dbo.FactSales
WHERE orderDate >= '2012-01-01'
    AND orderDate < '2013-01-01';
```

We are now ready to execute the package! Press F5 or navigate to Debug ➤ Start Debugging. Your successfully executed package should look similar to Figure 8-14.

Figure 8-14. *The successfully executed package*

Summary

We've covered a lot of material in this chapter. You have learned about the architecture of Microsoft SQL Server Parallel Data Warehouse (PDW) and some of the differences between SMP and MPP systems. You have learned about different loading methods and discussed how to improve load performance. You have also discovered some best practices along the way. Lastly, you walked through a step-by-step exercise to load data from SQL Server into PDW.

## CHAPTER 9

XML Patterns

XML is a popular format for exchanging data between systems. SSIS provides an XML Source adapter, but because of the flexible nature of XML, it can sometimes be tricky to get your data to fit into the tabular format that the SSIS data flow expects. This chapter describes the formats that work best with the XML Source and two alternative patterns for reading XML data with SSIS.

Using the XML Source

Like most Data Flow components, the XML Source component requires column metadata to be set at design time. This is done using an XML schema file (.xsd). The XML Source component uses the XML structure defined in the schema to create one or more outputs, and it also uses the element and attribute data types to set the column metadata. Changing the schema file will refresh the component's metadata and may cause validation errors if you have already mapped some of its outputs.

If you don't already have an XML schema defined for your document, SSIS can generate one for you. Click the Generate Schema button on the XML Source editor UI, and the component will infer the schema from the current document. Note that while this schema is guaranteed to work with the current XML file, it might not work for others if there are optional elements or values that are longer than expected. You may need to modify the generated schema file by hand to ensure that the minOccurs and maxOccurs attribute values are correct for each element and that the data types were set correctly.

The XML Source is easiest to use when your input file has a simple element/subelement structure. Listing 9-1 shows an example of that structure.

Listing 9-1. Simple XML Format Using Elements

```
<root>
    <node>
        <subnode> value</subnode>
        <anothersubnode> 1</anothersubnode>
    </node>
    <node>
        <subnode> value</subnode>
        <anothersubnode> 2</anothersubnode>
    </node>
</root>
```

Alternatively, the XML Source works well when values are listed as attributes, as shown in Listing 9-2. This format is similar to the output you would get from a SELECT ... FROM XML RAW statement in SQL Server.

Listing 9-2. Simple XML Format Using Attributes

```
<root>
    <row CustomerID="1" TerritoryID="1" AccountNumber="AW00000001" />
    <row CustomerID="2" TerritoryID="1" AccountNumber="AW00000002" />
</root>
```

Dealing with Multiple Outputs

The XML samples in Listings 9-1 and 9-2 will produce a single output in the XML Source. If your XML format has multiple levels of nested elements, the XML Source will start to produce more than one output. These outputs will be linked by automatically generated _Id columns, which you may need to join further down stream using a Merge Join transform.

■ **Note**   This pattern works well if you have a single level of nested XML elements that you need to join. If you have multiple levels of XML elements and you need to join more than two of the XML Source outputs, you'll need to use the Sort transformation.

Listing 9-3 contains an XML document with customer information. We'll use this document as our example for the remainder of the chapter.

Listing 9-3. Sample XML Document

```
<?xml version="1.0" encoding="utf-8"?>
<Extract Date="2011-07-04">
  <Customers>
    <Customer Key="11000">
      <Name>
        <FirstName>Jon</FirstName>
        <LastName>Yang</LastName>
      </Name>
      <BirthDate>1966-04-08</BirthDate>
      <Gender>M</Gender>
      <YearlyIncome>90000</YearlyIncome>
    </Customer>
    <Customer Key="11001">
      <Name>
        <FirstName>Eugene</FirstName>
        <LastName>Huang</LastName>
      </Name>
      <BirthDate>1965-05-14</BirthDate>
      <Gender>M</Gender>
      <YearlyIncome>60000</YearlyIncome>
    </Customer>
  </Customers>
</Extract>
```

The XML Source component will generate a separate output for each nested XML element. There will be three outputs for the XML document in Listing 9-3: Customers, Customer, and Name. Each output contains the elements and attributes that were defined in the schema, as well as an < element_name> _Id column, which acts as a primary key for the row. Outputs generated for child elements will contain _Id column for their parent element's output, which allows the data to be joined later in your data flow if needed.

Figure 9-1 shows the outputs and column names generated by the XML Source component for the XML document in Listing 9-3.

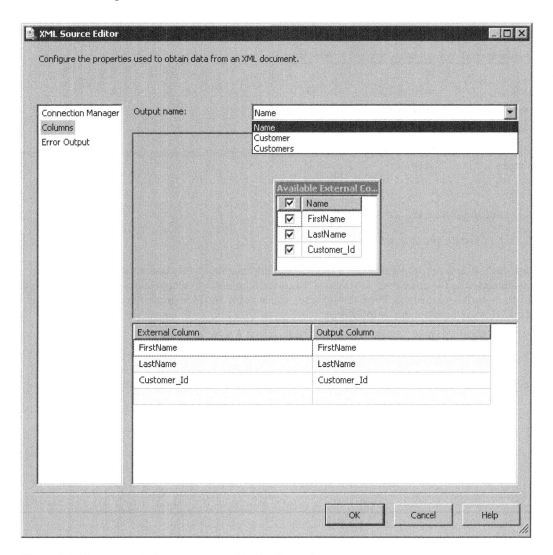

Figure 9-1. *Outputs and columns generated for the Name element*

■ **Note** The XML Source will not pick up any attribute values found on the root element of the document. To include this value in your output, you'll need to reformat the document to include a new root element node.

Figure 9-2 shows the schema of the destination table we will be storing the customer data in. As we can see, the table wants all of the columns shown in a single row, which means we'll have to merge the Customer and Name outputs before we can insert the data. The Merge Join transform is well suited for this, but it requires that both of its inputs are sorted the same way. We could add a Sort transform on each path before the Merge Join, but performing a sort can adversely affect performance and we should try to avoid doing so.

Customers

	Column Name	Data Type	Allow Nulls
	[Key]	int	☐
	FirstName	nvarchar(50)	☑
	LastName	nvarchar(50)	☑
	BirthDate	date	☑
	Gender	nvarchar(1)	☑
	YearlyIncome	money	☑
			☐

Figure 9-2. *Customers database table schema*

Although the XML Source component doesn't set any sort information on the columns it produces, the output is already sorted on the generated _Id columns. To get the Merge Join to accept these inputs without using the Sort transform, we'll have to manually set the IsSorted and SortKeyPosition properties using the Advanced Editor for the XML Source component, as follows:

- Right-click the XML Source component and select Show Advanced Editor.

- Select the Input and Output Properties tab.

- Select the Name output and set the IsSorted property to **True**, as shown in Figure 9-3.

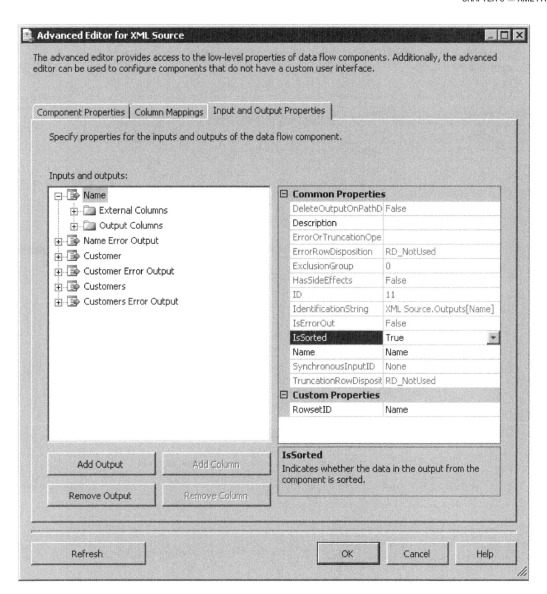

Figure 9-3. *Setting the IsSorted property value in the Advanced Editor for the XML Source*

- Expand the Name output and then expand the Output Columns folder.

- Select the Customer_Id field and set the SortKeyPosition property to **1**, as shown in Figure 9-4.

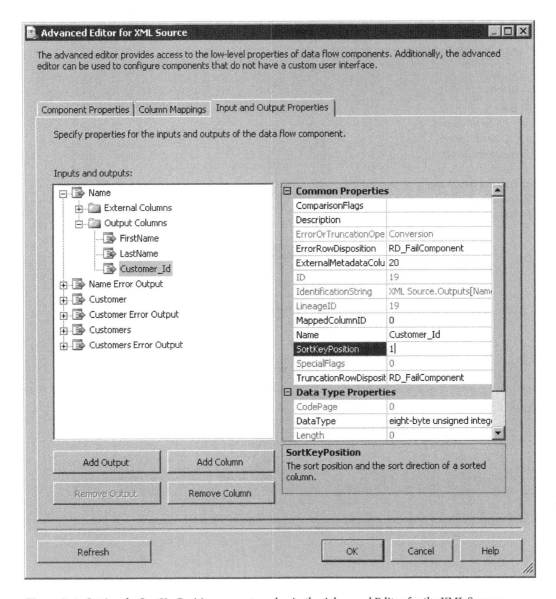

Figure 9-4. *Setting the SortKeyPosition property value in the Advanced Editor for the XML Source*

- Repeat steps 3–5 for the Customer output.

- Click OK to save the changes and return to the designer.

By setting the SortKeyPosition value for the Customer_Id columns in the Name and Customer outputs, we've told SSIS that the rows will be sorted. We can now map both outputs directly to the Merge Join transform (as shown in Figure 9-5), and select the columns we want for our destination table (as shown in Figure 9-6).

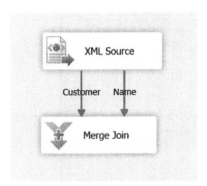

Figure 9-5. *Connecting the XML Source component to a Merge Join transform*

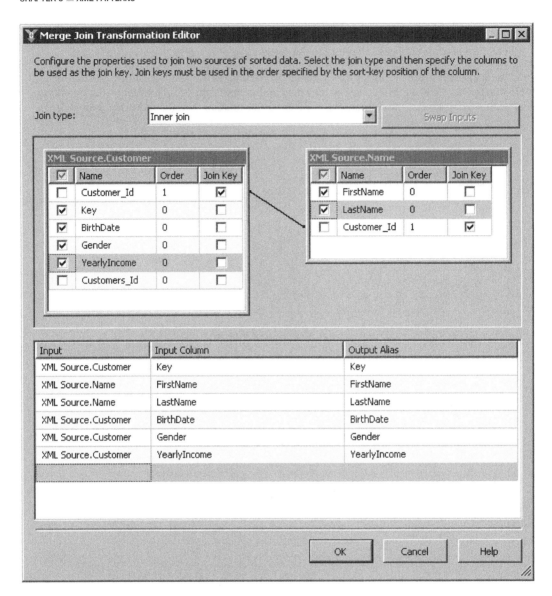

Figure 9-6. *Mapping columns from the Merge Join transform*

Making Things Easier with XSLT

You can simplify the handling of complex XML documents by preprocessing a source file with XSLT. Using XSLT, you can shape the XML to a format that closely resembles the destination schema, remove the fields that you don't need to capture, or transform it into a simple format that is easily handled by the XML Source component.

The sample XML from Listing 9-3 produced three separate outputs for the XML Source component. To insert the data into our destination, we had to merge the outputs into the format we wanted. Using the XSLT script in Listing 9-4, we can "flatten" or denormalize the data so that the XML Source component will have a single output.

Listing 9-4. *XSLT Script to Simplify Our XML Sample*

```xml
<?xml version="1.0" encoding="utf-8"?>
<xsl:stylesheet version="1.0" xmlns:xsl="http://www.w3.org/1999/XSL/Transform">
<xsl:output method="xml" indent="yes"/>
<xsl:template match="/Extract">
    <Customers>
        <xsl:for-each select="Customers/Customer">
        <Customer>
            <Key>
                <xsl:value-of select="@Key"/>
            </Key>
            <FirstName>
                <xsl:value-of select="Name/FirstName"/>
            </FirstName>
            <LastName>
                <xsl:value-of select="Name/LastName"/>
            </LastName>
            <BirthDate>
                <xsl:value-of select="BirthDate"/>
            </BirthDate>
            <Gender>
                <xsl:value-of select="Gender"/>
            </Gender>
            <YearlyIncome>
                <xsl:value-of select="YearlyIncome"/>
            </YearlyIncome>
        </Customer>
        </xsl:for-each>
    </Customers>
</xsl:template>
</xsl:stylesheet>
```

We can apply this XSLT using an XML Task. Here is the process for doing that:

1. Save your XSLT script to a file.

   - Add an XML Task to your package.

   - Double-click the task to open the editor.

   - Set the OperationType property to XSLT and the SaveOperationResult property to **True**.

   - Set the SecondOperandType and SecondOperand properties to point to your XSLT script file.

2. Enter the appropriate connection information for SourceType, Source, DestinationType, and Destination, similar to what is shown in Figure 9-7.

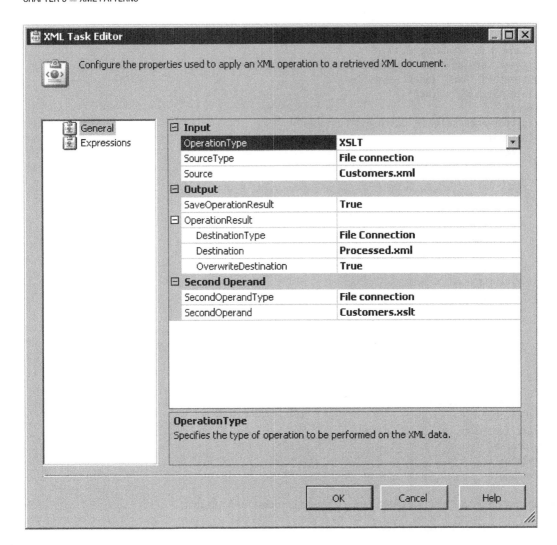

Figure 9-7. *XML Task configuration*

■ **Note** The XML Task was updated in the SQL Server 2012 release to use the latest .NET XML technologies. The performance of applying XSLT scripts is much better than in previous versions.

Listing 9-5 shows us what our sample XML document looks like after applying the XSLT script from Listing 9-4. We can see that all of the fields we need to extract are now under a single parent element. The schema for this new XML format gives us a single output with the XML Source component, removing the need to join outputs later on in the data flow.

Listing 9-5. Simplified XML Document

```
<?xml version="1.0" encoding="utf-8"?>
<Customers>
```

```
<Customer>
  <Key> 11000</Key>
  <FirstName> Jon</FirstName>
  <LastName> Yang</LastName>
  <BirthDate> 1966-04-08</BirthDate>
  <Gender> M</Gender>
  <YearlyIncome> 90000</YearlyIncome>
</Customer>
<Customer>
  <Key> 11001</Key>
  <FirstName> Eugene</FirstName>
  <LastName> Huang</LastName>
  <BirthDate> 1965-05-14</BirthDate>
  <Gender> M</Gender>
  <YearlyIncome> 60000</YearlyIncome>
</Customer>
</Customers>
```

Using a Script Component

An alternatve to processing an XML document with the XML Source is to use a Script Component. This pattern requires some custom coding, but it gives you full control over the way the data is output. The .NET Framework provides a number of ways to parse and load an XML document, each with their own strengths and performance characteristics. This section describes two separate patterns for processing XML documents with a Script Component.

The first pattern uses the XML Schema Definition Tool (Xsd.exe) to generate a set of .NET classes that can be used by an SSIS Script Component. It uses the XmlSerializer class to convert the source XML document into a set of easy-to-use .NET objects. While XmlSerializer is not the fastest way to process an XML document in .NET, the strongly typed classes allow for code that is straightforward and easy to maintain. This approach is a recommended alternative to the XML Source when you're working with complex XML documents that can easily fit into memory (for example, smaller than 100MB).

The second pattern uses a combination of LINQ to XML and the XmlReader class to process XML documents in a streaming manner. This approach is more sensitive to changes to the XML format; it may be harder to maintain, but it will output scripts that use the XmlSerializer class. This pattern is recommended when you are processing very large XML documents, or when performance is critical.

Configuring the Script Component

The Script Components in both patterns are configured the same way, but they will contain different code. Both will use a file connection manager to locate the source XML file at runtime, and both will define the same set of output columns. Use the following steps to configure your Script Component:

1. Add a file connection manager to your package.

   - Set Usage type to **Existing file** and set the path to our XML source file as shown in Figure 9-8.

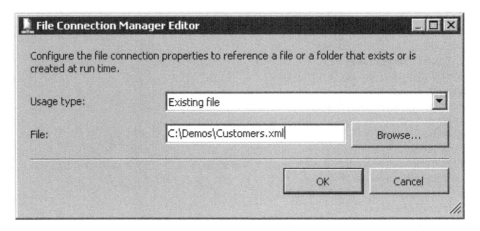

Figure 9-8. Configure the File Connection Manager

- Add a data flow to your package, and drag a Script Component transform from the toolbox.

- Select **Source** from the Select Script Component Type dialog as shown in Figure 9-9.

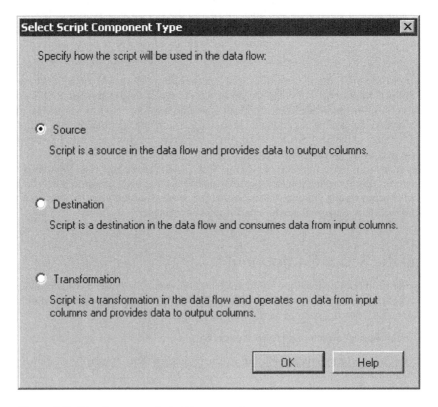

Figure 9-9. Creating a new Script Component source

- Double-click the component to bring up the Script Transform editor.

- Click the Inputs and Outputs page.

- Rename your output from "Output 0" to something more meaningful. Since our sample XML is outputting a set of "Customers," that is the name we'll use for this example.

- Define the columns as you'd like them to be output. Make sure the data types for the columns match what has been defined in your schema. Your column definition should look similar to Figure 9-10.

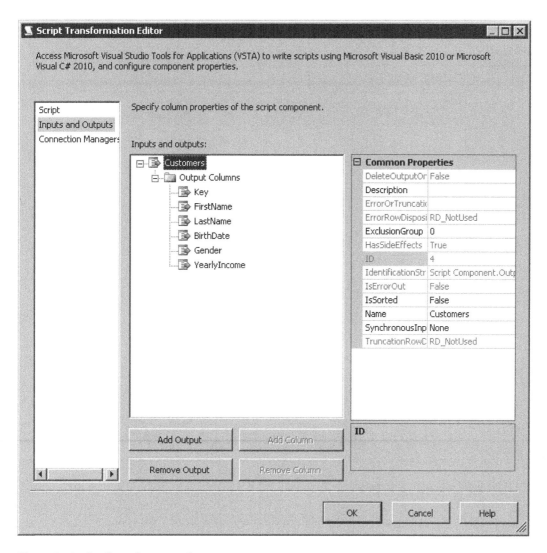

Figure 9-10. Configured output columns

- Go to the Connection Managers page and add a reference to the file connection manager you created in step 1.

- Give the connection manager a meaningful name, such as "CustomerFile." The page will look similar to Figure 9-11.

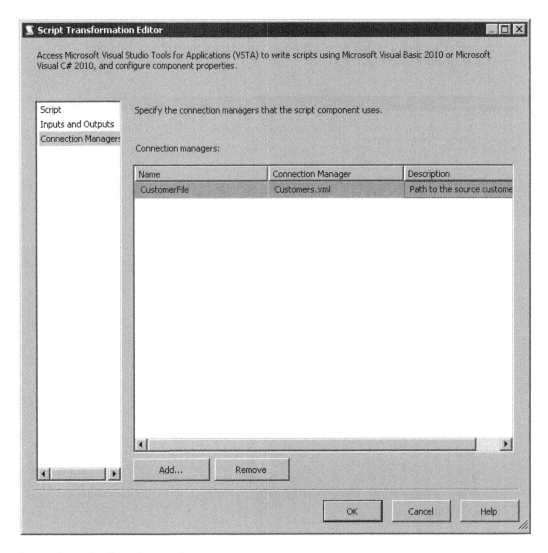

Figure 9-11. *Configured connection manager*

- Go to the Script page and click the Edit Script button to launch the VSTA editor.

We'll be adding code to the PreExecute and CreateNewOutputRows methods of the ScriptMain class, as well as overriding two additional methods from the base class: AcquireConnection and ReleaseConnection.

The AcquireConnection method will retrieve the path to our XML file from the connection manager we configured in step 10.

The PreExecute method will verify that the file actually exists, and it will raise an error if it is not found.

The CreateNewOutputRows method does the majority of the script's work. It is responsible for extracting data from our source document and outputting it to the data flow. The code that goes in here will depend on which pattern you select.

Finally, the ReleaseConnection method will release the file connection, indicating to the runtime that we are finished with it.

■ **Note** While calling ReleaseConnection for a file connection manager isn't needed, it's good to get into the habit of calling ReleaseConnection anytime you have a matching call to AcquireConnection. Certain connection managers, such as the OLE DB connection manager, will leave the underlying database connections open and keep resources in memory until the connection object has been released.

Listing 9-6 shows the code that we will be using for both Script Component patterns.

Listing 9-6. Full Source Code Listing

```csharp
using System;
using System.Data;
using Microsoft.SqlServer.Dts.Pipeline.Wrapper;
using Microsoft.SqlServer.Dts.Runtime.Wrapper;
using System.IO;
using System.Xml.Serialization;
using System.Xml;

[Microsoft.SqlServer.Dts.Pipeline.SSISScriptComponentEntryPointAttribute]
public class ScriptMain : UserComponent
{
    string pathToXmlFile;

    public override void AcquireConnections(object Transaction)
    {
        // Call the base class
        base.AcquireConnections(Transaction);

        // The file connection manager's AcquireConnection() method returns us the path as a
string.
        pathToXmlFile = (string)Connections.CustomerFile.AcquireConnection(Transaction);
    }

    public override void PreExecute()
    {
        // Call the base class
        base.PreExecute();

        // Make sure the file path exists
        if (!File.Exists(pathToXmlFile))
        {
            string errorMessage = string.Format("Source XML file does not exist. Path: {0}",
pathToXmlFile);
            bool bCancel;
```

```
            ComponentMetaData.FireError(0, ComponentMetaData.Name, errorMessage, string.Empty,
0, out bCancel);
        }
    }
    public override void CreateNewOutputRows()
    {
        // TODO - This is where we will load our XML document
    }

    public override void ReleaseConnections()
    {
        // Call the base class
        base.ReleaseConnections();

        // Release our connection
        Connections.CustomerFile.ReleaseConnection(pathToXmlFile);
    }
}
```

Once your script component is configured, you can plug in the `CreateNewOutputRows` logic from one of the following patterns.

Processing XML with XmlSerializer

To process the XML file using the `XmlSerializer` class, we'll use the XML Schema Definition Tool to generate a set of .NET classes from our XML Schema file. From the command line, we'll specify that we want to generate classes (`/classes`), the language we'd like to use (in this example, we'll use C#, but VB could be used as well), the namespace of the resulting class, and the path to our schema file. We'll use the schema file (`Customer.xsd`) for the customer data XML from Listing 9-3. The command line and `xsd.exe` output is shown in Listing 9-7.

Listing 9-7. XML Schema Definition Tool Command Line

```
C:\demos> xsd.exe /classes /language:CS /namespace:DesignPatterns.Samples Customer.xsd

Microsoft (R) Xml Schemas/DataTypes support utility
[Microsoft (R) .NET Framework, Version 2.0.50727.3038]
Copyright (C) Microsoft Corporation. All rights reserved.
Writing file 'Customer.cs'.
```

The resulting `Customer.cs` file will have the classes we'll use in our Script Component. When used with the `XmlSerializer` class, we can read the entire XML source file into an easy-to-manipulate set of objects.

■ **Note** The XML Schema Definition Tool is part of the Windows SDK. On most machines, it will be found in the `C:\Program Files (x86)\Microsoft SDKs\Windows\v7.0A\Bin` directory. For more information on the XML Schema Definition Tool, see its MSDN entry at `http://msdn.microsoft.com/en-us/library/x6c1kb0s.aspx`.

Before we begin writing the CreateNewOutputRows logic, we'll need to include the Customer.cs file that we generated using xsd.exe. To do this, perform the following steps from within the VSTA script editor environment:

1. Right-click the project node in the solution explorer (this will start with "sc_", followed by a string of numbers) and choose **Add ➤ Existing Item**.

   • Browse to the Customer.cs file that you generated with xsd.exe.

   • Open main.cs from the Solution Explorer.

   • Include the namespace for the Extract class by adding Using DesignPatterns. Samples; to the top of the file.

Once the file has been added to your project, you can write the code in CreateNewOutputRows that will read and manipulate the XML data. The source code for the CreateNewOutputRows function is in Listing 9-8.

Listing 9-8. Script Logic for Using the XmlSerializer Class

```
public override void CreateNewOutputRows()
{
    // Load our XML document
    Extract extract = (Extract) new XmlSerializer(typeof(Extract)).Deserialize(XmlReader.
Create(pathToXmlFile));

    // Output a new row for each Customer in our file
    foreach (ExtractCustomer customer in extract.Customers)
    {
        CustomersBuffer.AddRow();

        CustomersBuffer.Key = customer.Key;
        CustomersBuffer.FirstName = customer.Name.FirstName;
        CustomersBuffer.LastName = customer.Name.LastName;
        CustomersBuffer.BirthDate = customer.BirthDate;
        CustomersBuffer.Gender = customer.Gender;
        CustomersBuffer.YearlyIncome = customer.YearlyIncome;
    }
}
```

Processing XML with XmlReader and LINQ to XML

This pattern makes use of the XmlReader class to stream in an XML document, as well as LINQ to XML functionality to extract the values you want to keep. It is ideal for processing large XML documents, as it does not require the entire document to be read into memory. It is also well suited for scenarios where you want to extract certain fields from the XML document and ignore the rest.

■ **Note** The idea for this pattern came from a post from SQL Server MVP, Simon Sabin. Sample code and other great SSIS content can be found on his blog at http://sqlblogcasts.com/blogs/simons/.

The key to this pattern is the use of the XmlReader class. Instead of using the XDocument class to read our source XML file (which is the typical approach when using LINQ to XML), we'll create a special function that returns the XML as a collection of XElements. This allows us to make use of the LINQ syntax while taking advantage of the streaming functionality provided by XmlReader.

Before adding the code, you'll need to make the following changes to your script project:

1. Add a reference to the System.Xml.Linq assembly.

   - Add the following namespaces to your Using statements:

2. System.Collections.Generic

3. System.Linq

4. System.Xml.Linq

Listing 9-9 contains the code for the XmlReader function (StreamReader), as well as the CreateNewOutputRows logic to consume the XML document.

Listing 9-9. Script Logic for Using the XmlReader Class

```
public override void CreateNewOutputRows()
{
    foreach (var xdata in (
        from customer in StreamReader(pathToXmlFile, "Customer")
        select new
        {
            Key = customer.Attribute("Key").Value,
            FirstName = customer.Element("Name").Element("FirstName").Value,
            LastName = customer.Element("Name").Element("LastName").Value,
            BirthDate = customer.Element("BirthDate").Value,
            Gender = customer.Element("Gender").Value,
            YearlyIncome = customer.Element("YearlyIncome").Value,
        }
    ))
    {
        try
        {
            CustomersBuffer.AddRow();
            CustomersBuffer.Key = Convert.ToInt32(xdata.Key);
            CustomersBuffer.FirstName = xdata.FirstName;
            CustomersBuffer.LastName = xdata.LastName;
            CustomersBuffer.BirthDate = Convert.ToDateTime(xdata.BirthDate);
            CustomersBuffer.Gender = xdata.Gender;
            CustomersBuffer.YearlyIncome = Convert.ToDecimal(xdata.YearlyIncome);
        }
    }
```

```
        catch (Exception e)
        {
            string errorMessage = string.Format("Error retrieving data. Exception message: {0}",
e.Message);
            bool bCancel;
            ComponentMetaData.FireError(0, ComponentMetaData.Name, errorMessage, string.Empty,
0, out bCancel);
        }
    }
}

static IEnumerable<XElement> StreamReader(String filename, string elementName)
{
    using (XmlReader xr = XmlReader.Create(filename))
    {
        xr.MoveToContent();

        while (xr.Read())
        {
            while (xr.NodeType == XmlNodeType.Element && xr.Name == elementName)
            {
                XElement node = (XElement)XElement.ReadFrom(xr);
                yield return node;
            }
        }
        xr.Close();
    }
}
```

Summary

The XML Source component lets you process XML documents from an SSIS Data Flow without writing any code. Although it can handle most XML schemas, it tends to work best with simple XML documents. When dealing with complex XML formats, consider using XSLT to reformat the source document to a format that is easily parsed. If you don't mind writing and maintaining .NET code, consider using one of the Script Component patterns described in this chapter when you need more control over how a document is parsed, are working with large XML documents, or have specific performance requirements.

## CHAPTER 10

Expression Language Patterns

Expression language in SSIS might appropriately be referred to as the "glue" that holds the product together. Expressions in SSIS provide a relatively simple and easy-to-use interface to allow data developers to introduce dynamic logic into the ETL infrastructure. Thinking through the various moving parts within Integration Services, it's safe to say that they can all be manipulated in one way or another through the use of expressions.

Expressions provide a fast, effective, and—dare I say—fun way to solve specific ETL challenges. In this chapter, we'll look into some of the basics of the expression language, and I'll describe a few instances where SSIS expressions are ideal (and a few where they might not be) for effectively solving difficult ETL problems.

Getting to Know the Expression Language

Before diving into the design patterns around the SSIS expression language, let's spend a little time defining and getting familiar with the nuances of the language. Since its behavior and syntax differ significantly from any other type of interpreted code, a review of the language-specific patterns can be of value here.

What is Expression Language?

The SSIS expression language is an interpreted language built into the SSIS runtime environment. This specialized language is used to craft scalar-valued snippets of code (individually referred to as *expressions*) that may be used at various points within the SSIS environment.

The SSIS designer exposes dozens of interfaces where expressions can be used in place of hard-coded values, allowing the BI professional to leverage that flexibility to create dynamic and reusable elements within SSIS. Conceptually, it's not unlike the product-specific dialects that exist in other Microsoft development environments. For example, when developing reports in SSDT or BIDS for deployment to SQL Server Reporting Services, one can use Visual Basic for Applications (VBA) code to generate dynamic behavior during report execution and rendering.

As you explore the expression language, you'll find it to be a very powerful addition to the natural capabilities of SQL Server Integration Services. It has a rich library of functionality that will be familiar to both developers and DBAs. Among the functional domains of the SSIS expression language is

- A full complement of mathematical functions and operators

- An impressive set of string functions that may be used in comparisons, analysis, and value manipulation

- Common date and time functionality, including date part extraction, date arithmetic, and comparison

The expression language serves two different roles within the package life cycle:

- *Evaluation:* Expressions can be used to determine whether a specified condition is true, and to change the behavior of the package accordingly. When used as part of the control flow, an expression used as an evaluation may check a certain value and dynamically alter the execution path based on the results of that comparison. Within the data flow, expressions allow the evaluation of data a row at a time to determine how to proceed in the ETL.

- *Assignment:* In addition to expressions as decision-making elements, we can use SSIS expressions to programmatically modify data during package execution. Typical uses of this include expression-based property settings, and transformation of in-process data within the data flow.

Expressions in SSIS may derive their comparisons or assignments from several fronts. Built-in system variables permit visibility into software environmental data such as package and container start times, machine environment information, package versioning metadata, and more. We can interrogate and manipulate the values of user-defined SSIS variables by using expressions and access values of package parameters to be leveraged elsewhere during package execution. In the data flow, expressions may interact with running data at the cellular level.

Expressions are value-driven at runtime. Unlike settings that are generally only configurable at design time (think: data flow column definitions), expressions will calculate their values when the package is actually executed. Further, a single expression may be evaluated many times (perhaps with a different result each time) during the execution life cycle of the package. Consider the case of the For Each Loop, a container that loops through a specified set of objects or values until it reaches the end of said collection. Expressions that are manipulated within the loop may be updated dozens or even hundreds of times during this process.

Why Use Expressions?

The ability to use expressions is one of the greatest strengths of SQL Server Integration Services. Simply put, expressions help to fill in the small gaps. Expression language isn't a tool in itself, but is rather an interface that helps other SSIS tools more effectively perform their respective functions. That's well and good, but in the interest of simplicity, why would an ETL developer choose to use expressions instead of other languages such as T-SQL, C#, or VB.NET? There are a few compelling reasons to employ the expression language in your SSIS packages:

- *Simplicity.* Expressions language can be used to quickly add flow logic or make small changes to in-pipeline data in the data flow. Small ETL changes that might otherwise be relegated to a script task or component can often be handled inline without the need to introduce extra code to the package.

- *Consistency.* Use of the expression language can lead to a consistent approach to data or program flow challenges. For example, if your ETL requires that you convert blank strings to NULLs, the approach and syntax would otherwise be different for flat files, Access databases, and relational database sources. Applying expression language to the same task would reduce the amount of distinct code one would have to write by relying on the built-in string manipulation functions in expression language.

- *Maintenance scope.* By applying the design pattern of using expression language for cleansing needs, you can eliminate much of the sleuth work required to track down and change cleansing rules as your business expectations change. Using expressions in the package itself provides a single point of maintenance rather than forcing you to inspect the upstream data sources each time you need to make a change.

I've done a number of presentations for novice SSIS developers, and when I bring up the topic of expression language, one question almost always seems to come up: Where do I use this expression language stuff? My answer: Everywhere! Part of the beauty of expressions is that they can be used almost anywhere within SSIS packages. You can employ expressions on the control flow in precedence constraints. It's convenient to make your SSIS package variables dynamic by replacing their static values with expressions. One can leverage expressions within the data flow to manipulate data and even control the execution path. The bottom line is that many of the common properties of packages, tasks, constraints, and data flow elements can be manipulated through the use of expressions.

Although its syntax is very unique, the expression language isn't difficult to learn. Anyone with logical scripting experience (even if that experience is limited to T-SQL) can quickly pick up on the basics and should be able to master the language with a reasonable amount of practice.

Language Essentials

Even for those who have experience scripting in other Microsoft development environments, the first exposure to the SSIS expression language can be a little unsettling. The syntax and functionality are unlike any other language, either interpreted or compiled. It appears to be a strange hybrid of several languages and is certainly a dialect all its own.

Developers who have spent time using the C-style languages (C, C++, C#, Java) will recognize some of the syntactical nuances within expression language, including

- Case sensitive column and variable names

- Case sensitive string comparisons

- Double-equal (==) comparison operator

- Simplified conditional (if/then/else) operator

- Data types

Similarly, anyone experienced in T-SQL will find a great deal of familiar behavior within the SSIS expression language:

- Case insensitive function names

- Date arithmetic and string manipulation functions much like those in T-SQL

The SSIS expression language is quite powerful, with its wide variety of functions and operators. With native behavior including equality tests, type casts, string manipulation, and date arithmetic, the use of expressions within SSIS packages can help to overcome ETL challenges both large and small.

Limitations

As useful as the expression language is, there are a few key limitations to its use. Bear in mind that these are relatively minor hang-ups; the SSIS expression language is not intended to be a full-featured programming language, but rather a lightweight tool to supplement the behavior of existing SSIS task and components. Among some of the challenges are the following:

- *Expressions are limited to single-value statements.* This almost goes without saying since it's an expression language and not a programming language. Still, it's worth mentioning that one can't, for example, use a single expression to iterate through a list or process a string character-by-character.

- *No Intellisense.* Unlike other scripting/expression environments, there is no built-in Intellisense within the native expression editors. Although the expression editor in SSIS does have field, variable, and function lists, the convenience and coding reliability of Intellisense has not yet made it into the product.

- *No error handling.* This limitation is most visible when attempting to change data type or length. Because there is no try/catch or TryParse() behavior found in the .NET based languages, you cannot, for example, attempt to cast a text value to a number and programmatically handle any type cast errors in the same expression.

- *No comments allowed.* The fact that there is no provision for code comments can be a significant downside when using lengthy or complex expressions. Any comments documenting the purpose of the expression would have to be done peripherally; for example, on the data flow or control flow surface as an SSIS annotation.

- *Complex statements can be difficult.* Simple assignments or comparisons are easy to do, and usually easy to understand after the fact. However, introducing even a moderate amount of complexity to an expression can make for a lengthy and convoluted statement. Consider the case of a multiconditional if statement. In most other dialects, one could simply perform an if/then/else if... operation to account for more than one test condition. However, the expression language doesn't have such behavior, so to build such logic requires one to nest conditional operators. Figure 10-1 shows how one might easily address four possible conditions in a CASE operation in Transact-SQL. By contrast, Figure 10-2 shows a similar example using expression language (note that I manually wrapped the text to fit it on the page). Although the result of the operation is the same, the latter has conditional operators nested two levels deep and is more difficult to develop and maintain.

```
SELECT CASE WHEN @TestCase=3 THEN 'Test case=Solid'
            WHEN @TestCase=2 THEN 'Test case=Liquid'
            WHEN @TestCase=1 THEN 'Test case=Gas'
            ELSE 'Unknown test case' END [TestCaseType]
```

Figure 10-1. *Multi-condition evaluation in T-SQL*

```
(TestCase == 1) ? "Test case=Gas" : (TestCase == 2 ? "Test case=Liquid" : (TestCase == 3 ?
"Test case=Solid" : "Unknown Test Case"))
```

Figure 10-2. *Multiconditional evaluation in expression language*

Despite its minor shortcomings, the SSIS expression language remains an integral part of the product, and as we'll see later in this chapter, has some very practical uses in a well-designed ETL ecosystem.

Putting Expression Language to Work

With an understanding of what the expression language is (and is not), let's talk about some design patterns where one might use it.

Package Expressions

Although not as common as other uses, it is possible to use SSIS expressions to configure package-level properties. There are a handful of properties that may be set at the package level by using expressions, including

- Disable

- Disable Event Handlers

- CheckpointFileName

- MaxConcurrentExecutables

- DelayValidation

- Description

Consider the example of MaxConcurrentExecutables, which defines how many executables (packages, tasks, etc.) can run concurrently. Setting of this property through an expression would allow the ETL developer to dynamically control this value based on any criteria visible through an expression.

Although these properties are configurable by using expressions, it's far more common to find package-level options set by using package parameters (with SQL Server 2012) or package configurations (SQL Server 2008 and earlier). The sharing of common values across package ancestries is usually best done using parameters or configurations, which allows for greater flexibility and easier maintenance. I expose this particular design pattern more for the purpose of identifying it as an antipattern than for defining parameters for its use. Unless there's some business case or regulation dictating otherwise, it's a better long-term solution to externalize these values rather than relying on expressions.

Variable Expressions

As shown in Figure 10-3, you can configure each variable with a static value in the Value field, or define a value expression that will be evaluated at runtime. Note that the variable window was improved starting in SQL Server 2012— in older versions, static values were shown in the variable window, but you had to use the Properties window to view or alter an expression for a variable.

Name	Scope	Data type	Value	Expression	
ClientName	Merge Vendor Data	String	"IonTech"	@[$Package::ClientName]	...
NumberOfFilesProcessed	Merge Vendor Data	Int32	0		...
OutputDirectory	Merge Vendor Data	String	d:\data\"IonTech"	"d:\\data\\" + @[User::ClientNa...	...

Figure 10-3. *Expressions with variables*

In practice, I often see expressions applied to variable values, and then using the resulting variable as a property on a task or component (as opposed to using an expression to set the property directly). I'm a fan of this design pattern for one simple reason: reusability. It's not uncommon for components to share certain properties, and building expressions on each of those shared properties for every applicable component is both redundant and unnecessary. For those properties that will be shared across multiple tasks or components, it's far easier to centralize the expression logic into a variable and then use that variable to set the shared properties. This approach allows for faster development as well as easier maintenance should the logic require changes down the road.

When using this design pattern, don't forget that you can also "stack" variable values. In the expression statement, you can leverage other variables to set the value of the current variable.

Connection Managers

One of the most practical and common places to use SSIS expressions is the Connection Managers tray. Generally speaking, it's typically preferable to store dynamic connection properties not in expressions but rather as parameters, particularly when dealing with structured data. Because of the sensitive and frequently changing nature of connection metadata (server names, user names, and passwords), most ETL professionals choose to externalize those settings to keep them stored securely and externally to the package so they can be globally changed (rather than modified package by package).

One recurring exception to this pattern is connections that interact with the file system. There are several cases where using expressions helps to lighten the load of processing file-based sources or destinations:

- When working with flat files, the files are to be named according to the current date and/or timestamp (such as Medicare_2012_03_01.txt, for example).

- The files are expected to be filed in the filesystem according to the date (such as D:\Data\2012\03\01\Medicare.txt).

- A scheduled job loads a text file that always has the same filename, but a copy of each day's file needs to be saved without overwriting the file processed on the previous day.

For the cases above, a little dab of expression language can be used to dynamically build directory paths and file names to be used by our connections in SSIS. Let's assume that we're generating a flat text file from within our package, and we want to use a dynamic file name based on the current date. By setting the ConnectionString property from within the Properties window of the instance of the Flat File Connection Manager, we can manipulate the runtime value of the file name. As shown in Figure 10-4 below, we're specifying the base filename and then appending the elements of the current date to build a customized file name.

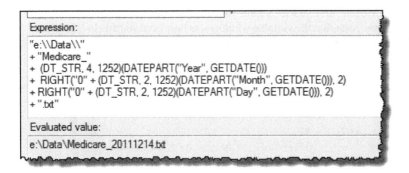

Figure 10-4. *Dynamic file name using expression*

Note that the pattern above could be further extended to include elements of time (hours/minutes/seconds) should your ETL requirements include a restraint for that level of granularity.

Since we're not going in-depth into all the syntactical elements of the expression language, I'll just point out a couple of things I've done here:

- Because the backslash (\) is a special character in the expression language, I have to "escape" it (to negate its status as a special character) by using a double backslash when including it as a string literal.

- Using (DT_STR, n, 1252), I'm converting the integer value returned by the DATEPART function to ASCII text. In this case, I'm using codepage 1252 with a maximum length of either 2 or 4 depending on the component of the date element.

- Using the RIGHT function, I'll pad any single-digit month or day value with zeroes (e.g., so that "3" becomes "03") to maintain consistency.

Remember that this pattern is highly flexible. It can be utilized with most any file connection, whether it's to be used as a source or a destination. We're not limited to just flat file connections here either; this logic can be extended to some of the other SSIS connections as well. I've used this same design pattern when dealing with

FTP data as both a source and destination. By embedding the same logic within the properties of an FTP source, one can programmatically "walk" the directory structure of a remote server when it is in a known and predictable format such as this.

Project-level Connection Managers

With the introduction of SQL Server 2012, we now have a new way to expose connection information across multiple packages in the same project by way of project connection managers. Using the traditional, pre-2012 model, any connection manager defined within a package is independent of those in other packages. Starting with SSIS in SQL Server 2012, however, we now have the ability to attach a connection manager to our workspace at the project level. These are accessible to all packages within the same project.

We'll not go deeply into the new deployment model in this chapter, but it is important to point out how the use of expressions impacts project connection managers. Because they are attached to the project and not one particular package, the properties of these shared connections are common to all packages in the project. As such, any property setting on these project connection managers—including the use of expressions—would be immediately reflected in all packages in the project. This is a welcome and much needed improvement to the way packages interact with one another, but for those who have worked with previous versions of SSIS, it's a bit of a paradigm shift. Don't get caught off guard when an expression applied to a project connection in one package gets applied to the other packages in the project!

Control Flow

Within the control flow, there are a couple of different ways to implement SSIS expressions. First, each of the tasks and containers will expose several properties which are configurable using expressions. In addition, the paths between them (known as precedence constraints) allow ETL developers to customize the decision path when moving from one task/container to another.

Conditional Execution Through Expressions and Constraints

The essential function of the control flow is to manage the execution of package elements. Through the use of precedence constraints, one can design a package so that tasks and containers are fired in the proper order and with the correct dependencies intact. For a simple example of this, think about a package that truncates and then loads a staging table. Both of these tasks can be performed in the same package, but without a precedence constraint to cause the insert operation to occur after the TRUNCATE TABLE execution, you run the risk of inadvertently *loading and then deleting* the same data.

Precedence constraints can be configured to manage flow-based successful completion of the preceding task (the default behavior), or may be set to cause the task to execute only if the preceding task fails. In addition, the constraint can be set to Completion, allowing the downstream task to fire when the upstream task is finished, regardless of its outcome. Tasks may have multiple precedence constraints, and these may be set such that all any or all of them must be satisfied before the task to which they are attached will execute. Figure 10-5 shows a fairly typical use of precedence constraints; note that the unlabeled arrows represent Success constraints, and the others are labeled as to their purpose. The dashed lines indicate that the task is configured to execute upon completion of *either* of the preceding tasks.

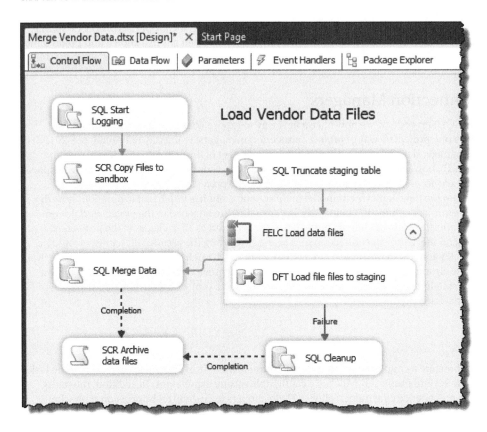

Figure 10-5. *Precedence constraints*

As useful as precedence constraints are, the domain of variability that they address is fairly limited: the only conditions that can be tested are whether a task completed as well as the success or failure of said task. In the brief example shown in Figure 10-5, you can probably infer that we're downloading one or more files from an external source, loading the data from those files into staging tables, and then merging (upserting) the data into a database table. Although there's nothing technically wrong here, there is room for improvement. For example, what happens if there are no files to be processed? In the example shown, the truncation of the staging table, the loop through the filesystem to find the downloaded files (even if none exist), and the merge operation will all be executed even if there are no files to process.

In the first job I ever held, I was responsible for, among other things, gathering stray shopping carts from the store parking lot and bringing them back inside. My boss once told me, "This job requires an excessive amount of walking, so do what you can to save steps." All these years later, that advice still holds true today. Why run through extra steps when we can simply skip past them if they are not needed? For the previous example, including a relatively simple expression can bypass the execution of the majority of the package when no files are found to process. Saving those steps saves CPU cycles, disk I/O, and other resources.

Precedence constraints also have the ability to use expressions to enforce proper package flow. In Figure 10-6, you'll see that the evaluation operation is set to **Expression and Constraint** to enforce both the execution value of the prior task as well as the value defined in the **Expression** box. For purposes of illustration, we're going to assume that we've populated an SSIS variable to store the number of files downloaded in the script task operation, and we're using the expression to confirm that at least one file was processed. From here, you can either type the expression into the window manually or use the ellipsis button to open the expression editor (note

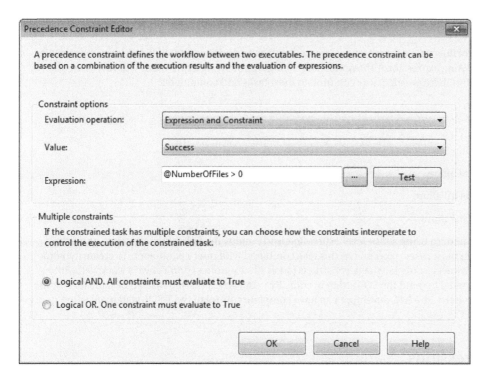

Figure 10-6. *Precedence constraint editor*

that the latter is new to SQL Server 2012—when using earlier versions of the product, you will have to enter the expression by hand without the benefit of the expression editor).

Referring back to our original package, you'll see that the precedence constraint between the first script task and the truncation SQL task now reflects the presence of an expression in the constraint Figure 10-7).

Figure 10-7. *Expression notation in precedence constraint*

It's worth noting that the example in Figure 10-7 shows a non-standard notation on the constraint. By default, only the function icon (f_x) will appear when using an expression as part of a constraint. Assuming that the expression is not a lengthy one, I typically change the ShowAnnotation option of the constraint to ConstraintOptions, which will include the expression itself on the label of the constraint. This is an easy reminder of the expression used in the constraint, and it doesn't require opening the properties window to see the expression.

Task-Level Expressions

In addition to the control flow uses of expressions, most every task and container in SSIS has its own properties that can be configured using expressions. The options for configuration using expressions will vary from one executable to the next, but there are elements common to most tasks and containers:

- Description
- Disable
- DisableValidation
- TransactionOption
- FailPackageOnFailure
- FailParentOnFailure

A common design pattern using a task-level expression is to employ the SqlStatementSource property of the Execute SQL Task. In most cases, you can use this task combined with query parameters to create dynamic statements in T-SQL. However, some language constructs (such as subqueries) don't always work well with parameters, exposing a need to build the SQL string in code. By using an expression instead of static text for the SqlStatementSource property, the ETL developer can have complete control of the T-SQL statement when query parameters don't fit.

Data Flow Expressions

Moving from the control flow into the data flow, we find the more traditional use of expressions as part of our ETL strategy. Like the higher-level executables, we find that every component in the data flow is affected either directly or indirectly by SSIS expressions.

Data Cleansing

Lightweight data cleansing is one of the most common uses of the expression language within the data flow of SSIS. Most frequently used within the derived column transformation, expressions can be used for certain cleanup tasks, including

- Changing the case of data
- Grabbing a substring from within a longer string
- Trimming extraneous space
- Replacing inappropriate characters (such as removing letters from text)
- Changing data length or type

Often, one can minimize the need for data cleansing in the data flow simply through well-designed query statements in the extraction from the various data sources. However, sometimes cleanup at the source is just not an option. Many sources of data are nonrelational: consider text files and web services as data sources, for example, which generally do not have the option of cleaning up the data before its arrival into the SSIS space. Sometimes even relational sources fit in this box as well: I've encountered a number of scenarios where the only interface to the data was through a predefined stored procedure that could neither be inspected nor changed by the ETL developer. For cases such as these where source cleansing is not possible, using expressions within the data flow is a good second-level defense.

One design pattern that I use frequently is to trim out extra whitespace and convert blank strings to NULL values. As shown in the following, such an operation could be performed with a single, relatively simple expression:

```
(LEN(TRIM([Street_Address]))>0) ? TRIM([Street_Address]) : (DT_WSTR, 100)NULL(DT_WSTR, 100)
```

Regarding data cleansing using the expression language, I will offer a brief word of caution: if you find yourself needing to do complex, multi-step cleansing operations within your SSIS packages, consider using some other means to do the heavy lifting. As I mentioned earlier, the expression language is best suited for lightweight data cleansing; because complex expressions can be difficult to develop and debug, you might instead use a richer tool such as the Script Task or Script Component, or perhaps Data Quality Services, for these advanced transformations.

Branching

Sometimes there arises the need to create forks in the road with ETL data flow. There are several reasons you might need to create branches within your data flow:

- *Different outputs*: For data that exists in a single data flow but is bound for different destinations, creating branches is an effective solution. I recall a case I worked on several years back when we were building a system to distribute data to several financial vendors. Each of these vendors required the same type of data, but each vendor would get a different "slice" of the data based on several criteria, and each required the data in a slightly different format. Rather than design multiple end-to-end data flows that would essentially duplicate much of the logic, I created a single package that employed a conditional split transformation to split the data flow based on a specified condition, and from there, the data branched out to the respective outputs.

- *Inline cleansing*: A very common ETL scenario in SSIS is to split "good" data from "bad" data within a single data flow, attempt to clean the bad data, and then merge the cleansed data with the good data. This allows you to leave intact any data that does not require cleansing, which may help to conserve processing resources.

- *Disparate data domains*: In cases where data is structurally similar but syntactically different, you might want to employ branching to handle the data differently within your data flow. Consider the example of geographical address data: although they both describe a physical address, you might need to process domestic addresses differently than you would handle international addresses. By using branching tools such as the conditional split, various address types from a single source types can be handled within one data flow task.

- *Varying metadata*: Although relatively rare, there will be the occasion where a source may contain rows with varying metadata. Consider a text file with a ragged structure in which some rows are missing columns at the end of the line. By splitting the data based on the absence of certain columns, you can account for the metadata differences inline.

Figure 10-8 exposes this design pattern by showing the use of expression logic to break apart a data stream into multiple outputs. In this case, we process a billing file by using comparison expressions within the conditional split transformation (see the callout) to determine whether each row is paid on time, not yet due, or past due, and then send it to the appropriate output accordingly.

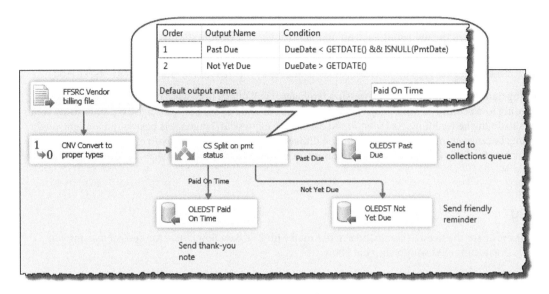

Figure 10-8. *Using expressions to define multiple paths*

One interesting caveat regarding the application of expressions within the data flow is the way in which SSIS exposes component-level expressions. Although the expression language is very useful within the pipeline of the data flow, most components do not actually expose properties that can be set using expressions. For those that do allow expressions on certain properties, these expressions are surfaced as elements of the data flow itself, and will appear as part of the options in the Data Flow Properties window while working in the control flow.

As shown in Figure 10-9, we are using the expression properties of the data flow to access the ADO.NET data source within that data flow. As you can see, the identifier in the Property column shows that this expression

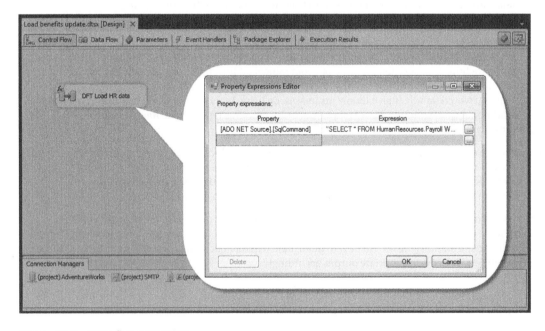

Figure 10-9. *Data flow expression*

belongs to the data source within the data flow, allowing us to set the SqlCommand property of that source. It's useful to note here that I used the ADO.NET source purposefully in this example. As this source does not currently allow the use of parameters, setting the SqlCommand property is often an acceptable substitute for dynamically retrieving data from a relational database using this component.

Application of Business Rules

Although they share some of the same methods, the application of business rules differs conceptually from data cleansing. For the most part, data cleansing is considered to be universal: misspelled words, inconsistent casing, extraneous spacing, and the NULL-versus-blank-versus-zero quandary are all common problems that must be dealt with in most every ETL process. Business rules, on the other hand, are specific use cases in which data is manipulated, extrapolated, or discarded based on custom logic that is specific to the business at hand. These rules may be general enough to apply to an entire industry (healthcare billing workflows, for example) or as specific as the arrangement of data to suit the preferences of an individual manager.

Generally speaking, the use of expressions to apply business logic works best when limited to a small number of simple business rule cases. As mentioned earlier, the expression language is not ideal for multiple test conditions, and therefore may not be ideally suited for multifaceted and complex business rules. For enterprise-level business rule application, consider other tools in SSIS such as the script component or Execute SQL task (for operations that can be performed at the relational database level), or perhaps a separate tool such as SQL Server Data Quality Services or Master Data Services.

CHOOSING BETWEEN COMPLEX EXPRESSIONS AND OTHER TOOLS

In my experience, the majority of uses of SSIS expressions involve short, simple expressions. Interrogating the value of a variable, modifying the contents of an existing column, comparing two variables, and other similar operations tend to require relatively brief and uncomplicated logic as an SSIS expression. However, there are many cases where a short-and-sweet expression just won't get it done.

In these cases of more complicated logic, is an SSIS expression still the best choice? In some instances, the answer is no. As mentioned earlier, there are instances in the ETL cycle where the expression language is ill-suited to solve the problem. In cases where the logic required involves complexity that exceeds that which is practical or convenient for the SSIS expression language, a common pattern is to engage a separate tool to address the problem hand. Some of the other methods for handling these complex logical scenarios are as follows:

- *Data source component*: Especially when working with relational source data, it can be simpler and faster (both design time and runtime) to build the necessary logic into the source component instead of using an expression in SSIS.

- *Execute SQL task*: Sometimes it's easier to load the data to a relational store and then perform transformation and cleansing there rather than doing it inline within the SSIS package. This methodology differs slightly from that of traditional ETL and is typically branded as ELT (extract/load/transform). Using this model, the Execute SQL Task could be used to transform the data once it has been loaded from the source to the relational database in which it will be transformed.

- *Script task*: When working in the control flow, you can substitute an instance of the script task in place of an overly complex SSIS expression. When using a script task for this purpose, you get the added benefits of Intellisense, error handling, multistep operations, and the ability to include comments in your code.

- *Script component*: Replaces complex expressions within the data flow, for the same reasons as above. In addition, the script component may be used as a source, transformation, or destination in the data flow surface, giving you even greater control of the manipulation of data than by strictly using expressions.

- *Custom task/component*: If you find yourself reusing the same complex logic in many packages, consider creating a custom task or component that you can distribute to multiple packages without having to copy and paste script code to each package.

- *Third party task/component*: Sometimes it's easier to buy (or borrow) than to build. There are hundreds, perhaps even thousands, of third party tasks and components designed to extend the native behaviors of SSIS. In fact, many of these tools are freely available—often with the underlying source code in case you need to further customize the behavior of the tool.

There are no hard-and-fast rules defining when an expression may not be the best solution. However, there are a few design patterns that I tend to follow when deciding whether to use an expression or some other tool when applying dynamic logic in my SSIS packages. Typically, I will avoid using expressions in situations where

- *The expression will be exceptionally lengthy.* If the logic required in an expression would exceed more than a few hundred characters, a script or other tool is often a better choice.

- *The expression requires more than three levels of nesting.* Especially in cases where if/then/else logic is required, there's frequently a need to respond to more than one condition (if/then/elseif/then/else), and unfortunately, the only way to accomplish this in the SSIS expression language is by nesting conditional operators.

- *Complex string interrogation or manipulation is required.* Simple string manipulation is easy enough through SSIS expressions with the use of well-known functions such as *SUBSTRING, REPLACE, LEFT/RIGHT, UPPER/LOWER*, and *REVERSE*. However, more advanced operations (extracting text from the middle of a string, replacing multiple patterns of character(s), extracting numbers embedded in text, etc.) usually requires overly complex expressions. Further, some text operations such as regular expression (RegEx) matching are not natively supported in the SSIS expression language.

- *The logic requires a volatile type cast.* Because the SSIS expression language has no error handling in itself, a conversion that is prone to failure (text to number, Unicode to ASCII, moving from a larger to smaller capacity of the same type) may cause an undesired interruption in your package flow. Often, I'll wrap these into a script task or script component using a TryParse() method or a try/catch block, which allows a greater amount of flexibility in the event of a type cast failure.

The bottom line is that not every ETL challenge within SSIS should be solved using expressions. The expression language was intended as a lightweight solution, and used in that context, is an outstanding supplement to the product line. Try to think of SSIS expressions as spackle; small, light, elegant, and used pervasively, but in small doses. As effective as spackle is, a building contractor would never think of building an entire house using only spackle. As with any tool, expressions in SSIS are best used in proper context and should not be considered as a one-size-fits-all solution to every problem.

Summary

ETL can be hard. Often, it's not the big design problems but the small "how do I…?" tactical questions that collectively cause the most friction during SSIS development. The SSIS expression language was designed for these types of questions. Its small footprint, somewhat familiar syntax, and extensive usability across the breadth of SSIS make it an excellent addition to the capabilities within Integration Services. Used properly, it can help to address a variety of problem domains and hopefully ease the burden on the ETL developer.

CHAPTER 11

■ ■ ■

Data Warehouse Patterns

SQL Server Integration Services is an excellent general-purpose ETL tool. Its versatility finds it used by DBAs, developers, BI professionals, and even business principals in many different scenarios. Sometimes it's a dump truck, used for the wholesale movement of enormous amounts of data. Other times it's more like a scalpel, carving out with precision just the right amount of data.

Though it is a great tool in other areas, SSIS truly excels when used as a data warehouse ETL tool. It would be hard to argue that data warehousing isn't its primary purpose in life. From native slowly changing dimension (SCD) elements to the new CDC processing tasks and components, SSIS has all the hooks it needs to compete with data warehouse ETL tools at much higher price points.

In this chapter, we'll discuss design patterns applicable to loading a data warehouse using SQL Server Integration Services. From incremental loads to error handling and general workflow, we'll investigate methodologies and best practices that can be applied in SSIS data warehouse ETL.

Incremental Loads

Anyone who has spent more than 10 minutes working in the data warehouse space has heard the term *incremental load*. Before we demonstrate design patterns for performing incremental loads, let's first touch on the need for an incremental load.

What Is an Incremental Load?

As the name implies, an incremental load is one that processes a partial set of data based only on what is new or changed since the last execution. While many consider incremental loads to be purely time based (for example, grabbing just the data processed on the prior business day), it's not always that simple. Sometimes, changes are made to historical data that should be reflected in downstream systems, and unfortunately it's not always possible to detect when changes were made. (As an aside, those ubiquitous "last update timestamp" fields are notorious for being wrong.)

Handling flexible data warehouse structures that allow not only inserts but updates as well can be a challenging proposition. In this chapter, we'll surface a few design patterns in SSIS that can be used when dealing with changing data in your data warehouse.

Why Incremental Loads?

Imagine you are hired by a small shoe store to create a system through which the staff can analyze their sales data. Let's say the store averages 50 transactions a day, amounting to an average of 100 items (2 items per transaction). If you do simple math on the row counts generated by the business, you'll end up with fewer than 200 rows of data per day being sent to the analysis system. Even over the course of the entire year, you're looking at less than 75,000 rows of data. With such a small volume of data, why would one want to perform an incremental load? After all, it would be almost as efficient to simply dump and reload the entire analytical database each night rather than try to calculate which rows are new, changed, or deleted.

In a situation like the one just described, the best course of action probably would be to perform a full load each day. However, in the real world, few, if any, systems are so small and simple. In fact, it's not at all uncommon for data warehouse developers to work in heterogeneous environments that generate millions of rows of data per day. Even with the best hardware money can buy, attempting to perform a daily full load on that volume of data simply isn't practical.

The incremental load seeks to solve this problem by allowing the systematic identification of data to be moved from transactional systems to the data warehouse. By selectively carving out only the data that requires manipulation—specifically, the rows that have been inserted, updated, or deleted since the last load—we can eliminate a lot of unnecessary and duplicate data processing.

The Slowly Changing Dimension

When you consider the application of incremental data loads in a data warehouse scenario, there's no better example than the slowly changing dimension (SCD). The nature of dimensional data is such that it often does require updates by way of manipulating existing rows in the dimension table (SCD Type 1) or expiring the current record and adding a new row for that value, thus preserving the history for that dimension attribute (SCD Type 2).

Although the slowly changing dimension is certainly not the only data warehouse structure to benefit from an incremental load, it is one of the most common species of that animal. As such, we'll focus mostly on SCD structures for talking points around incremental loads.

Incremental Loads of Fact Data

Although it is a less frequently used design pattern, some data warehouse scenarios require the changing of fact data after it has been loaded to the data warehouse. This scenario is typically handled through a secondary load with a negating entry and a delta record, but some designs require the original fact record to be corrected.

In such cases, the same methodology used for slowly changing dimension data may also apply to fact data. However, be aware that careful consideration for performance must be paid to applying SCD methods to fact data. Fact data is exponentially more voluminous than dimension data and typically involves millions, and sometimes billions, of records. Therefore, apply the SCD pattern to fact data only if you must. If there's any flexibility at all in the DW design, use the delta record approach instead.

Incremental Loads in SSIS

Microsoft SQL Server, and SSIS specifically, have several tools and methodologies available for managing incremental data loads. This section discusses design patterns around the following vehicles:

- Native SSIS components (Lookup + Conditional Split)
- Slowly Changing Dimension Wizard
- MERGE statement in T-SQL
- Change data capture (CDC)

Each of these tools is effective when used properly, though some are better suited than others for different scenarios. We'll step through the design patterns with each of these below.

Native SSIS Components

The first incremental load pattern we'll explore is that of using native components within SSIS to perform the load. Through the use of lookups, conditional splits, and OLEDB command components, we can create a simple data path through which we can processes new and changed data from our source system(s).

This design pattern is one of the most common ways to perform an incremental load using SSIS. Because all of the components used in this pattern have been around since SSIS was introduced in 2005, it's a very mature and time-tested methodology. Of all of the incremental methodologies we'll explore, this is certainly the most flexible. When properly configured, it can perform reasonably well. This is also the design pattern with the fewest external dependencies; almost any data can be used as a source, it does not require the enabling of database engine features such as CDC, and it does not require any third-party components to be installed.

The Moving Parts

Using this design pattern, the most common operations will include the following steps:

1. Extract data from the data source(s). If more than one source is used, they can be brought together using the appropriate junction component (Merge, Merge Join, or Union All transformation).

2. Using the lookup transformation, join the source data with the target table based on the business key(s).

3. Route changed rows to the target table. Unmatched rows from the above step can then be routed directly to the target table using the appropriate database destination component.

4. For the source rows that have a business key match in the target table, compare the other values that may change. If any of those source values differs from the value found for that row in the destination table, those rows in the destination table will be updated with the new values.

Figure 11-1 shows a typical data flow design for these operations. You can see in the first callout that we need to set the option on the lookup transformation to "Redirect rows to no match output." Using this setting, any source rows that are not resolved to an existing row in the destination table are sent down an alternate path—in this case, directly to the destination table.

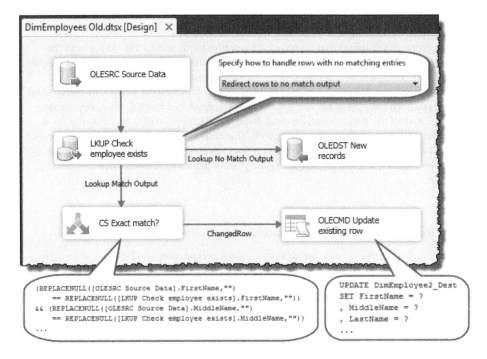

Figure 11-1. *Incremental load using atomic SSIS components*

Next, we'll apply the conditional split transformation to the matched rows. As shown in the snippet within the callout on the lower left, we'll use a bit of the SSIS expression language to compare equivalent columns between source and destination. Any rows with an exact match will not go through any further processing (though you could send them to a row count transformation if you want to capture the count of source rows with no action taken).

Finally, the rows that matched the business key but not the subsequent attribute values will be sent to the OLEDB command transformation. The callout on the lower right in Figure 11-1 shows a snippet of the SQL code in which we perform a parameterized update of each row in the destination table. It is important to note that the OLEDB command transformation performs a row-by-row update against the target table. We can typically leverage this pattern as shown because most incremental operations are heavy on new rows and have far fewer updates than inserts. However, if a particular implementation requires the processing of a very large amount of data, or if your data exploration indicates that the number of updates is proportionally high, consider modifying this design pattern to send those rows meant for update out to a staging table where they can be more efficiently processed in a set-based operation.

Typical Uses

As mentioned previously, this incremental load design pattern is quite useful and mature. This pattern fits especially well when dealing with non-relational source data, or when it's not possible to stage incoming data before processing. This is often the go-to design for incremental loads, and it fits most such scenarios reasonably well.

Do keep in mind that, because we're performing the business key lookup and the column equivalency tests within SSIS, some resource costs are associated with getting the data into the SSIS memory space and then performing said operations against the data. Therefore, if a particular implementation involves a very large amount of data, and the source data is already in a SQL Server database (or could be staged there), another design pattern such as the T-SQL MERGE operation (to be covered shortly) might be a better option.

The following subsections describe components of the incremental load pattern and configuration options for each.

Lookup Caching Options

When performing lookup operations, you want to consider the many options available for managing lookup caching. Depending on the amount of data you're dealing with, one of the following caching design patterns may help to reduce performance bottlenecks.

Table Cache

A table cache for lookups is populated prior to executing a Data Flow Task requiring the lookup operation. The table can be created and dropped as needed by SSIS using Execute SQL Tasks. It can be populated via Execute SQL Task or a Data Flow Task. Most of the time, the data needed to build a table cache is local to the destination and contains data from the destination, so I often use T-SQL in an Execute SQL Task to populate it.

Maintaining the table cache can be accomplished via truncate-and-load. For larger sets of lookup data, you may wish to consider maintaining the table cache using incremental load techniques. This may sound like overkill, but when you need perform a lookup against a billion-row table (it happens, trust me), the incremental approach starts to make sense.

Cache Transformation and Cache Connection Manager

If you find you need to look up the same data in multiple Data Flow Tasks, consider using the Cache Tranformation along with the Cache Connection Manager. The Cache Connection Manager provides a memory-resident copy of the data supplied via the Cache Transformation. The Cache is loaded prior to the first Data Flow Task that will consume the lookup data, and the data can be consumed directly by a Lookup Transformation. Pre-caching data in this manner supports lookups, but it also provides a way to "mark" sets of rows for other considerations such as loading. Later in this chapter, we will explore late-arriving data and discuss patterns for managing it. One way to manage the scenario of data continuing to arrive *after* the load operation has started is to create a cache of primary and foreign keys that represent completed transactions, and then join to those keys in Data Flow Tasks throughout the load process. Will you miss last-second data loading in this way? Yes, you will. But your data will contain complete transactions. One benefit of executing incremental loads with table-caches is the ability to execute the load each month, week, evening, or every five minutes; only complete transactions that have arrived since the last load executed will be loaded.

If you find you need to use the same lookup data across many SSIS packages (or that the cache is larger than the amount of available server RAM), the Cache Connection Manager can persist its contents to disk. The Cache Connection Manager makes use of the new and improved RAW file format, a proprietary format for storing data directly from a Data Flow Task to disk, completely bypassing Connection Managers. Reads and writes are very fast as a result, and the new format persists column names and data types.

Load Staging

Another pattern worth mentioning here is Load Staging. Consider the following scenario: a data warehouse destination table is large and grows often. Since the destination is used during the load window, dropping keys and indexes is not an option to improve load performance. All related data must become available in the data warehouse at roughly the same time to maintain source-transactional consistency. By nature, the data does not lend itself to partitioning. What to do?

Consider load staging, where all the data required to represent a source-transaction is loaded into stage tables on the destination. Once these tables are populated, you can use Execute SQL Tasks to insert the staged rows into the data warehouse destination table. If timed properly, you may be able to use a bulk insert to accomplish the load. Often, data loads between tables in the same SQL Server instance can be accomplished more efficiently using T-SQL rather than the buffered SSIS Data Flow Task. How can you tell which will perform better? Test it!

The Slowly Changing Dimension Wizard

The Slowly Changing Dimension Wizard is another veteran of the SSIS incremental load arsenal. As its name implies, it is designed specifically for managing SCD elements in a data warehouse. However, its use is certainly not limited to dimension processing.

The SCD Wizard has been a part of SSIS ever since the product's introduction in 2005. At first glance, it is the natural choice for handling slowly changing dimension data in SSIS. This tool is built right into Integration Services, and it is designed specifically for the purpose of SCD processing.

The SCD Wizard is surfaced as a transformation in SSIS and is leveraged by connecting the output of a data source (the incoming data) to the input of the SCD transformation. Editing the SCD transformation will kick off the wizard, as shown in Figure 11-2.

Figure 11-2. *The SCD Wizard showing alignment of columns between source and destination*

From there, the wizard will guide you through the selection of the necessary elements of the slowly changing dimension configuration, including the following:

- Which columns should be engaged as part of the slowly changing dimension, along with the option to handle changes as simple updates (Type 1) or historical values (Type 2)

- How to identify current vs. expired rows, if any Type 2 columns are present; you can specify either a flag or a date span to indicate currency of SCD records

- How to handle inferred members (discussed in more depth shortly)

Upon completion of the SCD Wizard, several new elements are automagically added to the data flow. Figure 11-3 shows an example of the transformations and destinations added when using a combination of Type 1 and Type 2 fields, fixed attribute (static) fields, and inferred member support. The SCD Wizard adds only those components pertinent to the design specified, so the final result may look a bit different than the example in this figure depending on how the wizard is configured.

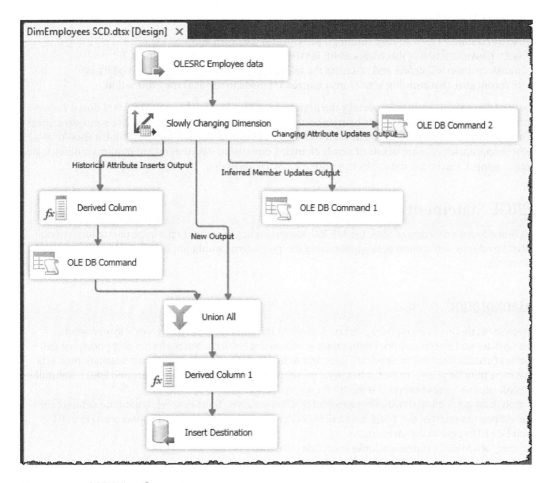

Figure 11-3. *SCD Wizard output*

Of all of the slowly changing dimension design patterns, the SCD Wizard is arguably the easiest to use for simple SCD scenarios, and it offers the fastest turnaround at design time. For small, simple dimensions, the wizard can be an effective tool for managing changing data.

However, the SCD Wizard does have some significant drawbacks.

- *Performance.* The wizard performs reasonably well against small sets of data. However, because many of the operations are performed on a row-by-row basis, leveraging this transformation against sizeable dimensions can cause a significant performance bottleneck. Some data warehouse architects have strong feelings against the SCD Wizard, and this is often the chief complaint.

- *Destructive changes.* As I mentioned, when you run the wizard, all of the required transformations and destinations are created automatically. Similarly, if you reconfigure the SCD transformation (for example, changing a column type from a Type 1 to a Type 2 historical), the existing design elements are removed and added back to the data flow. As a result, any changes that you've made to that data path will be lost if you make a change to the SCD transformation.

- *No direct support for auditing.* Although you can add your own auditing logic, it's not a native function of this component. Further, because any changes to the SCD transformation will delete and re-create the relevant elements of the data flow, you'll have to reconfigure that auditing logic if any changes are made to the SCD transformation.

As a result of these shortcomings (especially the performance implications), the SCD Wizard doesn't see a lot of action in the real world. I don't want to beat up on this tool too much because it does have some usefulness, and I don't necessarily recommend that you avoid it completely. However, like any specialty tool, it should be used only where appropriate. For small sets of slowly changing dimension data that do not require complex logic or specialized logging, it can be the most effective option for SCD processing.

The MERGE Statement

Although technically not a function of SSIS, the MERGE statement has become such a large part of incremental data loads that any discussion around data warehousing design patterns would not be complete without coverage of this tool.

A Little Background

Prior to version 2008, there was no native upsert (UPdate/inSERT) in Microsoft SQL Server. Any operation that blended updates and inserts required either the use of a cursor (which often performs very poorly) or two separate queries (usually resulting in duplicate logic and redundant effort). Other relational database products have had this capability for years—in fact, it has been present in Oracle since version 9i (around 2001). Naturally, SQL Server professionals were chomping at the bit for such capabilities.

Fortunately, they got their wish with the release of SQL Server 2008. That version featured the debut of the new MERGE statement as part of the T-SQL arsenal. MERGE allows three simultaneous operations (INSERT, UPDATE, and DELETE) against the target table.

The anatomy of a MERGE statement looks something like this:

1. Specify the source data.

2. Specify the target table.

3. Choose the columns on which to join the source and target data.

4. Indicate the column alignment between the two sets of data, to be used for determining whether matched records are different in some way.

5. Define the logic for cases when the data is changed, or if it exists in only either the source or the destination.

The new MERGE capabilities are useful for DBAs and database developers alike. However, for data warehouse professionals, MERGE was a game changer in terms of managing slowly changing dimension data. Not only did this new capability provide an easier way to perform upsert operations, but it also performed very well.

MERGE in Action

Since there are no native (read: graphical) hooks to the MERGE statement in Integration Services, the implementation of MERGE in an SSIS package is done through an Execute SQL task.

To explore this design pattern, let's first examine the typical flow for using the T-SQL MERGE functionality within a data warehouse SSIS load package. Again, we'll use the slowly changing dimension scenario as a basis for exploration, but much of the same logic would apply to other uses of MERGE.

As part of an SCD MERGE upsert process, our SSIS package would contain tasks to perform the following functions:

1. Remove previously staged data from the staging table.

2. Load the staging table from the source system.

3. Clean up the staged data (if required).

4. Execute the MERGE statement to upsert the staged data to the dimension table.

5. Log the upsert operation (optional).

A typical control flow design pattern is shown in Figure 11-4.

```
DimEmployees MERGE.dtsx [Design]  ×

  [ ] SQL Truncate        [ ] DFT Load data to      [ ] SQL Cleanse         [ ] SQL Merge data
      Stage Tbl               stage tbl                 staged data


MERGE dbo.DimEmployee2_Dest AS target                    -- Destination table
USING (SELECT * FROM staging.DimEmployee) AS source       -- Staging table
ON target.PersonID = source.PersonID                      -- Match parameters
WHEN MATCHED AND NOT (
    source.FirstName = ISNULL(target.FirstName, '')
    AND source.MiddleName = ISNULL(target.MiddleName, '')
    AND source.LastName = ISNULL(target.LastName, '')
    AND source.Gender = ISNULL(target.Gender, '')
    AND source.MaritalStatus = ISNULL(target.MaritalStatus, '')
    AND source.BirthDate = ISNULL(target.BirthDate, '1/1/1900')
    AND source.LoginID = ISNULL(target.LoginID, '')
    AND source.JobTitle = ISNULL(target.JobTitle, '')
    AND source.HireDate = ISNULL(target.HireDate, '1/1/1900')
    AND source.EmpStatus = ISNULL(target.EmpStatus, 1)
)
THEN UPDATE                      -- PersonID exists but records are different :: UPDATE
    SET target.FirstName = source.FirstName
    , target.MiddleName = source.MiddleName
    , target.LastName = source.LastName
    , target.Gender = source.Gender
    , target.MaritalStatus = source.MaritalStatus
    , target.BirthDate = source.BirthDate
    , target.LoginID = source.LoginID
    , target.JobTitle = source.JobTitle
    , target.HireDate = source.HireDate
    , target.EmpStatus = source.EmpStatus
WHEN NOT MATCHED BY target       -- PersonID does not exist in target table :: Insert
THEN INSERT (PersonID, FirstName, MiddleName, LastName, Gender, MaritalStatus
    , BirthDate, LoginID, JobTitle, HireDate, EmpStatus
    )
    Values (source.PersonID, source.FirstName, source.MiddleName, source.LastName
    , source.Gender, source.MaritalStatus, source.BirthDate, source.LoginID
    , source.JobTitle, source.HireDate, source.EmpStatus
    )
OUTPUT $action, inserted.*;      -- Capture updated/inserted data for auditing
```

Figure 11-4. *Using MERGE against a slowly changing dimension table*

Also note the large callout in Figure 11-4 with the T-SQL code used for the MERGE statement. In the interest of maintaining focus, I won't try to provide comprehensive coverage of the MERGE statement here, but I'll point out a couple of the high points:

- The ON clause (third line) indicates the field on which we join the source data with the destination data. Note that we can use multiple fields on which to align the two sets.

- The 10-line code block following WHEN MATCHED AND NOT... indicates which of the fields will be checked to see if the data in the destination table differs from the source data. In this case, we're checking ten different fields, and we'll process an update to the destination if any of those fields is different between source and destination. Also note the liberal use of the ISNULL() function against the destination table. This is recommended to ensure that NULL values in the destination table are not inadvertently skipped during the MERGE.

- In the code block immediately following, we'll update rows in the target table that have a valid match against the source but have one or more values that differ between the two.

- In the code block beginning with WHEN NOT MATCHED BY target ..., any source rows not matched to the specified key column(s) of an existing dimension record will be written as new rows to that dimension table.

- Finally, we use the OUTPUT clause to select the action description and insert data. We can use the output of this to write to our auditing table (more on that momentarily).

You'll notice that we're handling this dimension processing as a Type 1 dimension, in which we intentionally overwrite the previous values and do not maintain an historical record of past values. It is possible to use the MERGE command to process Type 2 dimensions that retain historical values, or even those with a mixture of Type 1 and Type 2 attributes. In the interest of brevity I won't try to cover the various other uses of MERGE as it applies to slowly changing dimensions, but I think you'll find that it's flexible enough to handle most Type 1 and Type 2 dimensions.

Also worth noting is that the MERGE statement can also be used to delete data in addition to performing inserts and updates. It's not as common in data warehouse environments as in other settings to delete data, but it may occasionally be necessary to delete data from the target table.

Auditing with MERGE

As with other data warehouse operations, it's considered a best practice to audit, at a minimum, the row counts of dimensional data that is added, deleted, or changed. This is especially true for MERGE operations. Because multiple operations can occur in the same statement, it's important to be able to track those operations to assist with troubleshooting, even if comprehensive auditing is not used in a given operation.

The MERGE statement does have a provision for auditing the various data operations. As shown in the example in Figure 11-4, we can use the OUTPUT clause to select out of the MERGE statement the insert, update, or delete operations. This example shows a scenario where the data changes would be selected as a result set from the query, which could subsequently be captured into a package variable in SSIS and processed from there. Alternatively, one could modify the OUTPUT clause to insert data directly into an audit table without returning a result set to SSIS.

Change Data Capture (CDC)

Along with the MERGE capability, another significant incremental load feature first surfaced in SQL Server 2008: change data capture. CDC is a feature of the database engine that allows the collection of data changes to monitored tables.

Without jumping too far off track, here's just a bit about how CDC works. CDC is a supply-side incremental load tool that is enabled first at the database level and then implemented on a table-by-table basis via capture instances. Once enabled for a table, the database engine uses the transaction log to track all DML operations (inserts, updates, and deletes), logging each change to the change table for each monitored table. The change table contains not only the fact that there was a change to the data, but it also maintains the history of those changes. Downstream processes can then consume just the changes (rather than the entire set of data) and process the inserts, updates, and deletes in any dependent systems.

CDC in Integration Services

SSIS can consume CDC data in a couple of different ways. First, using common native SSIS components, you can access the change table to capture the data changes. Keeping track of which changes have been processed by SSIS can be done by capturing and storing the log sequence number (LSN) by using a set of system stored procedures created when CDC is enabled.

The manual methods are still valid; however, new to SSIS in SQL Server 2012 is an entirely new set of tools for interfacing with CDC data. Integration Services now comes packaged with a new task and two new components that help to streamline the processing of CDC data:

- *CDC Control Task.* This task is used for managing the metadata around CDC loads. Using the CDC Control Task, you can track the start and end points of the initial (historical) load, as well as retrieve and store the processing range for an incremental load.

- *CDC Source.* The CDC Source is used to retrieve data from the CDC change table. It receives the CDC state information from the CDC Control Task by way of an SSIS variable, and it will selectively retrieve the changed data using that marker.

- *CDC Splitter.* The CDC Splitter is a transformation that will branch the changed data out into its various operations. Effectively a specialized conditional split transformation, it will use the CDC information received from the CDC Source and send the rows to the Insert, Update, Delete, or Error path accordingly.

For the purposes of reviewing CDC capabilities as part of an SSIS incremental load strategy, we'll stick with the new task and components present in SSIS 2012. In systems using SQL Server 2008, know that the same objectives can be met by employing the manual extraction and LSN tracking briefly described previously.

Change Detection in General

Detecting changes in data is a sub-science of data integration. Much has been written on the topic from sources too numerous to list. Although CDC provides handy change detection in SQL Server, it was possible (and necessary!) to achieve change detection before the advent of CDC. It is important to note that CDC is not available in all editions of SQL Server; it is also not available in other relational database engines.

Do not fear: CDC is not required to detect data changes!

Checksum-Based Detection

One early pattern for change detection was using the Transact-SQL Checksum function. Checksum accepts a string as an argument and generates a numeric hash value. But Checksum performance has proven less than ideal, generating the *same* number for different string values. Steve Jones blogged about this behavior in a post entitled SQL Server Encryption - Hashing Collisions (`www.sqlservercentral.com/blogs/steve_jones/2009/06/01/sql-server-encryption-hashing-collisions/`). Michael Coles provided rich evidence to support Steve's claims in the post's comments (`www.sqlservercentral.com/blogs/steve_jones/2009/06/01/sql-server-encryption-hashing-collisions/#comments`). In short, the odds of collision with Checksums are substantial, and you should not use the Checksum function for change detection.

What can you use?

Detection via Hashbytes

One good alternative to Checksum is the Hashbytes function. Like Checksum, Hashbytes provides value hashing for a string value or variable. Checksum returns an integer value; Hashbytes returns a binary value. Checksum uses an internal algorithm to calculate the hash; Hashbytes uses standard encryption algorithms. The sheer number of values available to each function is one reason Hashbytes is a better choice. Checksum's int data type can return roughly $+/-2^{31}$ values, whereas Hashbytes can return $+/-2^{127}$ values for MD2, MD4, and MD5 algorithms and $+/-2^{159}$ values for SHA and SHA1 algorithms.

Brute Force Detection

Believe it or not, a "brute force" value comparison between sources and destinations remains a viable option for change detection. How does it work? You acquire the destination values by way of either a second Source component or a Lookup Transformation in the SSIS Data Flow Task. You match the rows in source and destination by alternate (or business) key—a value or combination of values that uniquely identifies the row in both source and destination—and then compare the non-key column values in the source row to the non-key values in the destination row.

Remember, you are attempting to isolate *changes*. It is assumed you have separated the new rows—data that exists in the source and not in the destination—and perhaps you have even detected deleted rows that exist in the destination but are no longer found in the source. Changed and unchanged rows remain. Unchanged rows are just that: the alternate keys align as do every other value in each source and destination column. Changed rows, however, have identical alternate keys and one or more *differences* in the source and destination columns. Comparing the column values as shown in Figure 1-1 earlier in this chapter—accounting for the possibility of NULLs—remains an option.

Historical Load

There should be a separate process to populate the historical data for each of the tracked CDC tables. This historical load is designed to be executed just once, and it would load data to the destination system from as far back as is required. As shown in Figure 11-5, two CDC control tasks are required. The first one (configured as shown in the callout) is used to set the beginning boundary of the data capture. With this information, the CDC Control Task writes the CDC state to the specified state table. The second CDC Control Task marks the end point of the initial load, updating the state table so the appropriate starting point will be used on subsequent incremental loads. Between these two tasks sits the data flow, which facilitates the historical load of the target table.

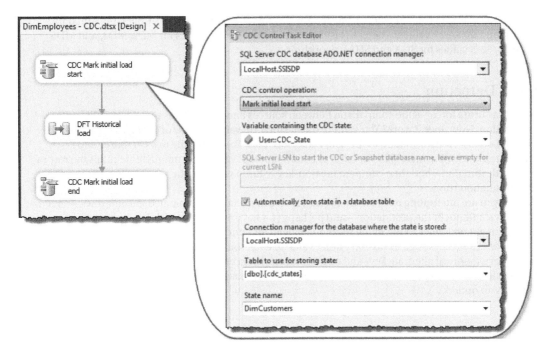

Figure 11-5. *CDC task for an initial historical load*

Incremental Load

Because of the inherent differences between historical loads and incremental loads, it's almost always preferable to create separate packages (or package groups) for each of these. Although there are similarities, there are enough differences to justify separating the logic into different sandboxes.

For the control flow elements of the historical load, this incremental load pattern will also use two CDC Control Tasks with a data flow between them. We'll need to slightly change the configuration of these tasks so that we retrieve and then update the current processing range of the CDC operation. As shown in Figure 11-6, we'll set the operation for the first of these as "Get processing range," which would be followed by "Update processing range" after the incremental load is complete.

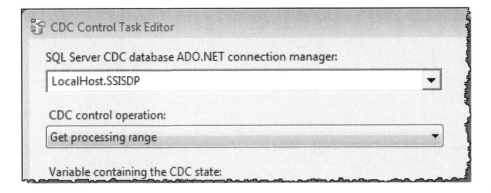

Figure 11-6. *Get processing range for CDC incremental load*

■ **Note**   The CDC Control Task is a versatile tool that includes several processing modes to handle various CDC phases, including dealing with a snapshot database or quiescence database as a source. A complete listing of the processing modes can be found here: `http://msdn.microsoft.com/en-us/library/hh231079.aspx`

Within the data flow, the CDC source should be set with the table from which to capture, the capture instance, and the processing mode. In this case, we're going to use "Net" to retrieve the net changes to the CDC table. See Figure 11-7.

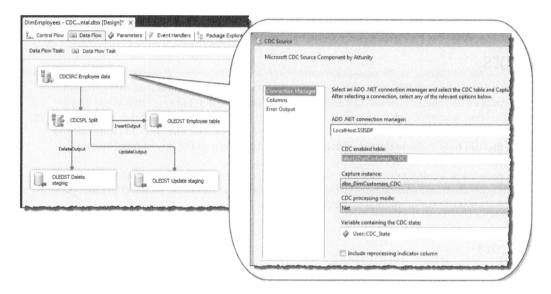

Figure 11-7. *CDC source*

The CDC Splitter breaks apart the data stream and sends rows out to the insert, update, and delete outputs. From there, we'll write the update and delete rows to a staging table so we can process those as high-performance, set-based operations. The insert records can go directly into the output table.

It's worth mentioning here that several CDC processing modes are available through the CDC Source component. The example in Figure 11-7 illustrated the use of the Net setting, which is the most common mode in most data warehouse scenarios. However, depending on the ETL requirements and source system design, you may opt for one of the other processing modes, as follows:

- *All:* Lists each change in the source, not just the net result

- *All with old values:* Includes each change plus the old values for updated records

- *Net with update mask:* Is for monitoring changes to a specific column in the monitored table

- *Net with merge:* Is similar to Net, but the output is optimized for consumption by the T-SQL MERGE statement

Typical Uses

CDC represents a shift in the incremental load methodology. The other methods described here apply a downstream approach to incremental loading, with a minimally restrictive extraction from the source and a decision point late in the ETL flow. CDC, on the other hand, processes the change logic further upstream, which can help lighten the load on SSIS and other moving parts in the ETL.

If CDC is in place (or could be implemented) in a source system, it's certainly worth considering using this design pattern to process incremental loads. It can perform well, can reduce network loads due to processing fewer rows from the source, and requires fewer resources on the ETL side. It's not appropriate for every situation, but CDC can be an excellent way to manage incremental loads in SQL Server Integration Services.

Keep in mind that the use of CDC as a design pattern isn't strictly limited to Microsoft SQL Server databases. CDC may also be leveraged against CDC-enabled Oracle database servers.

Data Errors

Longfellow once wrote, "Into each life some rain must fall." The world of ETL is no different, except that rain comes in the form of errors, often as a result of missing or invalid data. We don't always know when they're going to occur. However, given enough time, something is going to go wrong: late-arriving dimension members, packages executed out of order, or just plain old bad data. The good news is that there are data warehousing design patterns that can help mitigate the risk of data anomalies that interrupt the execution of Integration Services packages.

To address patterns of handling missing data, we're going to concentrate mostly on missing dimension members, as this is the most frequent cause of such errors. However, you can extend some of the same patterns to other elements that are part of or peripheral to data warehousing.

Simple Errors

The vast majority of errors can and should be handled inline, or simply prevented before they occur. Consider the common case of data truncation: you have a character type field that's expected to contain no more than 50 characters, so you set the data length accordingly. Months later, you get a late-night phone call (most likely when you're on vacation or when you're out at a karaoke bar with your fellow ETL professionals) informing you that the SSIS package has failed because of a truncation error. Yep, the party's over.

We've all been bitten before by the truncation bug or one of its cousins—the invalid data type error, the unexpected NULL/blank value error, or the out-of-range error. In many cases, however, these types of errors can be handled through defensive ETL strategies. By using tasks and components that detect and subsequently correct or redirect nonconforming rows, we can handle minor data errors such as this without bubbling up a failure that stops the rest of the ETL from processing.

Missing Data

With respect to data warehousing, a more common example of handling errors inline is the case of late arriving dimension data. As shown in Figure 11-8, the typical pattern is to load the dimensions first, followed by a load of the fact tables. This helps to ensure that the fact records will find a valid dimension key when the former is loaded to the data warehouse.

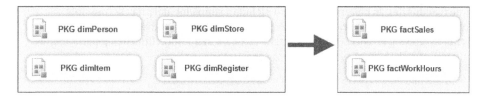

Figure 11-8. *Typical data warehouse methodology of loading dimensions, then facts*

However, this pattern breaks down when attempting to process fact records that reference dimension data that does not yet exist in the data warehouse. Consider the case of holiday retail sales: because things happen so quickly at the retail level during the end-of-year holiday season, it's not uncommon for last-minute items to appear at a store's dock with little or no advance notice. Large companies (retailers included) often have multiple systems used for different purposes that may or may not be in sync, so a last-minute item entered in the point-of-sale (POS) system may not yet be loaded in the sales forecasting system. As a result, an attempt to load a data warehouse with both POS and forecasting data may not fit this model because we would have fact data from the sales system that does not yet have the required dimension rows from the forecasting system.

At this point, if the decision is made to handle this issue inline, there are a few different methodogies we can use. These are described next.

Use the Unknown Member

The fastest and simplest pattern to address the issue of missing dimension members is to push fact records with missing dimension data into the fact table while marking that dimension value as unknown. In this case, the fact records in question would be immediately available in the data warehouse; however, all of the unknowns would, by default, be grouped together for analytical purposes. This pattern generally works best when the fact record alone does not contain the required information to create a unique new dimension record.

This design pattern is fleshed out in Figure 11-9. Using the No Match output of the lookup transformation, we're sending the fact records not matched to an existing [Item] dimension member to an instance of the derived column transformation, which sets the value of the missing dimension record to the unknown member for that dimension (in most cases, represented by a key value of -1). The matched and unmatched records are then brought back together using the "union all" transformation.

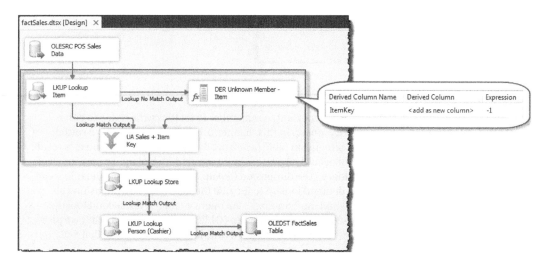

Figure 11-9. *Using Unknown Member for missing dimension member*

It is important to note that this design pattern should also include a supplemental process (possibly consisting of just a simple SQL statement) to periodically attempt to match these modified facts with their proper dimension records. This follow-up step is required to prevent the fact data in question from being permanently linked to the unknown member for that dimension.

Add the Missing Dimension Member

Using this design pattern, missing dimension records are added on the fly as part of the fact package, using as much dimension data as is provided by the fact data. In this scenario, the fact records are immediately available in the data warehouse, just like the previous design pattern, but this methodology has the added benefit of matching the fact record to its proper dimension member. In most cases, this allows the immediate association to the correct dimension data rather than grouping the unmatched data into the unknown member bucket.

Like the previous pattern, this method does come with a couple of caveats. First of all, the fact record must contain all of the information to 1) satisfy the table constraints (such as NOT NULL restrictions) on the dimension table, and 2) create a uniquely identifiable dimension row using the business key column(s). Also, since we're deriving the newly added dimension member from the incoming fact records, it can be reasonably assumed in most cases that the incoming fact data will not completely describe the dimension member. For that reason, this design pattern should also be complemented with a process that attempts to fill in the missing dimension elements (which may already be addressed as part of a comprehensive slowly changing dimension strategy).

As shown in Figure 11-10, we use a methodology similar to the previous example. However, instead of simply assigning the value of the unknown member using the derived column transformation, we leverage an instance of the OLEDB command transformation to insert into the dimension table the data for that missing dimension record in the fact table. The SQL statement is shown in the callout, and in the properties of the OLEDB command we map the placeholders (indicated by question marks) to the appropriate values from the fact record.

After adding the missing member, we send those rows to a secondary ItemID lookup, which will attempt (successfully, unless something goes terribly wrong) to match the previously unmatched data with the newly

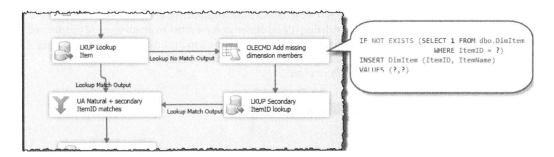

Figure 11-10. Add missing dimension member

added dimension records in the DimItem table. It is important to remember to set the cache mode to either Partial Cache or No Cache when using a secondary lookup in this manner. The default lookup cache setting (Full Cache) will buffer the contents of the Item dimension table *before* the data flow is initiated, and as a result none of the rows added during package execution would be present in this secondary lookup. To prevent all of these redirected fact rows from failing the secondary Item dimension lookup, use one of the non-default cache methods to force the package to perform an on-demand lookup to include the newly added dimension values.

Regarding the secondary lookup transformation methodology, one might wonder if the second lookup is even necessary. After all, if we perform the insert in the previous step (OLEDB command), couldn't we just collect the new Item dimension key value (a SQL Server table identity value, in most cases) using that SQL statement? The answer is a qualified *yes*, and in my experience that is the simpler of the two options. However, I've also found that some ETL situations—in particular, the introduction of parallel processes performing the same on-the-fly addition of dimension members—can cloud the issue of collecting the identity value of the most recently inserted record. From that perspective, I lean toward using the secondary lookup in cases such as this.

Triage the Lookup Failures

For missing dimension records, the most common approaches typically involve one of the preceding. However, on occasion it will be necessary to delay the processing of fact records that do not match an existing dimension record. In cases such as this, you'll need to create a triage table that will store the interim records until they can be successfully matched to the proper dimension.

As shown in Figure 11-11, we're adding a couple of additional components to the ETL pipeline for this design pattern. At the outset, we need to use two separate sources of data: one to bring in the new data from the source system, and the other for reintroducing previously triaged data into the pipeline. Further into the data flow, the example shows that we are redirecting the unmatched fact records to another table rather than trying to fix the data inline.

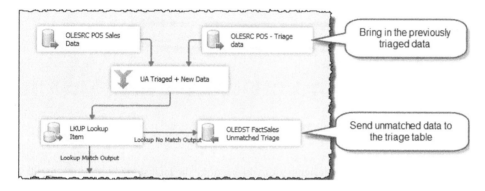

Figure 11-11. *Use triage table to store unmatched fact data*

As an aside, this pattern could be modified to support manual intervention for correcting failed lookups as well. If the business and technical requirements are such that the unmatched fact data must be reviewed and corrected by hand (as opposed to a systematic cleanup), you could eliminate the triage source so that the triage data is not reintroduced into the data flow.

Coding to Allow Errors

Although it may sound like an oxymoron, it's actually a common practice to code for known errors. In my experience, the nature of most ETL errors dictates that the package execution can continue, and any errors or anomalies that cannot be addressed inline are triaged as shown in the previous example (with the appropriate notification to the person responsible, if manual intervention is required) for later resolution. However, there are situations where the data warehouse ETL process should be designed to fail if error conditions arise.

Consider the case of financial data. Institutions that store or process financial data are subject to frequent and comprehensive audits, and for inconsistent data to appear in a governmental review of the data could spell disaster for the organization and its officers. Even though a data warehouse may not be subject to the same to-the-penny auditing scrutiny as OLTP systems, there is still an expectation of consistency when matters of money and governmental regulation are involved. In the case of a data warehouse load where nonconforming data is encountered, quite possibly the best thing to occur is that the package would fail gracefully, rolling back any changes made as part of the load.

Fail Package on Error

Extending the financial data example mentioned previously, let's examine the design pattern to facilitate a failure in the event of a lookup error. In reality, this is the default behavior. As shown in Figure 11-12, we use the default setting of Fail component on the lookup components, which stops the execution of the package if a row is encountered that cannot be matched to either the GL Account or GL Subaccount lookup.

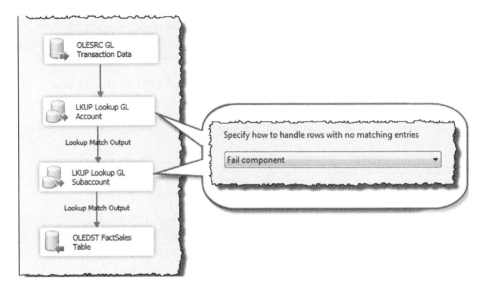

Figure 11-12. *Allow package to fail upon error*

It's worth noting here that a proper use of this design pattern does require the inclusion of some logic to roll back changes due to a partial load. If a fact row not matching one of the lookup components is encountered, the package will still fail; however, rows preceding the errored row that have already been sent to the destination may be commited to that table before the failure and could cause the whole of the data to be in an inconsistent state.

There are several ways to accomplish this rollback behavior:

- *SSIS transactions:* Integration Services natively has the ability to wrap tasks and containers into transactions and, in theory, will reverse any durable changes to the relational database in the event of an error in the scope of that transaction. In practice, however, I've found that using the SSIS transaction functionality can be challenging even on a good day. Leveraging transactions directly in SSIS requires a lot of things to align at once: all involved systems must support DTC transactions, the DTC service must be running and accessible at each of those endpoints, and all relevant tasks and connections in SSIS must support transactions.

- *Explicit SQL transactions:* This method involves manually creating a transaction in SSIS by executing the T-SQL command to engage a relational transaction on the database engine. Using this method, you essentially create your own transaction container by explicitly declaring the initialization and COMMIT point (or ROLLBACK, in the event of an error) using the Execute SQL Task. On the database connection, you'll need to set the RetainSameConnection property to True to ensure that all operations reuse the same connection and, by extension, the same transaction. Although this method does require some additional work, it's the more straightforward and reliable of the two transactional methods of strategic rollback.

- *Explicit cleanup:* This design pattern involves creating your own environment-specific cleanup routines to reverse the changes due to a failed partial load, and it typically does not engage database transactions for rollback purposes. This method requires the most effort in terms of development and maintenance, but it also allows the greatest amount of flexibility if you need to selectively undo changes made during a failed package execution.

Unhandled Errors

I'm certain that the gentleman who came up with Murphy's Law was working as a data warehouse ETL developer. Dealing with data from disparate systems is often an ugly process! Although we can defensively code around many common issues, eventually some data anomaly will introduce unexpected errors.

To make sure that any error or other data anomaly does not cause the ETL process to abruptly terminate, it's advisable to build in some safety nets to handle any unexpected errors. You'll find more information about capturing errors in Appendix A.

Data Warehouse ETL Workflow

Most of what has been covered in this chapter so far has been core concepts about the loading of data warehouses. I'd like to briefly change gears and touch on the topic of SSIS package design with respect to workflow. Data warehouse ETL systems tend to have a lot of moving parts, and the workload to develop those pieces is often distributed to multiple developers. Owing to a few lessons learned the hard way, I've developed a workflow design pattern of package atomicity.

Dividing Up the Work

I've told this story in a couple of presentations I've done, and it continues to be amusing (to me, anyway) to think about ever having done things this way. The first production SSIS package of any significance that I deployed was created to move a large amount of data from multiple legacy systems into a new SQL Server database. It started off rather innocently; it initially appeared that the ETL logic would be much simpler than what it eventually became, so I wrapped everything into a single package. I realized once I was well into the project that it might get ugly, but, like pulling at a loose thread on a fine sweater, I couldn't find a smooth point at which to stop.

In the end, the resulting SSIS package was enormous. There were 30, maybe 40, different data flows (some with multiple sources/destinations and complex transformation logic) and dozens of other helper tasks intermingled. The resulting .dtsx file size was about 5MB just for the XML metadata! Needless to say, every time I opened this package in Visual Studio, it would take several minutes to run through all of the validation steps.

This extremely large SSIS package worked fine, and technically there was nothing wrong with the design. Its sheer size did bring to light some challenges that are present in working with large, do-everything packages, and as a result of that experience I reengineered my methodology for atomic package design.

One Package = One Unit of Work

With respect to data warehouse ETL, I've found that the best solution in most cases is to break apart logical units of work into separate packages, in which each package does just one thing. By splitting up the workload, you can avoid a number of potential snags and increase your productivity as an ETL developer. Some of the considerations for smaller SSIS packages include the following:

- *Less time spent waiting on design-time validation.* SQL Server Data Tools has a rich interface that provides, among other things, a near real-time evaluation of potential metadata problems in the SSDT designer. If, for example, a table that is accessed by the SSIS package is changed, the developer will be presented with a warning (or an error, if applicable) in SSDT indicating that metadata accessed by the package has changed. This constant metadata validation is beneficial in that it can help to identify potential problems before they are pushed out for testing. There's also a performance cost associated with this. The length of time required for validation increases as the size of the package increases, so naturally keeping the packages as small as practical will cut down on the amount of time you're drumming your fingers on your desk waiting for validation to complete.

- *Easier testing and deployment.* A single package that loads, say, 10 dimensions has a lot of moving parts. When developing each of the dimensions within the package, there is no easy way to test just one element of the package (apart from manually running it in the SSDT designer, which isn't a completely realistic test for a package that will eventually be deployed to the server). The only realistic test for such a package would be to test the entire package as a server-based execution, which may be overkill if you're only interested in one or two changed properties. Further, it's not uncommon for organizations with formal software testing and promotion procedures to require that the entire thing be retested, not just the new or changed elements. By breaking up operations into smaller units, testing and deployment are usually less of a burden because you are only operating on one component at a time.

- *Distributed development.* If you work in an environment where you are the only person developing SSIS packages, this is less of a concern. However, if your shop has multiple ETL developers, those do-everything packages are quite inconvenient. Although it's much easier in SQL Server 2012 than in previous releases to compare differences between versions of the same package file, it's still a mostly manual process. By segmenting the workload into multiple packages, it's much easier to farm out development tasks to multiple people without having to reconcile multiple versions of the same package.

- *Reusability.* It's not uncommon for the same logic to be used more than once in the same ETL execution, or for that same logic to be shared among multiple ETL processes. By encapsulating these logical units of work into their own packages, it's much easier to share that logic and avoid duplicate development.

It is possible to go overboard here. For example, if, during the course of the ETL execution, you need to drop or disable indexes on 20 tables, you probably don't need to create a package for each index! Break operations up into individual packages, but be realistic about what constitutes a logical unit of work.

These aren't hard and fast rules, but with respect to breaking up ETL work into packages, here are a few design patterns that I've found work well when populating a data warehouse:

- Each dimension has a separate package.

- Each fact table has a separate package.

- Staging operations (if used) each have their own package.

- Functional operations unrelated to data movement (for example, dropping or disabling indexes on tables before loading them with data) are separated as well. Some of these operations can be grouped together in common packages where appropriate; for example, if you truncate tables and drop indexes in a staging database, those operations typically reside in the same package.

Further, it's often a good practice to isolate in separate packages any ETL logic that is significantly different in terms of scope or breadth of data. For example, an historical ETL process that retrieves a large chunk of old data will likely have different performance expectations, error handling rules, and so on than a more frequently executed package that collects just the most recent incremental data. As such, creating a separate package structure to address those larger sets of data helps to avoid the issue of trying to force a single package to handle these disparate scenarios.

Summary

SQL Server Integration Services isn't just another ETL tool. At its root, it is ideally suited for the unique challenges of data warehouse ETL. This chapter has shown some specific methodologies for how to leverage SSIS against common and realistic DW challenges.

CHAPTER 12

Logging Patterns

In any effective ETL system, there lies an unseen but valuable system of event and error logging designed to aid in troubleshooting problems, heading off potential issues, and tracking historical trends in data movement and transformation.

In this chapter, we're going to discuss logging patterns. If you are a lumberjack and are looking for career tips, you can stop reading now—this is a different type of logging.

Essentials of Logging

Let's be honest—event and error logging probably isn't at the top of the list when the average ETL professional thinks of his or her favorite things. Consider the types of things we brag about: "I moved 100 million rows in 19 minutes;" "I cleaned up this ugly mess of data without a single line of code;" "I integrated twelve different sources of data into this fact table." These are the things that, in our geeky culture, would result in a pat on the back or at least an "Attaboy." For people like us, this is the home run in the bottom of the ninth, the last-second winning field goal, or the goal from center ice.

Event and error logging, on the other hand, rarely evokes such emotion. I doubt if anyone has ever given a high-five over an effective logging strategy. In the board room or the sales pitch, logging gets about as much attention as the color of ink that will be used to sign the contract.

However, when it comes to tasks that can make or break a successful ETL implementation, having an effective and understandable logging strategy is near the top of the list. While not an outwardly visible element of the project deliverables, error and event logging provides a means with which ETL professionals can measure the health of the data pipeline. Capturing the necessary information during ETL execution will allow easier analysis of the fidelity of the downstream data stores.

Why Logging?

Before diving into the discussion of logging patterns, it's essential to understand why error and event logging is so critical in an ETL project.

It tells you what has happened in the past

Consider for a moment that you fire up SQL Server Management Studio on Monday morning and discover your central SSIS package ran for 23 minutes yesterday, processing a total of ten million records. On their own, those numbers sound very reasonable. But what if this process typically runs for 30 seconds? What if the typical run processes 100 million rows? It's important to monitor when packages fail, but in the space between package success and failure is the stuff you really need to worry about. An SSIS package that fails on execution instantly tells me that something bad has happened. However, packages that complete without any errors may still present issues that need to be investigated, and only properly logging key metrics will provide the information necessary to track down these latent clues.

Capturing and storing logging information allows you to evaluate over time the expected runtimes, row counts, and anomalies. This is important not only as a troubleshooting mechanism but for proper capacity planning. Capturing data volume patterns over time is essential for ensuring that your organization is proactive about addressing disk space and other capacity constraints.

It tells you what's happening now

Although the greatest value of logging resides in the ability to analyze execution data over time, another benefit of an effective logging strategy is that it tells you what's happening right now in your ETL domain. Consider the case of a package that is running for much longer than expected. What tasks are currently running right now? Have any tasks failed? How much data have I processed so far? Without a good system of information logging, it's going to be difficult to answer these questions while the ETL process is still running.

Properly logged, however, your in-progress SSIS packages and other ETL elements will no longer be a mystery. Good logging practices ensure that you won't have to wait until the package actually fails before you know something is wrong.

Elements of Logging

Logging consists of the following elements:

- **Error logging.** The most common and visible element of logging is the capturing of information about any errors that occur during process execution. Sadly, this is sometimes the only logging done. Accurate error logging should ideally contain not just a declaration of failure but an accurate description of the cause of the failure.

- **Event logging.** Event logging takes error logging to the next level. Rather than simply capturing when something generates a failure in the ETL, a well-designed event logging system will store enough information about the ETL flow that its execution can be evaluated, not just on a Boolean succeed/fail state but on its overall health.

- **Start and ending information** (for the entire process as well as elements therein).

- **Amount of information processed**, generally described in terms of row counts. Note that this can be especially useful to log at the data flow or component level, particularly if your packages have allowances for dropping or generating rows during transformation.

- **Notifications.** Though not purely a function of the logging system, having a means by which system administrators or other responsible individuals can be notified of sentinel events is crucial to ensuring timely response to ETL anomalies. Notifications are typically associated with error events; when a package fails, someone gets notified. However, in mission-critical systems, other scenarios may also need to generate a notification to the ETL administrator. Consider a long-running ETL process that threatens to impact contracted service level agreements (SLAs): even though it may not generate a failure, such a delay would probably need to be dealt with immediately rather than allowing that SLA to fall into breach. With a system of appropriate notifications, support personnel can quickly respond to potential issues before they get out of hand.

Logging in SSIS

As with other tedious tasks, SQL Server Integration Services has integrated facilities to eliminate some of the time and guesswork involved with error and event logging. Starting with the first version of SSIS in 2005, package-level logging was provided as a way to associate executable objects with events, allowing the logging of those intersections to database or file destinations. Starting with SQL Server 2012, the SSIS catalog was introduced, bringing along with it a brand new way to log information. Using the SSIS catalog to log information adds more to the logging footprint.

In addition to these native logging platforms, many ETL developers choose to craft their own homegrown logging solutions to either replace or, more frequently, supplement the information provided by the built-in SSIS logging tools.

A question that comes up frequently about logging is whether or not the native SSIS logging elements are sufficient for capturing all of the information necessary to properly track the inner workings of the ETL operations. In prior versions of SQL Server, the logging capabilities built into SSIS provided some of the information required by ETL logging systems but failed to accommodate the direct logging of other information (most notably, the row counts for various data flow operations). As a result, for capturing logging information, many enterprising SSIS professionals built their own frameworks that blended native SSIS logging with custom logging processes.

For those working with a SQL Server 2012 ETL environment, the integrated logging facilities are greatly improved. In addition to the replacement of package-level logging with server-wide logging, ETL professionals can now enjoy row count logging among the improvements for the current version.

The bottom line is to find the right combination of logging tools to suit the needs of your organization. For shops using older versions of Integration Services or that have highly specialized logging requirements, native logging supplemented by a custom solution may be the best bet. In most cases, though, the logging facilities built into SQL Server 2012 will suffice for common logging needs.

SSIS Catalog Logging

Any conversation about event and error logging in SSIS should begin with server-based logging through the SSIS catalog. Introduced with SQL Server 2012, this vehicle helps to automate and make consistent the process of logging information and events during package execution. With logging in the SSIS catalog, keeping track of the ETL goings-on no longer requires logic embedded in the package.

When packages stored in the catalog are executed, event and error logging information is written to special tables in the SSIS catalog database (SSISDB). Information stored in those tables can then be accessed through a series of views created specifically for reporting from the SSISDB event log tables. Among the key views in this scenario:

- [catalog].[executions]: This view exposes the high-level details of each executable that runs during the ETL operation. The information stored here includes the start time and end time of the execution, the current status of the execution, and metadata about the executable itself.

- [catalog].[event_messages]: This view shows the logged messages associated with each execution. Depending on the size of the SSIS package and the specified logging level (more on the latter momentarily), the number of entries for each execution could be sizeable.

- [catalog].[execution_data_statistics]: This view shows an entirely new segment of native logging capabilities: intrapackage row counts. The data presented through this view includes the names of the source and destination components, the name of the data path itself, and the number of rows transferred.

As you explore the catalog views in the SSISDB database, you'll find that these are just a few of many such views. Because these are simply views in a user database, you can consume the information logged here just as you would any other data in the system. You can use the SSIS catalog views to build SSRS reports, expose the information through Excel, generate alerts, etc.

Logging Levels

First introduced in SQL Server 2012, the concept of the logging levels eliminates much of the guesswork from selecting which events to log. These predefined levels allow the ETL professional to specify at a broad level how much information should be written to the logging tables in the SSIS catalog.

Before the SSIS catalog was introduced, native logging involved the selection of specific tasks and events for which information would be logged. While this does allow a lot of flexibility, it also lends itself to an all-or-nothing logging approach (especially for beginners—spoken from experience!). Unless one chooses to log all events for all components—which can be expensive in terms of performance overhead and storage—it takes some experience and tweaking to get all of the settings right.

With the introduction of logging levels, ETL professionals can now choose from one of four settings to specify how much information will be captured and stored during execution.

- **None.** As the name implies, no detailed logging will be performed. It's important to note that this does not mean that there will be no logging for that execution; a record will still be added to the [catalog].[executions] table to track the package execution, but the details (specifically those tracked in the [catalog].[event_messages] table) are not stored when the logging level is set to None.

- **Basic.** This is the default logging level, providing a reasonable starting point for SSIS catalog logging.

- **Performance.** This logging level resides between None and Basic in terms of the logging detail.

- **Verbose.** This gets you everything and the kitchen sink. Verbose logging is a great way to capture everything you might possibly need regarding the execution of SSIS packages. The downsides are that this level of logging can hurt performance and that it requires more attention to the amount of space required to store those logs. It's important to note that the Verbose setting is the only level that captures row count information.

■ **Note:** For an excellent walk-through the new features of SSIS catalog logging, I recommend a blog post by Jamie Thompson—it's an older post based on a CTP version of SQL Server, but it provides a great overview of the internals of this platform. You can find that post here: http://sqlblog.com/blogs/jamie_thomson/archive/2011/07/16/ssis-logging-in-denali.aspx.

Built-In Reports

Although having the flexibility to craft your own custom ETL process reports is great, I suspect that many such custom reports look very much alike: Package Name, Start Time, End Time, Execution Status. Maybe even a Duration column for those who can't do date math in their heads. Fortunately, SQL Server Management Studio comes equipped with canned reports that display a common set of execution data for packages stored in the SSIS catalog.

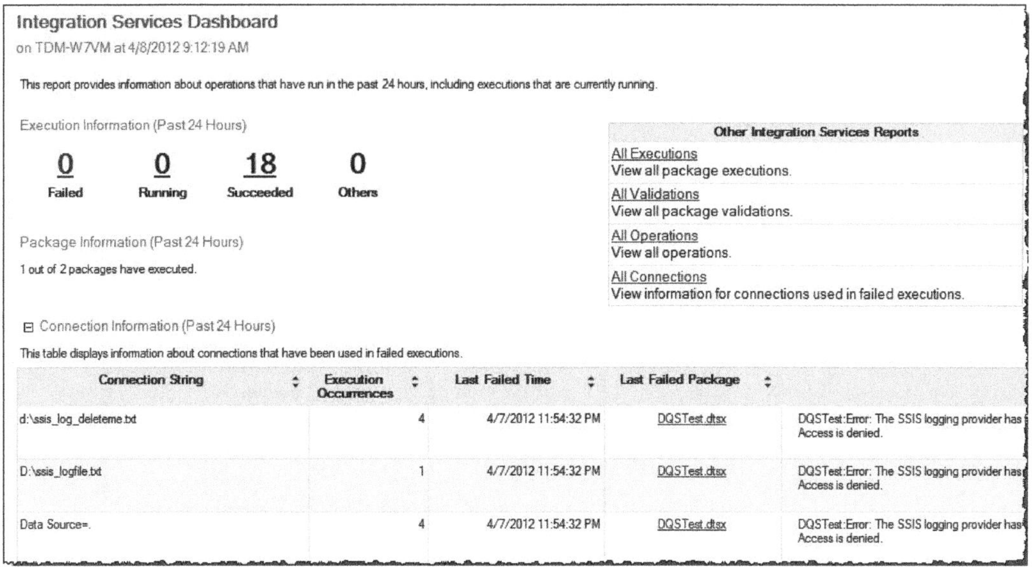

Integration Services Dashboard
on TDM-W7VM at 4/8/2012 9:12:19 AM

This report provides information about operations that have run in the past 24 hours, including executions that are currently running.

Execution Information (Past 24 Hours)

0	**0**	**18**	**0**
Failed	Running	Succeeded	Others

Other Integration Services Reports

All Executions
View all package executions.

All Validations
View all package validations.

All Operations
View all operations.

All Connections
View information for connections used in failed executions.

Package Information (Past 24 Hours)

1 out of 2 packages have executed.

⊟ Connection Information (Past 24 Hours)

This table displays information about connections that have been used in failed executions.

Connection String	Execution Occurrences	Last Failed Time	Last Failed Package	
d:\ssis_log_deleteme.txt	4	4/7/2012 11:54:32 PM	DQSTest.dtsx	DQSTest:Error: The SSIS logging provider has Access is denied.
D:\ssis_logfile.txt	1	4/7/2012 11:54:32 PM	DQSTest.dtsx	DQSTest:Error: The SSIS logging provider has Access is denied.
Data Source=.	4	4/7/2012 11:54:32 PM	DQSTest.dtsx	DQSTest:Error: The SSIS logging provider has Access is denied.

Figure 12-1. *Integration Services Dashboard*

As shown in Figure 12-1, SSMS offers a built-in dashboard report that provides a high-level snapshot of the current status and recent history. Other reports include execution detail report, failed connections report, and one of my favorites, the execution history report shown in Figure 12-2. This report outlines the recent history on a given package, including the most recent execution stats (complete with a data flow component analysis), and a chart showing the execution duration over time.

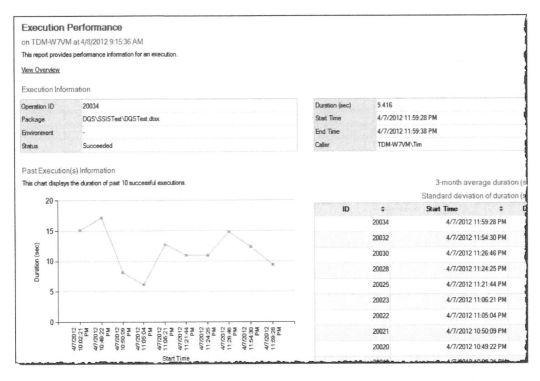

Figure 12-2. *Package Execution Performance report*

If there is a downside to be found in these integrated reports, it's that they are designed purely for consumption within SQL Server Management Studio—there's no path to push the reports to a standard format (for example, an .rdl file for use in Reporting Services). Furthermore, the information in these reports cannot be directly exported, though it is possible to print the report to a format such as PDF with the right client software.

On the plus side, however, these built-in reports will likely eliminate much of the need to craft custom reports around the SSIS logging subsystem. Almost every ETL professional who has gone through the exercise of adding logging information to an ETL system has also performed the simple but tedious task of creating reports to access said information. Couple these standard reports with the catalog logging, and there's the potential for significant time savings on each ETL project. Having built from scratch a number of reports very similar to these, I can attest that the built-in execution reports in SSMS are one of the most convenient features of this version of the product.

Package Logging

In addition to the server-based SSIS catalog event logging in SQL Server 2012, ETL developers also have the option of logging events and errors at the package level. Although designed with a similar purpose, the package-level logging in SSIS is a completely separate beast from the catalog logging mentioned earlier.

Package logging has been around since SSIS was first introduced, and is an effective way to track basic information about executions in SSIS. It has been, and remains for many legacy packages, the default mechanism for logging when custom event and error logging is not required.

Although very mature and heavily-used, this type of logging does come with a few downsides:

- The responsibility of logging package events rests on the shoulders of the ETL developers. This is a process that must be repeated for every package, and although the logic can be wrapped into a reusable template, almost any change to the logging specification would require the modification of every package.

- There's no easy way to add or change logging at runtime. Changing the logging properties on a per-execution basis is technically possible, but to do this, the ETL developer must have set up a logging connection in the package.

- There is no server-wide repository for logging. Unlike logging to the SSIS catalog, which logs to the SSISDB databaseon the SQL Server instance on which the package is executed, package-level logging requires the specification of a destination provider. On the plus side, package logging affords more flexibility than logging to the SSIS catalog. While the latter stores information only in SSISDB, the former allows you to specify both the destination type (SQL Server database, text file, XML file, etc.) and the location (local or remote file or database). To that end, package logging provides a standout benefit not offered through the SSIS catalog: centralized enterprise logging.

- There is no row count logging in the data flow. Given that row count logging is one of the most significant elements of effective ETL data collection, this is a significant downside.

For those working with SSIS versions earlier than 2012, package logging is the only native option available to you; the SSIS catalog first appears in SQL Server 2012.

Package logging is largely unchanged since the first version of SSIS in 2005. To engage logging at the package level, the ETL developer will specify the logging provider, either a file or a SQL Server database, and the events that will be logged to said provider. As shown in Figure 12-3, this provides a great deal of flexibility in terms of which ETL elements should be logged and to what degree.

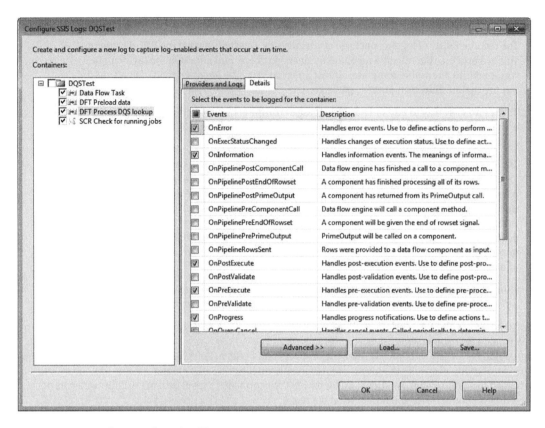

Figure 12-3. *Configure package-level logging*

So let's assume that you've got an existing ETL infrastructure using package-level logging. You're happy with what it gives you, but you're wondering if it's worth leaning on server logging in the SSIS catalog instead. What's the tipping point at which you should upgrade?

Based on what I've seen, I'm inclined to recommend the SSIS catalog logging in most cases over native package logging. Admittedly you lose some measure of flexibility, but catalog logging is more straightforward, easier to configure at runtime, and provides more coverage. However, if you're dependent on having task-level configuration for logging events, consider sticking with the package-level logging.

Also worth noting is that there is no restriction against using both SSIS catalog logging in addition to package-level logging. However, if you blend two different logging methods, make sure you take some time to evaluate what you're capturing to avoid any unnecessary duplication.

Custom Logging

There comes a time in every ETL developer's life when he or she must drive off the paved road. In terms of logging, creating your own custom logging elements is the equivalent of leaving the pavement. Even though creating these customized structures represents a departure from the "proper" native logging components in SSIS, it's actually quite common, particularly in shops with a large number of SSIS packages.

Almost every custom logging scenario has its own purpose, its own nuances, and its own dedicated resources. However, after observing many different custom SSIS logging setups, I find that there is a common component fingerprint found in many of them:

- Parameterized, reusable stored procedures that write logging information are created in the database to which the logging information will be written.

- Execute SQL Tasks designed to log informational messages are created in SSIS packages. These are either added inline in the control flow of the package, or added to an event handler (usually the OnPostExecute event).

- Separately, additional Execute SQL Tasks are added to log errors or anomalies in the package. These are most often added to OnError event handlers for tasks or the package itself, though they are sometimes used at the business end of a failure constraint in the control flow.

- Occasionally, highly customized logging requirements may introduce the need for a script task or script component to assist with meeting those requirements.

Custom logging is the most difficult to create and maintain because you're essentially on your own in terms of metadata. However, because there is no real framework (apart from whatever native SSIS tasks you use), you have very few constraints on what you can and can't do. It certainly takes more elbow grease to get it done, but custom logging allows for flexibility not found in native logging facilities.

Although custom logging has been a part of SSIS since it was SSIS (and even earlier, as DTS), I suspect that the need for custom logging design patterns will diminish as improvements are made in the native logging capabilities of SSIS. Now that one of the principal deficiencies in prior versions regarding logging—the inability to capture row counts—has been addressed in SQL Server 2012, it could be expected that native logging will take the place of custom structures as the go-to mechanism for package execution information.

What to Capture?

The quintessential question: Now that I've decided to log information in my SSIS packages, what information should I capture? This question is central to every ETL project. Gather too much information and you waste processing time and storage space. Capture too little data and you risk not getting enough to properly troubleshoot errors or head off potential problems.

Every scenario will have different requirements, but the answer to the question "How much information should I log?" will always be the same: Capture the information required. No more, no less.

I realize this isn't a silver-bullet answer, but it does tell you that the decision of what to capture in your logging strategy isn't quick or easy. You need to get all of the data you'll need to figure out what happened in the event of a package failure, analyze patterns to discover data anomalies or other irregularities, and abide by governmental regulations and/or company policies. However, every additional logging element adds processing time and storage to your system, so it's usually not practical to take a "log everything just in case" approach, particularly on high-volume systems.

To find the right strategy for you, think about the following:

- What do you hope to accomplish by logging? Do you just want to know where and when the ETL process failed, or do you expect to consume the logging information in a proactive system intended to head off problems before they occur?

- How much horsepower do you have? If you have state of the art ETL hardware and network, you can be more liberal in your logging expectations. However, if your SSIS server is a virtual machine on a shared set of disks, you need to be much more careful.

- Are you in a highly-regulated environment? Healthcare and financial institutions are under particular scrutiny, but other shops may have similar reporting and/or auditing requirements. As a rule, I'm a big fan of doing things that keep me from going to jail, so I'm happy to recommend that you design your ETL logging in such a way that it fully complies with federal law. If you need to make shortcuts in logging, this isn't something you want to play around with.

Creating an effective logging strategy that balances the need for information with the need to maintain a stable and well-performing system isn't always done on the first swipe. Know that designing a proper logging pattern, like the core ETL process itself, tends to be an iterative process.

Logging Systems

We discussed three different logging platforms—SSIS catalog logging, package logging, and custom logging—earlier in the chapter. Early in the process of designing your logging system, you'll need to pick which of these will be used to capture logging information from your packages.

There are no hard and fast rules for selecting which logging system should be used in a given scenario. However, the following tips may help point you in the right direction:

- Remember that you're not limited to a single logging mechanism. You can add custom logging to either package logging or SSIS catalog logging, or even mix all three of them together if you're daring. When using multiple logging vehicles, take care that you don't log the same information in multiple ways.

- If you are in a SQL Server 2012 environment, seriously consider using the SSIS catalog for event and error logging. The improvements over prior versions are significant and can address many of the scenarios previously left for custom logging.

- If you need to centralize logging across multiple SSIS servers, you'll need to lean on package logging or custom logging.

- Consider using custom logging to supplement another logging platform, not as a single means through which to log all required data. As mentioned, custom logging takes significantly more effort than the native facilities, so don't reinvent the wheel if you don't have to.

Summary

In this chapter, we've discussed design patterns around logging in SSIS, including an exploration of the various high-level approaches to error and event logging. Even though event and error logging isn't one of the more exciting aspects of data movement, it's still a critical piece of the puzzle. Effective logging works as an insurance policy, a troubleshooting tool, and even a capacity planning guide. The time invested in building proper logging is rarely wasted.

CHAPTER 13

Slowly Changing Dimensions

Processing Slowly Changing Dimensions (SCDs) is a common ETL operation when dealing with Data Warehouses. The SSIS Data Flow has a Slowly Changing Dimension Transform, which provides a wizard that outputs a set of transforms needed to handle the multiple steps of processing SCDs. While the built-in SCD Transform can be useful, it is not ideal for all data loading scenarios. This chapter describes how to make the most of the SCD Transform, and provides a couple of alternative patterns you can use.

Note   There are many different types of SCD, but this chapter will focus on the two most common types: Type 1 and Type 2. For more information about the different types of Slowly Changing Dimensions, see the Wikipedia entry at http://en.wikipedia.org/wiki/Slowly_changing_dimensions

---

Slowly Changing Dimension Transform

To best understand the SCD Transform, let's consider two key scenarios it was designed for.

> **Type 1 - A small number of change rows.** You are performing change data capture (CDC) at the source, or as close to the source as possible. Unless you are dealing with a very active dimension, most SCD processing batches will contain a small number of rows.

> **Type 2 - Large dimension.** You are working against large dimensions, but only processing a small number of change rows. You will want to avoid operations which cause full table scans of your dimension.

Because of these target scenarios, the SCD Transform does not cache the existing dimension data (like a Lookup Transform does), and performs all of its comparisons row-by-row against the destination table. While this allows the transform to avoid full scans of the destination dimension, and reduces memory usage, it does affect performance when processing a large number of rows. If your scenario does not match the ones listed above, you might want to consider using one of the other patterns in this chapter. If it does match, or if you prefer using in-the-box components over third party solutions (or would just like to avoid hand crafted SQL statements required for the Merge Pattern), consider applying the optimizations listed at the end of this pattern.

Running the Wizard

Unlike other SSIS Data Flow components, when you drop the Slowly Changing Dimension Transform onto the design surface in BIDS, a wizard pops up and walks you through the steps of setting up your SCD processing.

The first page of the Wizard (Figure 13-1) allows you to select the dimension you'll be updating, and select the column or columns that make up the business key (also known as the natural key).

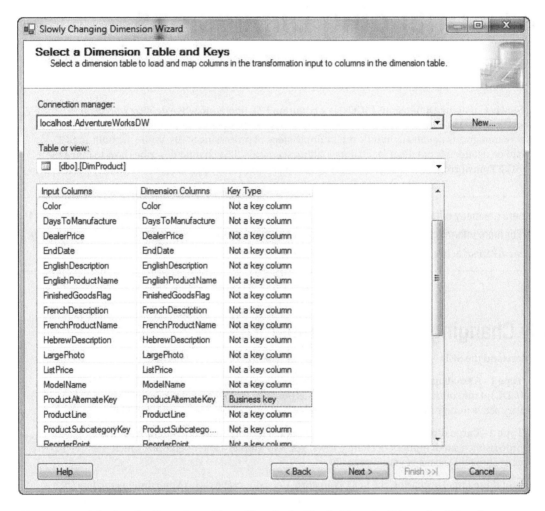

Figure 13-1. *Selecting the dimension table and keys in the Slowly Changing Dimension Wizard*

On the next page (Figure 13-2) you specify the columns that you'll be processing, and determine how you'd like the wizard to treat them. You have the three choices (as shown in Table 13-1).

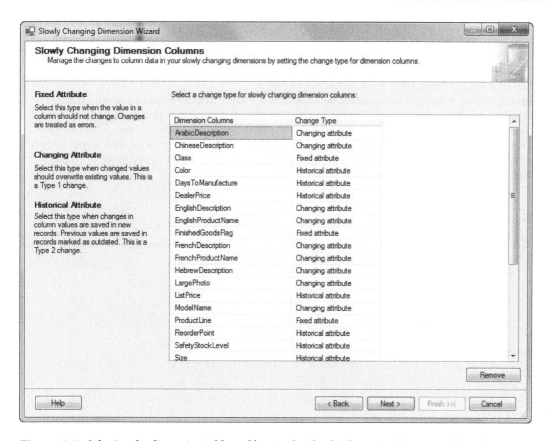

Figure 13-2. *Selecting the dimension table and keys in the Slowly Changing Dimension Wizard*

Table 13-1. *Column Change Types*

Change Type	Dimension Type	When to Use
Fixed Attribute	--	Fixed Attributes are columns that should not change, or require special handling when changes are made. By default, a change on one of these columns is treated as an error.
Changing Attribute	Type 1	When a change is made to a Changing Attribute column, existing records are updated to reflect the new value. These are typically columns that aren't used as part of business logic or time sensitive reporting queries, such as a Product Description.
Historical Attribute	Type 2	Historical Attributes are columns for which you need to maintain history for. These are frequently numeric columns that are used in time sensitive reporting queries, such as a Sales Price, or Weight.

On this page, you should not map columns that will not be updated as part of your SCD processing, such as foreign keys to other dimension tables, or columns related to the tracking of historical changes, such a Start and End Date columns, an expiry flag, and the surrogate key. The SCD Transform does not support LOB columns (columns that would be treated as DT_IMAGE, DT_TEXT and DT_NTEXT types in the SSIS Data Flow), so these columns should be handled separately, and also not mapped here.

The next pages of the wizard allow you to configure options for how you'd like to handle Fixed Attributes (Figure 13-3), as well as Type 1 and Type 2 changes (Figure 13-4). When dealing with Historical Attributes, the wizard knows how to generate the logic needed to update the dimension in two different ways; using a single column, or using start and end date columns to indicate whether the record is current or expired. If your table is using a combination of these, or some other method of tracking the current record, you will need to update the generated transforms to contain this logic.

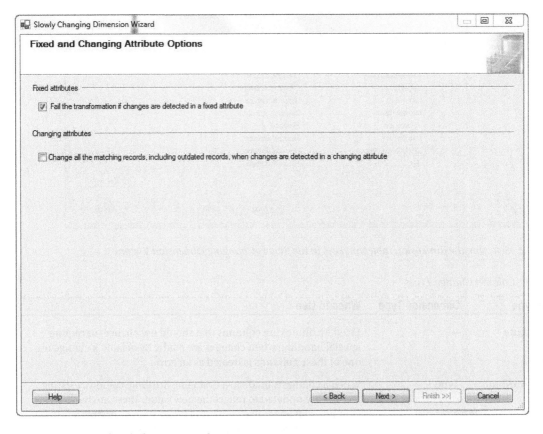

Figure 13-3. *Fixed and Changing Attribute Options*

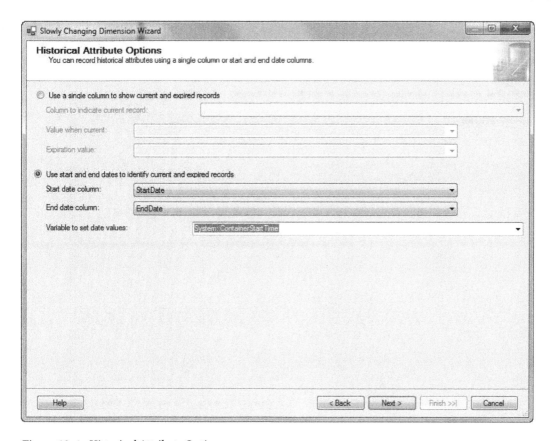

Figure 13-4. *Historical Attribute Options*

The final page of the wizard (Figure 13-5) lets you enable support for inferred members. An inferred member is created with minimal information, typically just the business and surrogate keys. It's expected that the remaining fields will be populated in subsequent loading of the dimension data. Although the wizard enables inferred member support by default, most forms of SCD processing will not need it.

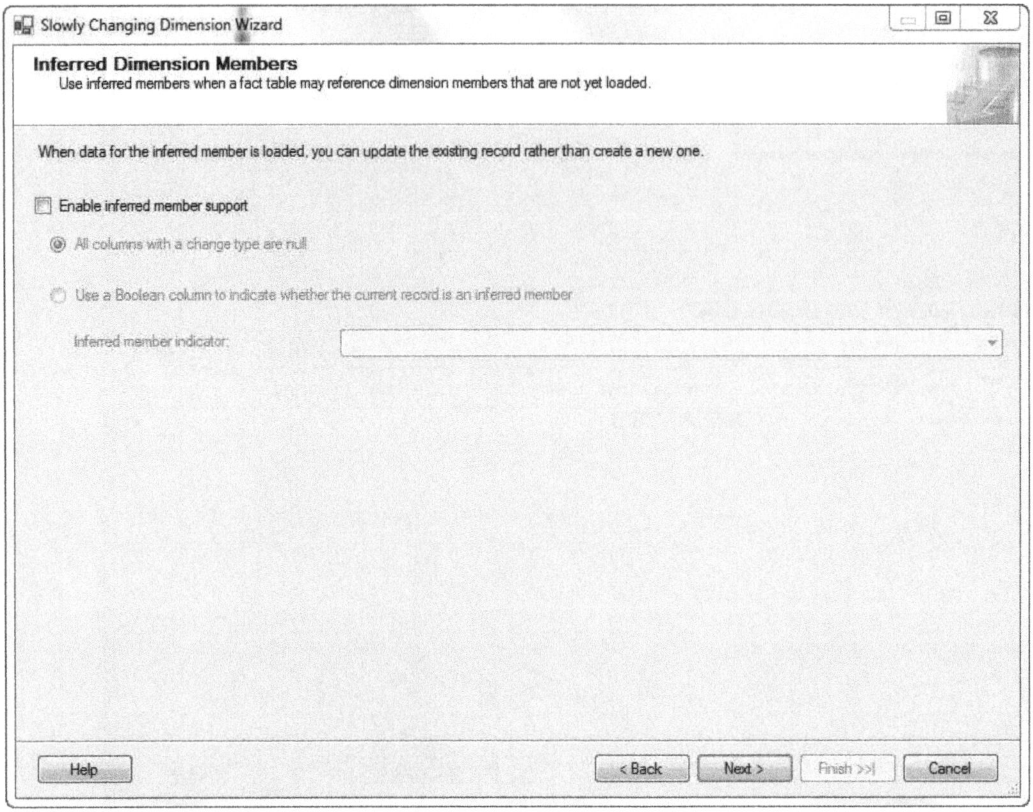

Figure 13-5. *Inferred Dimension Members*

Using the Transformations

When the wizard completes, it will output a number of different data flow components in addition to the main "Slowly Changing Dimension" component (Figure 13-6). The main component checks incoming data against the destination table, and sends incoming rows down one of its outputs if the record is new or modified. Records without any changes are ignored. The components connected to these outputs will be configured according to the options you selected in the wizard dialogs.

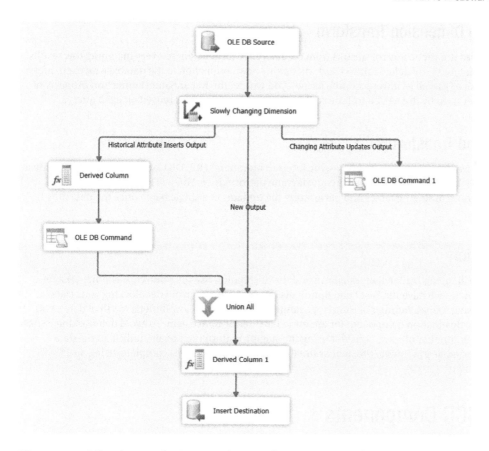

Figure 13-6. *Wizard output for Type 1 and Type 2 changes, and no inferred member support*

You can further customize the SCD processing logic by modifying these components. Double clicking the main "Slowly Changing Dimension" transform will re-launch the wizard. The wizard remembers your settings from the previous run; however, it will overwrite any changes or customizations you've made to the existing transforms. This includes any layout and resizing changes you might have done.

■ **Note**   When re-running the SCD Wizard, the default options selected in the UI are not inferred from the components. Instead, they are persisted as part of the package in < designTime > elements. If you have a deployment process which removes package layout information, note that you will also lose your choices in the wizard.

Optimizing Performance

The components output from the SCD Wizard are not configured for optimal performance. By changing some settings and moving to a set based pattern, you can drastically improve the performance of your SCD processing.

Slowly Changing Dimension Transform

The main transform does not cache any row results from the reference dimension, so every incoming row results in a query against the database. By default, the wizard will open a new connection to the database on each query. For a gain in performance (as well as lower resource usage), you can set the RetainSameConnection property of the connection manager used by the wizard to True so that the same connection is reused on each query.

OLE DB Command Transforms

The wizard will output two (or three if you're processing inferred members) OLE DB Command transforms. These transforms perform row-by-row updates, which greatly degrade performance. You will get a big performance boost by placing these rows in staging tables and performing the updates in a single batch once the data flow completes.

OLE DB Destination

Since the main Slowly Changing Dimension transform and the destination use the same connection manager, the destination component will have the Fast Load option disable by default to avoid deadlocking your Data Flow. If you are processing a small number of rows (for example, a single Data Flow Buffer's worth of data), you enable Fast Load on the destination component for an immediate performance gain. To avoid deadlocking issues when processing a larger number of rows, consider using the staging pattern once again. Bulk load the data into a temporary staging table and update the final destination once the data flow is complete, using an INSERT INTO . . . SELECT statement.

Third Party SCD Components

A couple of popular third party alternatives to the SCD Transform are available. Both have similar architectures and usage patterns, but offer different capabilities.

- The Table Difference component is available through CozyRoc.com. This transform takes in the source and destination tables as inputs, and does row by row comparisons in memory. It has three outputs – New, Updated, and Deleted. It can also be used to do general purpose table comparisons, in addition to SCD processing.

■ **Note**   For more information about the Table Difference component, please see the CozyRoc web page at http://www.cozyroc.com/ssis/table-difference.

- The Dimension Merge SCD component is available through PragmaticWorks.com. It was designed to handle dimension loading as per the Kimball Method. Like the Table Difference component, it takes in the source and destination dimension tables and does the comparisons in memory. Also like the Table Difference component, it does not modify the destination table directly. It will apply row updates in memory, and provides a number of outputs that you hook up your own destination tables to.

■ **Note**   For more information about the Dimension Merge SCD component, please see the Pragmatic Works web site page at `http://pragmaticworks.com/Products/Business-Intelligence/TaskFactory/Features.aspx#TSDimensionMergeSCD`.

The main draw of these components is their performance. Since the transforms take both source and destination tables into memory, they are able to do fast in-memory comparisons, without multiple queries to the destination server. They also provide additional functionality over the SCD Transform, such as detecting deleted rows, and can be easier to maintain as all of the logic is contained within a single component.

However, bringing in both the source and destination dimension tables means that you're doing a full table scan of the destination (and typically the source as well). As the Data Flow does not end until all sources are done reading their rows, the entire destination dimension will be read even if you are only processing a small number of changed source rows. While the third party components will perform well in many cases, you should consider if they will be ideal for your scenario.

MERGE Pattern

SQL Server 2008 introduced support for the T-SQL MERGE statement. This statement will perform insert, update, and delete operations on a destination table based on the results of a join with a source table. It is very efficient, and provides a good alternative for SCD processing.

■ **Note**   For more information about MERGE, please see the Books Online entry "Using MERGE in Integration Services Packages" at `http://technet.microsoft.com/en-us/library/cc280522.aspx`

There are three steps to using MERGE from within SSIS:

1. Stage the data in a Data Flow

2. Optimize the staging table (optional)

3. Run the MERGE statement(s) using an Execute SQL Task

MERGE allows a single statement to be run when it detects a row has been updated ("matched" using the MERGE terminology), and when a row is new ("not matched"). Since processing Type 1 and Type 2 changes require different types of processing, we'll use two MERGE statements to complete the SCD processing (as shown in Figure 13-7).

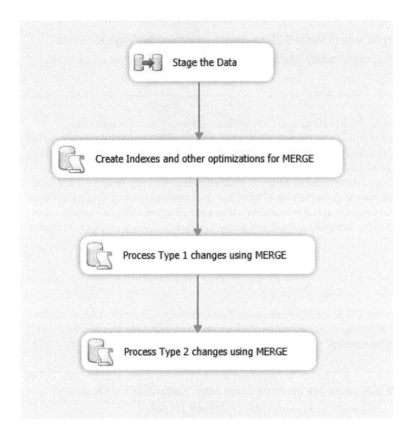

Figure 13-7. *Control flow for the MERGE Pattern*

Handling Type 1 Changes

Listing 13-1 shows the first MERGE statement we'll run to update all of our Type 1 columns in the destination table. The ON ( ) section specifies the keys that we'll be matching on (in this case, the business key for the table). In the WHEN MATCHED section, we include DEST.EndDate is NULL to ensure that we are only updating the current record (this is optional – in many cases you do want to update all records, and not just the current one). The THEN UPDATE section contains the list of our Type 1 columns that we want to update.

Listing 13-1. MERGE Statement for Type 1 Columns

```
MERGE INTO [DimProduct] AS DEST
USING [Staging] AS SRC
ON (
        DEST.ProductAlternateKey = SRC.ProductAlternateKey
)
WHEN MATCHED AND DEST.EndDate is NULL -- update the current record
THEN UPDATE SET
          DEST.[ArabicDescription] = SRC.ArabicDescription
         ,DEST.[ChineseDescription] = SRC.ChineseDescription
         ,DEST.[EnglishDescription] = SRC.EnglishDescription
```

```
        ,DEST.[FrenchDescription] = SRC.FrenchDescription
        ,DEST.[GermanDescription] = SRC.GermanDescription
        ,DEST.[HebrewDescription] = SRC.HebrewDescription
        ,DEST.[JapaneseDescription] = SRC.JapaneseDescription
        ,DEST.[ThaiDescription] = SRC.ThaiDescription
        ,DEST.[TurkishDescription] = SRC.TurkishDescription
        ,DEST.[ReorderPoint] = SRC.ReorderPoint
        ,DEST.[SafetyStockLevel] = SRC.SafetyStockLevel
;
```

Handling Type 2 Changes

Since the MERGE statement allows a single statement for each action, updating Type 2 columns is a little more challenging. Remember, for Type 2 changes we need to perform two operations: 1) mark the current record as expired and 2) insert the new record as current. To accomplish this, we'll use the MERGE inside of a FROM clause, and use its OUTPUT to feed an INSERT INTO statement (as shown in Listing 13-2)

Listing 13-2. MERGE Statement for Type 2 Columns

```
INSERT INTO [DimProduct]
([ProductAlternateKey],[ListPrice],[EnglishDescription],[StartDate])
SELECT [ProductAlternateKey],[ListPrice],[EnglishDescription],[StartDate]
FROM (
        MERGE INTO [DimProduct] AS FACT
        USING [Staging] AS SRC
        ON ( FACT.ProductAlternateKey = SRC.ProductAlternateKey )
        WHEN NOT MATCHED THEN
        INSERT VALUES (
                SRC.ProductAlternateKey
                ,SRC.ListPrice
                ,SRC.EnglishDescription
                ,GETDATE()       -- StartDate
                ,NULL            -- EndDate
                )
        WHEN MATCHED AND FACT.EndDate is NULL
        THEN UPDATE SET FACT.EndDate = GETDATE()
        OUTPUT $Action Action_Out
                ,SRC.ProductAlternateKey
                ,SRC.ListPrice
                ,SRC.EnglishDescription
                ,GETDATE() StartDate
) AS MERGE_OUT
WHERE MERGE_OUT.Action_Out = 'UPDATE'
```

Summary

There are many ways to process Slowly Changing Dimensions in SSIS. While the built-in SCD Transform can get you up and running quickly, it may not perform as well as the alternatives. You may prefer using the Merge Pattern due to its overall performance, but the maintenance of the SQL statements may be an inhibitor in the long run. If you prefer a visual designer experience, consider trying one of the third party component options.

Table 13-2 summarizes the advantages and disadvantages described in this chapter.

Table 13-2. *Slowly Changing Dimension Processing Patterns*

Pattern	Use For
Slowly Changing Dimension Transform	• Quick prototyping
	• Processing a small number of rows
	• Very large dimensions
Third Party Components	• Full or historical dimension loads
	• Small-medium sized dimensions
	• Non-SQL Server destinations
Merge Pattern	• Best overall performance
	• Cases when you don't mind hand-crafting SQL statements

## CHAPTER 14

Loading the Cloud

It is 2012 and cloud technology is becoming ubiquitous. As more applications are hosted in various cloud service providers, the desire to locate their associated data in the cloud increases. Thanks to forethought and good engineering, Microsoft SQL Server is well-positioned to assist. The user experience when interacting with Microsoft SQL Azure databases is nearly identical to interacting with local servers or servers on the enterprise network. Make no mistake, this is by design – and it is good design.

In this chapter, we will consider SSIS design patterns used to integrate data in the cloud. These patterns are useful when connecting to any repository that shares cloud technology characteristics. Because interacting with data in the cloud is similar to interacting with data that are more local, the patterns aren't revolutionary. "So why write a chapter about loading the cloud?" Excellent question.

First, the cloud is here to stay – the djin will not fit back into the bottle. The more we, as data professionals, learn about using the cloud, the better. Second, the cloud offers interesting challenges to data integration; challenges to be addressed and solved by the data integration developer. Loading the cloud isn't just about interacting with buzz-worthy technology. It is an opportunity to design good architecture.

Interacting with the Cloud

For the purposes of this chapter, "the cloud" will refer to "containers of data" or data repositories that:

- Reside off-enterprise-premises
- Are hosted by a third party
- Are outside of the physical enterprise domain

I understand these points are subject to debate. I will not debate them here. This definition will likely not survive the years following this writing (2012). And even now, there is ambiguity and a blurring of lines between what is and is not considered "in the cloud".

For demonstration, I am using data collected from my local weather station in Farmville, Virginia. The weather data are exposed and available at AndyWeather.com. AndyWeather.com is hosted by a large hosting company that provides remotely-accessible SQL Server database connectivity. As such, the data are stored in the cloud (according to my definition).

I also host weather data using Microsoft SQL Azure: the same data, stored in a different location. "Why?" The simple answer: Fault tolerance. Fault tolerance is the same reason DBAs perform database backups and test database restores. The difference between a technician and an engineer – or a developer and an architect – is that a technician builds systems that succeed while engineers build systems that don't fail. It's about mindset. Technicians get it working and stop there. Engineers consider many ways the system can fail and try to fix these things before they break.

Incremental Loads to SQL Azure

An incremental load is one in which only new or updated rows (and sometimes deleted) rows are loaded or changed. Incremental loads can be contrasted with the truncate-and-load pattern, where the existing data in the destination is deleted and all data is reloaded from the source. Sometimes truncate-and-load is most efficient. As data scale – especially at the destination – truncate-and-load performance often suffers. How do you know which will perform best? Test, measure, rinse, and repeat.

One benefit to truncate-and-load is simplicity. It is difficult to mess up a simple mechanism. Imcremental loads introduce complexity, and Change Detection is the first place complexity to enter the solution.

■ **Note**   Chapter 11 discusses some incremental load patterns.

Change Detection

Change detection is functionality designed to separate rows that have never been sent from the source (New Rows) to the destination from rows that have been sent. Change detection also separates source rows that exist in the destination into rows that have changed in the source (Changed Rows) and rows that remain unchanged since they were last loaded or updated in the destination (Unchanged Rows). Change detection can also encompass rows that have been deleted from the destination that need to be deleted (or "soft-deleted") from the source. We will ignore the Deleted Rows use case in this chapter.

We will consider using change detection to determine and discriminate between Unchanged Rows, Changed Rows, and New Rows. The block diagram for an incremental load pattern is shown in Figure 14-1:

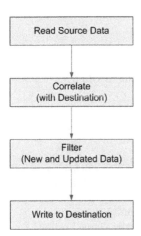

Figure 14-1. *Incremental Load Block Diagram*

New Rows (Only)

You would think detecting new rows would be simple, regardless of the technology behind the destination database. You would be right. But when loading SQL Azure, there is an economic consideration. As I write this in 2011, uploads are free. As a data provider, you are charged when your data is consumed. How does this fact impact your incremental load?

Here is where good data integration architecture and design comes in. Part of the job of the data integration architect is to know your data. This goes beyond knowing there is a column in the CleanTemperature table that contains the Average Dew Point for a given hour. Knowing your data means that you understand how and when it changes – or if. Certain types of data, like weather data, do not get updated after they are captured and recorded.

If you have read Tim's description of a typical incremental load pattern in Chapter 11, you will note a Lookup Transformation configured to connect to the destination and read data. In SQL Azure, you will pay for that reading. At the time of this writing, there are almost 30,000 rows present in my SQL Azure AndyWeather database. If I load all the rows from my source into a Data Flow Task and use a Lookup Transformation to "join" between my source and SQL Azure, I pay for reading rows that haven't changed. What's more, I know they *will never change*. One ramification: there will be no Changed Rows.

Each hour, a few rows of new data are generated for each subject area in the AndyWeather database. If I use a Lookup, I load all 30,000 rows for no good reason – and I pay for the privilege. No thank you.

To limit the amount of data read, and thereby lower the costs of the solution, I could execute a query that selects a "marker" indicating the latest or last row loaded. For this, I could select the maximum value from a field containing the date and time the table was last load; something like Max(LastUpdatedDateTime) or even a data integration lineage or metadata field like Max(LoadDate). I could similarly select another marker such as the Max(ID) from an integer column reliably maintained by either a sequence, identity, trigger, or other mechanism. The reliability of the mechanism represents the maximum confidence a data integration architect can place in the value. I will demonstrate building an incremental loader using an identity column maintained on the source data.

Before I do, I wish to point out that Chapter 11 contains a great section on the Incremental Load design pattern. There is a discussion of another solution I will not touch upon: Change Data Capture. I encourage you to review Chapter 11 before you complete your data integration design.

Building the Cloud Loader

To demonstrate, you will need a SQL Azure account and database. Creating the account and database is beyond the scope of this book, but you can learn more at `www.windowsazure.com/en-us/home/features/sql-azure`. Once SQL Azure is set up and configured, create a database. In this database, create a table named "dbo. LoadMetrics" using the T-SQL shown in Listing 14-1.

Listing 14-1. Creating the LoadMetrics Table

```
Create Table dbo.LoadMetrics
  (ID int identity(1,1)
    Constraint PK_LoadMetrics_ID Primary Key Clustered
  ,LoadDate datetime
    Constraint DF_LoadMetrics_LoadDate Default(GetDate())
  ,MetricName varchar(25)
  ,MetricIntValue int)
```

The LoadMetrics table will hold the last ID loaded for each table in the cloud destination. We will write this row once, read and update it each load cycle. Accessing this table in this manner is the simplest and least processor-intensive manner to acquire the information we seek: the value of the last ID column loaded for a particular table. Why store this value in a table? Why not simply execute a Max(ID) select statement on the data table? Currently, SQL Azure charges for reads and not writes. Billing may change – it has in the past. What if we're billed according to cycles or execution plans? You never know.

While connected to the SQL Azure instance, create a table to hold your data. My data table will hold temperature information collected from my weather station in Farmville Virginia. The table I use contains temperature and humidity related data and is shown in Listing 14-2.

Listing 14-2. Creating the CleanTemperature Table

```
Create Table dbo.CleanTemperature
  (ID int identity(1,1)
    Constraint PK_Cleantemperature_ID Primary Key Clustered
  ,MeasDateTime datetime
  ,MinT real
  ,MaxT real
  ,AvgT real
  ,MinH smallint
  ,MaxH smallint
  ,AvgH smallint
  ,ComfortZone smallint
  ,MinDP real
  ,MaxDP real
  ,AvgDP real
  ,MinHI varchar(7)
  ,MaxHI varchar(7)
  ,AvgHI varchar(7)
  ,LoadDate datetime
  ,LowBatt bit
 .,SensorID int)
```

Once the cloud tables have been created, we can begin work on an SSIS loader.

Locally, create a new SSIS solution and project named "CloudLoader". Rename the default SSIS package "SimpleCloudLoader.dtsx". Add a Sequence Container and rename it "SEQ Pre-Load Operations". Add an Execute SQL Task to the Sequence Container and rename it "Get AWCleanTempMaxID From AndyWeather". Set the ResultSet property to "Single row" and change the ConnectionType property to "ADO.Net". Create the ADO. Net connection manager using information from your SQL Azure account. To acquire the latest ID from the LoadMetrics table, I use the following query.

```
Select Coalesce(MetricIntValue, 0) As CleanTempMaxID
From dbo.LoadMetrics
Where MetricName = 'CleanTempMaxID'
```

On the Result Set page, I store the value in an SSIS variable of Int32 data type named "SQLAzureCleanLoadMaxID".

Add another Execute SQL Task to the Sequence Container and rename it "Get CleanTempMaxID from the local table". Configure the connectionto your source database and table. For me, it's a local default instance of SQL Server hosting the WeatherData database and the clean.CleanTemperature table. I use the following T-SQL to extract the current maximum value from the table, configuring a single row result set to push this value into the CleanTempLocalMaxID SSIS variable (Int32 data type).

```
Select Max(ID) As CleanTempLocalMaxID
From clean.CleanTemperature
```

Add a Data Flow Task outside the "SEQ Pre-Load Operations" Sequence Container and rename it "Load SQL Azure". Connect an OnSuccess precedence constraint between the Sequence Container and the Data Flow Task. Open the Data Flow Task editor and add an OLE DB Source adapter. Connect the OLE DB Source adapter to a local source database you wish to load in the cloud and write a query to pull the latest data from the desired table. In my case, I am pulling data from my "clean.CleanTemperature" table. To accomplish the load, I use the source query shown in Listing 14-3.

Listing 14-3. WeatherData Source Query

```
SELECT ID
       ,MeasDateTime
       ,MinT
       ,MaxT
       ,AvgT
       ,MinH
       ,MaxH
       ,AvgH
       ,ComfortZone
       ,MinDP
       ,MaxDP
       ,AvgDP
       ,MinHI
       ,MaxHI
       ,AvgHI
       ,LoadDate
       ,LowBatt
       ,SensorID
  FROM clean.CleanTemperature
WHERE ID Between ? And ?
```

Click the Parameters button and map Parameter0 and Parameter1 to the SQLAzureCleanLoadMaxID and CleanTempLocalMaxID variables as shown in Figure 14-2.

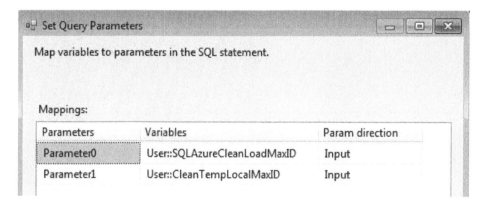

Figure 14-2. *Mapping the SQLAzureCleanLoadMaxID variable to Parameter0*

The question marks in the source query shown in Listing 14-3 are replaced with the values stored in the respective mapped variables. This query will only return rows where the ID is greater than the value stored in the cloud. Why do we grab the maximum ID from the source table before the load? In a word, latency. In the WeatherData database, the latency is minimal. But think about loading highly active systems – latency can be an issue.For example, suppose several transactions per second are entering the source table and it takes a few second to load the destination. If we wait until the load is complete to capture the source table's Max ID value that value will likely include data we didn't load. The technical term for that is "bad". So we design the package to grab the Max ID value before the load starts and only load rows between the last ID loaded into SQL Azure and the Max ID value captured at the start of the SSIS package. And we never miss a row.

Returning to the demo package, add an ADO.Net Destination adapter and rename it "SQL Azure ADO NET Destination". Connect a Data Flow Path from the OLE DB Source adapter to the ADO.Net Destination. Why an ADO.Net Destination? SQL Azure only allows ADO.Net connections.

Connect a data flow path between the source and destination adapters, edit the destination, and map the columns.

The last step is to update the LoadMetrics table in the SQL Azure database. To accomplish this update, add an Execute SQL Task to the Control Flow and rename it appropriately and descriptively. I named mine "Update AndyWeather LoadMetrics Table" and configured it to use ADO.Net to connect to my SQL Azure database. My query looks like this one shown in Listing 14-4.

Listing 14-4. Updating the SQL Azure LoadMetrics Table

```
Update dbo.LoadMetrics
Set MetricIntValue = (@MaxID + 1)
, LoadDate = GetDate()
Where MetricName = 'CleanTempMaxID'
```

Map the value of CleanTempLocalMaxID into the @MaxID parameter on the Parameter Mapping page. And that's it. This script makes the current maximum ID the minimum ID of the next load.

Summary

In this chapter we examined aspects of the architecture and design for loading cloud destinations. We designed a sound solution after weighing the architectural and economic considerations.

CHAPTER 15

Logging and Reporting Patterns

An essential part of managing any application is knowing what happens during the day-to-day usage of the application. This theme holds especially true in ETL solutions, in which the data being manipulated can be used for reporting, analysis, or financial reporting. Administrators satisfy this need through logging and reporting of the executions, errors, and statuses of the applications, which fits perfectly into the management framework concept.

The past few chapters have discussed how to set up other pieces of the management framework, including how to execute parent-child packages and how to implement centralized custom logging. This chapter will describe how to use the built-in logging in Integration Services to report on all aspects of an Integration Services application.

Integration Services provides two primary methods to help satisfy the logging and reporting need.

- Package logging and reporting
- Catalog logging and reporting

Let's walk through how to set up each of these methods and then utilize patterns that best highlight these methods.

Package Logging and Reporting

The *package logging and reporting* method has been around since the first edition of Integration Services. This method is characterized by setting up logging during development of the package. A logging provider can log to different outputs, including SQL server tables, text files, and more. The log information is stored in one object, such as one file or the sysssislog table.

Each log can be restricted to store only certain types of events, such as OnError, OnPreExecute, and OnVariableValueChanged. An administrator can then look at the logs to see what happened during the execution of the package. Once the package has been deployed to the server, you cannot change the type or amount of logging that occurs.

Package logging is the best and only option when using Integration Services 2005 or 2008 or when using Integration Services 2012 in Package Deployment mode. In Integration Services 2012's Project Deployment mode, you can use package logging on a regular basis to keep track of errors that may occur or to ensure that packages are executing when expected. For more in-depth logging and reporting, you will want to use *catalog logging and reporting*, which will be discussed later in this chapter.

Let's take a look at setting up package logging and then how to use the output.

Setting Up Package Logging

To set up logging at a package level, you will go to the package itself and turn on logging. Each package needs to be set up separately to log to the database. You can do this by right-clicking on the package and selecting the Logging option or going to the SSIS menu at the top of the SQL Server Data Tools (SSDT) and selecting the Logging option.

Within the Logging menu, you will decide what type of logging you want to use. Among the options are text files, XML files, and SQL Server tables. Once the type of logging has been decided, you will select which events you want to log and at what level you want to log these events. If you select events at the highest package level, you will be able to see all events for all lower containers, too. The logging menu with the SQL Server option set is shown in Figure 15-1.

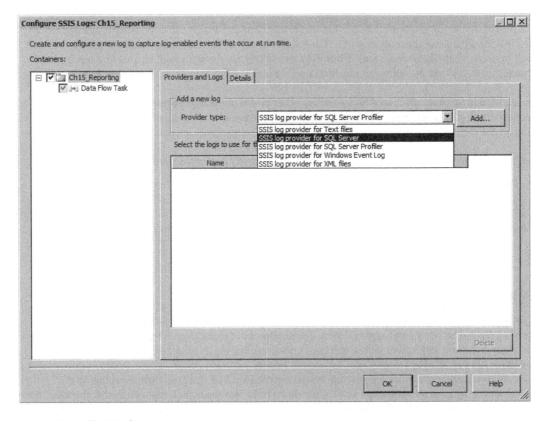

Figure 15-1. *The SSIS logging menu*

■ **Note**　While this chapter focuses on package logging to a SQL Server database table to facilitate reporting, you can learn more about all logging methods in Chapter 12.

When the package runs, Integration Services creates a new table, if one is not already available, and stores the logging information within it. The table sysssislog contains the data for all recorded events.

Reporting on Package Logging

Once you've run the package with logging, you'll want to know what happened! The table that contains all of the information you need is called `sysssislog`. By default, it will be created in the `msdb` database on the server of the connection manager you selected in the `Logging` menu; however, you can change the database by specifying it directly in the connection manager.

Let's take a look at the data in the table once we've run the package by running the following SQL query:

```
select * from msdb.dbo.sysssislog
```

This statement returns results similar to those in Figure 15-2.

	id	event	computer	operator	source	sourceid	executionid	starttime	endtime	datacode	datab
1	1	OnPreValidate	SQLSERVER2012	SQLSE...	Ch19_Reporting	D3F185D9...	6B1E706F-D...	2012-06-13 08:39:49.000	2012-06-13 08:39:49.000	0	0x
2	2	OnPostValidate	SQLSERVER2012	SQLSE...	Ch19_Reporting	D3F185D9...	6B1E706F-D...	2012-06-13 08:39:49.000	2012-06-13 08:39:49.000	0	0x
3	3	PackageStart	SQLSERVER2012	SQLSE...	Ch19_Reporting	D3F185D9...	6B1E706F-D...	2012-06-13 08:39:49.000	2012-06-13 08:39:49.000	0	0x
4	4	Diagnostic	SQLSERVER2012	SQLSE...	Ch19_Reporting	D3F185D9...	6B1E706F-D...	2012-06-13 08:39:49.000	2012-06-13 08:39:49.000	0	0x
5	5	DiagnosticEx	SQLSERVER2012	SQLSE...	Ch19_Reporting	D3F185D9...	6B1E706F-D...	2012-06-13 08:39:49.000	2012-06-13 08:39:49.000	0	0x
6	6	OnPreExecute	SQLSERVER2012	SQLSE...	Ch19_Reporting	D3F185D9...	6B1E706F-D...	2012-06-13 08:39:49.000	2012-06-13 08:39:49.000	0	0x
7	7	OnPostExecute	SQLSERVER2012	SQLSE...	Ch19_Reporting	D3F185D9...	6B1E706F-D...	2012-06-13 08:39:50.000	2012-06-13 08:39:50.000	0	0x
8	8	DiagnosticEx	SQLSERVER2012	SQLSE...	Ch19_Reporting	D3F185D9...	6B1E706F-D...	2012-06-13 08:39:50.000	2012-06-13 08:39:50.000	0	0x

Figure 15-2. *Results from the SSIS log table*

Design Pattern: Package Executions

While it is possible to use the information in the table directly, you can also combine the information to make it a little more readable. If you want to see the package executions and how long each page took to run, you can use the following query, in Listing 15-1:

Listing 15-1. Query to Return Package Durations

```
select ssis.source
       , min(starttime) as package_start
       , max(endtime) as package_end
       ,DATEDIFF(ms, min(starttime), max(endtime)) as duration_ms
from msdb.dbo.sysssislog ssis
where event in ('PackageStart', 'PackageEnd')
group by ssis.source, ssis.executionid
```

Catalog Logging and Reporting

The catalog logging and reporting method is new in Integration Services 2012 and is the best logging method to use if available. It can be used only if you have set up the Project Deployment Model type. The nice thing about this type of logging is you don't need to prepare anything in the package to utilize it. Let's jump right into how to set up the logging and design patterns to report on that data.

Setting Up Catalog Logging

As I mentioned earlier, the benefit of catalog logging is that you don't need to modify the package at all to use the logging output. The only preparation you need is to make sure your package is set to project deployment type and deploy the package to the SSIS catalog.

To begin setting up catalog logging and reporting, you will create an SSIS catalog. You can do this by connecting to the database instance. If Integration Services is installed, you will see a node entitled Integration Services Catalogs. If you create a new catalog named SSISDB, it will look like Figure 15-3.

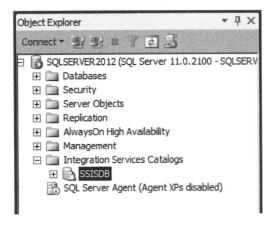

Figure 15-3. *The SSISDB catalog*

At this point, you are ready to deploy your package. First, though, you should make sure the project is set to use the Project Deployment Model. You can do this by right-clicking on the project. If you see Package Deployment Model, as shown in Figure 15-4, you are in this mode.

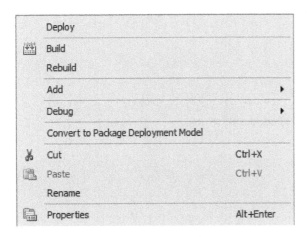

Figure 15-4. *A project in project deployment mode*

Finally, you will deploy the package to the SSIS catalog. This stores the package in the msdb database and allows for some default and some configurable logging.

Next, we will look at the tables where the information for both types of logging is stored.

Catalog Tables

When a package runs, all of the information is stored in a set of tables that reside in the SSISDB database on the same server where the Integration Services package was deployed. While there is a series of internal tables, you will do most of your reporting from the catalog views. Figure 15-5 shows a database diagram of the SSIS internal tables, while Figure 15-6 shows a list of the SSIS catalog views.

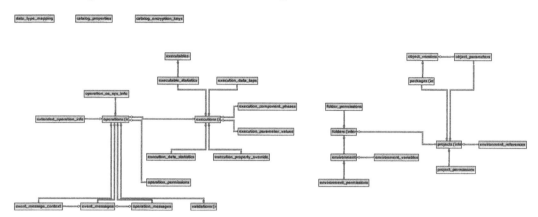

Figure 15-5. *SSIS catalog internal tables*

Figure 15-6. *SSIS catalog views*

Changing Logging Levels After the Fact

Even after the package has been deployed to the Integration Services server, you can change the amount of logging that occurs. But why would you want to do this? If you initially set up your package with a defined set of logging events, you will see only that set of data. However, you may want to include more events if you are doing more advanced troubleshooting or if you have a specific error you need to track down. On the other hand, you may want to increase the performance of a package by reducing the number of events that are recorded.

Modifying logging at the package level is not a best practice. By opening up the package to change even the slightest item, you increase the risk of a breaking change, whether it be fat-fingering a value or choosing an unavailable logging option. In some organizations, this may even result in the package having to go through the change control process again. Ideally, we want to make logging changes in an external location without touching the package at all.

In Integration Services 2012, you can choose from four different logging levels, as described in Table 15-1.

Table 15-1. *SSIS Logging Levels*

Logging Level ID	Level	Events	Notes
0	None	None	Captures enough information to say whether the package succeeded or failed but does not log any messages to the [operation_messages] view
1	Basic	OnPreValidate	Captures similar information to what is displayed on the console by the default when a package is run with dtexec
		OnPostValidate	
		OnPreExecute	
		OnPostExecute	
		OnInformation	
		OnWarning	
		OnError	
2	Performance	OnWarning	Required to track the performance information for the run (how long it took to run each task or component, how many rows were processed, etc.) but does not log all of the events captured by the Basic log level
		OnError	
3	Verbose	All events	Captures all log events, including performance and diagnostic events; can introduce some overhead on performance

Design Patterns

Now that you know how to set up and log information, let's walk through the following design patterns:

1. Changing the logging level

2. Utilizing existing reports

3. Creating new reports

Changing the Logging Level

Now that you know what the different logging levels are and when you would use each one, let's walk through changing the logging level. You can do this in either of two ways: through the execution interface or through a command-line execution.

To modify the logging level through the execution interface, you will connect your Integration Services catalog, right-click on the desired package, and select Execute. On the execution wizard, you will see the Logging option on the Advanced tab. By default, the option is set to Basic, as shown in Figure 15-7. Alternatively, you can modify this value to another logging level to see more or less in the logging tables.

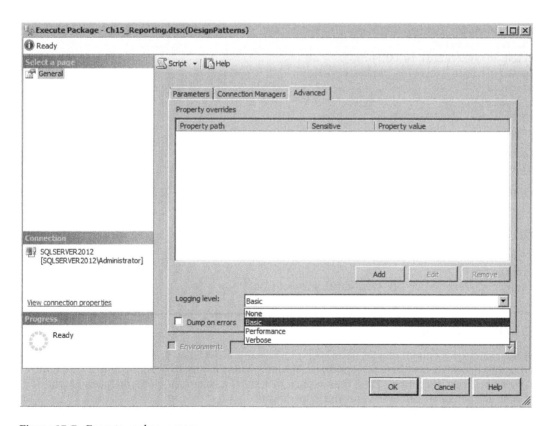

Figure 15-7. *Execute package screen*

The other option is to modify logging through the command line. All packages can be executed through the command line, and you can set a logging level associated with an individual execution.

■ **Note**   Much of the functionality associated with administering Integration Services packages can be accessed through a command-line interface. By using the command line, you can integrate your Integration Services administration with your other maintenance tasks.

Run the following code in Listing 15-2 to change the logging level to log all Verbose records for a new execution:

Listing 15-2. Statement to Modify the Logging Level for an Execution

```
DECLARE @execution_id INT
EXECUTE [catalog].[create_execution]
   @folder_name = 'DesignPatterns'
  ,@project_name = 'DesignPatterns'
  ,@package_name = 'Ch15_Reporting.dtsx'
  ,@reference_id = null
  ,@use32bitruntime = false
  ,@execution_id = @execution_id OUTPUT
EXECUTE [catalog].[set_execution_parameter_value]
   @execution_id
  ,@object_type = 50
  ,@parameter_name = 'LOGGING_LEVEL'
  ,@parameter_value = 3 --Verbose

EXECUTE [catalog].[start_execution]
   @execution_id
```

Once you've done this, you can see the output from the newly set logging level by running the query in Listing 15-3:

Listing 15-3. Query to Return All Messages

```
select * from catalog.event_messages
where operation_id =
        (select max(execution_id) from catalog.executions)
```

Utilizing Existing Reports

Our next design pattern is an important one: use what is provided to you. Included in the SSIS catalog are reports that use the logging information we have just discussed. The information in these reports includes an in-depth view of all of your packages' executions. These reports are a great start for you to see when your packages run, if any errors occur, and potential trouble areas for you to investigate.

Figure 15-8 shows all of the reports available to you. You can access all reports through the Management Studio interface and the Integration Services Catalog node.

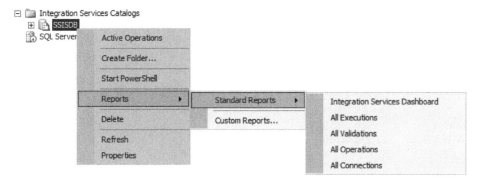

Figure 15-8. *Available catalog reports*

If you are looking at a specific execution, you will always want to start with the Overview report, which can be run by selecting the Overview link on any of the provided reports. In fact, at the end of an execution through the interface, you will be asked if you want to see this report. If you select yes, you will see something similar to Figure 15-9.

Figure 15-9. *An overview report*

Creating New Reports

Now that you've seen the reports that are available to you without doing any work, you may be perfectly happy. If not, you may want to dig into the data a little deeper. You can create new reports by looking at the catalog views that were described earlier. Particular reasons why you may want to do this include

1. Seeing the longest-running executions

2. Finding out why a package failed

3. Understanding the inner workings of a particular component

Let's start with the first reason. This report is interesting because it uses the main output view, but based on the query and transformations, it becomes a helpful little tool. Listing 15-4 shows the query that lists the five longest-running packages over the past day:

Listing 15-4. Query for Five Longest-Running Packages

```
select top 5 e.execution_id, e.package_name, DATEDIFF(ms, start_time, end_time) as
duration_ms
from catalog.executions e
where e.start_time>DATEADD(dd, -1, getdate())
order by duration_ms desc
```

The second reason you may want a new report is to see why a package failed. You will use an additional view for this information, the catalog.event_messages view. Restricting the data on both the executions and the event_ messages view will ensure that you get only packages that failed entirely and see only the events that caused them to fail. This query can be seen in Listing 15-5:

Listing 15-5. Failed-Packages Query

```
select e.execution_id, e.package_name, em.*
from catalog.executions e
inner join catalog.event_messages em on e.execution_id=em.operation_id
where e.status=4 and em.event_name='OnError'
```

The final reason is to understand the inner workings of a particular component. You can see the individual steps that occurred during the execution of each component in the data flow. For example, the query in Listing 15-6 returns each step that occurs in the execution of the sources, transformations, and destinations and how long each step takes.

Listing 15-6. Query to Return Component Phases and Times

```
select subcomponent_name, phase
              , DATEDIFF(ms, start_time, end_time) as duration_ms
from catalog.execution_component_phases
where package_name='Ch15_Reporting.dtsx'
              and task_name='Data Flow Task'
```

Once you have your desired query, you can either run it directly from Management Studio or embed it into a Reporting Services report to make it look like the Standard reports available in the solution. To make the report through Management Studio, you can store the folders in your local Documents folder, under the structure SQL Server Management Studio\Custom Reports. To access them, you will then select the Custom Reports option under the Reports menu on the Integration Services node, as shown in Figure 15-10.

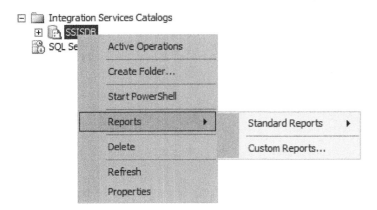

Figure 15-10. *Selection of custom reports*

Summary

This chapter has discussed many ways to monitor your Integration Services packages. Whether you are using an older version of the tool or the latest and greatest, you will be able to understand the internal workings of the package by following the design patterns described here. Discussions of both package logging and reporting and catalog logging and reporting have shown you how to modify the types of events you log and how to retrieve that information.

CHAPTER 16

■ ■ ■

Parent-Child Patterns

In earlier versions of Integration Services, the data movement platform did not include a management framework, which is the implementation of the execution, logging, and deployment of the Integration Services packages. To try to fill this hole, developers created their own management framework to use in their organizations. As with any custom solution, the management framework needed to be cared for and upgraded when new versions or new packages were introduced into the system.

Previous chapters have covered ETL instrumentation, focusing on metadata collection and validation. The metadata discussed include key information necessary to manage your packages. Not only can these metadata be used standalone, they can also be used as part of a management framework. This chapter starts the Integration Services Framework section, where we will discuss management frameworks. Specifically, Chapter Four covers parent-child patterns, where an Integration Services package can execute another package from within its own execution.

Integration Services 2012 contains its own management framework, including logging and execution through the Integration Services service. In this and subsequent chapters, we will show how to use the available framework and enhance it to provide more information while still working around the issues we discussed.

The following are the three parent-child patterns we'll discuss in this chapter:

- Master Package Pattern
- Dynamic Child Package Pattern
- Child to Parent Variable Pattern

Using these patterns, you can implement the Integration Services management functionality out of the box.

Master Package Pattern

When setting up a framework, one of the first things we want to do is find a way to organize how our packages execute. This organization could include parallel versus serial processing, conditional execution, and categorical batching. While some of this organization could occur in a job scheduler such as SQL Agent or Tivoli, wouldn't it be easier if we could manage our package execution in an environment we already know?

Luckily for us, Integration Services already provides this ability! By using the workflow designer and the Execute Package Task, we can execute other packages, creating a "Parent-Child" package relationship. When we use the parent-child relationship to execute a series of packages, we call this a master package. There are two steps we need to complete in order to set up one child package for our master package:

1. Assign the child package
2. Configure parameter binding

Assign the Child Package

Once we have created our initial package, we begin by using the Execute Package Task from the SSIS Toolbox. Drag the task to the Control Flow, and open the task to see multiple menus that we can modify. Let's begin by configuring the **Package** menu, as shown in Figure 16-1.

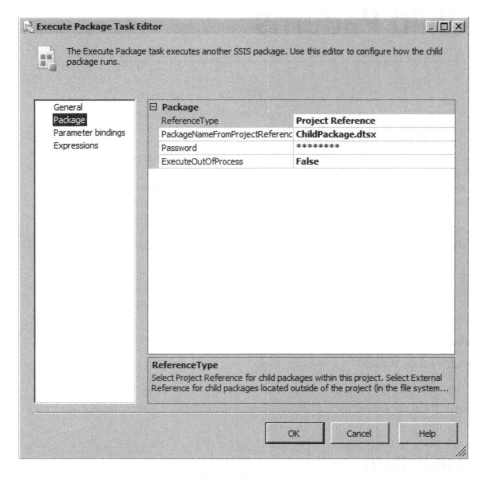

Figure 16-1. *Execute Package Task Editor Package Screen*

This is where we set up the package that we want to execute. A new addition to the Execute Package Task is the ReferenceType property, which enables developers to use the master package to run a package that is included in this project or a package that is external to the project. For this example, we will just use an existing package in our solution.

At this point, we could click the OK button and have a perfectly acceptable master package. Before we do that; however, we should delve into passing information between the packages using parameters in the next menu, **Parameter bindings**.

Configure Parameter Binding

Just calling a child package isn't very exciting. What is exciting is tying the child package into something that the master package is doing! We do this through parent package parameters. This option can only be used if we are using a child package from the same project as the master package. Once we complete the setup for our package parameters, we should see the screen shown in Figure 16-2.

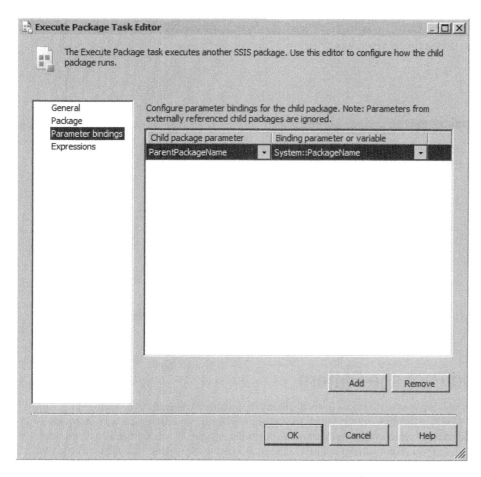

Figure 16-2. *Execute Package Task Editor Parameter Bindings Screen*

To achieve the result shown in Figure 16-2, we need to look at the Execute Package Task Editor and go to the **Parameter bindings** menu. Click the Add button to set up a parameter. For the Child Package Parameter, we can either select a parameter that has already been created or add our own parameter, in case we have not created the child package's parameter yet. Keep in mind that this will not automatically create the variable in the child package. That is up to you to do! Next, we will assign either a parameter or variable from the master package to be stored in the child parameter. In the scenario shown in Figure 16-2, we are storing the name of the parent package in a parameter in the child package, which could be used to record the package that called the child package.

If we want to test the package, we can create a Script Task in the child package, using the code shown in Listing 16-1. Make sure to put the $Package::ParentPackageName parameter in the ReadOnlyVariables property. If everything is mapped correctly, when we run the package, we should see the name of the parent package in a message box, as shown in Figure 16-3.

Listing 16-1. *Visual Basic Code to Display the Parent Package Name*

```
Public Sub Main()
    MsgBox("The name of the parent package is: " & _
            Dts.Variables("$Package::ParentPackageName").Value.ToString)
    Dts.TaskResult = ScriptResults.Success
End Sub
```

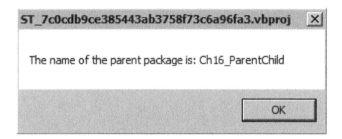

Figure 16-3. *Message box showing the name of the Parent Package*

Now that we have a working parent child package, let's take it to the next level by creating a dynamic child package.

Dynamic Child Package Pattern

One of the nice things about Integration Services is the flexibility it provides if you want to do something a little different. For example, if you are not sure exactly which packages need to run, you can create a master package that has a dynamic child package which will only execute the desired packages. This is a great idea if you have a series of files coming in, but you're not sure which files come in at a certain time. Our end goal is to create a package that looks like Figure 16-4. Let's walk through an example of creating the master package and list of the dynamic packages that we want to execute.

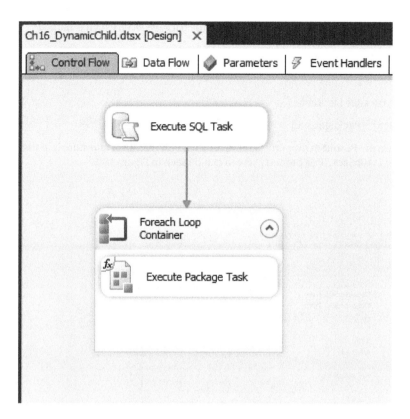

Figure 16-4. *Completed Dynamic Child Package Pattern Package*

To create the table that contains the package names, run the Create and Insert statements found in Listing 16-2.

Listing 16-2. T-SQL Code to Create and Populate a Package List Table

```
USE [DesignPatterns]
GO

CREATE TABLE [dbo].[PackageList](
        [ChildPackageName] [varchar](50) NULL
)
GO

INSERT INTO [dbo].[PackageList] ([ChildPackageName])
     VALUES ('ChildPackage.dtsx')
GO

INSERT INTO [dbo].[PackageList] ([ChildPackageName])
     VALUES ('ChildPackage2.dtsx')
GO
```

Now we will create the master package. Starting with a blank SSIS package, create a variable that is scoped to the package level. The variable should be named packageListObject and have a data type of Object. You do not need to put a value for the variable. Secondly, add a variable, also scoped to the package level, which is named packageName. This is data type String and also contains an empty value.

Next, add an Execute SQL Task in the Control Flow. Use the query in the Execute SQL Task shown in Listing 16-3 against the database you just created your table.

Listing 16-3. T-SQL Code to Query the Package List Table

```
SELECT [ChildPackageName] FROM [dbo].[PackageList]
```

In addition to the SQL query, ensure the ResultSet property is set to return a **Full result set** and store it in the variable we just created called packageListObject. This property screen can be seen in Figure 16-5.

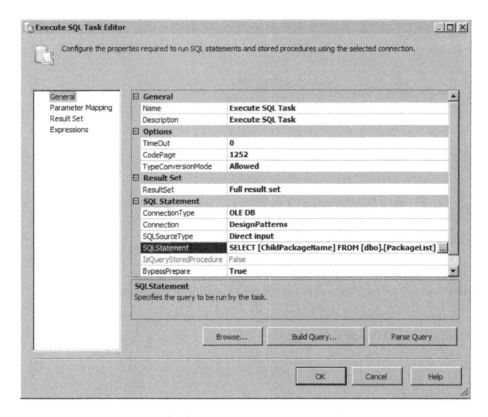

Figure 16-5. Execute SQL Task Editor Screen

Attach a ForEach Loop Container to the Execute SQL Task. This is where we will execute the package. Within the Collection menu of the ForEach Loop Container, set the enumerator to use Foreach ADO Enumerator, which will loop through the variable object. The ADO object source variable field should contain `User::packageListObject`. This screen can be seen in Figure 16-6.

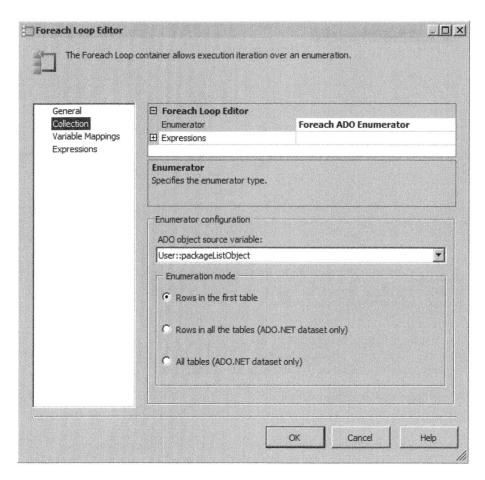

Figure 16-6. *Foreach Loop Editor Screen that enumerates through each row in the packageListObject variable*

Then, we need to tell Integration Services what to do with the value it retrieves when enumerating through the object list. On the Variable Mappings menu, set the variable to `User::packageName` and the Index to 0. This will put each value into the variable.

Finally, we're at a point to add the part that executes the package. Similar to the creation of the master-child package, we want to use an Execute Package Task. Begin by setting the DelayValidation property to **True** to allow us to make the decision of what package to run at runtime. Rather than walk through the same steps as we did in the master-child package, we will go directly to the Expressions menu in the Execute Package Task Editor. This is where we set up the dynamic portion of the package. Set the Package Name Property to use the Expression `@[User::packageName]`. The final Expressions screen should look like Figure 16-7.

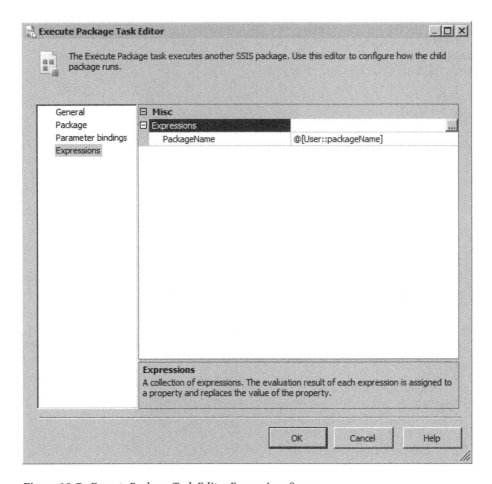

Figure 16-7. *Execute Package Task Editor Expressions Screen*

When the package runs, it will loop through each row in the PackageList table, set the package name property of the Execute SQL Task to the current row, and execute only the packages that you need. Keep in mind that this will always run the child packages serially, unless you create multiple loops and specifically code your master package to handle parallelism.

Next, we will describe how a child package can send information back to the parent package in the Child to Parent Variable pattern.

Child to Parent Variable Pattern

Parent-child patterns are an essential part of a management framework. For example, you could use the master package pattern to group similar packages together and make sure they are executed in the correct order. You could also use the dynamic child package pattern to run a variable number of packages. To ensure that we store all of this information, it is important to pass important information between packages, not only from the parent to the child, but also from the child back to the parent. While this feature is not readily known, it is possible to do this using the Script Task. Let's use our existing packages to show how to pass the name of a file from the child package to its parent.

The first step is to create a variable in the parent package. In our scenario, we are going to create a variable named ChildFileName of datatype String that is scoped at the package level. Attached to the Execute Package Task we created previously in this chapter, we'll add a Script Task. Add the ChildFileName variable as a ReadOnly variable, and add the code in Listing 16-4 inside the Visual Basic script.

Listing 16-4. Visual Basic Script to Display the Child File Name

```
Public Sub Main()
    MsgBox("The name of the child file is: " & _
           Dts.Variables("User::ChildFileName").Value.ToString)
    Dts.TaskResult = ScriptResults.Success
End Sub
```

Next, we will modify our child package. In the Script Task, add the variable User::ChildFileName to the ReadWriteVariables property list. Add the line of code found in Listing 16-5 to the Visual Basic script task.

Listing 16-5. Visual Basic Script to Set the Child File Name Value

```
Dts.Variables("User::ChildFileName").Value = "SalesFile.txt"
```

Once run, the package will finish with the figure seen in Figure 16-8.

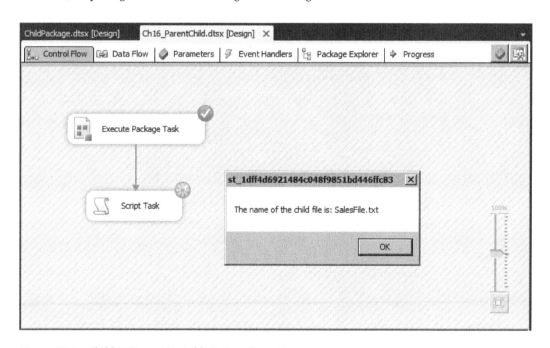

Figure 16-8. Child To Parent Variable Pattern Execution

The passing of variable values from child to parent package works because of how containers work in Integration Services. Inside of a package, any child container, such as a Sequence Container, can access its parent's properties. Likewise, any child task, such as an Execute SQL Task, can access its parent's properties. This paradigm allows us to use variables and properties without having to recreate them for every object in our package. When we add a child package using the Execute Package Task, we add another layer to the parent-child hierarchy, and allow the child package to set the parent package's variable.

Summary

SQL Server enthusiasts everywhere embraced Integration Services when it was first introduced as part of SQL Server 2005. The latest edition of Integration Services has been enhanced to make ETL developers even more excited than before. Integration Services 2012 includes the basis for a management framework and the ability to create parent child relationships, as this chapter discussed. We also discussed master package patterns and management frameworks.

## CHAPTER 17

Business Intelligence Markup Language

You likely purchased this book to learn how to be a more productive SQL Server Integration Services developer. I applaud your desire and decision, and I sincerely hope the information contained herein has provided ideas and information to help you be more productive. I am always on the lookout for ways to become a better data integration developer. Specifically, I seek out ways to improve code quality and reduce the amount of time required to build solutions. Those goals motivated me to begin practicing patterns-based development in the first place, which eventually led to the idea for this book.

Business Intelligence Markup Language – or Biml – represents SSIS packages using XML. By storing metadata that describes SSIS packages in XML, Biml approaches data integration development from the perspective of a domain-specific language. Business Intelligence Markup Language provides another means to materialize SSIS design patterns – something other than an SSIS package library containing template packages. Regardless of which mechanism used, storing design patterns facilitates code production at a consistent and repeatable quality. That may sound innocuous but I assure it is important; and it is one of the primary reasons to use design patterns in the first place.

Biml is a complex language. You would do well to gain an understanding of domain-specific languages, XML, and .Net development before diving into Biml development proper. I will not delve into the underlying architecture of Biml in this chapter. I will show you some of the mechanisms and direct you to the Biml documentation website: `www.varigence.com/documentation/biml/`. I believe this is enough to whet your appetite while demonstrating the power of Biml.

A Brief History of Business Intelligence Markup Language

In early 2007, the Microsoft Customer Service and Support (CSS) business incubated a new approach to building business intelligence solutions. As the organization responsible for managing all front-line customer support interactions, CSS has significant analytical and predictive business intelligence needs – across data from a wide variety of sources. To accelerate the development of its internal solutions, CSS began the development of the Vulcan project, which used an XML-based markup language to describe a subset of SQL Server Integration Services packages. This created a model where business intelligence solutions could be developed more rapidly and iteratively by globally distributed teams of BI developers.

After a period of significant success building new BI capabilities, CSS and the SQL Server product team decided to publish the source code for the Vulcan project on CodePlex to enable customers to try the technology and begin building a community around it (`http://vulcan.codeplex.com`). Feedback from customers recognized that the approach was powerful and promising, but that the implementation reflected the project's status as an internal tool used to accelerate an operational delivery team. Without documentation and training resources, usability considerations, and additional features, the cost of adopting Vulcan was prohibitive for all but the most determined customers.

In late 2008, Scott Currie, who worked with the Vulcan technology in CSS, founded Varigence, Inc. Varigence created the Business Intelligence Markup Language (Biml), along with tools to enable its design and development. While Biml didn't directly use any code or technology from Vulcan, the approach taken by the Vulcan project inspired the Varigence team to build Bimlas an Xml-based markup language with rapid, iterative global team development capabilities in mind.

Biml is now available in proprietary products, open source projects, and has been published as an open language specification. Varigence has developed a Biml-compiler that enables a wide variety of automation and multi-targeting capabilities. Additionally, Varigence offers an Integrated Development Environment (IDE) for Biml called Mist. Mist enables rapid and visual design and debugging features for Biml. The open source BIDSHelper project includes Biml functionality, enabling anyone to write and execute Biml code for free.[1]

In this chapter, we will leverage the free Biml functionality included with BIDSHelper to dynamically generate SSIS packages.

■ **Note** An object containing Business Intelligence Markup Language is a "Biml File". Biml files are "executed" to generate SSIS Packages.

Building Your First Biml File

Before we get started with Business Intelligence Markup Language, you will need to download and install the latest version of BIDSHelper from http://bidshelper.codeplex.com. Once installed, create a new SSIS solution and project named "Biml." In Solution Explorer, right-click the project name and click "Add New Biml File." The new file, BimlScript.biml, will be created and assigned to the Miscellaneous virtual folder in Solution Explorer. Double-click the file to open it in the editor.

The file begins with the most basic Biml construct, as shown in Listing 17-1.

Listing 17-1. Initial Biml Code

```
<Biml xmlns = "http://schemas.varigence.com/biml.xsd">
</Biml>
```

Add XML so that your Biml file reads as shown in Listing 17-2.

Listing 17-2. Biml After Adding Package XML Metadata

```
<Biml xmlns = "http://schemas.varigence.com/biml.xsd">
  <Packages>
    <Package Name = "TestBimlPackage" ConstraintMode = "Parallel">
    </Package>
  </Packages>
</Biml>
```

Save the file, right-click BimlScript.biml in Solution Explorer, and then click "Generate SSIS Packages." Figure 17-1 shows a new SSIS package named TestBimlPackage.dtsx is created in the project and file system. The packageshows up in Solution Explorer as part of this project:

---

[1] From an interview with Scott Currie of Varigence, Inc.

Figure 17-1. *TestBimlPackage.dtsx*

Let's return to the BimlScript.biml file and add a task. Create a new XML node beneath the `<Package>` tag named "Tasks." Between the `<Tasks>` and `</Tasks>` tags, add a new node named "ExecuteSQL."

■ **Tip** If you are not seeing Intellisense with Biml, follow this link: `http://bidshelper.codeplex.com/ wikipage?title=Manually%20Configuring%20Biml%20Package%20Generator&referringTitle= xcopy%20deploy` for Biml Intellisense configuration instructions.

Add an attribute to the ExecuteSQL root node named "Name" and set its value to "Test Select." Create a new XML node between the `<ExecuteSQL>` and `</ExecuteSQL>` tags named "DirectInput." Between the `<DirectInput>` and `</DirectInput>` add the T-SQL statement "Select 1 As One." If you are playing along at home, your BimlScript.biml file should look like Listing 17-3.

Listing 17-3. Biml After Adding Initial Metadata Describing an Execute SQL Task

```
<Biml xmlns="http://schemas.varigence.com/biml.xsd">
  <Packages>
    <Package Name="TestBimlPackage" ConstraintMode="Parallel">
      <Tasks>
        <ExecuteSQL Name="Test Select">
          <DirectInput>Select 1 As One</DirectInput>
        </ExecuteSQL>
      </Tasks>
    </Package>
  </Packages>
</Biml>
```

To test, save the file and generate the SSIS package from BimlScript.biml in Solution Explorer. Do you get an error similar to that displayed in Figure 17-2? You should get such an error.

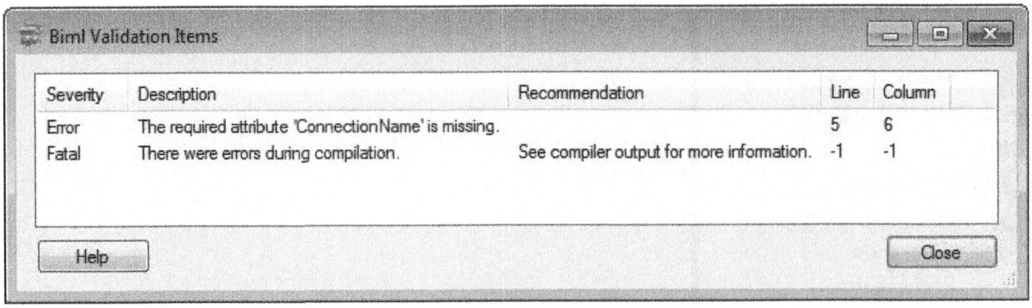

Figure 17-2. *Missing "ConnectionName" attribute*

The Business Intelligence Markup Language engine includes validation functionality and it caught the error in Figure 17-2. You can invoke a validation from Solution Explorer; simply right-click BimlScript.biml and then click "Check Biml for Errors."

To fix the error we need to add a Connection Name attribute to the "ExecuteSQL" tag. But we don't have a connection specified at this time. To create a connection, return to the top of BimlScript.biml and add a new line just after the "Biml" tag and before the "Packages" tag. On this line, add the "Connections" XML node. Inside the < Connections > and </Connections > tags, add a "Connection" XML node. A Connection requires two attributes, Name and ConnectionString. I created a connection to the AdventureWorks2012 database on the default instance of the local SQL Server. Once the Connection metadata is configured, I added a ConnectionName attribute to the "ExecuteSQL" tag. My BimlScript.biml file now contains the code listed in Listing 17-4.

Listing 17-4. Biml After Adding Connection Metadata

```
<Biml xmlns="http://schemas.varigence.com/biml.xsd">
  <Connections>
    <Connection Name="AdventureWorks2012" ConnectionString="Data Source=.;Initial
Catalog=AdventureWorks2012;Provider=SQLNCLI10.1;Integrated Security=SSPI;Auto Translate=False;" />
  </Connections>
  <Packages>
    <Package Name="TestBimlPackage" ConstraintMode="Parallel">
      <Tasks>
        <ExecuteSQL Name="Test Select" ConnectionName="AdventureWorks2012">
          <DirectInput>Select 1 As One</DirectInput>
        </ExecuteSQL>
      </Tasks>
    </Package>
  </Packages>
</Biml>
```

Let's test by regenerating the TestBimlPackage.dtsx SSIS package from BimlScript.biml. When we attempt to generate the SSIS package, we see a dialog that confirms we would like to overwrite the existing TestBimlPackage. dtsx SSIS package. When you confirm this intention, the TestBimlPackage.dtsx SSIS package is regenerated from the metadata contained in the updated BimlScript.biml file. Open the TestBimlPackage.dtsx SSIS package: it should appear as shown in Figure 17-3.

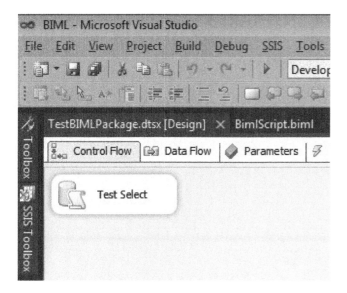

Figure 17-3. *A Biml-Generated SSIS package*

Building a Basic Incremental Load SSIS Package

The Incremental Load Pattern is fundamental in data integration solutions; especially Extract, Transform, and Load (ETL) solutions. Biml provides a mechanism for codifying the Incremental Load pattern in a repeatable fashion.Creating Databases and Tables.

Let's prepare for this demo by building a couple databases and tables. Execute the T-SQL statements from Listing 17-5 to build and populate the test databases and tables.

Listing 17-5. Building and Populating Demo Databases and Tables

```
Use master
Go

If Not Exists(Select name
              From sys.databases
              Where name = 'SSISIncrementalLoad_Source')
 CREATE DATABASE [SSISIncrementalLoad_Source]

If Not Exists(Select name
              From sys.databases
              Where name = 'SSISIncrementalLoad_Dest')
 CREATE DATABASE [SSISIncrementalLoad_Dest]

Use SSISIncrementalLoad_Source
Go

If Not Exists(Select name
              From sys.tables
              Where name = 'tblSource')
```

```
CREATE TABLE dbo.tblSource
 (ColID int NOT NULL
 ,ColA varchar(10) NULL
 ,ColB datetime NULL constraint df_ColB default (getDate())
 ,ColC int NULL
 ,constraint PK_tblSource primary key clustered (ColID))

Use SSISIncrementalLoad_Dest
Go

If Not Exists(Select name
              From sys.tables
              Where name = 'tblDest')
CREATE TABLE dbo.tblDest
 (ColID int NOT NULL
 ,ColA varchar(10) NULL
 ,ColB datetime NULL
 ,ColC int NULL)

 If Not Exists(Select name
               From sys.tables
               Where name = 'stgUpdates')
 CREATE TABLE dbo.stgUpdates
  (ColID int NULL
  ,ColA varchar(10) NULL
  ,ColB datetime NULL
  ,ColC int NULL)

Use SSISIncrementalLoad_Source
Go
 -- insert an "unchanged", a "changed", and a "new" row
INSERT INTO dbo.tblSource
 (ColID,ColA,ColB,ColC)
 VALUES
 (0, 'A', '1/1/2007 12:01 AM', -1),
 (1, 'B', '1/1/2007 12:02 AM', -2),
 (2, 'N', '1/1/2007 12:03 AM', -3)

Use SSISIncrementalLoad_Dest
Go

-- insert a "changed" and an "unchanged" row
INSERT INTO dbo.tblDest
 (ColID,ColA,ColB,ColC)
 VALUES
 (0, 'A', '1/1/2007 12:01 AM', -1),
 (1, 'C', '1/1/2007 12:02 AM', -2)
```

The T-SQL statements in Listing 17-5 create two databases; SSISIncrementalLoad_Source and SSISIncrementalLoad_Dest. A table named tblSource is created in SSISIncrementalLoad_Source database and populated with three rows. Another table named tblDest is created in the SSISIncrementalLoad_Dest database and populated with two rows.

The configuration created by Listing 17-5 is a basic setup for an incremental load. ColID is the business key. This value should never change and should also uniquely identify the row in the Source and Destination systems.

The character values in ColA of the Source and Destination tables indicate clues to the type of row. The "A" row is present and identical in both the Source and Destination tables. It is an *Unchanged* row. The row with a ColID value of 1 contains the ColA value "B" in the Source and the ColA value "C" in the Destination table. This row has *Changed* in the Source since it was initially loaded into the Destination table. The row with a ColID value of 2 exists only in the Source. It is a *New* row.

Adding Metadata

In this section, we will:

- Add metadata that defines the Connection Managers used in the Incremental Load SSIS design pattern
- Add a new Biml file to the Biml project and rename it "IncrementalLoad.biml"
- Add a "Connections" XML node just after the `<Biml>` tag
- Add two "Connection" XML nodes configured to connect with the SSISIncremental_ Source and SSISIncremental_Dest databases.

Your code should appear as shown in Listing 17-6.

Listing 17-6. Configured Connections for IncrementalLoad.biml

```
<Biml xmlns="http://schemas.varigence.com/biml.xsd">
  <Connections>
    <Connection Name="SSISIncrementalLoad_Source" ConnectionString="Data Source=(local);Initial
Catalog=SSISIncrementalLoad_Source;Provider=SQLNCLI11.1;Integrated Security=SSPI; " />
    <Connection Name="SSISIncrementalLoad_Dest" ConnectionString="Data Source=(local);Initial
Catalog=SSISIncrementalLoad_Dest;Provider=SQLNCLI11.1;OLE DB Services=1;Integrated
Security=SSPI; " />
  </Connections>
</Biml>
```

Add a "Packages" node between the `</Connections>` and `</Biml>` tags. Just after, add a "Package" XML node, followed by a "Tasks" node. Immediately thereafter, add an "ExecuteSQL" node configured as shown in Listing 17-7.

Listing 17-7. Configured Packages, Package, Tasks, and ExecuteSQL Nodes

```
<Packages>
  <Package Name="IncrementalLoadPackage" ConstraintMode="Parallel"
ProtectionLevel="EncryptSensitiveWithUserKey">
    <Tasks>
      <ExecuteSQL Name="Truncate stgUpdates" ConnectionName="SSISIncrementalLoad_Dest">
        <DirectInput>Truncate Table stgUpdates</DirectInput>
      </ExecuteSQL>
    </Tasks>
  </Package>
</Packages>
```

The Execute SQL Task defined in the Biml in Listing 17-7 will truncate a staging table that will hold rows that have been changed in the Source table since being loaded into the Destination table.

Specifying a Data Flow Task

After the </ExecuteSQL> tag, add a "Dataflow" XML node. Include a "Name" attribute and set the value of the Name attribute to "Load tblDest". Inside the < Dataflow > tag, add a "PrecedenceConstraints" node. Place an "Inputs" node inside the < PrecedenceConstraints > tag, and an "Input" node that includes an "OutputPathName" attribute with the value "Truncate stgUpdates.Output" inside the < Inputs > tag – as shown in Listing 17-8.

Listing 17-8. Adding a Precedence Constraint from the "Truncate stgUpdates" Execute SQL Task to the "Load tblDest" Data Flow Task

```
<Dataflow Name="Load tblDest">
  <PrecedenceConstraints>
    <Inputs>
      <Input OutputPathName="Truncate stgUpdates.Output" />
    </Inputs>
  </PrecedenceConstraints>
</Dataflow>
```

This code defines an OnSuccess Precedence Constraint between the "Truncate stgUpdates" Execute SQL Task to the "Load tblDest" Data Flow Task.

Adding Transformations

We are now ready to add metadata that define transformations, the heart of a Data Flow Task. In this section, we will design an Incremental Load that includes an OLEDB Source adapter, Lookup transformation, Condition Split transformation, and a couple OLEDB Destination adapters.

To begin, Add a "Transformations" node just after the < /PrecedenceConstraints > tag. Inside the < Transformations > tags, add an "OleDbSource" tag with following the attribute and value pairs:

- Name: tblSource Source
- ConnectionName: SSISIncrementalLoad_Source

Inside the < OleDbSource > tag, add an "ExternalTableInput" node with a "Table" attribute whose value is "dbo.tblSource". This metadata constructs an OLEDB Source adapter named "tblSource Source" that connects to the SSISIncrementalLoad_Source Connection defined above inside the < Connections > tag. The OLE DB Source adapter will connect to the table "dbo.tblSource" as specified in the "ExternalTableInput" tag. The "Dataflow" XML node will now appear as shown in Listing 17-9.

Listing 17-9. The Dataflow Node Containing an OLEDB Source Adapter

```
<Dataflow Name="Load tblDest">
  <PrecedenceConstraints>
    <Inputs>
      <Input OutputPathName="Truncate stgUpdates.Output" />
    </Inputs>
  </PrecedenceConstraints>
  <Transformations>
    <OleDbSource Name="tblSource Source" ConnectionName="SSISIncrementalLoad_Source">
      <ExternalTableInput Table="dbo.tblSource" />
    </OleDbSource>
  </Transformations>
</Dataflow>
```

To continue, add a "Lookup" XML node immediately after the </OleDbSource> tag. Include the following attribute and value pairs in the < Lookup > tag:

- Name: Correlate

- OleDbConnectionName: SSISIncrementalLoad_Dest

- NoMatchBehavior: RedirectRowsToNoMatchOutput

The Name attribute sets the name of the Lookup transformation. The OleDbConnectionName instructs Biml to use the Connection Manager defined in the < Connections > tag above. The NoMatchBehavior attribute is configured to redirect non-matching rows to the "NoMatch" output of the Lookup transformation.

Continue configuring the metadata that define the Lookup transformation by adding a "DirectInput" node immediately after the < InputPath > tag. Enter the following T-SQL statement between the < DirectInput > and </DirectInput> tags.

```
SELECT ColID, ColA, ColB, ColC FROM dbo.tblDest
```

Add an "Inputs" node immediately following the </DirectInput> tag. Inside the < Inputs > tag, add a "Column" node. Include the following attribute name: value pairs.

- SourceColumn: ColID

- TargetColumn: ColID

The preceding metadata provides the mapping between the Available Input Columns and Available Lookup Columns on the Columns page of the Lookup transformation.

Add an "Outputs" node immediately following the </Inputs> tag. Inside the < Outputs > tag, add three "Column" nodes with the following attribute name and value pairs.

1.
   a. SourceColumn: ColA
   b. TargetColumn: Dest_ColA

2.
   a. SourceColumn: ColB
   b. TargetColumn: Dest_ColB

3.
   a. SourceColumn: ColC
   b. TargetColumn: Dest_ColC

The preceding metadata "selects" the columns returned from the Lookup transformation's Available Lookup Columns on the Columns page. Once added, the Lookup transformation metadata should appear as shown in Listing 17-10.

Listing 17-10. Transformations Including Lookup Metadata

```
<Transformations>
  <OleDbSource Name="tblSource Source" ConnectionName="SSISIncrementalLoad_Source">
    <ExternalTableInput Table="dbo.tblSource" />
  </OleDbSource>
  <Lookup Name="Correlate" OleDbConnectionName="SSISIncrementalLoad_Dest"
NoMatchBehavior="RedirectRowsToNoMatchOutput">
    <InputPath OutputPathName="tblSource Source.Output" />
```

```
  <DirectInput>SELECT ColID, ColA, ColB, ColC FROM dbo.tblDest</DirectInput>
  <Inputs>
    <Column SourceColumn="ColID" TargetColumn="ColID" />
  </Inputs>
  <Outputs>
    <Column SourceColumn="ColA" TargetColumn="Dest_ColA" />
    <Column SourceColumn="ColB" TargetColumn="Dest_ColB" />
    <Column SourceColumn="ColC" TargetColumn="Dest_ColC" />
  </Outputs>
</Lookup>
</Transformations>
```

Immediately following the `</Lookup>` tag, add an "OleDbDestination" XML node with the following attribute name and value pairs.

- Name: tblDest Destination

- ConnectionName: SSISIncrementalLoad_Dest

Inside the `<OleDbDestination>` tag, add an "InputPath" node with an "OutputPathName" attribute set to the value "Correlate.NoMatch". After the `<InputPath>` tag, add an "ExternalTableOutput" node with a "Table" attribute set to the value "dbo.tblDest."

The preceding metadata defines an OLEDB Destination adapter and configures it to connect the Lookup transformation's "NoMatch" output to the "SSISIncrementalLoad_Dest" Connection defined above.

Add a "ConditionalSplit" XML node immediately after the `</OleDbDestination>` tag. Add an attribute called "Name" and set its value to "Filter". Inside the `<ConditionalSplit>` tags, add an "InputPath" XML node with an "OutputPathName" attribute set to "Correlate.Match". Now we need to add a conditional output path. Immediately following the `<InputPath>` tag, add an "OutputPaths" node, followed in turn by a "OutputPath" node containing an "Name" attribute set to "Changed Rows". Inside the `<OutputPaths>` tags, create an "Expression" node. Between the `<Expression>` and `</Expression>` tags, add the following SSIS Expression.

```
(ColA != Dest_ColA) || (ColB != Dest_ColB) || (ColC != Dest_ColC)
```

Once this step is complete, the "Transformations" XML should appear as shown in Listing 17-11.

Listing 17-11. Transformations Node Including an OLEDB Source, Lookup, Conditional Split, and one OLEDB Destination

```
<Transformations>
  <OleDbSource Name="tblSource Source" ConnectionName="SSISIncrementalLoad_Source">
    <ExternalTableInput Table="dbo.tblSource" />
  </OleDbSource>
  <Lookup Name="Correlate" OleDbConnectionName="SSISIncrementalLoad_Dest"
NoMatchBehavior="RedirectRowsToNoMatchOutput">
    <InputPath OutputPathName="tblSource Source.Output" />
    <DirectInput>SELECT ColID, ColA, ColB, ColC FROM dbo.tblDest</DirectInput>
    <Inputs>
      <Column SourceColumn="ColID" TargetColumn="ColID" />
    </Inputs>
    <Outputs>
      <Column SourceColumn="ColA" TargetColumn="Dest_ColA" />
      <Column SourceColumn="ColB" TargetColumn="Dest_ColB" />
      <Column SourceColumn="ColC" TargetColumn="Dest_ColC" />
    </Outputs>
  </Lookup>
```

```xml
<OleDbDestination Name="tblDest Destination" ConnectionName="SSISIncrementalLoad_Dest">
  <InputPath OutputPathName="Correlate.NoMatch" />
  <ExternalTableOutput Table="dbo.tblDest" />
</OleDbDestination>
<ConditionalSplit Name="Filter">
  <InputPath OutputPathName="Correlate.Match"/>
  <OutputPaths>
    <OutputPath Name="Changed Rows">
      <Expression>(ColA != Dest_ColA) || (ColB != Dest_ColB) ||
(ColC != Dest_ColC)</Expression>
    </OutputPath>
  </OutputPaths>
</ConditionalSplit>
</Transformations>
```

The Conditional Split metadata most recently added configures a single output named "Changed Rows" and assigns an SSIS Expression designed to detect changes in rows that exist in both the Source and Destination tables.

The final component in our Data Flow Task is an OLEDB Destination adapter designed to stage rows that will be updated *after* the data flow completes execution. Immediately following the </ConditionalSplit> tag, add an "OleDbDestination" node with the following attribute name and value pairs.

- Name: stgUpdates

- ConnectionName: SSISIncrementalLoad_Dest

Inside the <OleDbDestination> tag, add a new node named "InputPath" with an attribute named "OutputPathName" and the value set to "Filter.Changed Rows". Immediately thereafter, add a node named "ExternalTableOutput" that includes a "Table" attribute set to "dbo.stgUpdates". This metadata defines an OLEDB Destination adapter that connects the "Changed Rows" output of the Conditional Split named "Filter" to a table named "dbo.stgUpdates" in the database defined by the "SSISIncrementalLoad_Dest" Connection defined above.

The complete Data Flow Task metadata is shown in Listing 17-12.

Listing 17-12. The Completed Dataflow XML Node

```xml
<Dataflow Name="Load tblDest">
  <PrecedenceConstraints>
    <Inputs>
      <Input OutputPathName="Truncate stgUpdates.Output" />
    </Inputs>
  </PrecedenceConstraints>
  <Transformations>
    <OleDbSource Name="tblSource Source" ConnectionName="SSISIncrementalLoad_Source">
      <ExternalTableInput Table="dbo.tblSource" />
    </OleDbSource>
    <Lookup Name="Correlate" OleDbConnectionName="SSISIncrementalLoad_Dest"
NoMatchBehavior="RedirectRowsToNoMatchOutput">
      <InputPath OutputPathName="tblSource Source.Output" />
      <DirectInput>SELECT ColID, ColA, ColB, ColC FROM dbo.tblDest</DirectInput>
      <Inputs>
        <Column SourceColumn="ColID" TargetColumn="ColID" />
      </Inputs>
```

```
      <Outputs>
        <Column SourceColumn="ColA" TargetColumn="Dest_ColA" />
        <Column SourceColumn="ColB" TargetColumn="Dest_ColB" />
        <Column SourceColumn="ColC" TargetColumn="Dest_ColC" />
      </Outputs>
    </Lookup>
    <OleDbDestination Name="tblDest Destination" ConnectionName="SSISIncrementalLoad_Dest">
      <InputPath OutputPathName="Correlate.NoMatch" />
      <ExternalTableOutput Table="dbo.tblDest" />
    </OleDbDestination>
    <ConditionalSplit Name="Filter">
      <InputPath OutputPathName="Correlate.Match"/>
      <OutputPaths>
        <OutputPath Name="Changed Rows">
          <Expression>(ColA != Dest_ColA) || (ColB != Dest_ColB) || (ColC !=
Dest_ColC)</Expression>
        </OutputPath>
      </OutputPaths>
    </ConditionalSplit>
    <OleDbDestination Name="stgUpdates" ConnectionName="SSISIncrementalLoad_Dest">
      <InputPath OutputPathName="Filter.Changed Rows" />
      <ExternalTableOutput Table="dbo.stgUpdates" />
    </OleDbDestination>
  </Transformations>
</Dataflow>
```

There remains one more Execute SQL Task to complete our Incremental Load SSIS package. This task will update the Destination table by applying the rows stored in the "dbo.stgUpdates" table using a single Update T-SQL statement. Applying the updates in this fashion is generally faster than updating each row individually.

To continue developing the demo code, add an "ExecuteSQL" XML node immediately following the </Dataflow> tag with the following attribute name and value pairs.

- Name: Apply stgUpdates
- ConnectionName: SSISIncrementalLoad_Dest

Immediately following the < ExecuteSQL > tag, add a "PrecedenceConstraints" node, followed by an "Inputs" node. Inside the < Inputs > tag add an "Input" node containing an attribute named "OutputPathName" set to the value "Load tblDest.Output". Add a "DirectInput" node immediately following the </PrecedenceConstraints > tag. Inside the < DirectInput > tags, add the following T-SQL statement.

```
Update Dest
Set Dest.ColA = Upd.ColA
   ,Dest.ColB = Upd.ColB
   ,Dest.ColC = Upd.ColC
From tblDest Dest
Join stgUpdates Upd
  On Upd.ColID = Dest.ColID
```

Believe it or not, that's it! If your Biml looks like Listing 17-13, you should have compilable metadata.

Listing 17-13. The Complete IncrementalLoad.biml Listing

```
<Biml xmlns="http://schemas.varigence.com/biml.xsd">
  <Connections>
```

```xml
    <Connection Name="SSISIncrementalLoad_Source" ConnectionString="Data Source=(local);
Initial Catalog=SSISIncrementalLoad_Source;Provider=SQLNCLI11.1;Integrated Security=SSPI" />
    <Connection Name="SSISIncrementalLoad_Dest" ConnectionString="Data Source=(local);
Initial Catalog=SSISIncrementalLoad_Dest;Provider=SQLNCLI11.1;OLE DB Services=1;Integrated
Security=SSPI;" />
  </Connections>
  <Packages>
    <Package Name="IncrementalLoadPackage" ConstraintMode="Parallel" ProtectionLevel="EncryptSe
nsitiveWithUserKey">
      <Tasks>
        <ExecuteSQL Name="Truncate stgUpdates" ConnectionName="SSISIncrementalLoad_Dest">
          <DirectInput>Truncate Table stgUpdates</DirectInput>
        </ExecuteSQL>
        <Dataflow Name="Load tblDest">
          <PrecedenceConstraints>
            <Inputs>
              <Input OutputPathName="Truncate stgUpdates.Output" />
            </Inputs>
          </PrecedenceConstraints>
          <Transformations>
            <OleDbSource Name="tblSource Source" ConnectionName="SSISIncrementalLoad_Source">
              <ExternalTableInput Table="dbo.tblSource" />
            </OleDbSource>
            <Lookup Name="Correlate" OleDbConnectionName="SSISIncrementalLoad_Dest"
NoMatchBehavior="RedirectRowsToNoMatchOutput">
              <InputPath OutputPathName="tblSource Source.Output" />
              <DirectInput>SELECT ColID, ColA, ColB, ColC FROM dbo.tblDest</DirectInput>
              <Inputs>
                <Column SourceColumn="ColID" TargetColumn="ColID" />
              </Inputs>
              <Outputs>
                <Column SourceColumn="ColA" TargetColumn="Dest_ColA" />
                <Column SourceColumn="ColB" TargetColumn="Dest_ColB" />
                <Column SourceColumn="ColC" TargetColumn="Dest_ColC" />
              </Outputs>
            </Lookup>
            <OleDbDestination Name="tblDest Destination" ConnectionName=
"SSISIncrementalLoad_Dest">
              <InputPath OutputPathName="Correlate.NoMatch" />
              <ExternalTableOutput Table="dbo.tblDest" />
            </OleDbDestination>
            <ConditionalSplit Name="Filter">
              <InputPath OutputPathName="Correlate.Match"/>
              <OutputPaths>
                <OutputPath Name="Changed Rows">
                  <Expression>(ColA != Dest_ColA) || (ColB != Dest_ColB) ||
(ColC != Dest_ColC)</Expression>
                </OutputPath>
              </OutputPaths>
            </ConditionalSplit>
            <OleDbDestination Name="stgUpdates" ConnectionName="SSISIncrementalLoad_Dest">
              <InputPath OutputPathName="Filter.Changed Rows" />
```

```xml
            <ExternalTableOutput Table="dbo.stgUpdates" />
          </OleDbDestination>
        </Transformations>
      </Dataflow>
      <ExecuteSQL Name="Apply stgUpdates" ConnectionName="SSISIncrementalLoad_Dest">
        <PrecedenceConstraints>
          <Inputs>
            <Input OutputPathName="Load tblDest.Output" />
          </Inputs>
        </PrecedenceConstraints>
        <DirectInput>
            Update Dest
            Set Dest.ColA = Upd.ColA
            ,Dest.ColB = Upd.ColB
            ,Dest.ColC = Upd.ColC
            From tblDest Dest
            Join stgUpdates Upd
            On Upd.ColID = Dest.ColID
        </DirectInput>
      </ExecuteSQL>
    </Tasks>
  </Package>
 </Packages>
</Biml>
```

We are now ready to test!

Testing the Biml

Testing the Biml will consist of generating the SSIS package, then executing it. We will look at the data to see if the Incremental Load executed as expected. To begin, I have prepared a T-SQL Reset Rows script shown in Listing 17-14.

Listing 17-14. Resetting the Incremental Load Source and Destination Values

```sql
Use SSISIncrementalLoad_Source
Go

TRUNCATE TABLE dbo.tblSource

-- insert an "unchanged" row, a "changed" row, and a "new" row
INSERT INTO dbo.tblSource
(ColID,ColA,ColB,ColC)
VALUES
 (0, 'A', '1/1/2007 12:01 AM', -1),
 (1, 'B', '1/1/2007 12:02 AM', -2),
 (2, 'N', '1/1/2007 12:03 AM', -3)

Use SSISIncrementalLoad_Dest
Go

TRUNCATE TABLE dbo.stgUpdates
TRUNCATE TABLE dbo.tblDest
```

```
-- insert an "unchanged" row and a "changed" row
INSERT INTO dbo.tblDest
(ColID,ColA,ColB,ColC)
VALUES
 (0, 'A', '1/1/2007 12:01 AM', -1),
 (1, 'C', '1/1/2007 12:02 AM', -2)
```

Listing 17-15 contains the test script we will use to examine and compare the contents of the Source and Destination.

Listing 17-15. Test Script for the IncrementalLoad.dtsx SSIS Package

```
Use SSISIncrementalLoad_Source
Go

SELECT TableName = 'tblSource'
         ,ColID
      ,ColA
      ,ColB
      ,ColC
  FROM dbo.tblSource
Go

Use SSISIncrementalLoad_Dest
Go

SELECT TableName = 'tblDest'
           ,[ColID]
      ,[ColA]
      ,[ColB]
      ,[ColC]
  FROM [dbo].[tblDest]

SELECT TableName = 'stgUpdates'
           ,[ColID]
      ,[ColA]
      ,[ColB]
      ,[ColC]
  FROM [dbo].[stgUpdates]
Go
```

Executing the Test script after executing the Reset script yields the results pictured in Figure 17-4.

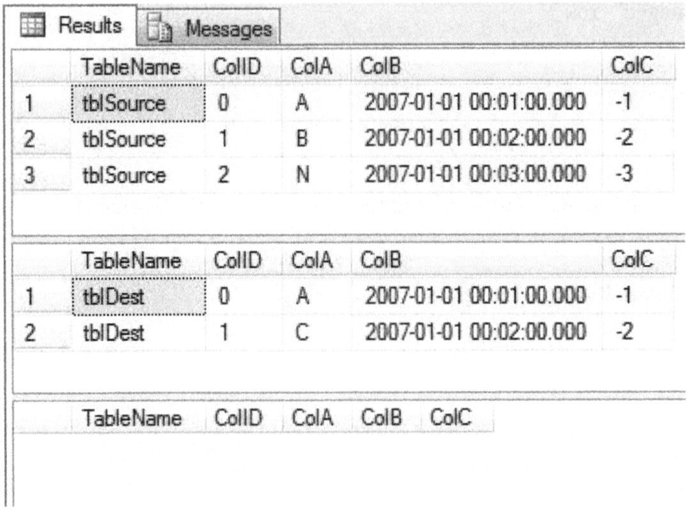

	TableName	ColID	ColA	ColB	ColC
1	tblSource	0	A	2007-01-01 00:01:00.000	-1
2	tblSource	1	B	2007-01-01 00:02:00.000	-2
3	tblSource	2	N	2007-01-01 00:03:00.000	-3

	TableName	ColID	ColA	ColB	ColC
1	tblDest	0	A	2007-01-01 00:01:00.000	-1
2	tblDest	1	C	2007-01-01 00:02:00.000	-2

	TableName	ColID	ColA	ColB	ColC

Figure 17-4. *Pre-SSIS-Package-Execution results of test script*

Return to Solution Explorer in SQL Server Data Tools. Right-click IncrementalLoad.biml and click "Generate SSIS Packages." If you receive no error, your Biml is sound and you should see an SSIS package named IncrementalLoadPackage.dtsx in the SSIS Packages virtual folder in Solution Explorer. If the SSIS package opens with no errors, press the F5 key to execute it in the Debugger. If all is as it should be, you should see results similar to those shown in Figure 17-5.

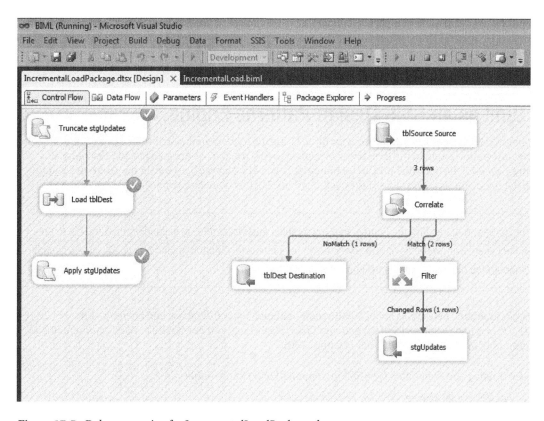

Figure 17-5. *Debug execution for IncrementalLoadPackage.dtsx*

Executing the Test script now returns evidence that SSISIncrementalLoad_Dest.dbo.tblDest has received the updates loaded from SSISIncrementalLoad_Source.dbo.tblSource, as shown in Figure 17-6.

	TableName	ColID	ColA	ColB	ColC
1	tblSource	0	A	2007-01-01 00:01:00.000	-1
2	tblSource	1	B	2007-01-01 00:02:00.000	-2
3	tblSource	2	N	2007-01-01 00:03:00.000	-3

	TableName	ColID	ColA	ColB	ColC
1	tblDest	0	A	2007-01-01 00:01:00.000	-1
2	tblDest	1	B	2007-01-01 00:02:00.000	-2
3	tblDest	2	N	2007-01-01 00:03:00.000	-3

	TableName	ColID	ColA	ColB	ColC
1	stgUpdates	1	B	2007-01-01 00:02:00.000	-2

Figure 17-6. *Results of a successful execution of IncrementalLoadPackage.dtsx*

317

By examining the results and comparing to Figure 17-4, we can see SSISIncrementalLoad_Dest.dbo.tblDest has been updated to match SSISIncrementalLoad_Source.dbo.tblSource. We can also see the updated row, with ColID = 1, was sent to the SSISIncrementalLoad_Dest.dbo.stgUpdates table.

Cool. But just wait: this is about to get awesome.

Using Biml as an SSIS Design Patterns Engine

Let's do something really cool and interesting with Biml. Using the IncrementalLoad.biml file as a template, and applying .Net integration found in the Biml library supplied to BISDHelper, we are going to add flexibility and versatility to a new Biml file that will build an Incremental Load SSIS Package between all the tables in a source and staging database. This is an example of the capital "E" in ETL; this is an Extraction SSIS Design Pattern.

■ **Note**   This pattern requires that the Source and Stage tables must exist prior to expanding the Biml file to create the SSIS Packages. Even with this caveat – which can be addressed, automated, and overcome – I believe this example demonstrates the power and game-changing attributes of Biml.

Let's begin by adding new tables to the SSISIncrementalLoad_Source database and creating – and populating – a new database named SSISIncrementalLoad_Stage. First, add new tables to SSISIncrementalLoad_Source by executing the T-SQL script shown in Listing 17-16.

Listing 17-16. Adding and Populating New SSISincrementalLoad_Source Tables

```
USE SSISIncrementalLoad_Source
GO

 -- Create Source1
If Not Exists(Select name
             From sys.tables
             Where name = 'Source1')
CREATE TABLE dbo.Source1
 (ColID int NOT NULL
 ,ColA varchar(10) NULL
 ,ColB datetime NULL
 ,ColC int NULL
 ,constraint PK_Source1 primary key clustered (ColID))
Go

 -- Load Source1
INSERT INTO dbo.Source1
(ColID,ColA,ColB,ColC)
VALUES
(0, 'A', '1/1/2007 12:01 AM', -1),
(1, 'B', '1/1/2007 12:02 AM', -2),
(2, 'C', '1/1/2007 12:03 AM', -3),
(3, 'D', '1/1/2007 12:04 AM', -4),
(4, 'E', '1/1/2007 12:05 AM', -5),
(5, 'F', '1/1/2007 12:06 AM', -6)
```

```
-- Create Source1
If Not Exists(Select name
             From sys.tables
             Where name = 'Source2')
CREATE TABLE dbo.Source2
 (ColID int NOT NULL
 ,Name varchar(25) NULL
 ,Value int NULL
 ,constraint PK_Source2 primary key clustered (ColID))
Go

  -- Load Source2
INSERT INTO dbo.Source2
(ColID,Name,Value)
VALUES
(0, 'Willie', 11),
(1, 'Waylon', 22),
(2, 'Stevie Ray', 33),
(3, 'Johnny', 44),
(4, 'Kris', 55)

-- Create Source3
If Not Exists(Select name
             From sys.tables
             Where name = 'Source3')
CREATE TABLE dbo.Source3
 (ColID int NOT NULL
 ,Value int NULL
 ,Name varchar(100) NULL
 ,constraint PK_Source3 primary key clustered (ColID))
Go

  -- Load Source3
INSERT INTO dbo.Source3
(ColID,Value,Name)
VALUES
(0, 101, 'Good-Hearted Woman'),
(1, 202, 'Lonesome, Onry, and Mean'),
(2, 303, 'The Sky Is Crying'),
(3, 404, 'Ghost Riders in the Sky'),
(4, 505, 'Sunday Morning, Coming Down')
```

The T-SQL in Listing 17-16 creates and populates three new tables.

- dbo.Source1

- dbo.Source2

- dbo.Source3

Execute the T-SQL shown in Listing 17-17 to build and populate the SSISIncrementalLoad_Stage database.

Listing 17-17. Building and Populating the SSISIncrementalLoad_Stage Database

```
Use master
Go

If Not Exists(Select name
              From sys.databases
                          Where name = 'SSISIncrementalLoad_Stage')
 Create Database SSISIncrementalLoad_Stage
Go

Use SSISIncrementalLoad_Stage
Go

CREATE TABLE dbo.tblSource(
      ColID int NOT NULL,
      ColA varchar(10) NULL,
      ColB datetime NULL,
      ColC int NULL
)

CREATE TABLE dbo.stgUpdates_tblSource(
      ColID int NOT NULL,
      ColA varchar(10) NULL,
      ColB datetime NULL,
      ColC int NULL
)
Go

INSERT INTO dbo.tblSource
 (ColID,ColA,ColB,ColC)
 VALUES
 (0, 'A', '1/1/2007 12:01 AM', -1),
 (1, 'B', '1/1/2007 12:02 AM', -2),
 (2, 'N', '1/1/2007 12:03 AM', -3)
Go

CREATE TABLE dbo.Source1(
      ColID int NOT NULL,
      ColA varchar(10) NULL,
      ColB datetime NULL,
      ColC int NULL
)

CREATE TABLE dbo.stgUpdates_Source1(
      ColID int NOT NULL,
      ColA varchar(10) NULL,
      ColB datetime NULL,
      ColC int NULL
)
Go

 INSERT INTO dbo.Source1
 (ColID,ColA,ColB,ColC)
 VALUES
 (0, 'A', '1/1/2007 12:01 AM', -1),
```

```
 (1, 'Z', '1/1/2007 12:02 AM', -2)
Go

CREATE TABLE dbo.Source2(
        ColID int NOT NULL,
        Name varchar(25) NULL,
        Value int NULL
)
CREATE TABLE dbo.stgUpdates_Source2(
        ColID int NOT NULL,
        Name varchar(25) NULL,
        Value int NULL
)
Go

 INSERT INTO dbo.Source2
 (ColID,Name,Value)
 VALUES
 (0, 'Willie', 11),
 (1, 'Waylon', 22),
 (2, 'Stevie', 33)
Go

CREATE TABLE dbo.Source3(
        ColID int NOT NULL,
        Value int NULL,
        Name varchar(100) NULL
)

CREATE TABLE dbo.stgUpdates_Source3(
        ColID int NOT NULL,
        Value int NULL,
        Name varchar(100) NULL
)
Go

 INSERT INTO dbo.Source3
 (ColID,Value,Name)
 VALUES
 (0, 101, 'Good-Hearted Woman'),
 (1, 202, 'Are You Sure Hank Done It This Way?')
Go
```

Let's continue by adding a new Biml file to the Biml project. Rename this file GenerateStagingPackages.biml. Before the < Biml > tag, add the code snippet shown in Listing 17-18.

Listing 17-18. Adding .Net Namespaces and Initial Method Calls to Biml

```
<#@ import namespace = "System.Data" #>
<#@ import namespace = "Varigence.Hadron.CoreLowerer.SchemaManagement" #>
<# var connection = SchemaManager.CreateConnectionNode("SchemaProvider", "Data
Source = (local);Initial Catalog = SSISIncrementalLoad_Source;Provider = SQLNCLI11.1;
Integrated Security = SSPI;"); #>
<# var tables = connection.GenerateTableNodes(); #>
```

The code in Listing 17-18 imports the System.Data and Varigence.Hadron.CoreLowerer. SchemaManagement namespaces into the Biml file. A variable named "connection" is created and assigned the value of a SchemaManager ConnectionNode object which is aimed at the SSISIncrementalLoad_Source database. The "Connection" variable supports another variable named "tables". The "tables" variable is populated from a call the "connection" variable's "GenerateTableNodes()" method which populates "tables" with the list of tables found in the SSISIncremetalLoad_Source database.

After the < Biml > tag, add a "Connections" XML Node that contains two "Connection" child nodes so that your Biml file now appears as shown in Listing 17-19.

Listing 17-19. Adding Connections to the GenerateStagingPackages.biml File

```
<#@ import namespace = "System.Data" #>
<#@ import namespace = "Varigence.Hadron.CoreLowerer.SchemaManagement" #>
<# var connection = SchemaManager.CreateConnectionNode("SchemaProvider", "Data
Source = (local);Initial Catalog = SSISIncrementalLoad_Source;Provider = SQLNCLI11.1;
Integrated Security = SSPI;"); #>
<# var tables = connection.GenerateTableNodes(); #>
<Biml xmlns = "http://schemas.varigence.com/biml.xsd">
<Connections>
  <Connection Name = "SSISIncrementalLoad_Source" ConnectionString = "Data Source = (local);
Initial Catalog = SSISIncrementalLoad_Source;Provider = SQLNCLI11.1;Integrated Security = SSPI;" />
  <Connection Name = "SSISIncrementalLoad_Stage" ConnectionString = "Data Source = (local);
Initial Catalog = SSISIncrementalLoad_Stage;Provider = SQLNCLI11.1;OLE DB Services = 1;Integrated
Security = SSPI;" />
</Connections>
```

As in the IncrementalLoad.biml file we designed in the last section, the Connection nodes are the templates for SSIS Connection Managers in the SSIS Package. Next, add a "Package" node immediately after the </Connections > tag. Here we will make a crucial modification to this Biml file and its capability. We begin a C# loop here that spans all but the last two lines of this Biml file. Your Biml file should now include the code from Listing 17-20, immediately after the </Connections > tag.

Listing 17-20. Adding the Packages Node and Starting a Loop

```
<Packages>
  <# foreach (var table in tables) { #>
```

The loop defined in Listing 17-20 will drive the Biml engine as it creates an SSIS Package for each table found in the SSISIncrementalLoad_Source database. Because we are using the SSIS Incremental Load Design Pattern as the template for this package, this Biml file will construct an Incremental Load SSIS Package for each of these tables.

The variables defined above are used later in the Biml file. Immediately after these variable declarations, add the "Package" node shown in Listing 17-21.

Listing 17-21. The Package Node with .Net Replacements

```
  <Package Name = "IncrementalLoad_ <#=table.Name#> " ConstraintMode = "Linear"
ProtectionLevel = "EncryptSensitiveWithUserKey">
```

This Biml code, like much in this Biml file, is copied from the IncrementalLoad.biml file and modified to accept .Net overrides from the foreach loop. Each SSIS Package generated when this Biml is expanded will be named consistently: "IncrementalLoad_< *Source Table Name*>".

Also note the "ConstraintMode" attribute of the 'Package' node is set to "Linear." In the IncrementalLoad. biml file, this was set to "Parallel." The differences are subtle but powerful. First, the Biml compiler will automatically create precedence constraints for you. Specifically, it will create an OnSuccess precedence constraint in the Control Flow from one task to the next, based on the order they appear in the Biml file. This functionality makes scripting and simple file authoring extremely quick. Second, you can eliminate InputPath nodes in the Data Flow Task because the InputPath will connect to the default output path of the transformation that appears directly before it.

Immediately following the < Package > tag, add a "Tasks" node, followed by an "ExecuteSQL" node configured as shown in Listing 17-22.

Listing 17-22. Adding Tasks and the "Truncate Staging Table" Execute SQL Task

```
<Tasks>
      <ExecuteSQL Name = "Truncate stgUpdates_<#=table.Name#>"
ConnectionName = "SSISIncrementalLoad_Stage">
         <DirectInput>Truncate Table stgUpdates_<#=table.Name#></DirectInput>
      </ExecuteSQL>
```

Again, note the generic naming of the Execute SQL Task that performs the truncate operation on the staging table. The name of the Source table will replace the < # = table.Name# > placeholder when the Biml file is expanded. It will be named differently for each table in the Source database, but it will also be descriptive and accurate.

In the next listing (Listing 17-23), I am simply going to show you the Biml for the incrementally loading Data Flow Task. Each component includes .Net code where necessary to make the Biml generic enough to respond to different Source table schemas.

Listing 17-23. The Generic Data Flow Task

```
<Dataflow Name="Load <#=table.Name#>">
  <Transformations>
    <OleDbSource Name="<#=table.Name#> Source" ConnectionName="SSISIncrementalLoad_Source">
      <DirectInput>SELECT <#=table.GetColumnList()#> FROM <#=table.SchemaQualifiedName#>
</DirectInput>
    </OleDbSource>
    <Lookup Name="Correlate" OleDbConnectionName="SSISIncrementalLoad_Stage"
NoMatchBehavior="RedirectRowsToNoMatchOutput">
      <DirectInput>SELECT <#=table.GetColumnList()#> FROM dbo.<#=table.Name#></DirectInput>
      <Inputs>
        <# foreach (var keyColumn in table.Keys[0].Columns) { #>
        <Column SourceColumn="<#=keyColumn.Column#>" TargetColumn="<#=keyColumn.Column#>" />
        <# } #>
      </Inputs>
      <Outputs>
        <# foreach (var col in table.Columns) { #>
        <Column SourceColumn="<#=col#>" TargetColumn="Dest_<#=col#>" />
        <# } #>
      </Outputs>
    </Lookup>
    <ConditionalSplit Name="Filter">
      <OutputPaths>
        <OutputPath Name="Changed Rows">
          <# string exp ="";
              foreach (var colex in table.Columns) { exp += "(" + colex + " != Dest_" + colex +
") || "; } #>
```

```
                <Expression><#=exp.Substring(0, exp.Length - 4)#></Expression>
            </OutputPath>
         </OutputPaths>
      </ConditionalSplit>
      <OleDbDestination Name="stgUpdates_<#=table.Name#>"
ConnectionName="SSISIncrementalLoad_Stage">
         <InputPath OutputPathName="Filter.Changed Rows" />
         <ExternalTableOutput Table="dbo.stgUpdates_<#=table.Name#>" />
      </OleDbDestination>
      <OleDbDestination Name="<#=table.Name#> Destination"
ConnectionName="SSISIncrementalLoad_Stage">
         <InputPath OutputPathName="Correlate.NoMatch" />
         <ExternalTableOutput Table="dbo.<#=table.Name#>" />
      </OleDbDestination>
   </Transformations>
</Dataflow>
```

The Biml / .Net code shown in Listing 17-24 dynamically generates an incrementally loading Data Flow Task, given the caveats listed near the beginning of this section. Let's complete the Biml file by creating a generic template for the final Execute SQL Task that performs the set-based update for Changed Rows between the staging table and destination, shown in Listing 17-24.

Listing 17-24. The Generic "Apply Staged Updates" Execute SQL Task

```
<ExecuteSQL Name="Apply stgUpdates_<#=table.Name#>"
ConnectionName="SSISIncrementalLoad_Stage">
   <# string upd ="Update Dest Set ";
      foreach (var colex in table.Columns.Where(column =>
!table.Keys[0].Columns.Select(keyColumn => keyColumn.Column).Contains(column))) {
         upd = upd + "Dest." + colex + " = Upd." + colex + ",";
      }
      var updc = upd.Substring(0,upd.Length-1) + " From " + table.SchemaQualifiedName + " Dest
Join [" + table.Schema.Name + "].[stgUpdates_" + table.Name + "] Upd On Upd." +
table.Keys[0].Columns[0].Column + " = Dest." + table.Keys[0].Columns[0].Column;#>
   <DirectInput><#=updc#></DirectInput>
</ExecuteSQL>
```

The final instructions contained in the Biml file are shown in Listing 17-25 and close out the "Tasks," "Package," "Packages," loop, and "Biml" nodes.

Listing 17-25. Closing out the Last Nodes and Loop in the Biml File

```
      </Tasks>
   </Package>
   <# } #>
   </Packages>
</Biml>
```

Time for a Test

In Solution Explorer, right-click the GenerateStagingPackages.biml file and click "Generate SSIS Packages". If all goes as planned, your Solution Explorer window should appear similar to that shown in Figure 17-7.

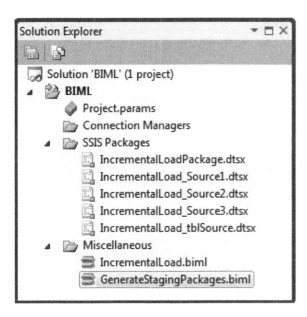

Figure 17-7. *Four SSIS packages from one Biml file!*

Conduct further testing by executing (and re-executing) each of the four SSIS Packages created by the Biml expansion. When I execute the SSIS package named "IncrementalLoad_tblSource.dtsx" I see results (shown in Figure 17-8) remarkably similar to those observed earlier (in Figure 17-5).

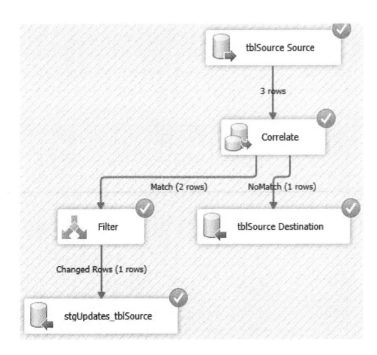

Figure 17-8. *Dynamically-Built Incremental Load SSIS package*

Testing will reveal the other SSIS packages perform similarly.

Summary

In this chapter, we have taken a brief tour of some of the functionality of Business Intelligence Markup Language. We have demonstrated its usefulness as a domain-specific language for generating SSIS Design Patterns, focusing on the Incremental Load pattern. In the final example, we demonstrated how Bimls are integrated .Net functionality can be used to create a patterns-based approach to building four SSIS packages using a tried and true data integration pattern (Incremental Load). On my machine, the four packages were generated in a matter of seconds. I assure you, based on testing, that Biml can produce hundreds of Incremental Load SSIS packages in a matter of minutes. This is game-changing technology, for generating hundreds of SSIS packages – even using templates and patterns – can easily consume data integration developer-months.

## CHAPTER 18

Configuration

SQL Server 2012 introduces Parameters – a new configuration model for SSIS. This new model is meant to simplify the configuration process, and make it easier for users to identify where values are coming from at runtime. While 2005/2008 style Package Configurations are still supported in SQL Server 2012, the two configuration models are not meant to be mixed. In fact, the menu option to use them will only appear when using the File Deployment Model, and on packages that have been upgraded from previous versions. New packages created in 2012 will use the new Parameter model by default.

This chapter describes the new Parameter model, and how it can be used to configure package properties at runtime. We'll look at how Parameters are exposed in the SSIS Catalog, and how you can set Parameter values as part of your build process using Visual Studio Configurations. Finally, we'll look at design patterns that can used to augment the functionality provided by the built-in Parameter model, providing dynamic runtime configuration.

Parameters

SSIS Parameters allow packages to define an explicit contract, much like function parameters do in programming languages like C#. Unlike package configurations, parameters are exposed to the callers, like SQL Agent, or the Execute Package Task, so users are able to see exactly what a package needs to run. Parameters are essentially read-only package variables in a special namespace. They follow the same type system as package variables, and will appear in all of the same UIs that variables do (for example, for setting property expressions). You'll make use of parameter values through Expressions, or by reading them in a Script Task. Parameter values are set before package execution begins, and their value cannot be changed while the package is running.

Parameters can be defined at the package level, and the project level. Package level parameters are visible only to tasks and components within that package – much like package variables. Package parameters are defined in the $Package namespace. Parameters defined at the Project level are global – all packages within the project are able to make use of them. Project parameters are defined in the $Project namespace.

Figure 18-1 shows the new Parameters tab in BIDS, which displays parameters defined at the package level. In addition to the standard properties you'd find on a package variable (such as Name, Type, and Value), Parameters expose three new properties: Description, Sensitive, and Required.

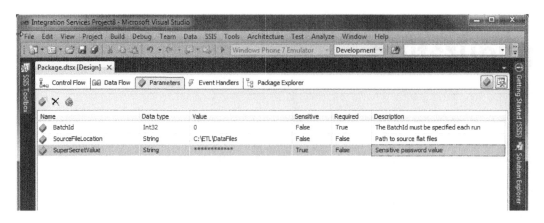

Figure 18-1. *Package level parameters are created and displayed on their own tab in BIDS*

The Description field provides an easy way for the SSIS package developer to document the arguments for their packages. It's recommended that you provide descriptions for your parameters, especially in cases where the person running or configuring the packages is not the same person that developed them.

If a parameter is marked as Sensitive, its value will be stored in an encrypted format within the package. Its value will also be masked when it is displayed in the UI, and will not be displayed in execution logs. Sensitive parameters can only be used in Expressions for properties that are marked as Sensitive (such as the Password property of a Connection Manager).

Parameters that are marked as Required must have their values specified at runtime. All parameters (and variables) need values set at design time for validation purposes. Required parameters will not use this design time value when the package runs – a new value must be specified by the caller (i.e., SQL Agent, or the parent Execute Package Task). If a parameter's Required property is set to False, the parameter becomes optional – its design time value will be used if no other value is supplied. Parameters that have no logical default value (such as a BatchID, or path to an input file) should be marked as Required.

Project level parameters can be found by accessing the new node in the Solution Explorer (as shown in Figure 18-2). Project parameters appear in their own node because they are stored in a separate file (Project. params) within the solution directory. Double clicking this node brings up the same parameter designer used for package parameters, with all of the same properties and options.

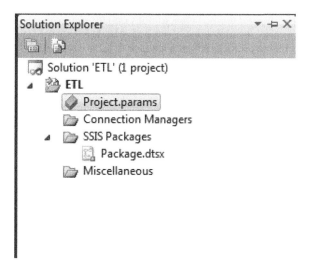

Figure 18-2. *Project level parameters can be found in the Project.params node in Solution Explorer*

Configuring Your Package Using Parameters

Parameter values are used in your package via SSIS Expressions. Expressions can be set on most Task properties, variables, and certain component properties in a Data Flow Task. To set an expression on a Task, open the Property Expressions Editor dialog (shown in Figure 18-3) by clicking on the Expressions property in a Task's

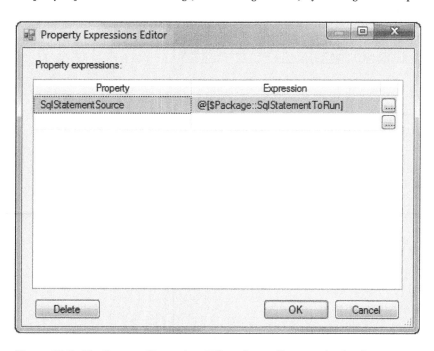

Figure 18-3. *The Property Expressions Editor shows all properties that have expressions set on them*

Properties window. Expressions can be set on variables directly from the Variables window (as shown in Figure 18-4). In SQL Server 2012, adding an expression to a variable automatically sets its `EvaluateAsExpression` property to True – in previous versions of the product, you had to perform this step yourself. You can disable expression evaluation for a variable by setting this property back to False.

Name	Scope	Data type	Value	Expression	
ConnectionString	1 Designer	String	Data Source= .;Initial Catalog= Test;Provide...		...
DatabaseName	1 Designer	String	Test Value		...
CurrentDate	1 Designer	DateTime	9/30/2011 5:12 PM	GETDATE()	...
IntVariable	1 Designer	Int32	0		...
SqlStatement	1 Designer	String	SELECT 1+1		...

Figure 18-4. *Expressions can be set directly from the Variables window in SQL Server 2012. Variables that have an expression set on them appear with a special icon.*

Figure 18-4 also shows a new feature in SQL Server 2012 – Expression Adorners. The icons for Tasks, Connection Managers, and Variables will change if any of the object's properties is set via expression, providing a visual way for a developer to identify which parts of a package are being set dynamically.

Setting expressions for Data Flow components is less straightforward than setting them on Tasks. The main differences are that the expressions are set on the Data Flow Task itself, and not all component properties are expressionable. Figure 18-5 shows how expressionable properties on a Lookup Transform "bubble up" and appear as properties on the Data Flow Task.

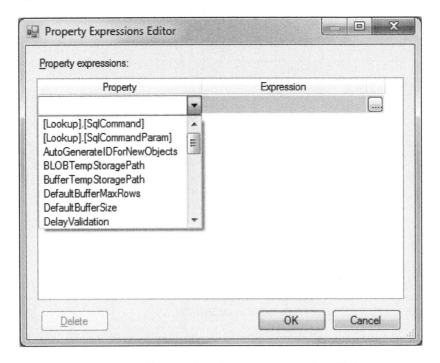

Figure 18-5. *Expressionable Data Flow Component properties will show up as properties on the Data Flow Task*

Package and Project level parameters will appear in all of the UIs that display the list of available Variables. On the Expression Builder dialog (Figure 18-6), all parameters appear under the "Variables and Parameters" folder.

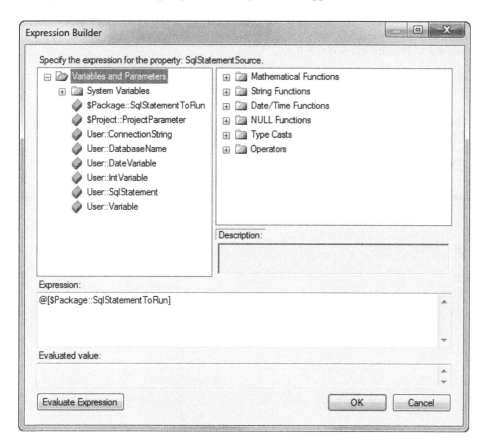

Figure 18-6. *Parameters appear alongside variables in the Expression Builder dialog*

Certain Tasks and Data Flow components are able to make use of variable and parameter values without the use of expressions. For example, the OLE DB Source provides a "SQL command from variable" data access mode that allows you to set the source query from a variable. Parameters can be used instead of variables for all such properties.

Using the Parametrize Dialog

SSIS provides a Parameterize UI (shown in Figure 18-7), which acts as a shortcut for making use of parameters in your packages. From this UI, you can create a new parameter, or make use of one that already exists. When you click OK, SSIS will automatically add an expression to the selected property. To launch the Parameterize UI, right click on and select "Parameterize" from the context menu.

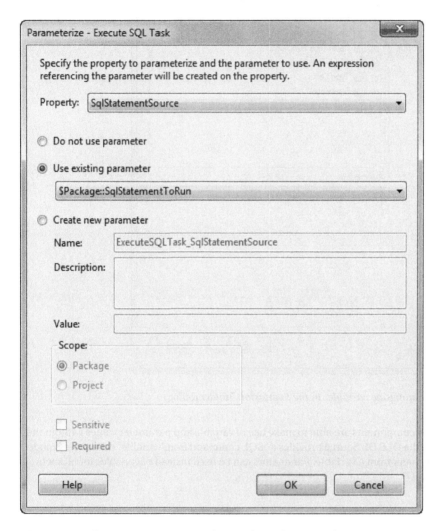

Figure 18-7. *The Parameterize UI is a shortcut for making use of parameters in your package*

Creating Visual Studio Configurations

Another new SSIS feature in SQL Server 2012 is the use of Visual Studio Configurations, which allow you to create multiple sets of parameter values within BIDS. Switching between configurations allows you to easily change parameter values during development, and also allows you to build multiple versions of your project deployment file with different default parameter values. Visual Studio Configurations are a way for developers to maintain their own settings in multi-developer or team environments.

When you first create a project within BIDS, you will have a default configuration called Development. You can create additional from the Configuration Manager dialog (shown in Figure 18-8). You can launch the Configuration Manager dialog from the Solution Configurations combo box on the Standard toolbar, or by right clicking on the project node in the Solution Explorer, selecting Properties, and clicking the Configuration Managers button. To create a new configuration, select the < New … > option from the Active solution configuration drop down.

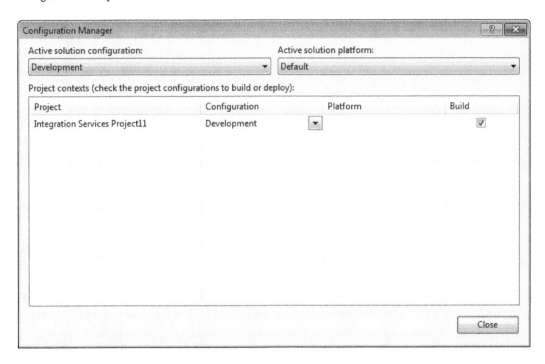

Figure 18-8. *Visual Studio Configurations can be managed from the Configuration Manager dialog*

To add a parameter to a configuration, click the Add Parameters to Configurations button on the package Parameters tab. Figure 18-9 shows the Manage Parameter Values dialog that will be displayed when adding package parameters to configurations. Clicking the Add button allows you to select a parameter – once a parameter is added, it will appear in all configurations in the solution. The Remove button will remove the selected parameter from configurations (which means it will always have the same default value at design time). The Sync button will apply the same value to all configurations – use this button as a shortcut when you're sure that the parameter's default value should change across all configurations. Currently only package parameters and project parameters can be added to Visual Studio Configurations, but they are configured from separate dialogs. To manage project level parameters, click the Add Parameters to Configurations button from the Project Parameters designer (Project.params). To manage a Connection Manager's settings with Visual Studio Configurations, you will first need to parameterize the Connection Manager. Shared Connection Managers cannot be configured using Visual Studio Configurations.

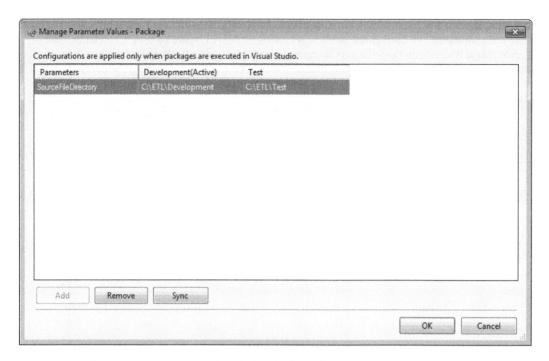

Figure 18-9. The Manage Parameter Values dialog displays all parameter currently set via configurations

---

■ **Note**   When a parameter is controlled by Visual Studio Configurations, its value is saved out to the Visual Studio project file (.dtproj). Be sure to save the project file after making updates to your configurations to make sure that the changes are not lost.

Specifying Entry Point Packages

SQL Server 2012 introduces another new concept for SSIS – Entry-point Packages. This feature allows the package developer to indicate that special attention should be paid to certain packages. This is very useful in projects that contain a small number of "master" packages that run a number of child packages. Note that packages that are not marked as entry point packages can still be run – the setting is meant to be a hint for the person configuring parameter values in the SSIS Catalog. Most SSIS UIs in SSMS allow you to quickly filter out parameters on non-entry point packages, allowing you to view only the parameters they need to set.

Packages are marked as entry points by default. To remove this setting, right click on the package name in the Solution Explorer, and unselect the Entry-point Package option.

Connection Managers

Most Connection Managers will require some form of configuration, and in SQL Server 2012 all Connection Manager properties are configurable when packages are run through the SSIS Catalog. As these properties are already exposed, in most cases you will not need to expose additional parameters for your Connection Managers.

However, you may encounter some scenarios where parameterized Connection Managers will be beneficial. Note that any Connection Manager property that is set via expression will not be exposed through the SSIS Catalog, which prevents a DBA from accidentally overriding property values are set at runtime.

■ **Note**   In previous versions of SQL Server Integration Services, it was very common for child packages to configure Connection Managers with variable values from the parent package. You may wish to keep this pattern in SQL Server 2012 if the connection string is determined at runtime; however, in many cases you'll want to use Shared Connection Managers instead.

Parameters can be set on Connection Managers using property expressions. The most common property to set via expression is the ConnectionString, as many Connection Managers derive their properties by parsing the ConnectionString value. When configuring Connection Managers, be sure to set expressions on either the ConnectionString, or individual properties – the order that expressions are resolved cannot be guaranteed, and certain properties may be overwritten when the ConnectionString is applied.

To parameterize a Shared Connection Manager, open up one of the packages in the project and right click on the Shared Connection Manager's name in the Connection Managers area of the design surface. Note that since Shared Connection Managers are declared at the project level, you can only use project level parameters or static strings in any property expressions on Shared Connection Managers. The expression dialog will not give you the option to use package parameters or variables.

Parameter Configuration on the Server

Parameters were designed to make it easier for the person scheduling and running SSIS packages. In many environments, this is typically a DBA or IT operations person – not the person who originally developed the package. By including descriptions with the parameters, an ETL developer can create self-documenting packages, making it very easy for whoever is configuring the package to see exactly what it needs to run.

This section describes how packages are configured through the SSIS Catalog, and how parameters are surfaced through SSMS. It covers how to set default parameter values after a project is deployed, the various package execution options, and how the built in reporting functionality in SQL Server 2012 make it easier to determine the exact configuration values set when the package was run.

Default Configuration

Default values for all parameters and connection managers are saved within the SSIS project deployment file (.ispac) when the file is built. These become the default values for the project once it is deployed to the SSIS Catalog. To change the default configuration, right click on the project name (or individual package names) and select Configure ... within the SSMS Object Explorer (as shown in Figure 18-10).

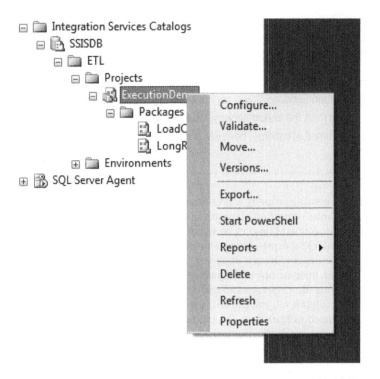

Figure 18-10. The default configuration for a project can be changed through SSMS after the project is deployed

Figure 18-11 shows the parameter configuration dialog in SSMS. Through this dialog, you can set default values for all parameters and connection manager properties for packages within this project. The Scope dropdown allows you to filter your view of the parameters and connection managers. The default view will display Entry-point packages only, but you can also view parameters for individual packages, and for the entire project. To change the value for parameter or connection manager property, click the ellipse button at the end of the row. You will have three options when changing a value: use the project default; set a literal value; or use a server environment variable. For more information about environments, see the next section.

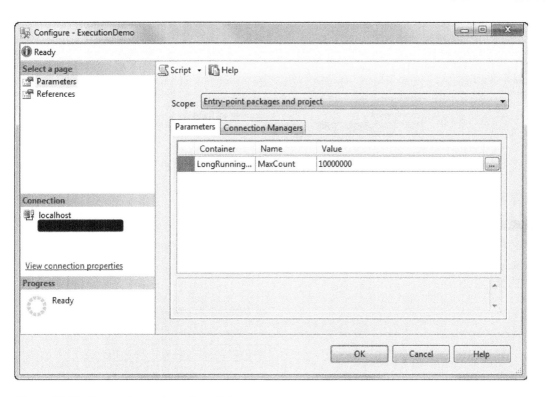

Figure 18-11. *Parameter configuration dialog*

Server Environments

Server Environments contain a set of variables – essentially name value pairs – that you can map to parameters and connection manager properties within your project. When you run a package through the SSIS Catalog, you can select an Environment to run it in. When a value is mapped to a server environment variable, its value will be determined by the environment is it currently running in.

Before you can map a value to server environment variable, you must associate the environment with the project. Figure 18-12 shows the References tab of the project configuration dialog which allows you to associate a project with one or more environments.

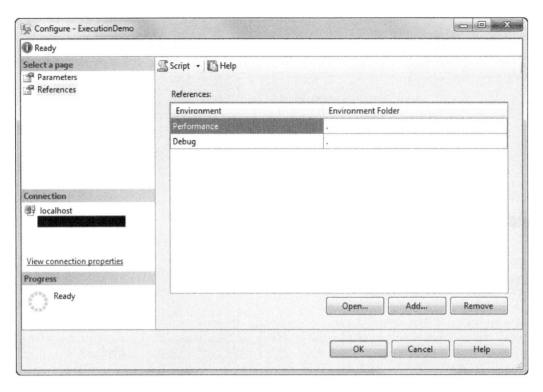

Figure 18-12. *The References tab of the Configure dialog lets you associate a project with environments*

Like Projects, Environments are contained within a Folder in the SSIS Catalog. A project may reference an environment in any folder in the Catalog – references are not limited to the current folder only. If you plan to use Environments throughout your projects, you might consider creating a separate folder as an area to store all of the common environments.

Environments support row-level security. Like Projects and Folders, you can configure which users or roles have access to individual Environments. Users will not be able to see Environments they do not have access to.

Once a project has been associated with one or more server environments, you are able to map parameter and connection manager values to variables contained within those environments.

■ **Note**   Environments can contain any number of Server Variables, and two environments might not contain variables with the same name. If a parameter or connection manager value is mapped to a Server Variable, only Environments which contain a variable with that name (and matching data type!) will be available when selecting the Environment to run the package in.

Default Parameter Values Using T-SQL

Default parameter values and connection manager properties can be set through the SSIS Catalog's T-SQL API. This allows a DBA to automate the setting of parameter values after a deployment, or after a project is moved to a new SSIS Catalog. An easy way to create a script is to make the changes through the parameter configuration UI, and then clicking the Script button. Listing 18-1 shows the T-SQL used to set default values for a two items; a package parameter (MaxCount) is to set 100, and a connection manager property (CM.SourceFile.ConnectionString) is set to 'C:\Demos\Data\RaggedRight.txt'.

Listing 18-1. Setting parameter values using T-SQL

```
DECLARE @var sql_variant = N'C:\Demos\Data\RaggedRight.txt'
EXEC [SSISDB].[catalog].[set_object_parameter_value]
        @object_type = 20,
        @parameter_name = N'CM.SourceFile.ConnectionString',
        @object_name = N'ExecutionDemo',
        @folder_name = N'ETL',
        @project_name = N'ExecutionDemo',
        @value_type = V,
        @parameter_value = @var
GO


DECLARE @var bigint = 100
EXEC [SSISDB].[catalog].[set_object_parameter_value]
        @object_type = 30,
        @parameter_name = N'MaxCount',
        @object_name = N'LongRunning.dtsx',
        @folder_name = N'ETL',
        @project_name = N'ExecutionDemo',
        @value_type = V,
        @parameter_value = @var
GO
```

■ **Note** For more information, see the set_object_parameter_value stored procedure entry in Books Online: http://msdn.microsoft.com/en-us/library/ff878162(sql.110).aspx

Package Execution through the SSIS Catalog

Default values for parameters and connection manager properties can be overridden when a package is executed. The Execute Package UI in SSMS (shown in Figure 18-13) allows you to specify the values to use for that specific execution of the package. Project and package level parameters are displayed on the Parameters tab, and shared connection managers and package level connection managers are shown in the Connection Managers tab. The advanced tab allows you to override property values that were not exposed as parameters. This feature – called Property Overrides – allows a DBA to make a quick configuration change to a value within a package without having to redeploy the entire project. The functionality is similar to using the /Set command line option with DTEXEC.

The Execute Package UI also has a Script button, which allows you to script out the creation of a package execution to T-SQL. Listing 18-2 provides an example of creating a new package execution and overriding a number of settings. This procedure involves a number of steps:

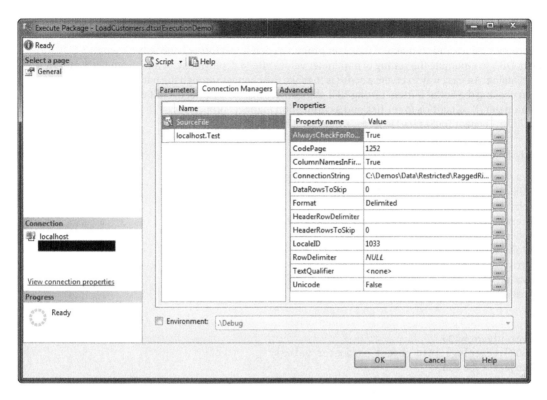

Figure 18-13. *Interactive package execution through SSMS*

1. Create a new Execution instance using [catalog].[create_execution]

2. Override parameter or connection manager values using [catalog].[set_execution_parameter_value]

3. Set property overrides using [catalog].[set_execution_property_override_value]

4. Start the package execution using [catalog].[start_execution]

Listing 18-2. Running a Package Using T-SQL

```
-- Create the package execution
DECLARE @exec_id bigint
EXEC [SSISDB].[catalog].[create_execution]
        @execution_id=@exec_id OUTPUT,
        @package_name=N'LoadCustomers.dtsx',
        @folder_name=N'ETL',
        @project_name=N'ExecutionDemo',
        @use32bitruntime=0

-- Set a new value for the AlwaysCheckForRowDelimiters property of the
-- SourceFile connection manager
EXEC [SSISDB].[catalog].[set_execution_parameter_value]
        @execution_id=@exec_id,
```

```
        @object_type = 20,
        @parameter_name = N'CM.SourceFile.AlwaysCheckForRowDelimiters',
        @parameter_value = 0

-- Set the logging level for this execution
EXEC [SSISDB].[catalog].[set_execution_parameter_value]
        @execution_id = @exec_id,
        @object_type = 50,
        @parameter_name = N'LOGGING_LEVEL',
        @parameter_value = 1

-- Create a property override for the MaxConcurrentExecutables property
EXEC [SSISDB].[catalog].[set_execution_property_override_value]
        @execution_id = @exec_id,
        @property_path = N'\Package.Properties[MaxConcurrentExecutables]',
        @property_value = N'1',
        @sensitive = 0

-- Start the package execution
EXEC [SSISDB].[catalog].[start_execution] @exec_id

-- Return the execution ID
SELECT @exec_id

GO
```

The Integration Services job steps in SQL Agent has been enhanced in SQL Server 2012 to support running packages stored in an SSIS Catalog. The user interface is the same as when you run a package interactively through SSMS, and provides the same configuration options. Alternatively, you can run SSIS packages using the T-SQL job step. However, as this step does not support the use of Proxy Accounts, you will be limited to running the packages as the SQL Server Agent service account.

Parameters with DTEXEC

The command prompt utility to run SSIS packages (DTEXEC) has been updated to support projects and parameters. DTEXEC is able to run packages stored within an SSIS project file (.ispac), as well as start a server-based execution of a package stored within an SSIS Catalog (local or remote). Both modes use different command line switches to set parameter values, and are described in separate sections below.

■ **Note** When working with individual SSIS package files (.dtsx), DTEXEC behaves the same as it did in previous versions of SQL Server. For more information on the various command line options for DTEXEC, see its entry in Books Online: http://msdn.microsoft.com/en-us/library/ms162810.aspx

---

Projects on the File System

While the new Project Deployment Model is primarily meant for use with the SSIS Catalog, it is possible to run packages within a project file using DTEXEC. Packages run this way are executed locally by the DTEXEC process. Individual parameter values can be set using the /Set option, and /ConfigFile can be used to set a number of parameter values from a 2005/2008 style XML configuration file. Table 18-1 provides a summary of the options related to running packages from projects stored on the file system.

Table 18-1. *DTEXEC Command Line Options for Using Project Files (.ispac)*

Parameter	Description
Proj[ect] = *path_to_project*	This option provides the path to the SSIS project file (.ispac).
	Example: /Proj c:\demo\project.ispac
Pack[age] = *package_name*	The name of the package within the project file you want to run. The value should include the .dtsx extension.
	Example: /Pack MyPackage.dtsx
Set = *parameter_name;value*	This option allows you to set a value for a parameter within the project. The syntax is similar to what you'd use to override package variable values on the command line. Use the $Project namespace to set values for parameters defined at the Project scope, and $Package for parameters defined at the Package scope.
	Example: /Set = \Package.Variables[$Project::IntParameter];1
Conf[igFile] = *path_to_file*	This option allows you to set multiple parameter values from an XML configuration file. The syntax for each parameter value is similar to what is used for the /Set option.
	Example: /Conf parameters.xml

Listing 18-3 provides an example of running a package (MyPackage.dtsx) contained within a project file (project.ispac). It sets the values for two parameters – BatchNumber, an integer parameter defined at the Project level, and HostName, a string parameter defined at the Package level.

Listing 18-3. Running Packages Within a Project File Using DTEXEC

```
dtexec.exe /Project c:\demo\project.ispac /Package MyPackage.dtsx /Set
\Package.Variables[$Project::BatchNumber];432 /Set
\Package.Variables[$Package::HostName];localhost
```

■ **Note** Although the syntax for setting parameter values is similar to setting values for variables and other package properties, there is one key difference. To set parameter values, you should not include the name of the property (i.e., ".Value") – you only specify the name of the parameter itself.

Projects in the SSIS Catalog

DTEXEC has been extended in SQL Server 2012 to support running packages contained within an SSIS Catalog. Unlike other execution modes, when running a package from a Catalog, the execution takes place on the SSIS Catalog's server, and not by the DTEXEC process. In this mode, you will use the /ISServer command line option to specify the path to the package you want to run, the /Parameter option to set parameter values, and the /EnvReference option if you wish to run your package in a specific server environment. Table 18-2 contains a full list of command line options for SSIS Catalog based execution with DTEXEC.

Table 18-2. *DTEXEC Command Line Options for the SSIS Catalog*

Parameter	Description
Ser[ver] = server_instance	The name of the SQL instance containing the SSIS Catalog. If this option is not specified, the default instance on the localhost is assumed.
	Example: /Ser ETLSERVER1
IS[Server] = *path_to_package*	The path of the package in the SSIS Catalog. This will contain the name of the catalog (SSISDB), the folder name, the project name, and the name of the package you want to run. This option cannot be used with the /DTS, / SQL, or /FILE options.
	Example: /IS \SSISDB\MyFolder\ETLProject\MyPackage.dtsx
Par[ameter] = *name[(type)];value*	Set a value for the given parameter. Include the namespace of the parameter along with the name to distinguish parameter scope ($Project for project level parameters, $Package for package level parameters, $CM for connection manager properties, and $ServerOption for server specific options). If the namespace is not included, the parameter is assumed to be at the package scope.
	Example: /Par $Project::BatchNumber;432
Env[Reference] = *environment_id*	This option allows you to specify a server environment to use when running a package. Any parameter values that have been bound to server environment variables will be resolved automatically. To get the ID for an environment, query for its name in the [catalog].[environments] view in SSISDB.
	Example: /Env 20

Listing 18-4 provides an example of running a package (MyPackage.dtsx) contained within a project (ETLProject) in a folder (MyFolder) on a remote SSIS Catalog server (ETLServer). It sets the values for two parameters – BatchNumber, an integer parameter defined at the Project level, and HostName, a string parameter defined at the Package level. It also sets the SYNCHRONIZED server option to True, which tells DTEXEC to run in a synchronous mode – more details on synchronous vs. asynchronous execution can be found below.

Listing 18-4. Running Packages Within an SSIS Catalog Using DTEXEC

```
C:\>dtexec.exe /Ser ETLServer /IS \SSISDB\MyFolder\ETLProject\MyPackage.dtsx /Par
$Project::BatchNumber;432 /Par $Package::HostName;localhost /Par
"$ServerOption::SYNCHRONIZED(Boolean)";True
```

```
Microsoft (R) SQL Server Execute Package Utility
Version 11.0.2100.60 for 64-bit
Copyright (C) Microsoft Corporation. All rights reserved.

Started:  4:46:44 PM
Execution ID: 4.
To view the details for the execution, right-click on the Integration Services Catalog,
and open the [All Executions] report
Started:  4:46:44 PM
Finished: 4:49:45 PM
Elapsed:  3 seconds
```

■ **Note**   You must use Windows Authentication to connect to your SQL Server instance when running packages contained in an SSIS Catalog. The /User and /Password command line options cannot be used with the /ISServer option. If you need to impersonate another user account, you can use the RunAs DOS command with DTEXEC.

When you run an SSIS Catalog package with DTEXEC, it will run in an asynchronous mode by default. This means that the process will return immediately, and will not tell you whether the package actually ran successfully. To get synchronous execution behavior (e.g., the same that you would get when running packages from the file system, or MSDB), you need to include the /Par "$ServerOption::SYNCHRONIZED(Boolean)"; True command line switch. When synchronous execution is used, the DTEXEC process will not return until the package has finished running.

Another difference between SSIS Catalog and other forms of DTEXEC execution is that the events that occur while the package is running are not displayed on the command line. Listing 18-4 shows a sample output from running a package in the SSIS Catalog – as you can see, there is only a single message telling you the server execution ID, and pointing you to the catalog reports.

Dynamic Configurations

Parameters on an entry point package allow a user to specify values, but they require that the values be known before the package starts running. There may be times where you'll need to determine configurations at runtime, or dynamically pull in values from other sources (such as an external file, or database table). The following sections provide design patterns that can be used to augment the capabilities provided by the Parameter model.

Configuring from a Database Table

The SSIS Catalog provides a central location for package configuration values, but your environment may already have alternative locations that store metadata that your packages need at runtime. This pattern shows how to retrieve values from a database table using an Execute SQL Task and configure properties within the package using property expressions. For this example, you'll be reading a directory and file name from a database, storing the values in variables, and then using them to dynamically set the ConnectionString for a Flat File Connection Manager.

Creating the Database Table

Listing 18-5 shows the SQL for the table that you will be reading your configuration values from. Each row in the table is a new flat file that you will want to process with this package. The two main columns you are interested in are directory and name – the id column is a surrogate key to uniquely identify each row in the table, and the processed column lets us easily filter out files that have already been processed. Sample values are shown in Table 18-3.

Listing 18-5. SQL definition of the table our package will read its configuration values from

```
CREATE TABLE [dbo].[PackageConfiguration]
(
        [id] int IDENTITY(1,1) NOT NULL,
        [directory] nvarchar(255) NOT NULL,
        [name] nvarchar(255) NOT NULL,
        [processed] bit NOT NULL
)
```

Table 18-3. *Sample Rows from the PackageConfiguration Table*

id	Directory	Name	processed
1	C:\ETL\Development	File1.txt	False
2	C:\ETL\Development	File2.txt	False
3	C:\ETL\Test	File1.txt	False

Retrieving Configuration Values with an Execute SQL Task

You will retrieve the list of files you need to process from the PackageConfiguration table you created using an Execute SQL Task. You will store the result set in a package variable, and then loop through each row with a Foreach Loop Container. You will use the processed field to mark the files that have already been processed – you will set the processed value to True once you have successfully loaded the file.

■ **Note** This example assumes that all of the flat files listed in the PackageConfiguration table have the same schema. It does not cover the logic needed to actually load the flat file into the database – it is meant to illustrate the pattern that you'd use as a template for processing a number of items in a loop.

Setting up the package takes the following steps:

1. Add four package variables

   a. FileID (Int32) – the row id for the file you are currently processing

   b. Directory (String) – the directory containing the flat file you need to process

   c. FileName (String) – the name of the file you are processing

   d. FilesToProcess (Object) – the result set of the Execute SQL Task

2. Add an Execute SQL Task to your package – name it "Retrieve File List"

3. Double click the Task to open its editor

4. Ensure the ConnectionType is OLE DB

5. Click on the Connection drop down and select < New connection ... >

6. Click New, and configure the connection manager to point to the database containing the PackageConfiguration table

7. Select all of the files that have not been processed from the PackageConfiguration table (as shown in Listing 18-6)

    Listing 18-6. Query to Pull Out All Entries in the Configuration Table that Have Not Been Processed Yet

    ```
    SELECT * FROM [PackageConfiguration] WHERE [processed]=0
    ```

8. Set the ResultSet value to Full Result Set. This means that the Execute SQL Task will retrieve the values as an ADO Recordset that can be processed by the Foreach Loop. Note that you could also use an ADO.NET Connection Manager here, which would cause the results to be returned as an ADO.NET DataTable.

9. Click on the Result Set tab

10. Click Add, and use these mappings

    a. Result Name – 0

    b. Variable Name – User::FilesToProcess

11. Click OK to save the changes to the Execute SQL Task

12. Add a Foreach Loop container to your package

13. Connect the Execute SQL Task to the Foreach Loop Container

14. Add a Data Flow task inside of the Foreach Loop Container

15. Add a new Execute SQL task inside of the Foreach Loop Container

16. Connect the Data Flow task to the Execute SQL Task

17. Double click the Execute SQL Task to open its editor

18. Set the Connection to the same connection manager you created in step 5

19. Listing 18-7 shows the SQLStatement to mark a row in the table as processed. Note that the statement contains a parameter marker (the question mark). You will map a variable value to this parameter in the next step.

    Listing 18-7. SQL statement to mark the file as processed

    ```
    UPDATE [PackageConfiguration] SET [processed]=1 WHERE  id=?
    ```

20. Click the Parameter Mapping tab

21. Click Add, and use these mappings

    a. Variable Name – User::FileID

    b. Data Type - LONG

    c. Parameter Name – 0

22. Click OK to save the changes to the Execute SQL Task

23. Add a new Flat File Connection Manager, and point it to an existing flat file

24. Right click on the Flat File Connection Manager, and select Properties

25. Select the Expression property, and bring up the Property Expression Editor

26. Set an expression on the ConnectionString property which makes use of the variable values retrieved from the PackageConfiguration table. Listing 18-8 provides an example of the expression.

Listing 18-8. Expression to Set the Path to the Input File on the Connectionstring Property

@[User::Directory] + "\\" + @[User::FileName]

Your package should now look like Figure 18-14.

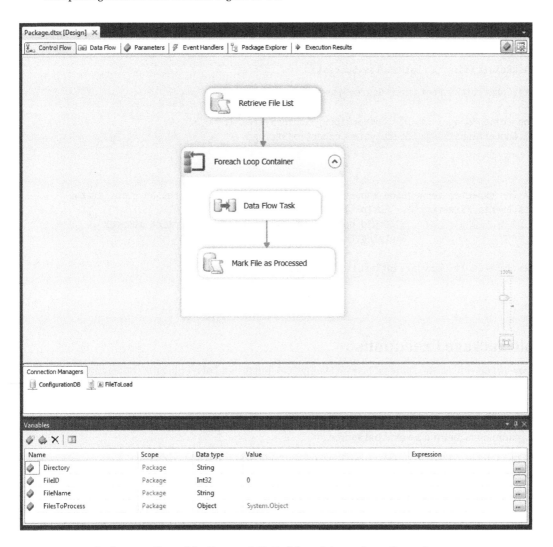

Figure 18-14. Package configured for Execute SQL Task based dynamic configurations

Setting Values using a Script Task

An alternative to retrieving your configuration with an Execute SQL Task and setting package properties through expressions is to use a Script Task. This approach can be useful if your values aren't coming from a database, or they require additional processing logic – for example, if they are coming from an encrypted source. From within a Script, you can easily read values from external configuration files (such as an XML file), and access shared configuration resources that might be used by other, non-SSIS parts of your data integration solution. The Script Task is able to read and modify package properties at runtime, including the variable values and all connection manager properties.

Listing 18-9 provides sample code a Script Task that sets a Connection Manager's `ConnectionString` at runtime.

Listing 18-9. Sample code to set package properties using a Script Task

```
public void Main()
{
    // TODO: This would be set from an external configuration file
    const string SourceSystemConnectionString = " ... ";

    Dts.TaskResult = (int)ScriptResults.Success;

    if (Dts.Connections.Contains("SourceSystem"))
    {
        ConnectionManager cm = Dts.Connections["SourceSystem"];
        cm.ConnectionString = SourceSystemConnectionString;
    }
    else
    {
        // The expected connection manager wasn't found - log is and set an error status
        Dts.Events.FireError(0, "Script Task",
                             "Could not find the SourceSystem connection manager",
                             string.Empty, 0);

        Dts.TaskResult = (int)ScriptResults.Failure;
    }
}
```

Dynamic Package Executions

In this approach, you will use the same table from Listing 18-5, but instead of reading the configuration values with an SSIS package, you'll use T-SQL to create dynamic package executions on the SSIS Catalog. The code in Listing 18-10 implements the following steps:

1. Declare script variables. Note that in a real world script, these values would be set through parameters, or from an external source.

2. Read the list of files to process from the `PackageConfiguration` table, and store the results in a table variable (`@FileList`).

3. Loop through the list of files. For each file, the code will:

   a. Retrieve the id and parameter values from the table variable.

   b. Create a new SSIS Catalog package execution.

c.   Set the parameter Directory and FileName parameter values.

d.   Start the execution.

e.   Update the PackageConfiguration table to mark that the file has been processed.

Listing 18-10. Dynamic Package Execution Script

```
DECLARE @FolderName NVARCHAR(50) = N'ExecutionDemo'
DECLARE @ProjectName NVARCHAR(50) = N'ETL'
DECLARE @DirectoryParameter NVARCHAR(50) = N'Directory'
DECLARE @FileNameParameter NVARCHAR(50) = N'FileName'
DECLARE @PackageName NVARCHAR(100) = N'LoadCustomers.dtsx'

DECLARE @PackageList TABLE
(
  RowNum smallint,
  Id int,
  Directory nvarchar(255),
  Name nvarchar(255)
)

INSERT INTO @FileList (RowNum, Id, Directory, Name)
        SELECT ROW_NUMBER() OVER (ORDER BY id), id, Directory, Name
        FROM [dbo].[PackageConfiguration]
        WHERE processed = 0

DECLARE @maxCount int = (SELECT MAX(RowNum) FROM @FileList)
DECLARE @count int = (SELECT MIN(RowNum) FROM @FileList)

WHILE (@count <= @maxCount)
BEGIN
        DECLARE @Id NVARCHAR(255) = (SELECT Id FROM @FileList WHERE RowNum = @count)
        DECLARE @DirectoryValue NVARCHAR(255) = (SELECT Directory FROM @FileList WHERE
RowNum = @count)
        DECLARE @NameValue NVARCHAR(255) = (SELECT Name FROM @FileList WHERE RowNum = @count)

        -- Create the package execution
        DECLARE @exec_id bigint
        EXEC [SSISDB].[catalog].[create_execution]
                @execution_id = @exec_id OUTPUT,
                @package_name = @PackageName,
                @folder_name = @FolderName,
                @project_name = @ProjectName

        -- Set the Directory parameter value
        EXEC [SSISDB].[catalog].[set_execution_parameter_value]
                @execution_id = @exec_id,
                @object_type = 20,
                @parameter_name = @DirectoryParameter,
                @parameter_value = @DirectoryValue
```

349

```
    -- Set the File Name parameter value
    EXEC [SSISDB].[catalog].[set_execution_parameter_value]
            @execution_id = @exec_id,
            @object_type = 20,
            @parameter_name = @FileNameParameter,
            @parameter_value = @NameValue

    -- Start the package execution
    EXEC [SSISDB].[catalog].[start_execution] @exec_id

    -- Return the execution ID
    SELECT N'Started package execution ' + CONVERT(nvarchar(20), @exec_id)

    -- Mark the file as processed
    DECLARE @UpdateSql nvarchar(1024) = N'UPDATE [dbo].[PackageConfiguration] SET processed = 1
WHERE id = ' + CONVERT(nvarchar(20), @Id)
    EXEC sp_sqlexec @UpdateSql

    SET @count = @count + 1
END
```

Summary

This chapter has covered some of the usage patterns for the new Parameter model, as well as some dynamic configuration scenarios. While the configuration patterns and best practices that were commonly used in SQL 2005 and 2008 continue to work in the latest version of SSIS, most users will see a benefit in migrating to the new model. The clarity of the Parameter model was designed to help everyone involved with an SSIS solutions life cycle, from those who develop the packages to those who deploy and schedule them.

## CHAPTER 19

Deployment

SQL Server 2012 has made great strides towards simplifying the deployment process for Integration Services projects. Projects within Visual Studio can now target two different deployment models – the Package Deployment Model, which is similar to what was used in previous versions of the product, and the Project Deployment Model, which was designed for the new SSIS Catalog.

This chapter will focus on patterns associated with the new Project Deployment Model and server based deployment. While the Project Model and SSIS Catalog are the recommended way to do deployment, organizations upgrading from previous versions may already have package execution frameworks that rely on file system based deployment.

Project Deployment Model

The new Project Model is the default target when creating SSIS projects in SQL Server 2012. With this model, packages and other project items such as Shared Connection Managers are bundled into a single file with an .ispac extension during the project's Build phase. This file can then be deployed to the SSIS Catalog using the Deployment Wizard, or executed directly using dtexec.exe.

If your project is targeting the Package Deployment Model, you can convert to the Project Deployment Model within Visual Studio. Right click on the project name in the Solution Explorer window, and select Convert to Project Deployment Model (as shown in Figure 19-1). Converting to the Project Deployment Model brings up the Project Conversion Wizard. The wizard helps you convert to the new model by updating Execute Package Tasks to use Project References, and changing Configurations to Parameters.

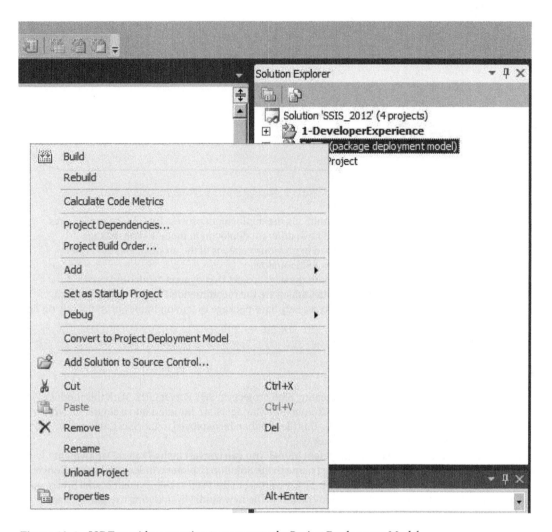

Figure 19-1. *SSDT provides an option to convert to the Project Deployment Model*

Integration Services projects in the Project Deployment Model can make use of new features such as Parameters, Shared Connection Managers, and Project References. Project References allow the Execute Package Task to locate child packages without the use of connection managers, and greatly simply the deployment process.

SSIS Catalog

The SSIS Catalog is a new feature in SQL Server 2012, and is the recommended deployment target for Integration Services projects. Deployment to the catalog is typically done using the SSIS Deployment Wizard, which can be launched from within SSDT, SSMS, double clicking an SSIS project file (.ispac) from windows explorer, or by running ISDeploymentWizard.exe.

To launch the Deployment Wizard from SSDT, right click on the project in the Solution Explorer and select the Deploy option. The wizard will automatically load your project file, putting you on the Select Destination page (as show in Figure 19-2).

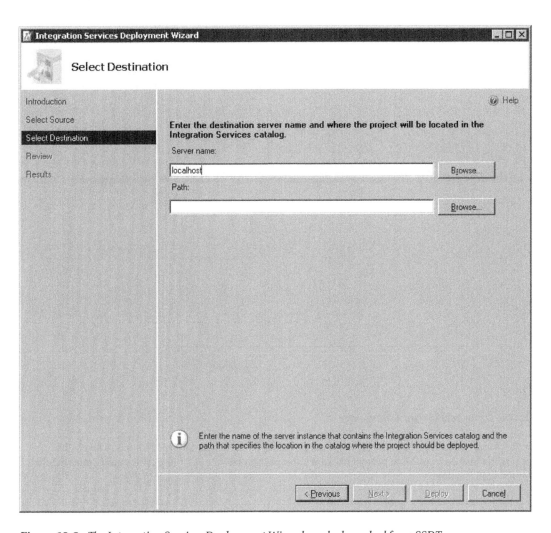

Figure 19-2. The Integration Services Deployment Wizard can be launched from SSDT

■ **Note** The Deployment Wizard is typically used to deploy files to the SSIS Catalog, but it can also be used to move projects between servers. To do this, choose the Integration Services catalog option on the Select Source page.

The Deployment Wizard allows you to select the server and folder you wish to deploy the project to. On the final page, the project file is sent to the server and stored in the SSIS Catalog. Note that, during deployment, the wizard indicates that it is changing the project's protection level (Figure 19-3). During this phase, sensitive

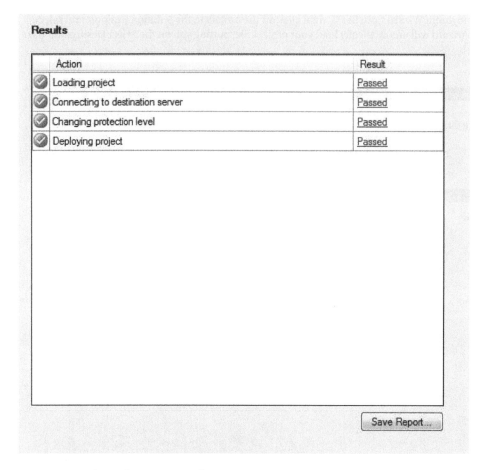

Results

	Action	Result
✅	Loading project	Passed
✅	Connecting to destination server	Passed
✅	Changing protection level	Passed
✅	Deploying project	Passed

Save Report...

Figure 19-3. The Deployment Wizard status page

data within the project is decrypted, and the project is converted to the Server Storage protection level. The server relies on database encryption to protect packages and parameter values – these tables are automatically encrypted in the SSIS Catalog.

■ **Note**   More information about package protection levels and secure deployments can be found in Books Online at http://msdn.microsoft.com/en-us/library/bb522558(v=SQL.110).aspx

Deployment Methods

This section describes the different deployment methods supported by the SSIS Catalog. The method you choose will depend on your environment, and what the people doing the deployment – whether they are developers, ETL operators, or DBAs – are most comfortable with. The deployment methods described here include:

- Deployment from the command line
- Deployment using custom code

- Deployment using PowerShell

- Deployment using SQL

Deployment from the Command Line

The Deployment Wizard (ISDeploymentWizard.exe) provides a command line interface, which allows you to deploy to the SSIS Catalog without a UI. This is very useful for deploying from scripts, or as part of a batch process. Table 19-1 shows the list of supported parameters. Listing 19-1 provides an example command line that deploys a project (C:\SSIS\Project.ispac) to a folder named MyFolder on a local SSIS Catalog.

Table 19-1. *Integration Services Deployment Wizard command line parameters*

Parameter	Short Version	Description
Silent[+|-]	S	When this option is true, the deployment will be done in a UI-less mode (command line only). Use this option when deploying from batch files. The default value is '-', which will display the UI.
		Example: /Silent+
SourceType:{File|Server}	ST	This option specifies whether the source project comes from the file system, or another SSIS Catalog. The default value is "File."
		Example: /SourceType:File
SourcePath:*path_to_project*	SP	The path to the .ispac file being deployed (when using the File source), or the path to the project name (when using the Server source).
		Example: /SourcePath:C:\ETL\project.ispac
SourceServer:*server_ instance*	SS	The name of the server instance when the SourceType is set to Server.
		Example: /SourceServer:localhost\SQL1
ProjectPassword:*password*	PP	If the source .ispac file is password protected, this parameter can be used to supply the password. Note that specifying a password on the command line is not recommended, as other users on the system might be able to see the arguments. If your project file is using password encryption, consider specifying the password in the response file (see the @ < file > option for more information)
DestinationServer:*server_ instance*	DS	The name of the server instance you are deploying to.
		Example: /DestinationServer:localhost
DestinationPath:*path*	DP	The path you want to deploy the project to on the destination server. The format of the path is "/<catalog>/<folder>/<project>".
		Example: /DestinationPath:/SSISDB/MyFolder/Project
@ < file>		This option allows you to specify all of your command line arguments in a text file, instead of entering them directly on the command line.
		Example: @arguments.txt

Listing 19-1. Deploying a project from the command line

```
ISDeploymentWizard.exe /Silent /SourcePath:"C:\ETL\Project.ispac"
/DestinationServer:"localhost" /DestinationPath:"/SSISDB/MyFolder/Project"
```

■ **Note**   When the Deployment Wizard is run in interactive (UI) mode, the Review page displays the equivalent parameters to do a command line based deployment. This can be a handy shortcut – simply copy the command line arguments into a batch file to perform automatic deployments in the future.

Deployment Using Custom Code

The SSIS Catalog has a managed .NET API called the Management Object Model (or MOM). This API allows you to programmatically perform that same management tasks that would normally be done through SQL Server Management Studio (SSMS), including Folder creation, and deployment of projects.

Listing 19-2 provides a sample C# application that makes use of the MOM to create a new Folder in an SSIS Catalog, and deploys a project to it. The core functionality can be found in the Microsoft.SqlServer.Management. IntegrationServices assembly, which is installed with SSMS and found in the Global Assembly Cache (GAC).

Listing 19-2. Deploying a project using the MOM

```
class Program
{
    const string ProjectFileLocation=@"C:\ETL\Project.ispac";

    static void Main(string[] args)
    {
        // Connect to the default instance on localhost
        var server=new Server("localhost");
        var store=new IntegrationServices(server);

        // Check that we have a catalog
        if (store.Catalogs.Count == 0)
        {
            Console.WriteLine("SSIS catalog not found on localhost.");
        }

        // Get the SSISDB catalog - note that there should only
        // be one, but the API may support multiple catalogs
        // in the future
        var catalog=store.Catalogs["SSISDB"];

        // Create a new folder
        var folder=new CatalogFolder(catalog,
                                "MyFolder",
                                "Folder that holds projects");
        folder.Create();

        // Make sure the project file exists
        if (!File.Exists(ProjectFileLocation))
        {
            Console.WriteLine("Project file not found at: {0}",
                        ProjectFileLocation);
        }
```

```
        // Load the project using the SSIS API
        var project = Project.OpenProject(ProjectFileLocation);

        // Deploy the project to the folder we just created
        folder.DeployProject(project);
    }
}
```

Deployment Using PowerShell

The SSIS Management Object Model (MOM) is accessible via PowerShell, which makes it possible to fully automate your deployment (and other management tasks) using PowerShell scripts. Listing 19-3 shows the PowerShell version of the simple deployment application from Listing 19-2.

Listing 19-3. Deploying a project using PowerShell

```
# Variables
$ProjectFilePath = "C:\ETL\Project.ispac"
$ProjectName = "Project"
$FolderName = "MyFolder"

# Load the IntegrationServices Assembly
$loadStatus =
[Reflection.Assembly]::Load("Microsoft.SqlServer.Management.IntegrationServices,
Version = 11.0.0.0, Culture = neutral, PublicKeyToken = 89845dcd8080cc91")

# Store the IntegrationServices Assembly namespace to avoid typing it every time
$ISNamespace = "Microsoft.SqlServer.Management.IntegrationServices"

Write-Host "Connecting to server ... "

# Create a connection to the server
$sqlConnectionString = "Data Source = localhost;Initial Catalog = master;Integrated Security = SSPI;"
$sqlConnection = New-Object System.Data.SqlClient.SqlConnection $sqlConnectionString

# Create the Integration Services object
$integrationServices = New-Object $ISNamespace".IntegrationServices" $sqlConnection
$catalog = $integrationServices.Catalogs["SSISDB"]

Write-Host "Creating Folder" $FolderName " ... "

# Create a new folder
$folder = New-Object $ISNamespace".CatalogFolder" ($catalog, $FolderName, "This is a folder
description")
$folder.Create()

Write-Host "Deploying" $ProjectName "project ... "

# Read the project file, and deploy it to the folder
[byte[]] $projectFile = [System.IO.File]::ReadAllBytes($ProjectFilePath)
$project = $folder.DeployProject($ProjectName, $projectFile)

Write-Host "All done."
```

Deployment Using SQL

If you prefer to do all of your database management and deployments using T-SQL, the SSIS Catalog exposes a full management interface through a set of Views and Stored Procedures. Listing 19-4 provides a sample that loads a project file in binary format, deploys it to a folder using the [catalog].[deploy_project] stored procedure, and then queries the status of the deployment from the [catalog].[operations] view.

Listing 19-4. Deploying a project using the SQL API

```
use SSISDB

DECLARE @ProjectBinary as varbinary(max)
DECLARE @OperationID as bigint

-- load the project file
SET @ProjectBinary =
(
  SELECT *
  FROM OPENROWSET
  (
    BULK 'C:\ETL\Project.ispac',
    SINGLE_BLOB
  ) as BinaryData
)

-- deploy the project
EXEC [catalog].[deploy_project]
        'MyFolder',        -- folder
        'Project',         -- project name
        @ProjectBinary,    -- binary data
        @OperationID out   -- operation id

--
-- Get the status of the last deployment
--

DECLARE @LastDeployment_id bigint;
SET @LastDeployment_id =
(
  SELECT MAX(operation_id)
  FROM    [catalog].[operations]
  WHERE   operation_type = 101      -- deploy
)

SELECT [object_name], start_time, end_time, [status], [value] =
  case
        when [status] = 1 then N'Created'
        when [status] = 2 then N'Running'
        when [status] = 3 then N'Canceled'
        when [status] = 4 then N'Failed'
        when [status] = 5 then N'Pending'
        when [status] = 6 then N'Unexpected Termination'
        when [status] = 7 then N'Succeeded'
        when [status] = 8 then N'Stopping'
```

```
        when [status]=9 then N'Completed'
  end
FROM    [catalog].[operations]
WHERE   [operation_id]=@LastDeployment_id
```

Package Deployment Model

SSIS projects created in SQL Server 2012 will default to the Project Deployment Model, but some users may want to continue using the Package Deployment Model from SQL Server 2005 and 2008. You can convert from the Project Deployment Model to the Package Deployment Model in Visual Studio by right clicking on the project name in Solution Explorer, and selecting Convert to Package Deployment Model (as shown in Figure 19-4). Projects that were originally created in previous versions of SQL Server will automatically start off in the Package Deployment Model when you open them in SSDT.

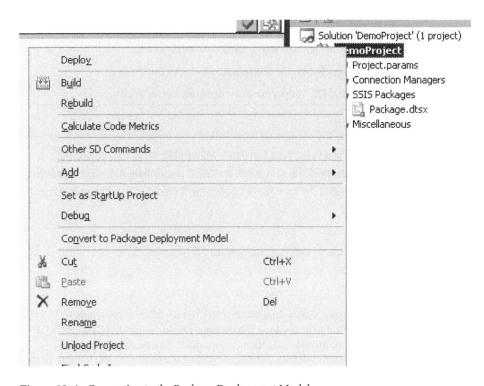

Figure 19-4. *Converting to the Package Deployment Model*

■ **Note**   When using the Package Deployment Model, you will not be able to use some of the new functionality introduced in SQL Server 2012, such as Parameters and Project References. If any of your packages are using these features, SSDT will not let you convert to the Package Deployment Model.

Table 19-2 lists the deployment locations you would use with the Package Deployment Model, and briefly describes the advantages of each approach.

Table 19-2. *Deployment locations when using the Package Deployment Model*

Location	Notes
File System	• Mirrors the structure you have when developing in SSDT • Doesn't require database permissions • Deployment is a simple file copy
SQL Server (MSDB)	• Backup and maintenance part of regular SQL functionality • Finer control over package access and security • Deploys through DTSInstall.exe (legacy deployment wizard), the SSIS object model, or dtutil.exe
Package Store (SSIS Service)	• Provides a façade over the File System and MSDB storage locations, allowing you to change the physical location of a package, yet keep the same logical path • Manages multiple storage locations from a single place • Deploys through SSMS, the SSIS object model, or dtutil.exe • Requires special DCOM permission configuration for access

■ **Note** You cannot use the Package Store interface to manage packages deployed to the SSIS Catalog. The service is only able to interact with packages stored in MSDB (the 2005, and 2008 deployment model), and is there to continue supporting users who have not migrated to the new Project Deployment Model. It may be depreciated in the future.

Summary

The deployment process for SSIS packages has been greatly simplified in SQL Server 2012. Although the deployment model used in SQL Server 2005 and 2008 (now called the Package Deployment Model) is still fully supported, moving to the new Project Deployment Model is highly recommended for new data integration projects. SSIS provides a number of ways to deploy to the SSIS Catalog, providing the flexibility you need to fit the deployment process into your environment.

## CHAPTER 20

Estimating ETL Projects

Out of the various duties assigned to the ETL project manager or architect, one of the most critical is the establishment of a project estimate. When considering a new project of any type, executives, managers, and other decision makers will ask first, "How long will it take?" Appropriately setting time frame expectations is critical to the success of the project.

In this chapter, I'll discuss the challenges and the various components of effective project estimation. Although I won't define a silver-bullet formula here, you should walk away with some things to keep in mind when constructing estimates for level of effort.

What is being measured?

When I talk about estimating ETL projects, I mean setting an expectation of the level of effort required to complete the initiative. Depending on the type of organization and the type of projects, one or more of the following metrics may be used to measure the expected effort:

- *Number of hours to complete the project.* In ETL projects where the work is hired out to a separate vendor, the sum of hours required to complete the work is most often the chief metric used for estimating the project effort.

- *Time to market.* ETL projects that are handled internally are most often estimated by the calendar time until the solution is implemented. Time to market may also be a key metric used to monitor outsourced projects where rapid development could lead to a competitive advantage.

- *Level of staff engagement.* Conscientious business leaders also take into account the impact of ETL projects on their internal staff, regardless of whether the development is handled internally or through a service provider. Even for outsourced projects, executives and other stakeholders will often demand to know how much time their nontechnical resources (those providing business input, testing, and validating results) must spend supporting the development initiative.

Why estimate?

Estimating the level of effort for ETL projects is as much a part of the process as deploying the SSIS package. Even in the smallest of organizations, responsible project owners will demand to know the impact of any such proposed solution. They will ask the following questions:

- *How much will it cost?*

- *How will my staff be impacted?*

- *How long will it take?*

Challenges

Any good project manager will tell you that the hardest part of almost any initiative (not just ETL projects) is properly estimating the level of effort and amount of time involved in getting to the finish line. Why is it so difficult?

It's difficult because it requires—communication

A large part of the reason that project estimation is hard is that a project requires excellent communication. Now, don't get me wrong—I don't want to paint the picture of the stereotypical computer geek sitting in a closet slinging code for 18 hours a day while his superiors toss in pizza and Mountain Dew to keep him fueled. Today's computer nerd is smart, eloquent, and good with people. (Okay, not all of them, but you get where I'm going.)

Even for the most skilled people person, finding the appropriate amount of communication for a project is difficult. Spend too much time talking and you don't get the work done; spend too little, and the developers work from specs that are pure fiction. Among the chief challenges and downfalls with regard to communication are the following:

- *Not asking enough of the right questions.* Properly engaging stakeholders (project champions, executives, and end users) to assess their expectations and business needs is critical. One of the most significant challenges—and most frequent mistakes—is a breakdown between those architecting ETL projects and those who will be impacted by them.

- *Incorrect assumptions.* The last point notwithstanding, it's almost impossible to interrogate stakeholders about every possible decision that will need to be made during architecture and development. Assumptions are a natural part of the project life cycle and are critical to the efficiency of any such initiative. At the risk of stating the obvious, the difficulty here is making the correct assumptions. There's a significant element of guesswork involved here, and the key to overcoming this challenge is making intelligent, fact-based assumptions.

- *Changing requirements.* Solution developers often point to this as the chief cause of blown timelines, and too often it is assumed to be caused by either incompetence or malice. Though I have seen a few occasions where project sponsors try to add to the required deliverables as a way to get a little extra work out of the developers, my experience tells me that changing requirements are generally the result of an evolution of understanding as the project moves along.

- *Language differences.* Here I'm referring not to technical programming languages, but to the way we communicate. Any project will likely engage a blend of technical and nontechnical personnel with various facets and depths of experience. As such, the languages we speak can be vastly different. Techies tend to speak geek, financial professionals have their own lingo, marketing folks use acronyms and industry terms, and so forth.

- *Engaging an inappropriate number of people.* There is a correct number of people for each ETL project. What is that number? As with everything else in the database world, *it depends.* Too few people and you risk not getting enough user perspective to address the possible points of failure.

Before becoming a consultant, I spent several years in the healthcare industry, and learned first-hand that even the most fundamental understandings can be fouled up by differences in communication. Think about the concept of a day: the most commonly accepted definition of a day is the period defined by the calendar and clock, from midnight to midnight. However, there are segments of business that use different definitions of a day. In my time in healthcare, I found that a day often is defined differently by business units within the same organization, especially when the day applies to a patient visit. Some divisions considered a day to be the common midnight-to-midnight calendar period. Others considered a day to be any 24-hour period, regardless of when it started or ended (for example, a patient visit lasting from 7 p.m. on a Friday to 6 p.m. on the following Saturday would be considered one day). Still others did not recognize the concept of multiple-day periods, and would consider any multi-day patient visit to be a series of single-day visits.

Needless to say, reconciling these differences in communication can be difficult, and just as importantly, can cost valuable time. As ETL professionals, a big part of our job is to integrate data from multiple sources and provide for accurate and consistent reporting across multiple domains of information. Certainly the alignment of these various data sets is a problem that can be solved, but getting out in front of this problem early is critical for an ETL project. If different groups of stakeholders expect differing definitions of something as fundamental as a day, it's essential to design the ETL solution with these expectations in mind. Otherwise, any project timeline estimate is likely to be completely off, since a retrofit would likely require far more effort than designing it properly the first time.

It's difficult because it requires guesswork

Those who develop ETL processes are, to some extent, scientists—we deal with rules, formulas, and algorithms that can usually be leveraged to predict output based on various input factors. Applying a specific mix of inputs in the right order ought to, within a small margin of error, result in predictable and reproducible output.

However, the same cannot always be said for predicting the life cycle of a development initiative. Although there are ways to predict some elements of ETL projects, the sheer number of unknowns—specifically, those things that cannot be fully known until the project is well underway—makes the process of building an accurate time sequence very difficult.

When estimating the effort required for a successful ETL initiative, we base our figures on all of the information we have at the time to create the best approximation possible. But even in the best-case scenario, it's still a guess (albeit an educated one).

It's difficult because it relies on technology

It goes without saying that any successful ETL endeavor requires reliable hardware and software. Getting the right tools, sharpening the skillset required to use those tools, and keeping everything up and running is essential. This is especially true when blending architectures during system consolidation or as part of a merger or acquisition.

Systems that speak different languages require the right blend of hardware and software tools to work well. The same could be said for very large ETL initiatives, where the sheer volume of data can bring even world-class systems to their knees. Further complicating matters, technical challenges are sometimes discovered late in the project, forcing a retrofit and costing valuable time.

Note that in the list of difficulties in ETL project estimation, I placed technical challenges at the end. I did so with a purpose. I don't want to diminish the role that technology plays in a successful and efficient ETL initiative: without the proper systems, professionals' ability to effectively do their jobs is inhibited, and the project timeline will suffer. However, in most cases, the technical components of an ETL project present far less risk than communication issues. Technical problems can usually be solved by writing a check (assuming the organization has deep enough pockets), but the same cannot be said for deficiencies in communication.

The secret to estimating ETL project timelines is….

… that there is no secret. As I mentioned earlier, there is no secret sauce, no multiplier, no algorithm that can determine with certainty the amount of time and effort required to bring an ETL project to completion.

Though there is no magic formula for creating an accurate estimate, there are some best practices that can help to make the process of creating realistic timelines a little easier.

Don't forget the little things

An ETL initiative is a development project. It's easy to get caught up in the "development" part and lose sight of the "project" component. Think about it—the typical picture of a development effort is a team of developers staring a bank of monitors, slinging code by the kilobyte. Although this is a realistic expectation, this is certainly not the only element of an ETL project.

Every project is different. However, there are groups of activities that are common to most any development iniative. Some of the elements you will need to consider include:

- *Requirements gathering*. Getting the green light to start on a project does not imply a license to start development. In most projects, the project manager, business analyst, and/or developer will need to research and document the required behaviors of the final product. This phase typically requires a number of user interviews, so don't be surprised by the amount of time required here.

- *Documentation*. I'll confess: I don't like creating documentation. (News flash: nobody does.) However, accurate documentation is essential for the long-term supportability of any ETL initiative, and in many cases will be contractually required as a deliverable. Remember to budget sufficient time not just to create the documentation, but to update it as the technical elements of the solution evolve during the development life cycle.

- *Testing*. This is one of the most frequently underestimated components of an ETL project. Testing an ETL solution often presents difficulties that don't necessarily exist in other development projects. For example, when developing a Windows application, it is usually possible to outsource wholesale testing to users who don't necessarily have deep knowledge of the information domain. On the other hand, testing and validating the results of an ETL process generally requires personnel who are deeply knowledgeable about the underlying data. The testing and validation cycles can be time-consuming. Don't underestimate here—be sure to allow enough wiggle room to adequately test and validate the results.

- *Environmental promotion.* ETL development may require you to move the solution between environments—for example, moving from development to testing to staging and finally to production. In some organizations, especially large companies, there are specific requirements that must be met before promoting a solution (particularly when targeting the final production environment). Furthermore, moving or changing code ad-hoc is usually disallowed; instead, specific deployment windows provide structure and documentation for any code changes.

- *Multiple iterations.* Depending on the chosen development methodology, the project may iterate over various cycles. Be sure to include the iterations in your timeline. Even if an iterative methodology is not used, these types of projects will still have repetitive components. For example, if the code has to go back through development for a correction or feature addition, remember that the solution will also have to go back through testing as well.

Plan for the unexpected

Let me lead by saying that I don't advocate the arbitrary padding of project estimates. Any knucklehead can create a rough timeline and multiply it by 100 just to be safe. You can get away with ridiculously padded estimates—but only for a little while.

Here's how it plays out: you create a bloated project timeline that gives enough time to complete the ETL initiative even if you were transforming the data with a chisel and stone tablets. The project hits a few bumps along the way but completes in a reasonable time, well ahead of your estimate. Next time you create the estimate, the project sponsor has less faith in your estimate, and encourages you to cut it down. From there, every time you come in ridiculously ahead of schedule you cut into your credibility, and project sponsors will no longer take seriously any of your estimates.

That being said, any project estimate should have *some* amount of wiggle room for the inevitable unexpected snafu. I've never worked on a single ETL initiative that didn't have some hiccup outside the scope and timeline of the initial estimate. It happens—regularly. The important thing here is to know the elements of the project that are most at risk for slowdowns, and take those risks into account when constructing the proposed timeline. Timelines can be impacted by various causes, but a few of the particularly risky elements include:

- *Key people who are unavailable, overworked, or disengaged.* ETL solutions are not developed in isolation. Even if the construction of the technical elements occurs quickly, if stakeholders critical to the success of the project can't get into it, the timeline is likely to swell. As much as possible, stay linked up with people. Know where they are in terms of their involvement, and make it easy for them to stay engaged.

- *Weak project champion.* The project champion is the one driving the bus, and typically has the most to gain or lose on the project. This is the person who keeps executives excited about the project, and generally serves as the cheerleader for the initiative (among other duties). If this person is lackadaisical or less than enthusiastic about the process, consider it a significant risk.

- *Many moving parts.* It goes without saying that integrating systems with three sources is far easier than a solution with 30 sources. Keep in mind that, in many cases, adding sources or destinations causes an exponential rather than a linear increase in the level of effort.

- *Previous failures.* Has this initiative been unsuccessfully attempted before? If it failed, are the key causes of failure still present? Don't underestimate a history of failure, especially if the conditions have not changed since the last attempt.

- *Technical time bombs.* Sometimes, technical problems lie in wait, eager to rear their ugly heads at the most inopportune moment. How's the disk space on the affected systems? Is the network burdened by slow links or excessive traffic? Is there a piece of equipment that represents a single point of failure in the ETL pipeline?

Sometimes these risks turn out to be benign, but don't be caught off guard. The more you understand how timelines can be affected by anomalies caused by these and other situations, the better you'll get at creating accurate project estimates.

Know the personalities involved

"If you think working with data is difficult, try working with people." Although this stereotypical geek speak is neither constructive nor politically correct, the fact remains that the personalities involved in a project present a significant element of unpredictability that can have a great deal of impact on the timeline of a project. It's not always possible to know which specific people will be taking part in a project when putting together your estimate. However, if that information is available, it's prudent to consider the abilities, temperament, and prior history of the people you know will be engaged on the project. Will you be working with a business liaison known for being unnecessarily difficult? Is the project manager a rock star with a history of on-time project delivery? If good fortune gives you access to this information before you create your estimate, it's perfectly reasonable to bias your estimate based on past performance of key players.

Learn to do it right by doing it wrong

There is no substitute for experience. Spending time getting to know the ETL process will help to create a better understanding of what is required for a successful ETL initiative, and will help to improve the accuracy of level-of-effort estimates. Whether the estimate is performed by the ETL developer, architect, project manager, or a combination of all three, experience is the most useful tool available.

Don't be overly afraid of being wrong. I mentioned earlier that estimates are essentially guesses. Sometimes when you guess, you're right. Sometimes you're wrong. You'll make mistakes in estimation, and you'll learn from them. The more mistakes you make, the more you'll learn how those little nuances, previously hidden or otherwise insignificant, can affect your project timeline.

When the timeline slips, communicate early and often

Bad news is never good, but it's easier to handle with a little warning. In the inevitable case where a risk event turns into a slipping point for the project, get out in front of it! Communicate with project staff members, the project champion, and other stakeholders as necessary. With some advance warning, it may be possible to realign resources or change the sequence of events to minimize or even neutralize a hiccup in the schedule.

Summary

Creating accurate project estimates is both difficult and necessary. It is a fragile process which often relies on sketchy information and many unknowns. Estimating project timelines will always require a significant bit of guesswork, but it doesn't have to be a complete shot in the dark. Accept that there are some things you cannot predict, but use the information you do have to craft a reasonable project timeline. Rarely will an estimate be 100 % correct, but with experience, attentiveness, and good communication, you can build your own estimating success story.

Evolution of an SSIS Framework

SSIS Frameworks are the next logical step after SSIS Design Patterns because frameworks comprise many patterns. At a minimum, an SSIS Framework should provide package execution control and monitoring. That sounds simple but we assure you, it is not. Execution control requires a working knowledge of the Integration Services Runtime API. An understanding of the subtleties of tight- and loose-coupling is not merely helpful; it can make or ruin your day (or data integration solution).

SSIS monitoring changed with the release of SSIS 2012. The SSIS Catalog, as discussed in Chapter 2, provided built-in support and instrumentation.

Instrumentation is a term used by engineers to describe devices—called "instruments"—placed into or near machinery or processes to measure pertinent indicators.

Why would anyone need an SSIS Framework if SSIS 2012 includes the SSIS Catalog? That is an excellent question. The SSIS 2012 Catalog utilizes the Project Deployment Model—the default for SSIS projects developed in SQL Server Data Tools (SSDT). But SSIS 2012 also includes the Package Deployment Model to support upgrading legacy SSIS projects to SSIS 2012. There are use cases for using the SSIS Catalog for execution and monitoring. There are also use cases for using a serial framework and the Package Deployment Model. As a data integration architect, I am very grateful to the Microsoft SSIS Team for both options.

In this appendix, we will walk you through designing and building a serial SSIS Execution and Monitoring Framework that will work with SSIS 2012's Package Deployment Model, complete with a SQL Server Reporting Services solution. Building an SSIS Framework is an advanced task, but we will build it from the ground up, using some of the design patterns covered earlier in this book.

Starting in the Middle

We begin at the heart of execution control with the Parent–Child Pattern. Create a new SSIS Solution and Project named "SSISConfig2012." Rename the default Package.dtsx to "Child1.dtsx." Open the Child1 SSIS package and add a Script Task to the Control Flow. Rename the Script Task "Who Am I?" and open the Script Task's editor. On the Script page, set the ScriptLanguage property to "Microsoft Visual Basic 2010." Click the ellipsis in the ReadOnlyVariables property value textbox and add the System::TaskName and System::PackageName variables. Open the script editor and add the following code in Sub Main().

```
Public Sub Main()

    Dim sPackageName As String = Dts.Variables("PackageName").Value.ToString
    Dim sTaskName As String = Dts.Variables("TaskName").Value.ToString

    MsgBox("I am " & sPackageName, , sTaskName)

    Dts.TaskResult = ScriptResults.Success
End Sub
```

Listing A-1. Sub Main From Who Am I? Script Task in Child1.dtsx Package

The code shown in Listing A-1 pops up a message box that informs an observer of the name of the package from which the message box originates. This is reusable code. Copy and paste this script task into any SSIS package and it will perform the same way each time.

Close the editor and execute the Child1.dtsx package in the SSDT debugger. When we execute the package, we see a message box similar to the one shown in Figure A-1.

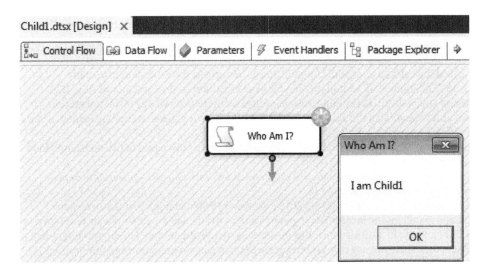

Figure A-1. Message Box from Child1.dtsx

Child.dtsx will be our first test package. We will use Child1.dtsx going forward to conduct tests of our SSIS Execution and Monitoring Framework.

Before we proceed, let's change the Deployment Model for the SSIS from "Project Deployment Model"—the default—to Package Deployment Model. To accomplish the conversion, right-click the SSIS Project in Solution Explorer and click "Convert to Package Deployment Model," as shown in Figure A-2.

Figure A-2. *Converting the Project to Package Deployment Model*

You will need to click the OK button on the dialog to acknowledge you understand that this will change the features available to use in SSIS. Once the conversion is complete, you will see a result pane informing you the project Child1.dtsx was converted to Package Deployment Model. The project in Solution Explorer will also indicate that the non-default deployment model has been selected, as shown in Figure A-3.

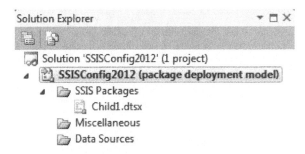

Figure A-3. *Package Deployment Model*

Add a new SSIS Package and rename it "Parent.dtsx." Add an Execute Package Task to the Control Flow of Parent.dtsx. Rename the Execute Package Task "Execute Child Package" and open the editor. On the Package page, set the Location property to "File System" and click the dropdown for the Connection property value. Click "<New connection . . .>" to configure a new File Connection Manager. Set the File Connection Manager Editor's Usage Type property to "Existing File." Browse to the location of your SSISConfig2012 project and select Child1. dtsx. Click the OK button to close the File Connection Manager editor and OK again to close the Execute Package Task editor. Note the File Connection Manager that was created during configuring the Execute Package Task. It is named "Child1.dtsx"–rename it "Child.dtsx."

Test the Parent.dtsx package by executing it in the SSDT debugger. If all goes as planned, then Child1. dtsx will execute and display the message box shown in Figure A-1. Acknowledge the message box and stop the debugger.

This is the Parent-Child pattern in action. We can improve upon the Parent-Child with a little metadata. How? We're glad you asked. First, add an SSIS Variable named ChildPackagePath (String). Click on the Child.dtsx Connection Manager, and then press F4 to display properties. The ConnectionString property of the File Connection Manager is the path to the file. Select the ConnectionString property, copy it to the clipboard, and then paste it into the Value property of the ChildPackagePath SSIS Variable. Return to the properties of the File Connection Manager named "Child.dtsx" and click the ellipsis in the Value textbox of the Expressions property. When the Property Expressions Editor displays, select ConnectionString from the Property dropdown, as shown in Figure A-4.

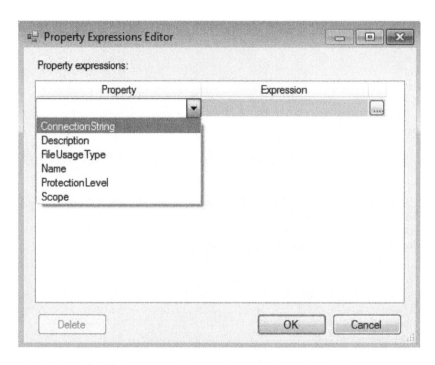

Figure A-4. *The File Connection Manager Property Expressions Editor*

Click the ellipsis in the Expression textbox beside the ConnectionString property. Expand the Variables and Parameters virtual folder in the upper left of the Expression Builder. Drag the variable "User::ChildPackagePath" from the virtual folder to the Expression textbox and click the Evaluate Expression button, as shown in Figure A-5.

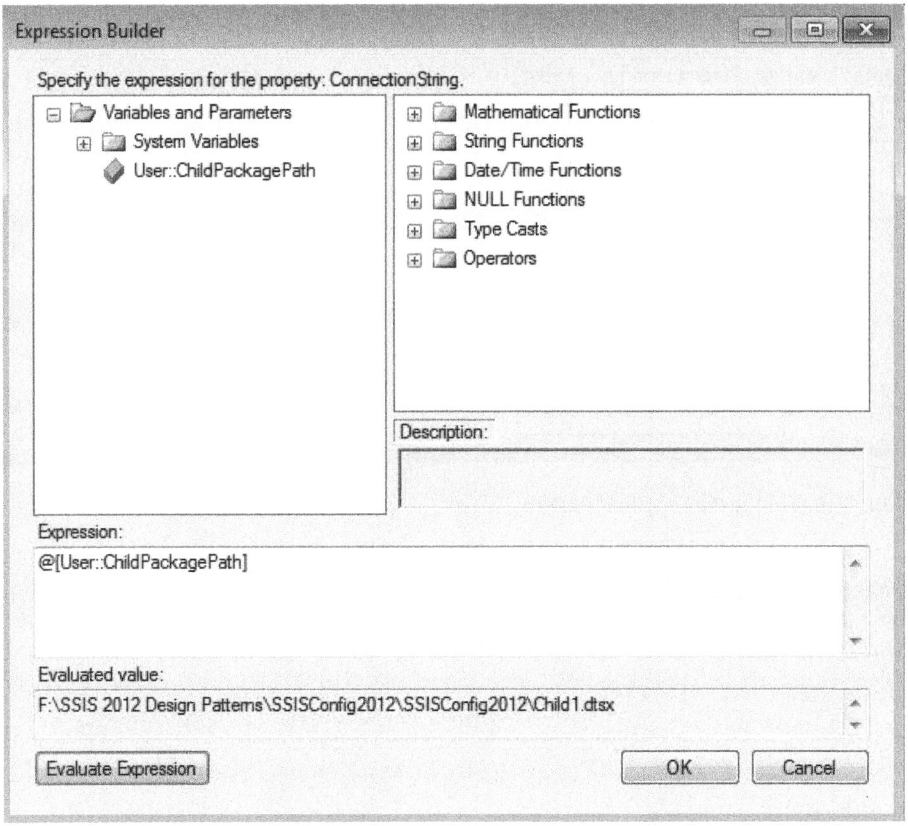

Figure A-5. *Assigning the User::ChildPackagePath Variable to the ConnectionString Expression*

Click the OK button to close the Expression Builder and then click the OK button to close the Property Expressions Editor. At this point, the ConnectionString property of the "Child.dtsx" File Connection Manager is managed by the User::ChildPackagePath SSIS Variable. We can test this functionality by creating a second test child package. Fortunately, creating a second test child package is relatively simple.

In Solution Explorer, right-click the Child1.dtsx SSIS package and then click Copy. Right-click the "SSIS Packages" virtual folder and click Paste. Change the name of the new package from "Child1 1.dtsx" to "Child2.dtsx."

Return to the Parent.dtsx package and change the value of the ChildPackagePath variable, substituting "Child2.dtsx" for "Child1.dtsx." Execute Parent.dtsx in the SSDT debugger and observe the results, as shown in Figure A-6.

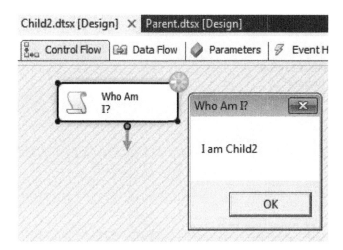

Figure A-6. *Executing Child2.dtsx in the Parent-Child Pattern*

Pretty cool, huh? We're just getting started!

Let's create a database to hold package metadata. Open SQL Server Management Studio (SSMS) and execute the T-SQL script shown in Listing A-2.

```
Use master
go
/* SSISConfig database */
If Not Exists(Select name
              From sys.databases
              Where name = 'SSISConfig')
 begin
  print 'Creating SSISConfig database'
  Create Database SSISConfig
  print 'SSISConfig database created'
 end
Else
 print 'SSISConfig database already exists.'
print ''
go
```

Listing A-2. Creating the SSISConfig Database

The script in Listing A-2 is re-executable. Plus, it informs the person executing the script about its actions via Print statements. The first time you execute this script, you will see the following messages in the SSMS Messages tab:

```
Creating SSISConfig database
SSISConfig database created
```

The second time—and each subsequent time—you execute the same script, you will see this message:

```
SSISConfig database already exists.
```

Writing re-executable T-SQL is not always feasible but when feasible, it is a good idea. Now that we have the database, let's build a table to hold SSIS package metadata. Listing A-3 contains T-SQL for such a table.

```
Use SSISConfig
go

/* cfg schema */
If Not Exists(Select name
              From sys.schemas
              Where name = 'cfg')
 begin
  print 'Creating cfg schema'
  declare @sql varchar(100) = 'Create Schema cfg'
  exec(@sql)
  print 'Cfg schema created'
 end
Else
 print 'Cfg schema already exists.'
print ''

/* cfg.Packages table */
If Not Exists(Select s.name + '.' + t.name
              From sys.tables t
              Join sys.schemas s
                On s.schema_id = t.schema_id
              Where s.name = 'cfg'
                And t.name = 'Packages')
 begin
  print 'Creating cfg.Packages table'
  Create Table cfg.Packages
  (
    PackageID int identity(1,1)
     Constraint PK_Packages
      Primary Key Clustered
   ,PackageFolder varchar(255) Not Null
   ,PackageName varchar(255) Not Null
  )
  print 'Cfg.Packages created'
 end
Else
 print 'Cfg.Packages table already exists.'
print ''
```

Listing A-3. Building the Cfg Schema and Cfg.Packages Table

The script in Listing A-3 creates a schema named "cfg" if one doesn't already exist; it then creates a table named "cfg.Packages," which contains three columns:

- PackageID is an identity column that serves as the Primary Key

- PackageFolder is a VarChar(255) column that holds the path to the folder containing the SSIS Package

- PackageName is a VarChar(255) column that contains the name of the SSIS Package.

I recently began identifying the stored procedures, functions, and views that support such a repository as a Database Programmers Interface, or DPI. Not an Applications Programmers Interface, or API because databases are *not* applications. Let's begin building the SSISConfig DPI with a stored procedure to load data into the cfg. Packages table, as shown in Listing A-4.

```
/* cfg.AddSSISPackage stored procedure */
If Exists(Select s.name + '.' + p.name
          From sys.procedures p
          Join sys.schemas s
            On s.schema_id = p.schema_id
          Where s.name = 'cfg'
            And p.name = 'AddSSISPackage')
 begin
  print 'Dropping cfg.AddSSISPackage stored procedure'
  Drop Procedure cfg.AddSSISPackage
  print 'Cfg.AddSSISPackage stored procedure dropped'
 end
print 'Creating cfg.AddSSISPackage stored procedure'
print ''
go

Create Procedure cfg.AddSSISPackage
  @PackageName varchar(255)
 ,@PackageFolder varchar(255
 ,@PkgID int output
As

   Set NoCount On

   declare @tbl table (PkgID int)

   If Not Exists(Select PackageFolder + PackageName
                 From cfg.Packages
                 Where PackageFolder = @PackageFolder
                   And PackageName = @PackageName)
    begin
     Insert Into cfg.Packages
     (PackageName
     ,PackageFolder)
     Output inserted.PackageID Into @tbl
     Values (@PackageName, @PackageFolder)
    end
   Else
    insert into @tbl
    (PkgID)
    (Select PackageID
    From cfg.Packages
    Where PackageFolder = @PackageFolder
    And PackageName = @PackageName)

    Select @PkgID = PkgID From @tbl
go
print 'Cfg.AddSSISPackage stored procedure created.'
print ''
```

Listing A-4. The Cfg.AddSSISPackages Stored Procedure

Note the cfg.AddSSISPackage stored procedure returns an integer value that represents the identity column—PackageID—from the cfg.Packages table. We will use this integer value later. Once this stored procedure is in place, we can use the T-SQL script in Listing A-5 to add the packages in our project.

```
/* Variable Declaration */
declare @PackageFolder varchar(255) = 'F:\SSIS 2012 Design
Patterns\SSISConfig2012\SSISConfig2012\'
declare @PackageName varchar(255) = 'Child1.dtsx'
declare @PackageID int

/* Add the Child1.dtsx SSIS Package*/
If Not Exists(Select PackageFolder + PackageName
              From cfg.Packages
              Where PackageFolder = @PackageFolder
                And PackageName = @PackageName)
 begin
  print 'Adding ' + @PackageFolder + @PackageName
  exec cfg.AddSSISPackage @PackageName, @PackageFolder, @PackageID output
 end
Else
 begin
  Select @PackageID = PackageID
  From cfg.Packages
  Where PackageFolder = @PackageFolder
     And PackageName = @PackageName
  print @PackageFolder + @PackageName + ' already exists in the Framework.'
 end

set @PackageName = 'Child2.dtsx'
/* Add the Child2.dtsx SSIS Package*/
If Not Exists(Select PackageFolder + PackageName
              From cfg.Packages
              Where PackageFolder = @PackageFolder
              And PackageName = @PackageName)
 begin
  print 'Adding ' + @PackageFolder + @PackageName
  exec cfg.AddSSISPackage @PackageName, @PackageFolder, @PackageID output
 end
Else
 begin
  Select @PackageID = PackageID
  From cfg.Packages
  Where PackageFolder = @PackageFolder
     And PackageName = @PackageName
  print @PackageFolder + @PackageName + ' already exists in the Framework.'
 End
```

Listing A-5. Adding our Packages to the Cfg.Packages Table

We now have enough to test the next step of our Execution and Monitoring SSIS Framework so let's return to SSDT. Add an Execute SQL Task to the Control Flow and rename it Get Package Metadata. Open the editor and change the ResultSet property to "Single row." Change the ConnectionType property to "ADO.Net." Click the dropdown in the Connection property and click "<New connection . . . >". Configure an ADO.Net connection to the SSISConfig database. Set the SQLStatement property to the following T-SQL script:

```
Select PackageFolder + PackageName
From cfg.Packages
Where PackageName = 'Child1.dtsx'
```

On the Result Set page, add a resultset. Set the Result Name to 0 and the Variable Name to User::ChildPackagePath. Execute the Parent.dtsx package to test it. What happens? The Execute SQL Task runs a query that returns the full path to the Child1.dtsx package stored in the SSISConfig.cfg.Packages table. The returned path is sent into the ChildPackagePath variable. Remember, this variable controls the Child.dtsx File Connection Manager, which is used by the Execute Package Task.

Alter the query in the "Get Package Metadata" Execute SQL Task to return Child2.dtsx and retest.

Introducing SSIS Applications

An SSIS Application is a collection of SSIS Packages that execute in a specified order. Let's start by adding a couple tables and supporting stored procedures to the SSISConfig database.

First, create a table named cfg.Applications, and a stored procedure to add them, in SSISConfig using the T-SQL in Listing A-6.

```
/* cfg.Applications table */
If Not Exists(Select s.name + '.' + t.name
              From sys.tables t
              Join sys.schemas s
              On s.schema_id = t.schema_id
              Where s.name = 'cfg'
              And t.name = 'Applications')
 begin
  print 'Creating cfg.Applications table'
  Create Table cfg.Applications
  (
      ApplicationID int identity(1,1)
       Constraint PK_Applications
        Primary Key Clustered
     ,ApplicationName varchar(255) Not Null
      Constraint U_Applications_ApplicationName
       Unique
  )
  print 'Cfg.Applications created'
 end
Else
 print 'Cfg.Applications table already exists.'
print ''
/* cfg.AddSSISApplication stored procedure */
If Exists(Select s.name + '.' + p.name
          From sys.procedures p
          Join sys.schemas s
            On s.schema_id = p.schema_id
          Where s.name = 'cfg'
            And p.name = 'AddSSISApplication')
```

```
begin
  print 'Dropping cfg.AddSSISApplication stored procedure'
  Drop Procedure cfg.AddSSISApplication
  print 'Cfg.AddSSISApplication stored procedure dropped'
end
print 'Creating cfg.AddSSISApplication stored procedure'
print ''
go

Create Procedure cfg.AddSSISApplication
  @ApplicationName varchar(255)
 ,@AppID int output
As

  Set NoCount On

  declare @tbl table (AppID int)

  If Not Exists(Select ApplicationName
                From cfg.Applications
                Where ApplicationName = @ApplicationName)
  begin
    Insert Into cfg.Applications
    (ApplicationName)
    Output inserted.ApplicationID into @tbl
    Values (@ApplicationName)
  end
  Else
    insert into @tbl
    (AppID)
    (Select ApplicationID
     From cfg.Applications
     Where ApplicationName = @ApplicationName)

  Select @AppID = AppID from @tbl
go
print 'Cfg.AddSSISApplication stored procedure created.'
print ''
```

Listing A-6. Building cfg.Applications and cfg.AddSSISApplication

Note the cfg.AddSSISApplication stored procedure returns an integer value that represents the identity column—ApplicationID—from the cfg.Applications table. We will use this integer value later. Let's add an SSIS Application to the table using the following T-SQL in Listing A-7.

```
declare @ApplicationName varchar(255) = 'SSISApp1'
declare @ApplicationID int

/* Add the SSIS First Application */
If Not Exists(Select ApplicationName
              From cfg.Applications
              Where ApplicationName = @ApplicationName)
  begin
    print 'Adding ' + @ApplicationName
    exec cfg.AddSSISApplication @ApplicationName, @ApplicationID output
```

```
 print @ApplicationName + ' added.'
 end
Else
 begin
 Select @ApplicationID = ApplicationID
 From cfg.Applications
 Where ApplicationName = @ApplicationName
 print @ApplicationName + ' already exists in the Framework.'
 end
print ''
```

Listing A-7. *Adding an SSIS Application*

The script in Listing A-7 uses the cfg.AddSSISApplication stored procedure to add the "SSISApp1" SSIS Application to the cfg.Applications table in the SSISConfig database.

A Note About Relationships

An SSIS Application is a collection of SSIS Packages that execute in a prescribed order, so it is pretty easy to determine that the relationship between SSIS Application and SSIS Packages is one-to-many. What may not be as obvious is the relationship between SSIS Packages and SSIS Applications. Herein is a key benefit for choosing patterns-based development: code reusability, specifically in reference to the SSIS Package code. Consider the Archive File Pattern from the end of the Flat File Design Patterns chapter. In an enterprise that loads data from dozens or hundreds of flat file sources, this package may be called many times by different SSIS Applications. From this, we gather that the relationship between SSIS Packages and SSIS Applications is *also* one-to-many. If you do the math, these relationships combine to create a many-to-many relationship between the Applications and Packages tables. This means we need a bridge or resolver table between them to create mappings between SSIS Applications and SSIS Packages.

We call this table cfg.AppPackages. Listing A-8 contains the T-SQL script that creates cfg.AppPackages and a stored procedure with which it is loaded.

```
/* cfg.AppPackages table */
If Not Exists(Select s.name + '.' + t.name
              From sys.tables t
              Join sys.schemas s
                On s.schema_id = t.schema_id
              Where s.name = 'cfg'
                And t.name = 'AppPackages')
 begin
  print 'Creating cfg.AppPackages table'
  Create Table cfg.AppPackages
  (
    AppPackageID int identity(1,1)
     Constraint PK_AppPackages
      Primary Key Clustered
   ,ApplicationID int Not Null
        Constraint FK_cfgAppPackages_cfgApplications_ApplicationID
          Foreign Key References cfg.Applications(ApplicationID)
   ,PackageID int Not Null
        Constraint FK_cfgAppPackages_cfgPackages_PackageID
          Foreign Key References cfg.Packages(PackageID)
```

```
   ,ExecutionOrder int Null
   )
   print 'Cfg.AppPackages created'
 end
Else
 print 'Cfg.AppPackages table already exists.'
print ''

/* cfg.AddSSISApplicationPackage stored procedure */
If Exists(Select s.name + '.' + p.name
          From sys.procedures p
          Join sys.schemas s
            On s.schema_id = p.schema_id
          Where s.name = 'cfg'
            And p.name = 'AddSSISApplicationPackage')
begin
  print 'Dropping cfg.AddSSISApplicationPackage stored procedure'
  Drop Procedure cfg.AddSSISApplicationPackage
  print 'Cfg.AddSSISApplicationPackage stored procedure dropped'
 end
print 'Creating cfg.AddSSISApplicationPackage stored procedure'
go

Create Procedure cfg.AddSSISApplicationPackage
  @ApplicationID int
 ,@PackageID int
 ,@ExecutionOrder int = 10
As

  Set NoCount On

  If Not Exists(Select AppPackageID
                From cfg.AppPackages
                Where ApplicationID = @ApplicationID
                  And PackageID = @PackageID)
  begin
   Insert Into cfg.AppPackages
   (ApplicationID
   ,PackageID
   ,ExecutionOrder)
   Values (@ApplicationID, @PackageID, @ExecutionOrder)
  end
go
print 'Cfg.AddSSISApplicationPackage stored procedure created.'
print '
```

Listing A-8. Creating Cfg.AppPackages and Cfg.AddSSISApplicationPackage

To create the mappings between SSIS Applications and SSIS Packages, we need the IDs of each. Executing the following queries returns the information we need:

```
Select * from cfg.Applications
Select * from cfg.Packages
```

379

We will now use that information to execute the cfg.AddSSISApplicationPackage stored procedure, building "SSISApp1" in the metadata of the SSISConfig database and assigning it "Child1.dtsx" and "Child2.dtsx"—in that order. We use the T-SQL script shown in Listing A-9 to accomplish the mapping.

```
declare @ExecutionOrder int = 10
declare @ApplicationID int = 1
declare @PackageID int = 1
declare @ApplicationName varchar(255) = 'SSISApp1'
declare @PackageFolder varchar(255) = 'F:\SSIS 2012 Design
Patterns\SSISConfig2012\SSISConfig2012\'
declare @PackageName varchar(255) = 'Child1.dtsx'

If Not Exists(Select AppPackageID
              From cfg.AppPackages
              Where ApplicationID = @ApplicationID
                And PackageID = @PackageID
                And ExecutionOrder = @ExecutionOrder)
 begin
  print 'Adding ' + @ApplicationName + '.' + @PackageName + ' to Framework with ExecutionOrder
' + convert(varchar, @ExecutionOrder)
  exec cfg.AddSSISApplicationPackage @ApplicationID, @PackageID, @ExecutionOrder
  print @PackageName + ' added and wired to ' + @ApplicationName
 end
Else
 print @ApplicationName + '.' + @PackageName + ' already exists in the Framework with
ExecutionOrder ' + convert(varchar, @ExecutionOrder)

/*Child2.dtsx */
set @PackageName = 'Child2.dtsx'
set @ExecutionOrder = 20
set @PackageID = 2

If Not Exists(Select AppPackageID
              From cfg.AppPackages
              Where ApplicationID = @ApplicationID
                And PackageID = @PackageID
                And ExecutionOrder = @ExecutionOrder)
 begin
  print 'Adding ' + @ApplicationName + '.' + @PackageName + ' to Framework with ExecutionOrder
' + convert(varchar, @ExecutionOrder)
  exec cfg.AddSSISApplicationPackage @ApplicationID, @PackageID, @ExecutionOrder
  print @PackageName + ' added and wired to ' + @ApplicationName
 end
Else
 print @ApplicationName + '.' + @PackageName + ' already exists in the Framework with
ExecutionOrder ' + convert(varchar, @ExecutionOrder)
```

Listing A-9. *Coupling the "Child1" and "Child2" SSIS Packages to the "SSISApp1" SSIS Application*

One note about the T-SQL script shown in Listing A-9. This is not the way we would load this metadata into Production (or even Test) environments. We would not "re-declare" the ApplicationName, PackageFolder, PackageName, ApplicationID, and PackageID variables; rather, we would reuse these values from the previous T-SQL scripts. We alluded to this earlier when we mentioned we will use the ApplicationID and PackageID values later. We will provide a full T-SQL Metadata Load script later in this appendix.

Retrieving SSIS Applications in T-SQL

We now have SSIS Application metadata stored in the SSISConfig database. Awesome, now what? Let's build a stored procedure to return the SSIS Package metadata we want for a given SSIS Application. Listing A-10 contains the T-SQL Data Definition Language (DDL) script to build such a stored procedure named cfg. GetSSISApplication.

```
/* cfg.GetSSISApplication stored procedure */
If Exists(Select s.name + '.' + p.name
          From sys.procedures p
          Join sys.schemas s
            On s.schema_id = p.schema_id
          Where s.name = 'cfg'
            And p.name = 'GetSSISApplication')
 begin
  print 'Dropping cfg.GetSSISApplication stored procedure'
  Drop Procedure cfg.GetSSISApplication
  print 'Cfg.GetSSISApplication stored procedure dropped'
 end
print 'Creating cfg.GetSSISApplication stored procedure'
go
/*
 (c) 2011,2012 Linchpin People, LLC
*/
Create Procedure cfg.GetSSISApplication
 @ApplicationName varchar(255)
As

Select p.PackageFolder + p.PackageName As PackagePath
     , ap.ExecutionOrder
     , p.PackageName
     , p.PackageFolder
     , ap.AppPackageID
From cfg.AppPackages ap
Inner Join cfg.Packages p on p.PackageID = ap.PackageID
Inner Join cfg.Applications a on a.ApplicationID = ap.ApplicationID
Where ApplicationName = @ApplicationName
Order By ap.ExecutionOrder
go
print 'Cfg.GetSSISApplication stored procedure created.'
print ''
```

Listing A-10. Creating the Cfg.GetSSISApplication Stored Procedure

The Cfg.GetSSISApplication stored procedure shown in Listing A-10 accepts a single parameter—ApplicationName—and uses this value to look up the SSIS Packages associated with the SSIS Application of that name. Note the columns returned are:

- PackagePath

- ExecutionOrder

- PackageName

- PackagePath

Also not the SSIS Packages are returned in the order specified by ExecutionOrder.

We can test the stored procedure using the existing metadata in the SSISConfig database by executing the following T-SQL statement:

```
exec cfg.GetSSISApplication 'SSISApp1'
```

My results appear as shown in Figure A-7.

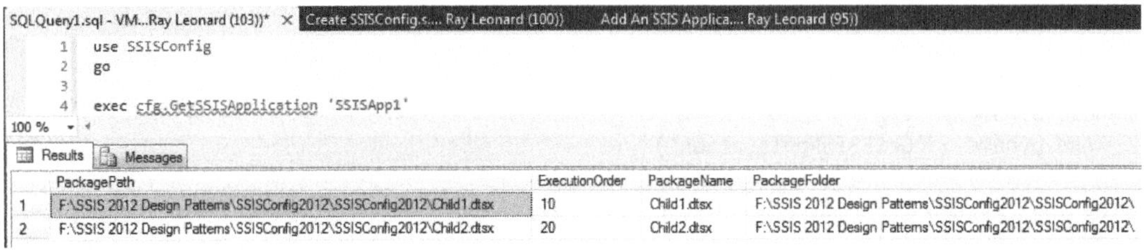

Figure A-7. *Results of Cfg.GetSSISApplication Statement*

Figure A-7 shows the results of the stored procedure statement execution, a result containing two rows of data, and this data represents the SSIS Packages metadata associated with the SSIS Application named "SSISApp1" in the SSISConfig database.

That was a lot of work! Fortunately, most of it will not need to be repeated. When we want to add SSIS Packages and associate them with SSIS Applications in the future, our script will look like the T-SQL shown in Listing A-11.

```
Use SSISConfig
go
/* Variable Declaration */
declare @PackageFolder varchar(255) = 'F:\SSIS 2012 Design
Patterns\SSISConfig2012\SSISConfig2012\'
declare @PackageName varchar(255) = 'Child1.dtsx'
declare @PackageID int
declare @ExecutionOrder int = 10

 declare @ApplicationName varchar(255) = 'SSISApp1'
 declare @ApplicationID int
/* Add the SSIS First Application */
If Not Exists(Select ApplicationName
             From cfg.Applications
             Where ApplicationName = @ApplicationName)
 begin
  print 'Adding ' + @ApplicationName
  exec cfg.AddSSISApplication @ApplicationName, @ApplicationID output
  print @ApplicationName + ' added.'
 end
Else
 begin
  Select @ApplicationID = ApplicationID
  From cfg.Applications
```

```
  Where ApplicationName = @ApplicationName
  print @ApplicationName + ' already exists in the Framework.'
 end
print ''

/* Add the Child1.dtsx SSIS Package*/
If Not Exists(Select PackageFolder + PackageName
              From cfg.Packages
              Where PackageFolder = @PackageFolder
                And PackageName = @PackageName)
 begin
  print 'Adding ' + @PackageFolder + @PackageName
  exec cfg.AddSSISPackage @PackageName, @PackageFolder, @PackageID output
 end
Else
 begin
  Select @PackageID = PackageID
  From cfg.Packages
  Where PackageFolder = @PackageFolder
    And PackageName = @PackageName
  print @PackageFolder + @PackageName + ' already exists in the Framework.'
 end

 If Not Exists(Select AppPackageID
               From cfg.AppPackages
               Where ApplicationID = @ApplicationID
                 And PackageID = @PackageID
                 And ExecutionOrder = @ExecutionOrder)
 begin
   print 'Adding ' + @ApplicationName + '.' + @PackageName + ' to Framework with ExecutionOrder
 ' + convert(varchar, @ExecutionOrder)
   exec cfg.AddSSISApplicationPackage @ApplicationID, @PackageID, @ExecutionOrder
   print @PackageName + ' added and wired to ' + @ApplicationName
 end
Else
 print @ApplicationName + '.' + @PackageName + ' already exists in the Framework with
ExecutionOrder ' + convert(varchar, @ExecutionOrder)

/*Child2.dtsx */
set @PackageName = 'Child2.dtsx'
set @ExecutionOrder = 20

If Not Exists(Select PackageFolder + PackageName
              From cfg.Packages
              Where PackageFolder = @PackageFolder
                And PackageName = @PackageName)
 begin
  print 'Adding ' + @PackageFolder + @PackageName
  exec cfg.AddSSISPackage @PackageName, @PackageFolder, @PackageID output
 end
Else
 begin
  Select @PackageID = PackageID
  From cfg.Packages
```

```
  Where PackageFolder = @PackageFolder
    And PackageName = @PackageName
  print @PackageFolder + @PackageName + ' already exists in the Framework.'
 end

If Not Exists(Select AppPackageID
              From cfg.AppPackages
              Where ApplicationID = @ApplicationID
                And PackageID = @PackageID
                And ExecutionOrder = @ExecutionOrder)
 begin
   print 'Adding ' + @ApplicationName + '.' + @PackageName + ' to Framework with ExecutionOrder
' + convert(varchar, @ExecutionOrder)
   exec cfg.AddSSISApplicationPackage @ApplicationID, @PackageID, @ExecutionOrder
   print @PackageName + ' added and wired to ' + @ApplicationName
 end
Else
 print @ApplicationName + '.' + @PackageName + ' already exists in the Framework with
ExecutionOrder ' + convert(varchar, @ExecutionOrder)
```

Listing A-11. *The Complete T-SQL Script for Adding "SSISApp1" and Associated SSIS Packages*

Retrieving SSIS Applications in SSIS

Return to SQL Server Data Tools and open the editor for the "Get Package Metadata" Execute SQL Task. Change the ResultSet property from "Single row" to "Full result set" and change the SQLStatement property to "cfg. GetSSISApplication." Set the IsQueryStoredProcedure property to True. On the Parameter Mapping page, click the Add button. Click the dropdown in the Variable Name column and select "<New variable . . . >" (you will probably need to scroll up to find "<New variable . . . >"). In the Add Variable window, make sure the Container property is set to Parent. Change the Name property to "ApplicationName." The NameSpace should be "User" and the Value Type property should be "String." For the Value property, enter "SSISApp1" without the double-quotes. Your Add Variable window should appear as shown in Figure A-8.

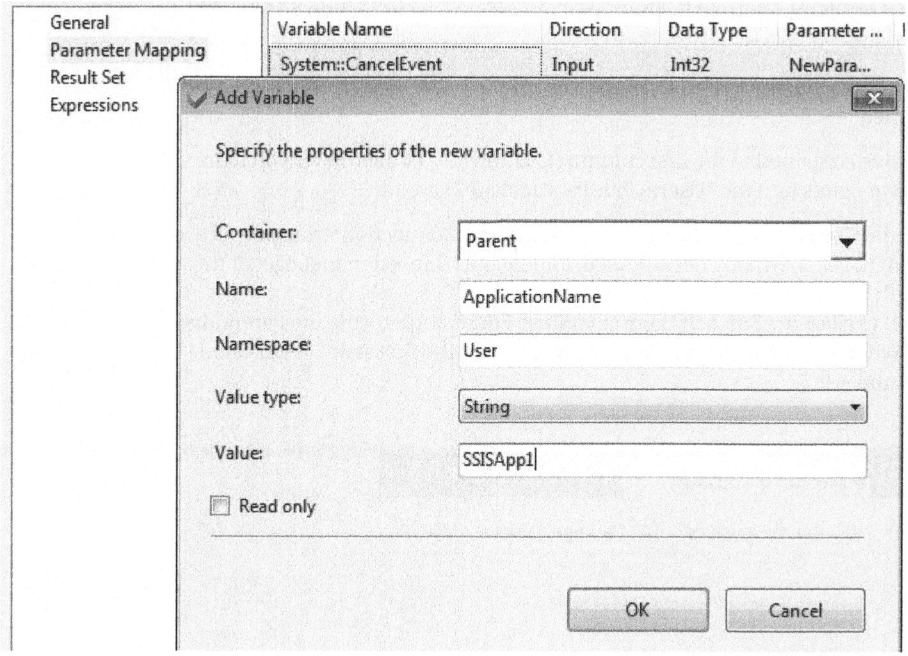

Figure A-8. Adding the ApplicationName Variable

Click the OK button to close the Add Variable window and change the Data Type of the ApplicationName variable to "String." Change the Parameter Name to "ApplicationName." Navigate to the Result Set page and change the "0" Result Name Variable from "User::ChildPackagePath" to a new variable with the following settings:

- Container: Parent
- Name: Packages
- Namespace: User
- Value Type: Object

Click the OK button to close the Add Variable window, and the OK button to close the Execute SQL Task Editor. Delete the precedence constraint between the "Get Package Metadata" Execute SQL Task and the "Execute Child Package" Execute Package Task. Drag a Foreach Loop Container onto the Control Flow and then drag the "Execute Child Package" Execute Package Task inside it. Add a precedence constraint from the "Get Package Metadata" Execute SQL Task to the new Foreach Loop Container, and rename the Foreach Loop Container "Foreach Child Package." Open the "Foreach Child Package" Foreach Loop Container's editor and navigate to the Collection page. Change the Enumerator to "Foreach ADO Enumerator." In the "ADO object source variable" dropdown, select the "User::Packages" variable. Accept the default Enumeration Mode: "Rows in the first table."

Navigate to the Variable Mappings page in the Foreach Loop Editor. Click on the Variable dropdown and select the "User::ChildPackagePath" variable. The Index property will default to 0—do not change it.

The changes we just made accomplish the following:

1. Execute the cfg.GetSSISApplications stored procedure in the SSISConfig database, passing it the value contained in the ApplicationName variable.

2. Push the full result set returned by the stored procedure execution into an SSIS Object Variable named "Packages."

3. Configure a Foreach Loop to point at each row stored in the "Packages" variable in the order returned.

4. Push the value contained in the first column (Column "0") of the row to which the Foreach Loop points into the "User::ChildPackagePath" variable.

When the value of the ChildPackagePath variable changes, the ConnectionString property of the "Child.dtsx" File Connection Manager is dynamically updated, aiming the connection manager at the path contained in "User::ChildPackagePath."

Click the OK button to close the Foreach Loop Container Editor and execute the Parent.dtsx SSIS package in the SSDT debugger. When we do this, we get two message boxes. The first states "I am Child1" and the second appears as shown in Figure A-9.

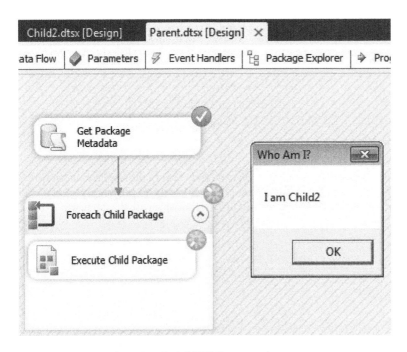

Figure A-9. *Executing a Test Serial SSIS Framework*

This code, as it stands, composes an SSIS Execution Framework. The database contains the metadata and the Parent package executes the SSIS packages. Monitoring is next.

Monitoring Execution

Most experienced Business Intelligence developers will tell you to start with the reports and work your way back to the source data. The source data in this particular case is information collected from the data integration process. What kind of information? Things like start and end execution times, execution status, error and event messages.

Instance data is recorded for each SSIS Application and SSIS Package execution. Each entry represents an execution, and there are two tables that hold these entries: Log.SSISAppInstance to hold execution metrics about SSIS Application instances; and Log.SSISPkgInstance to hold execution metrics for SSIS Child Package instances. When an SSIS Application starts, a row is inserted into the log.SSISAppInstance table. When the SSIS Application completes, the row is updated. Log.SSISPkgInstance works the same way for each SSIS package in an SSIS Application. An SSIS Application Instance is logically comprised of an Application ID and a start time. An SSIS Package Instance is comprised of an Application Instance ID, Application Package ID, and a start time.

Error and event logging is relatively straightforward. We store a Description of the error or event, the time it occurred, and the instance IDs. That's what the reports will reflect, and that's all there is to logging.

Building Application Instance Logging

Let's return to SSMS to build the tables and stored procedures to support logging. Execute the T-SQL script shown in Listing A-12 to build the Instance tables and stored procedures.

```
/* log schema */
If Not Exists(Select name
              From sys.schemas
              Where name = 'log')
 begin
  print 'Creating log schema'
  declare @sql varchar(100) = 'Create Schema [log]'
  exec(@sql)
  print 'Log schema created'
 end
Else
 print 'Log schema already exists.'
print ''

/* log.SSISAppInstance table */
If Not Exists(Select s.name + '.' + t.name
              From sys.tables t
              Join sys.schemas s
                On s.schema_id = t.schema_id
              Where s.name = 'log'
                And t.name = 'SSISAppInstance')
 begin
  print 'Creating log.SSISAppInstance table'
  Create Table [log].SSISAppInstance
  (
     AppInstanceID int identity(1,1)
      Constraint PK_SSISAppInstance
       Primary Key Clustered
    ,ApplicationID int Not Null
          Constraint FK_logSSISAppInstance_cfgApplication_ApplicationID
             Foreign Key References cfg.Applications(ApplicationID)
    ,StartDateTime datetime Not Null
     Constraint DF_cfgSSISAppInstance_StartDateTime
       Default(GetDate())
    ,EndDateTime datetime Null
    ,[Status] varchar(12) Null
  )
```

```
 print 'Log.SSISAppInstance created'
 end
Else
 print 'Log.SSISAppInstance table already exists.'
print ''

/* log.LogStartOfApplication stored procedure */
If Exists(Select s.name + '.' + p.name
          From sys.procedures p
          Join sys.schemas s
            On s.schema_id = p.schema_id
          Where s.name = 'log'
            And p.name = 'LogStartOfApplication')
 begin
  print 'Dropping log.LogStartOfApplication stored procedure'
  Drop Procedure [log].LogStartOfApplication
  print 'Log.LogStartOfApplication stored procedure dropped'
 end
print 'Creating log.LogStartOfApplication stored procedure'
go

Create Procedure [log].LogStartOfApplication
 @ApplicationName varchar(255)
As

declare @ErrMsg varchar(255)
declare @AppID int = (Select ApplicationID
                      From cfg.Applications
                      Where ApplicationName = @ApplicationName)

If (@AppID Is Null)
 begin
  set @ErrMsg = 'Cannot find ApplicationName ' + Coalesce(@ApplicationName, '<NULL>')
  raiserror(@ErrMsg,16,1)
  return-1
 end

Insert Into [log].SSISAppInstance
 (ApplicationID, StartDateTime, Status)
 Output inserted.AppInstanceID
 Values
 (@AppID, GetDate(), 'Running')
go
print 'Log.LogStartOfApplication stored procedure created.'
print ''


/* log.LogApplicationSuccess stored procedure */
If Exists(Select s.name + '.' + p.name
          From sys.procedures p
          Join sys.schemas s
            On s.schema_id = p.schema_id
          Where s.name = 'log'
            And p.name = 'LogApplicationSuccess')
```

```
begin
 print 'Dropping log.LogApplicationSuccess stored procedure'
 Drop Procedure [log].LogApplicationSuccess
 print 'Log.LogApplicationSuccess stored procedure dropped'
 end
print 'Creating log.LogApplicationSuccess stored procedure'
go

Create Procedure [log].LogApplicationSuccess
 @AppInstanceID int
As

 update log.SSISAppInstance
 set EndDateTime = GetDate()
   , Status = 'Success'
 where AppInstanceID = @AppInstanceID
go
print 'Log.LogApplicationSuccess stored procedure created.'
print ''

/* log.LogApplicationFailure stored procedure */
If Exists(Select s.name + '.' + p.name
          From sys.procedures p
          Join sys.schemas s
            On s.schema_id = p.schema_id
          Where s.name = 'log'
            And p.name = 'LogApplicationFailure')
 begin
  print 'Dropping log.LogApplicationFailure stored procedure'
  Drop Procedure [log].LogApplicationFailure
  print 'Log.LogApplicationFailure stored procedure dropped'
 end
print 'Creating log.LogApplicationFailure stored procedure'
go

Create Procedure [log].LogApplicationFailure
 @AppInstanceID int
As

 update log.SSISAppInstance
 set EndDateTime = GetDate()
   , Status = 'Failed'
 where AppInstanceID = @AppInstanceID
go
print 'Log.LogApplicationFailure stored procedure created.'
print ''
```

Listing A-12. Building the Application Instance Tables and Stored Procedures

Return to SSDT and let's add Application Instance logging to the Parent.dtsx package. Drag a new Execute SQL Task to the Control Flow and rename it "Log Start of Application." Set the ResultSet property to "Single row." Set the ConnectionType property to "ADO.Net" and the Connection to the SSISConfig connection manager. Set the SQLStatement property to "log.LogStartOfApplication" and the IsQueryStoredProcedure property to "True." Navigate to the Parameter Mapping page and add a new parameter: mapping the User::ApplicationName SSIS variable to the ApplicationName parameter for the log.LogStartOfApplication stored procedure. On the Result Set page, add a new Result named "0" and map it to a new Int32 variable named "AppInstanceID." Close the Execute SQL Task Editor and connect a precedence constraint from the "Log Start of Application" Execute SQL Task to the "Get Package Metadata" Execute SQL Task.

Drag another Execute SQL Task onto the Control Flow beneath the "Foreach Child Package" Foreach Loop Container and rename it "Log Application Success." Open the editor, change the ConnectionType property to "ADO.Net," and set the Connection property to the SSISConfig connection manager. Enter "log. LogApplicationSuccess" in the SQLStatement property and set the IsQueryStoredProcedure property to "True." Navigate to the Parameter Mapping page and add a mapping between the User::AppInstanceID SSIS variable and the Int32 AppInstanceID parameter for the log.LogApplicationSuccess stored procedure. Close the Execute SQL Task Editor and connect a precedence constraint from the "Foreach Child Package" Foreach Loop Container to the "Log Application Success" Execute SQL Task.

What did we just accomplish? We added SSIS Application Instance logging to the Control Flow of the Parent. dtsx SSIS Package. Execute Parent.dtsx in the SSDT debugger to test.

Once execution completes, execute the following query to observe the logged results:

```
Select * From [log].SSISAppInstance
```

When we execute this query, we get the results that are shown in Figure A-10.

Figure A-10. *Observing the Results of Querying the Application Instance Log*

What happens when an SSIS Application fails? We want to update the log.SSISAppInstance row with an EndDateTime and set the Status to "Failed." For this, we will us an Execute SQL Task configured to execute the log.LogApplicationFailure stored procedure. The question is: Where? The answer is: The Parent.dtsx package's OnError Event Handler.

In SSDT, click the Event Handlers tab on Parent.dtsx. In the Executable dropdown, select "Parent"; in the Event Handler dropdown, select "OnError" as shown in Figure A-11.

Figure A-11. *Configuring the Parent Package's OnError Event Handler*

Click the "Click here to create an 'OnError' event handler for executable 'Parent'" link on the surface of the Event Handler to create the OnError event handler for the Parent.dtsx package. We could walk you through building another Execute SQL Task to log the SSIS Application failure; however, it's easier and simpler to copy the "Log Application Success" Execute SQL Task from the bottom of the Control Flow and paste it into the Parent.dtsx OnError event handler. Change the name to "Log Application Failure" and the SQLStatement property to log.LogApplicationFailure.

We are now ready to test, but we have no real way to test the application failure unless we modify a package—and that just seems tragic. We are likely going to need to test errors after this, too. So why not build an ErrorTest.dtsx SSIS package and add it to our SSIS Application? We like this plan. Let's do it!

Create a new SSIS Package and rename it "ErrorTest.dtsx." Add a Script Task to the Control Flow and rename it "Succeed or Fail?" Open the editor and add the "System::TaskName" and "System::PackageName" variables to the ReadOnlyVariables property. Open the Script Editor and add the code shown in Listing A-13 to Sub Main().

```
Public Sub Main()

    Dim sPackageName As String = Dts.Variables("PackageName").Value.ToString
    Dim sTaskName As String = Dts.Variables("TaskName").Value.ToString
    Dim sSubComponent As String = sPackageName & "." & sTaskName

    Dim iResponse As Integer = MsgBox("Succeed Package?", MsgBoxStyle.YesNo,
sSubComponent)
    If iResponse = vbYes Then
        Dts.TaskResult = ScriptResults.Success
    Else
        Dts.TaskResult = ScriptResults.Failure
    End If

End Sub
```

Listing A-13. Code to Succeed or Fail SSIS Package

Let's unit-test by executing ErrorTest.dtsx in the SSDT debugger, as shown in Figure A-12.

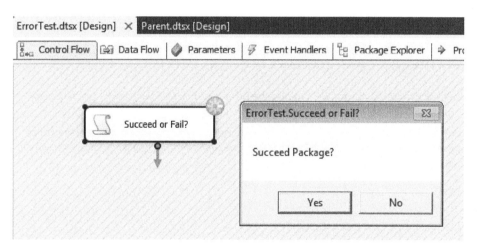

Figure A-12. Unit-testing the ErrorTest.dtsx SSIS Package

To add this SSIS Package to the "SSISApp1" SSIS Application, append the T-SQL script in Listing A-14 to the T-SQL script in Listing A-11.

```
/*ErrorTest.dtsx */
set @PackageName = 'ErrorTest.dtsx'
set @ExecutionOrder = 30

If Not Exists(Select PackageFolder + PackageName
              From cfg.Packages
              Where PackageFolder = @PackageFolder
                And PackageName = @PackageName)
```

```
begin
 print 'Adding ' + @PackageFolder + @PackageName
 exec cfg.AddSSISPackage @PackageName, @PackageFolder, @PackageID output
end
Else
 begin
  Select @PackageID = PackageID
  From cfg.Packages
  Where PackageFolder = @PackageFolder
    And PackageName = @PackageName
  print @PackageFolder + @PackageName + ' already exists in the Framework.'
 end

If Not Exists(Select AppPackageID
              From cfg.AppPackages
              Where ApplicationID = @ApplicationID
                And PackageID = @PackageID
                And ExecutionOrder = @ExecutionOrder)
 begin
   print 'Adding ' + @ApplicationName + '.' + @PackageName + ' to Framework with ExecutionOrder
' + convert(varchar, @ExecutionOrder)
   exec cfg.AddSSISApplicationPackage @ApplicationID, @PackageID, @ExecutionOrder
   print @PackageName + ' added and wired to ' + @ApplicationName
 end
Else
 print @ApplicationName + '.' + @PackageName + ' already exists in the Framework with
ExecutionOrder ' + convert(varchar, @ExecutionOrder)
```

Listing A-14. *Append this T-SQL Script to Listing A-11 to Add the ErrorTest.dtsx SSIS Package to the "SSISApp1" SSIS Application*

Open Parent.dtsx and execute it in the SSDT debugger. Once prompted by the ErrorTest.dtsx message box, click the No button to cause the ErrorTest.dtsx to fail. This should cause the Parent.dtsx package OnError event handler to fire, as shown in Figure A-13.

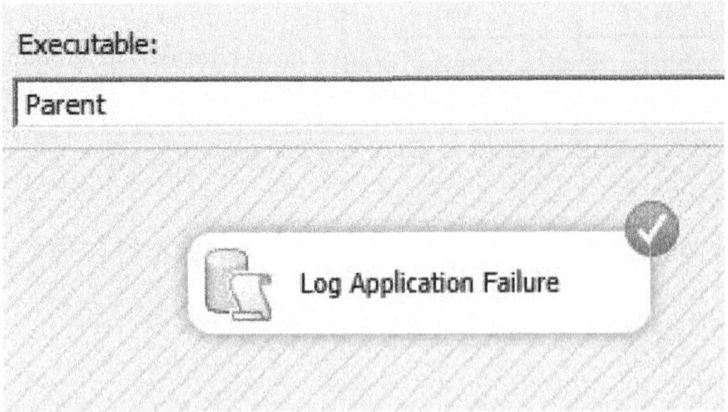

Figure A-13. *I Have Mixed Emotions About Successful OnError Event Handlers.*

A couple successful and failed executions later, and the log.SSISAppInstance table contains the rows shown in Figure A-14.

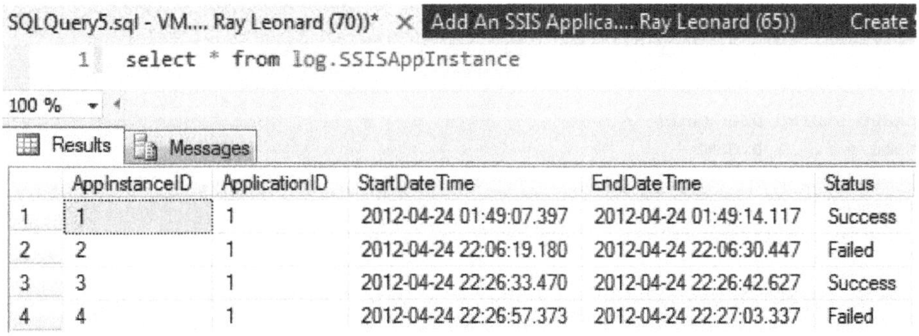

```
SQLQuery5.sql - VM.... Ray Leonard (70))*   ✕   Add An SSIS Applica.... Ray Leonard (65))      Create
    1   select * from log.SSISAppInstance
100 %   ▼  ◂
```

	AppInstanceID	ApplicationID	StartDateTime	EndDateTime	Status
1	1	1	2012-04-24 01:49:07.397	2012-04-24 01:49:14.117	Success
2	2	1	2012-04-24 22:06:19.180	2012-04-24 22:06:30.447	Failed
3	3	1	2012-04-24 22:26:33.470	2012-04-24 22:26:42.627	Success
4	4	1	2012-04-24 22:26:57.373	2012-04-24 22:27:03.337	Failed

Figure A-14. Successes and Failures of SSISApp1

That's a wrap on Application Instance logging! Next, let's build out Child Package Instance logging.

Building Package Instance Logging

Package Instance logging works like Application Instance logging, only on a different scale. An Application Instance consists of an Application ID and an execution start time. A Package Instance consists of an Application Package ID, an Application Instance ID, and an execution start time.

Let's start by creating the log.SSISPkgInstance table and stored procedures. Listing A-15 contains these database objects.

```
/* log.SSISPkgInstance table */
If Not Exists(Select s.name + '.' + t.name
              From sys.tables t
              Join sys.schemas s
                On s.schema_id = t.schema_id
              Where s.name = 'log'
                And t.name = 'SSISPkgInstance')
 begin
  print 'Creating log.SSISPkgInstance table'
  Create Table [log].SSISPkgInstance
  (
     PkgInstanceID int identity(1,1)
       Constraint PK_SSISPkgInstance Primary Key Clustered
    ,AppInstanceID int Not Null
         Constraint FK_logSSISPkgInstance_logSSISAppInstance_AppInstanceID
          Foreign Key References [log].SSISAppInstance(AppInstanceID)
    ,AppPackageID int Not Null
         Constraint FK_logSSISPkgInstance_cfgAppPackages_AppPackageID
          Foreign Key References cfg.AppPackages(AppPackageID)
    ,StartDateTime datetime Not Null
      Constraint DF_cfgSSISPkgInstance_StartDateTime
        Default(GetDate())
    ,EndDateTime datetime Null
    ,[Status] varchar(12) Null
  )
  print 'Log.SSISPkgInstance created'
 end
```

393

```
Else
 print 'Log.SSISPkgInstance table already exists.'
print ''

/* log.LogStartOfPackage stored procedure */
If Exists(Select s.name + '.' + p.name
          From sys.procedures p
          Join sys.schemas s
            On s.schema_id = p.schema_id
          Where s.name = 'log'
            And p.name = 'LogStartOfPackage')
 begin
  print 'Dropping log.LogStartOfPackage stored procedure'
  Drop Procedure [log].LogStartOfPackage
  print 'Log.LogStartOfPackage stored procedure dropped'
 end
print 'Creating log.LogStartOfPackage stored procedure'
go

Create Procedure [log].LogStartOfPackage
 @AppInstanceID int
,@AppPackageID int
As

declare @ErrMsg varchar(255)

Insert Into log.SSISPkgInstance
 (AppInstanceID, AppPackageID, StartDateTime, Status)
 Output inserted.PkgInstanceID
 Values
 (@AppInstanceID, @AppPackageID, GetDate(), 'Running')
go
print 'Log.SSISPkgInstance stored procedure created.'
print ''

/* log.LogPackageSuccess stored procedure */
If Exists(Select s.name + '.' + p.name
          From sys.procedures p
          Join sys.schemas s
            On s.schema_id = p.schema_id
          Where s.name = 'log'
            And p.name = 'LogPackageSuccess')
 begin
  print 'Dropping log.LogPackageSuccess stored procedure'
  Drop Procedure [log].LogPackageSuccess
  print 'Log.LogPackageSuccess stored procedure dropped'
 end
print 'Creating log.LogPackageSuccess stored procedure'
go

Create Procedure [log].LogPackageSuccess
 @PkgInstanceID int
As

 update log.SSISPkgInstance
```

```
set EndDateTime = GetDate()
   , Status = 'Success'
 where PkgInstanceID = @PkgInstanceID
go
print 'Log.LogPackageSuccess stored procedure created.'
print ''

/* log.LogPackageFailure stored procedure */
If Exists(Select s.name + '.' + p.name
           From sys.procedures p
           Join sys.schemas s
             On s.schema_id = p.schema_id
           Where s.name = 'log'
             And p.name = 'LogPackageFailure')
 begin
  print 'Dropping log.LogPackageFailure stored procedure'
  Drop Procedure [log].LogPackageFailure
  print 'Log.LogPackageFailure stored procedure dropped'
 end
print 'Creating log.LogPackageFailure stored procedure'
go

Create Procedure [log].LogPackageFailure
 @PkgInstanceID int
As

 update log.SSISPkgInstance
 set EndDateTime = GetDate()
   , Status = 'Failed'
 where PkgInstanceID = @PkgInstanceID
go
print 'Log.LogPackageFailure stored procedure created.'
print ''
```

Listing A-15. Building the Package Instance Logging Table and Stored Procedures

The log.SSISPkgInstance table will hold the SSIS Package Instance data. Log.LogStartofPackage inserts a row into the Package Instance table; log.LogPackageSuccess updates the row with an EndDateTime and a "Success" status, while log.LogPackageFailure updates the record with an EndDateTime and a "Failed" status.

In Parent.dtsx, open the editor for the "Foreach Child Package" Foreach Loop Container. Navigate to the Variable Mappings page and add a new variable. Configure the following settings in the Add Variable window:

- Container: Parent

- Name: AppPackageID

- Namespace: User

- Value Type: Int32

- Value: 0

Click the OK button to close the Add Variable window. The AppInstanceID—which exists in the dataset inside the "User::Packages" SSIS variable—is returned from executing the cfg.GetSSISApplication stored procedure. The AppPackageID column is returned as the fifth column. Therefore, the AppPackageID variable's Index column on the Variable Mappings page of the "Foreach Child Package" Foreach Loop Container should be set to 4 (the fifth value in a 0-based array). Click the OK button to close the "Foreach Child Package" Foreach Loop Container Editor.

Add an Execute SQL Task to the "Foreach Child Package" Foreach Loop Container. Rename the new Execute SQL Task "Log Start of Package." Open the editor and set the ResultSet property to "Single row." Set the ConnectionType property to "ADO.Net" and the Connection to the SSISConfig connection manager. Set the SQLStatement property to "log.LogStartOfPackage" and the IsQueryStoredProcedure property to "True." Navigate to the Parameter Mapping page and add two new parameters:

- Variable Name: User::AppInstanceID

- Direction: Input

- Data Type: Int32

- Parameter Name: AppInstanceID

- Variable Name: User::AppPackageID

- Direction: Input

- Data Type: Int32

- Parameter Name: AppPackageID

On the Result Set page, add a new Result named "0" and map it to a new Int32 variable named "PkgInstanceID." Close the Execute SQL Task Editor. Connect a precedence constraint from the "Log Start of Package" Execute SQL Task to the "Execute Child Package" Execute Package Task.

Add two more Execute SQL Tasks to the "Foreach Child Package" Foreach Loop Container. Rename the first "Log Package Success," set the connection properties from the ADO.Net connection manager used to connect to the SSISConfig database, the SQLStatement property to "log.LogPackageSuccess," and the IsQueryStoredProcedure property to True. On the Parameter Mapping page, add a parameter and map the User::PkgInstanceID variable to the PkgInstanceID parameter for the log.LogStartofPackage stored procedure. Connect a precedence constraint (OnSuccess) from the "Execute Child Package" Execute Package Task to the "Log Package Success" Execute SQL Task.

Rename the second "Log Package Failure," set the connection properties from the ADO.Net connection manager used to connect to the SSISConfig database, the SQLStatement property to "log.LogPackageFailure," and the IsQueryStoredProcedure property to True. On the Parameter Mapping page, add a parameter and map the User::PkgInstanceID variable to the PkgInstanceID parameter for the log.LogStartofPackage stored procedure. Connect a precedence constraint (OnFailure) from the "Execute Child Package" Execute Package Task to the "Log Package Failure" Execute SQL Task.

Test the Package Instance logging by running a few test executions. Allow one to succeed and the other to fail. When we check the Application and Package Instance tables, the results should appear as shown in Figure A-15.

```
1 ⊟select * from log.SSISAppInstance order by AppInstanceID DESC
2 │select * from log.SSISPkgInstance order by PkgInstanceID DESC
```

100 %

Results | Messages

	AppInstanceID	ApplicationID	StartDateTime	EndDateTime	Status
1	6	1	2012-04-25 17:24:46.870	2012-04-25 17:24:53.257	Failed
2	5	1	2012-04-25 17:24:28.557	2012-04-25 17:24:40.800	Success

	PkgInstanceID	AppInstanceID	AppPackageID	StartDateTime	EndDateTime	Status
1	6	6	3	2012-04-25 17:24:49.950	2012-04-25 17:24:53.353	Failed
2	5	6	2	2012-04-25 17:24:48.120	2012-04-25 17:24:49.920	Success
3	4	6	1	2012-04-25 17:24:46.953	2012-04-25 17:24:48.080	Success
4	3	5	3	2012-04-25 17:24:36.397	2012-04-25 17:24:40.750	Success
5	2	5	2	2012-04-25 17:24:30.560	2012-04-25 17:24:36.360	Success
6	1	5	1	2012-04-25 17:24:28.670	2012-04-25 17:24:30.530	Success

Figure A-15. *Examining the Application and Package Instance Logs*

We can tell by examining the Application Instance and Package Instance log tables that AppInstanceID 5 started at 5:24:28 PM 25 Apr 2012. We can also see three SSIS packages—with PkgInstanceID's 1, 2, and 3—were executed as part of the SSIS Application. Each package succeeded, and the SSIS Application succeeded as well. We also know AppInstanceID 6 started at 5:24:46 PM 25 Apr 2012 and executed PkgInstanceID's 4, 5, and 6. PkgInstanceID's 4 and 5 succeeded, but PkgInstanceID 6 failed; failing the SSIS Application.

Cool? Cool. Let's move to Error and Event logging.

Building Error Logging

Instrumenting data integration processes to capture and preserve error and exception metadata is the most important and useful type of logging. Exceptions and errors are going to happen. SSIS provides a fairly robust model for capturing and reporting errors as long as you realize you can mostly ignore the error codes. The error descriptions, however, are mostly good. So it balances out.

Before we demonstrate how to capture error messages in SSIS, let's discuss why. I used to manage a team of data integration developers. The team ranged in size from 28 to 40 developers and we built very large ETL solutions for US government interests. Part of my job was to figure out best practices. Having all SSIS packages log error data in the same format to the same location is a best practice. But how do you do this with 40 developers? Have you ever tried to get 40 developers to do the same thing the same way? It's like herding cats. The problem was half of them thought they were smarter than me; and half of those were correct in thinking that. But this isn't the kind of problem that required deep thinking; this required strategy. So what's the best strategy for getting every developer to build the exact same kind of log for every SSIS package every time? You guessed it: Don't let them. Take error logging completely out of their hands.

Soon after learning how to use the Execute Package Task, I learned events "bubble" from child to parent packages. For the purposes of error logging, this means we can capture and record any error at the parent package. Even better, it means we can do this *with no code in the child package*. Problem solved.

Let's take a look at how to implement this functionality into an SSIS Framework. First, let's add a table and a stored procedure to record and preserve errors, as shown in Listing A-16.

```
/* log.SSISErrors table */
If Not Exists(Select s.name + '.' + t.name
             From sys.tables t
             Join sys.schemas s
               On s.schema_id = t.schema_id
             Where s.name = 'log'
               And t.name = 'SSISErrors')
 begin
  print 'Creating log.SSISErrors table'
  Create Table [log].SSISErrors
  (
     ID int identity(1,1)
      Constraint PK_SSISErrors Primary Key Clustered
    ,AppInstanceID int Not Null
        Constraint FK_logSSISErrors_logSSISAppInstance_AppInstanceID
          Foreign Key References [log].SSISAppInstance(AppInstanceID)
    ,PkgInstanceID int Not Null
        Constraint FK_logSSISErrors_logPkgInstance_PkgInstanceID
          Foreign Key References [log].SSISPkgInstance(PkgInstanceID)
    ,ErrorDateTime datetime Not Null
      Constraint DF_logSSISErrors_ErrorDateTime
```

```
           Default(GetDate())
      ,ErrorDescription varchar(max) Null
      ,SourceName varchar(255) Null
  )
  print 'Log.SSISErrors created'
 end
Else
 print 'Log.SSISErrors table already exists.'
print ''

/* log.LogError stored procedure */
If Exists(Select s.name + '.' + p.name
          From sys.procedures p
          Join sys.schemas s
            On s.schema_id = p.schema_id
          Where s.name = 'log'
            And p.name = 'LogError')
 begin
  print 'Dropping log.LogError stored procedure'
  Drop Procedure [log].LogError
  print 'Log.LogError stored procedure dropped'
 end
print 'Creating log.LogError stored procedure'
go

Create Procedure [log].LogError
 @AppInstanceID int
,@PkgInstanceID int
,@SourceName varchar(255)
,@ErrorDescription varchar(max)
As

 insert into log.SSISErrors
 (AppInstanceID, PkgInstanceID, SourceName, ErrorDescription)
 Values
 (@AppInstanceID
,@PkgInstanceID
,@SourceName
,@ErrorDescription)
go
print 'Log.LogError stored procedure created.'
print ''
```

Listing A-16. Building the Error Logging Table and Stored Procedure

Each row in the log.SSISErrors table contains an AppInstanceID and PkgInstanceID for identification purposes. Why both? It is designed to capture and preserve errors that originate in both the Parent and Child Packages. An error in the Parent.dtsx package will have a PkgInstanceID of 0. The remaining columns capture metadata about the error proper: the date and time the error occurred (ErrorDateTime), the error message (ErrorDescription), and the SSIS task from which the error originated (SourceName).

Adding a row to the log.SSISErrors table with a PkgInstanceID of 0 will actually raise a foreign key constraint violation at this time, but we will address this matter later in the appendix.

It is important to note that Error Events are "raised" by SSIS tasks. When an error event is instantiated, its fields are populated with information such as the Error Description and Source Name (the name of the task raising the error). These data do not change as the event navigates—"bubbles"—inside the SSIS package execution stack. When the event arrives at the Parent.dtsx package in our framework, it will contain the name of the task that originated the error (SourceName) and the description of the error from that task (ErrorDescription).

When the error "bubbles" to the Parent.dtsx package, we will call the log.LogError stored procedure to populate the log.SSISErrors table. In SSDT, return to the Parent.dtsx package's On Error event handler we configured earlier. Add an Execute SQL Task and rename it "Log Error." Open the editor and configure the ConnectionType and Connection properties to connect to the SSISConfig database via ADO.Net. Set the SQLStatement property to "log.LogError" and the IsQueryStoredProcedure property to True. Navigate to the Parameter Mapping page and add the following parameters:

- Variable Name: User::AppInstanceID

- Direction: Input

- Data Type: Int32

- Parameter Name: AppInstanceID

- Variable Name: User::PkgInstanceID

- Direction: Input

- Data Type: Int32

- Parameter Name: PkgInstanceID

- Variable Name: System::SourceName

- Direction: Input

- Data Type: String

- Parameter Name: SourceName

- Variable Name: System::ErrorDescription

- Direction: Input

- Data Type: String

- Parameter Name: ErrorDescription

We created the AppInstanceID and PkgInstanceID SSIS variables earlier in this appendix. We are using the two variables from the System namespace—SourceName and ErrorDescription—which are two of the fields populated when an Error event is first raised by the originating task.

Once these parameters are mapped, close the Execute SQL Task Editor and connect a precedence constraint from the "Log Error" Execute SQL Task to the "Log Application Failure" Execute SQL Task, as shown in Figure A-16.

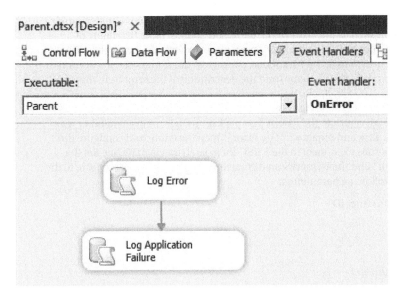

Figure A-16. *Adding the Log Error Execute SQL Task to the Parent Package OnError Event Handler*

Test the new error logging functionality by running Parent.dtsx in the SSDT debugger. When prompted from the ErrorTest.dtsx package, click the "No" button to generate an error. In SSMS, execute the following query to examine the error metadata:

```
Select * From log.SSISErrors
```

Your results should appear similar to those shown in Figure A-17.

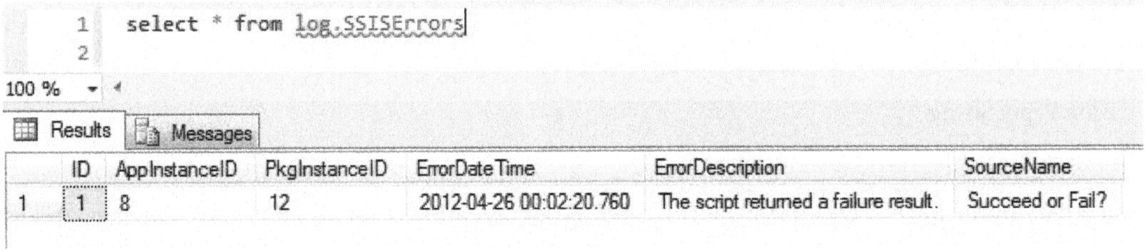

Figure A-17. *Error Metadata in the Log.SSISErrors Table*

As you can see from the preceding image (and hopefully your own code at this point), error logging can make troubleshooting SSIS issues much simpler.

Event logging is very similar to error logging in SSIS. Part of the reason is SSIS reuses the object model for the OnError event handler in the OnInformation event handler.

Let's begin by adding another table and stored procedure to the SSISConfig database. The T-SQL script in Listing A-17 accomplishes this task.

```
/* log.SSISEvents table */
If Not Exists(Select s.name + '.' + t.name
```

```
                From sys.tables t
                Join sys.schemas s
                  On s.schema_id = t.schema_id
                Where s.name = 'log'
                  And t.name = 'SSISEvents')
 begin
  print 'Creating log.SSISEvents table'
  Create Table [log].SSISEvents
  (
      ID int identity(1,1)
       Constraint PK_SSISEvents Primary Key Clustered
     ,AppInstanceID int Not Null
          Constraint FK_logSSISEvents_logSSISAppInstance_AppInstanceID
           Foreign Key References [log].SSISAppInstance(AppInstanceID)
     ,PkgInstanceID int Not Null
          Constraint FK_logSSISEvents_logPkgInstance_PkgInstanceID
           Foreign Key References [log].SSISPkgInstance(PkgInstanceID)
     ,EventDateTime datetime Not Null
      Constraint DF_logSSISEvents_ErrorDateTime
         Default(GetDate())
     ,EventDescription varchar(max) Null
     ,SourceName varchar(255) Null
  )
  print 'Log.SSISEvents created'
 end
Else
 print 'Log.SSISEvents table already exists.'
print ''

/* log.LogEvent stored procedure */
If Exists(Select s.name + '.' + p.name
          From sys.procedures p
          Join sys.schemas s
            On s.schema_id = p.schema_id
          Where s.name = 'log'
            And p.name = 'LogEvent')
 begin
   print 'Dropping log.LogEvent stored procedure'
   Drop Procedure [log].LogEvent
   print 'Log.LogEvent stored procedure dropped'
 end
print 'Creating log.LogEvent stored procedure'
go

Create Procedure [log].LogEvent
 @AppInstanceID int
,@PkgInstanceID int
,@SourceName varchar(255)
,@EventDescription varchar(max)
As

 insert into [log].SSISEvents
 (AppInstanceID, PkgInstanceID, SourceName, EventDescription)
```

```
Values
 (@AppInstanceID
,@PkgInstanceID
,@SourceName
,@EventDescription)
go
print 'Log.LogEvent stored procedure created.'
print ''
```

Listing A-17. Building the Event Logging Table and Stored Procedure

With the exception of the column names, the log.SSISEvents table is precisely the same design as the log. SSISErrors table. Return to SSDT and copy the "Log Error" Execute SQL Task from the Parent.dtsx OnError event handler. Change the Event Handler dropdown from OnError to OnInformation and create the OnInformation event handler by clicking the link. Next, paste the contents of the clipboard onto the OnInformation event handler surface. Open the editor and change the name of the task to "Log Event." Edit the SQLStatement property to read "log.LogEvent." On the Parameter Mapping page, change the "ErrorDescription" Parameter Name from "ErrorDescription" to "EventDescription." Close the Execute SQL Task Editor and you are done.

But what about all that 'Error' stuff in the parameter mapping? The OnInformation event handler message is conveyed via an SSIS variable named "System::ErrorDescription." That is not a typo. You might expect it to be InformationDescription, but it's not, which makes less work for us.

If we execute Parent.dtsx now to test the new Event logging functionality, then we don't see any events logged. Bummer. How do we get events from SSIS? Several tasks provide information via OnInformation events. The Data Flow Task, for example, provides lots of helpful metadata about rows read from sources and written to destinations; and lookup cache sizes, rows, and time to populate, for example. You can also inject OnInformation events into the execution stream using a Script Task.

We like to include Script Tasks that summarize the information we have about a SSIS Applications and Packages in SSIS Framework Parent packages. Let's add those now.

Drag a Script Task onto the Parent.dtsx package's Control Flow and rename it "Log Application Variables." Open the editor and change the ScriptLanguage to "Microsoft Visual Basic 2010." Add the following variables to the ReadOnlyVariables property:

- System::TaskName

- System::PackageName

- User::AppInstanceID

- User::ApplicationName

Edit the script and place the code shown in Listing A-18 in Sub Main().

```
Public Sub Main()

    Dim sPackageName As String = Dts.Variables("PackageName").Value.ToString
    Dim sTaskName As String = Dts.Variables("TaskName").Value.ToString
    Dim sSubComponent As String = sPackageName & "." & sTaskName
    Dim sApplicationName As String = Dts.Variables("ApplicationName").Value.ToString
    Dim iAppInstanceID As Integer = _
Convert.ToInt32(Dts.Variables("AppInstanceID").Value)

    Dim sMsg As String = "ApplicationName: " & sApplicationName & vbCrLf & _
                        "AppInstanceID: " & iAppInstanceID.ToString
    Dts.Events.FireInformation(1001, sSubComponent, sMsg, "", 0, True)
```

```
    Dts.TaskResult = ScriptResults.Success
End Sub
```

Listing A-18. Raising an Information Event from a Script Task

The purpose of the script is the Dts.Events.FireInformation call near the end. The first argument for this function is the InformationCode. Depending on the nature and purpose of the SSIS Framework, we may or may not enter a value (other than 0) here. The SubComponent argument is next and we usually construct a string identifying the names of the package and task. The description argument follows and this contains the message we want to inject into the log.SSISEvents table. The next two arguments are help-related—we usually blank and zero them, respectively. The last argument is FireAgain, and we are uncertain if it does anything (anymore); we always set it to True.

Close the script editor and the Script Task Editor. Connect a precedence constraint from the "Log Start of Application" Execute SQL Task to the "Log Application Variables" Script Task and another precedence constraint from the "Log Application Variables" Script Task to the "Get Package Metadata" Execute SQL Task.

Drag another Script Task into the "Foreach Child Package" Foreach Loop Container and rename it "Log Package Variables." Open the editor and change the ScriptLanguage to "Microsoft Visual Basic 2010." Add the following variables to the ReadOnlyVariables property:

- System::TaskName

- System::PackageName

- User::PkgInstanceID

- User::ChildPackagePath

- User::AppPackageID

Edit the script and place the code shown in Listing A-19 in Sub Main().

```
Public Sub Main()

    Dim sPackageName As String = Dts.Variables("PackageName").Value.ToString
    Dim sTaskName As String = Dts.Variables("TaskName").Value.ToString
    Dim sSubComponent As String = sPackageName & "." & sTaskName
    Dim sChildPackagePath As String = Dts.Variables("ChildPackagePath").Value.ToString
    Dim iAppPackageID As Integer = Convert.ToInt32(Dts.Variables("AppPackageID").Value)
    Dim iPkgInstanceID As Integer = _
Convert.ToInt32(Dts.Variables("PkgInstanceID").Value)

    Dim sMsg As String = "ChildPackagePath: " & sChildPackagePath & vbCrLf & _
                         "AppPackageID: " & iAppPackageID.ToString & vbCrLf & _
                         "PkgInstanceID: " & iPkgInstanceID.ToString
    Dts.Events.FireInformation(1001, sSubComponent, sMsg, "", 0, True)

    Dts.TaskResult = ScriptResults.Success
End Sub
```

Listing A-19. Raising an Information Event from a Script Task

If you execute Parent.dtsx now, you will get a foreign key constraint error when you try to log the Application Variables. Why? PkgInstanceID is set to a default value, "0", and there is no "0" row in the log.SSISPkgInstance table. Let's remedy that now with the following script shown in Listing A-20.

```
/* Add "0" rows */
If Not Exists(Select ApplicationID
```

```
                From cfg.Applications
                        Where ApplicationID = 0)
 begin
   print 'Adding 0 row for cfg.Applications'
   Set Identity_Insert cfg.Applications ON
   Insert Into cfg.Applications
   (ApplicationID
   ,ApplicationName)
   Values
   (0
   ,'SSIS Framework')
   Set Identity_Insert cfg.Applications OFF
   print '0 row for cfg.Applications added'
 end
Else
 print '0 row already exists for cfg.Applications'
print ''

If Not Exists(Select PackageID
                From cfg.Packages
                        Where PackageID = 0)
 begin
   print 'Adding 0 row for cfg.Packages'
   Set Identity_Insert cfg.Packages ON
   Insert Into cfg.Packages
   (PackageID
   ,PackageFolder
   ,PackageName)
   Values
   (0
   ,'\'
   ,'parent.dtsx')
   Set Identity_Insert cfg.Packages OFF
   print '0 row for cfg.Packages added'
 end
Else
 print '0 row already exists for cfg.Packages'
print ''

If Not Exists(Select AppPackageID
                From cfg.AppPackages
                        Where AppPackageID = 0)
 begin
  print 'Adding 0 row for cfg.Packages'
  Set Identity_Insert cfg.AppPackages ON
  Insert Into cfg.AppPackages
  (AppPackageID
  ,ApplicationID
  ,PackageID
  ,ExecutionOrder)
  Values
  (0
  ,0
```

```
 ,0
 ,10)
  Set Identity_Insert cfg.AppPackages OFF
  print '0 row for cfg.AppPackages added'
 end
Else
 print '0 row already exists for cfg.AppPackages'
print ''

If Not Exists(Select AppInstanceID
               From [log].SSISAppInstance
                        Where AppInstanceID = 0)
 begin
   print 'Adding 0 row for cfg.Packages'
   Set Identity_Insert [log].SSISAppInstance ON
   Insert Into [log].SSISAppInstance
   (AppInstanceID
   ,ApplicationID
   ,StartDateTime
   ,EndDateTime
   ,[Status])
   Values
   (0
   ,0
   ,'1/1/1900'
   ,'1/1/1900'
   ,'Unknown')
   Set Identity_Insert [log].SSISAppInstance OFF
   print '0 row for log.SSISAppInstance added'
 end
Else
 print '0 row already exists for log.SSISAppInstance'
print ''

If Not Exists(Select PkgInstanceID
               From [log].SSISPkgInstance
                        Where PkgInstanceID = 0)
 begin
   print 'Adding 0 row for cfg.Packages'
   Set Identity_Insert [log].SSISPkgInstance ON
   Insert Into [log].SSISPkgInstance
   (PkgInstanceID
   ,AppInstanceID
   ,AppPackageID
   ,StartDateTime
   ,EndDateTime
   ,[Status])
   Values
   (0
   ,0
   ,0
   ,'1/1/1900'
   ,'1/1/1900'
```

```
 ,'Unknown')
 Set Identity_Insert [log].SSISPkgInstance OFF print '0 row for log.SSISPkgInstance added'
 end
Else
 print '0 row already exists for log.SSISPkgInstance'
print ''
```

Listing A-20. Adding "0" ID Rows to Selected Tables in the SSISConfig Database

Now that these event-generating Script Tasks are in place, test-execute the Parent.dtsx package and then observe the log.LogEvents table by executing the following T-SQL in SSMS:

```
Select * From [log].SSISEvents
```

My results appear as shown in Figure A-18.

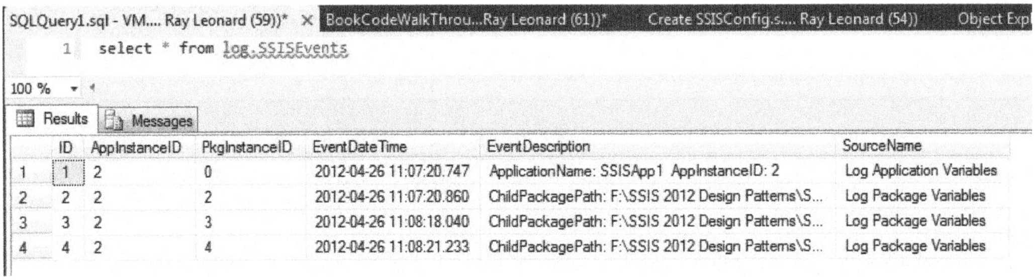

Figure A-18. SSIS Framework Events!

Viewing the log.SSISEvents table in SSMS is disappointing. The data is accurate and SSMS is doing its job, but the user experience could be better for this type of data. Fortunately, SQL Server 2012 ships with SQL Server Reporting Services, which provides a better user experience! Let's look at building reports to display this data.

Reporting Execution Metrics

SQL Server Reporting Services (SSRS) allows us to create reports that display SSIS Framework metadata and metrics in a more user-friendly format. We can add visualizations to the reports that will assist in identifying the status of SSIS Applications and SSIS Packages.

To begin, open a new instance of SQL Server Data Tools (SSDT) and create a new Report Server project named "SSISConfig2012Reports." In Solution Explorer, right-click Shared Data Source and click "Add New Data Source." When the Shared Data Source Properties window displays, set the Name property to "SSISConfig" and click the Edit button to configure the connection to your instance of the SSISConfig database. When we configure the Shared Data Source, it appears as shown in Figure A-19.

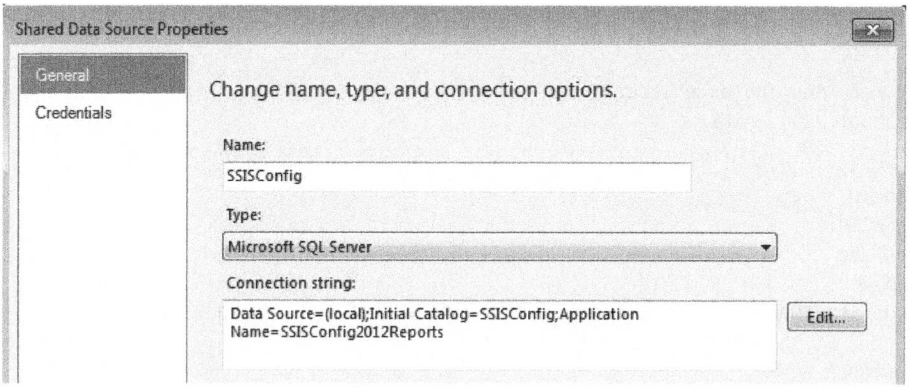

Figure A-19. *Configuring the SSISConfig Shared Data Source*

We are now ready to build reports! Let's begin by creating a report to display Application Instance data.

Before we jump into report development, let's create supporting objects in the SSISConfig database. Listing A-21 contains the T-SQL script required to build the "rpt" schema and the "rpt.ReturnAppInstanceHeader" stored procedure.

```
/* rpt schema */
If Not Exists(Select name
               From sys.schemas
               Where name = 'rpt')
 begin
  print 'Creating rpt schema'
  declare @sql varchar(100) = 'Create Schema rpt'
  exec(@sql)
  print 'Rpt schema created'
 end
Else
 print 'Rpt schema already exists.'
print ''

/* rpt.ReturnAppInstanceHeader stored procedure */
If Exists(Select s.name + '.' + p.name
          From sys.procedures p
          Join sys.schemas s
            On s.schema_id = p.schema_id
          Where s.name = 'rpt'
            And p.name = 'ReturnAppInstanceHeader')
 begin
  print 'Dropping rpt.ReturnAppInstanceHeader stored procedure'
  Drop Procedure rpt.ReturnAppInstanceHeader
  print 'Rpt.ReturnAppInstanceHeader stored procedure dropped'
 end
```

```
print 'Creating rpt.ReturnAppInstanceHeader stored procedure'
go

Create Procedure rpt.ReturnAppInstanceHeader
 @ApplicationName varchar(255) = NULL
As

  Select a.ApplicationID
       ,ap.AppInstanceID
       ,a.ApplicationName
       ,ap.StartDateTime
       ,DateDiff(ss,ap.StartDateTime,Coalesce(ap.EndDateTime,GetDate())) As RunSeconds
       ,ap.Status
  From log.SSISAppInstance ap
  Join cfg.Applications a
    On ap.ApplicationID = a.ApplicationID
  Where a.ApplicationName = Coalesce(@ApplicationName,a.ApplicationName)
  Order by AppInstanceID desc

go
print 'Rpt.ReturnAppInstanceHeader stored procedure created.'
print ''
```

Listing A-21. Creating the Rpt Schema and Rpt.ReturnAppInstanceHeader Stored Procedure

Return to SSDT, right-click the Reports virtual folder in Solution Explorer, and click "Add New Report." If the welcome screen displays, then click the "Next" button. On the "Select the Data Source" screen, select the Shared Data Source named "SSISConfig" and click the "Next" button. The "Design the Query" window displays next; add "rpt.ReturnAppInstanceHeader" (without the double-quotes) to the Query String textbox and click the "Next" button. Select "Tabular" on the "Select the Report type" page and click the "Next" button. When the "Design the Table" page displays, multi-select all the columns listed in the Available Fields listbox and click the "Details" button. Your Report Wizard will appear as shown in Figure A-20.

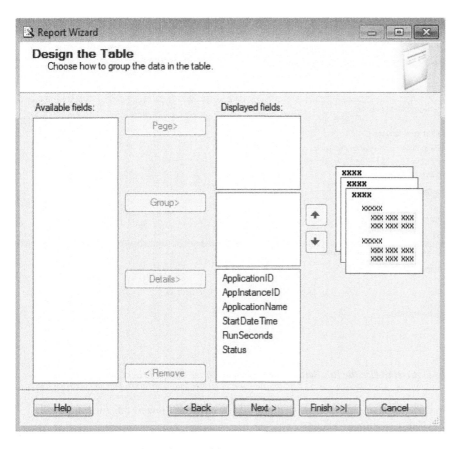

Figure A-20. *Selecting All Available Fields as Details*

Click the "Next" button. Select a theme on the "Choose the Table Style" page and click the "Next" button. On the "Completing the Wizard" page, enter "Application Instance" in the Report Name property textbox and click the "Finish" button.

The SSRS Report Wizard will generate the report, but it doesn't manage stored procedures effectively. We need to change this so we get the maximum performance out of the reports. Click View → Report Data to display the Report Data sidebar. Expand the Datasets virtual folder. Right-click "DataSet1" and click "Dataset Properties." When the Dataset Properties window displays, rename the dataset "rpt_ReturnAppInstanceHeader" (the Dataset Name property does not like periods . . .). Copy "rpt.ReturnAppInstanceHeader" out of the Query property and click the "Stored Procedure" option in the Query Type property. Paste "rpt.ReturnAppInstanceHeader" into the "Select or enter stored procedure name" dropdown. Your Dataset Properties window should appear similar to what is shown in Figure A-21.

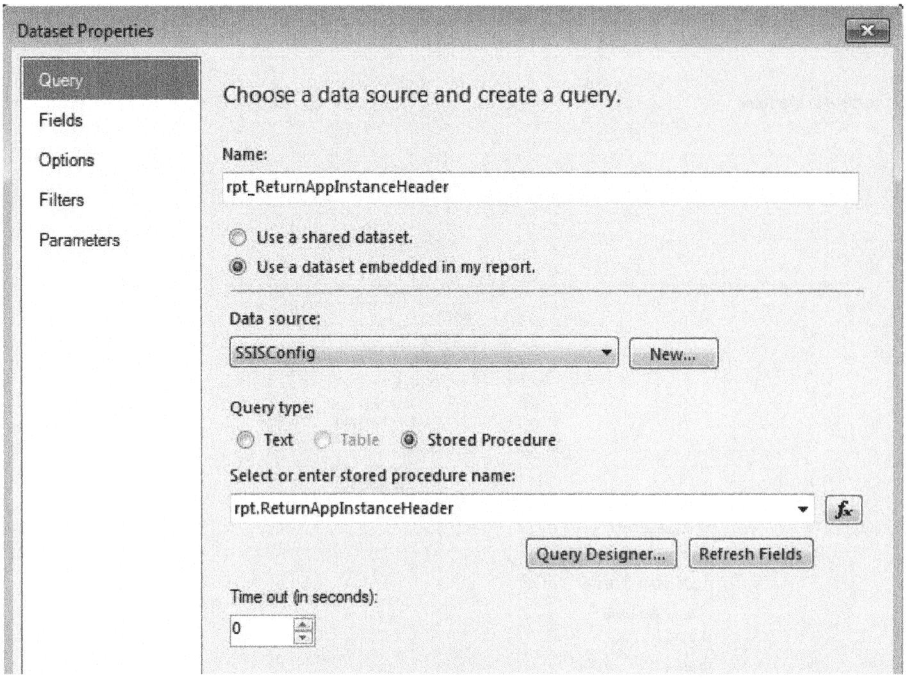

Figure A-21. *Configuring the Dataset to Use the Rpt.ReturnAppInstanceHeader Stored Procedure*

Click the "OK" button to close the Dataset Properties window. If you click the Preview tab, the report will prompt you for an Application Name as shown in Figure A-22.

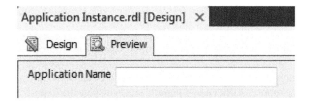

Figure A-22. *Prompting for Application Name*

Supply "SSISApp1" to the textbox (without the double-quotes) and click the "View Report" button in the upper right corner. We don't want the user to supply an SSIS Application each time they use the report, so let's configure the Report Parameter named "@ApplicationName." Return to the Report Data sidebar and expand the Parameters virtual folder. Double-click "@ApplicationName" to open the Report Parameter Properties window. On the General page, check the "Allow null value" checkbox and change the "Select parameter visibility" option to "Hidden." On the Default Values page, select the "Specify values" option and click the "Add" button. A "(Null)" row will be added to the Value grid, which is what we want. Click the "OK" button to close the Report Parameter Properties window.

Test the changes by clicking the Preview tab. The report should display all Application Instance rows stored in the database, as shown in Figure A-23.

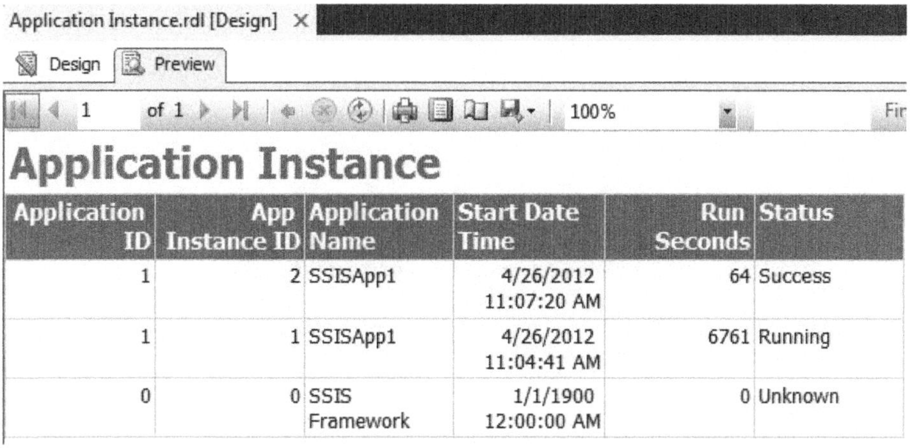

Figure A-23. *Displaying the Application Instance Data*

We do not want to see the "0" rows displayed in these reports. Modify the rpt.ReturnAppinstanceHeader stored procedure to eliminate these records from the returned results by executing the T-SQL shown in Listing A-22.

```
/* rpt.ReturnAppInstanceHeader stored procedure */
If Exists(Select s.name + '.' + p.name
          From sys.procedures p
          Join sys.schemas s
            On s.schema_id = p.schema_id
          Where s.name = 'rpt'
            And p.name = 'ReturnAppInstanceHeader')
 begin
  print 'Dropping rpt.ReturnAppInstanceHeader stored procedure'
  Drop Procedure rpt.ReturnAppInstanceHeader
  print 'Rpt.ReturnAppInstanceHeader stored procedure dropped'
 end
print 'Creating rpt.ReturnAppInstanceHeader stored procedure'
go

Create Procedure rpt.ReturnAppInstanceHeader
 @ApplicationName varchar(255) = NULL
As

  Select a.ApplicationID
       ,ap.AppInstanceID
       ,a.ApplicationName
       ,ap.StartDateTime
       ,DateDiff(ss,ap.StartDateTime,Coalesce(ap.EndDateTime,GetDate())) As RunSeconds
       ,ap.Status
  From log.SSISAppInstance ap
  Join cfg.Applications a
    On ap.ApplicationID = a.ApplicationID
  Where a.ApplicationName = Coalesce(@ApplicationName,a.ApplicationName)
  And a.ApplicationID > 0
  Order by AppInstanceID desc
```

```
go
print 'Rpt.ReturnAppInstanceHeader stored procedure created.'
print ''
```

Listing A-22. Updating the Rpt.ReturnAppInstanceHeader Stored Procedure

Refresh the Application Instance report Preview and it now appears as shown in Figure A-24.

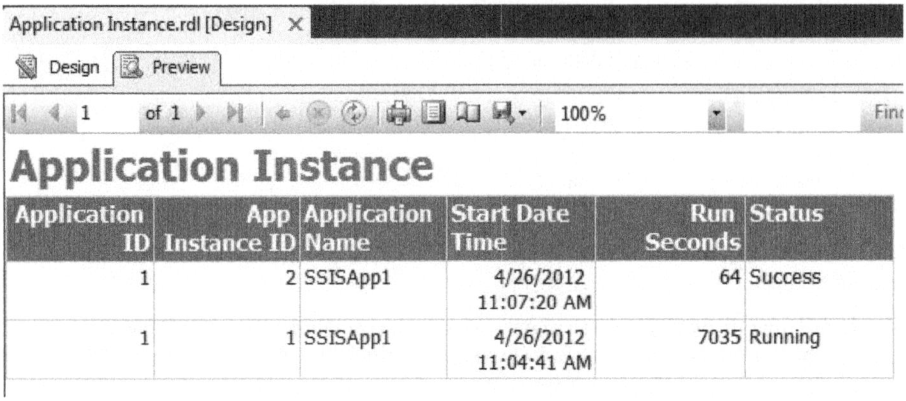
Application Instance.rdl [Design]
Design
Preview
1 of 1
100%
Application Instance
Application ID | App Instance ID | Application Name | Start Date Time | Run Seconds | Status
1 | 2 | SSISApp1 | 4/26/2012 11:07:20 AM | 64 | Success
1 | 1 | SSISApp1 | 4/26/2012 11:04:41 AM | 7035 | Running

Figure A-24. *Refreshed Application Instance Report, sans the "0" Row*

Color helps identify the state better than most visual cues. To add background color to the data rows, return to the Design tab and select the row that displays data values (the bottom row) in the table. Press the F4 key to display Properties and click on the BackgroundColor property. In the BackgroundColor property's value dropdown, select "Expression . . . ." When the Expression window opens, change the text in the "Set expression for: BackgroundColor" textbox from "No Color" (the default) to the following expression:

```
=Switch(Fields!Status.Value="Success", "LightGreen"
, Ficlds!Status.Valuc="Failed", "LightCoral"
, Fields!Status.Value="Running", "Yellow")
```

By cleaning up the report by resetting font sizes, changing text alignment, and adjusting column widths, our report appears as shown in Figure A-25:

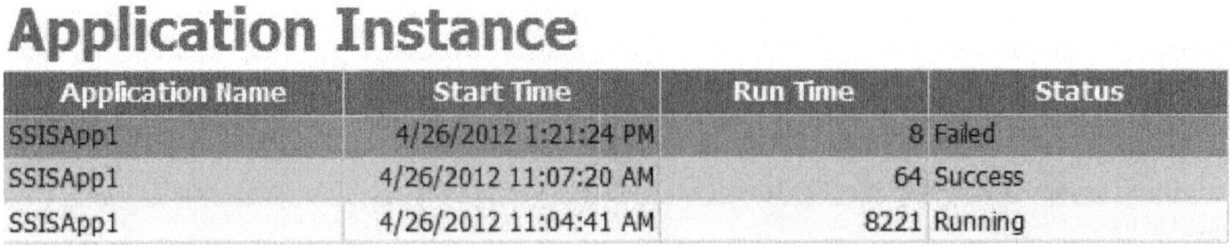
Application Instance
Application Name | Start Time | Run Time | Status
SSISApp1 | 4/26/2012 1:21:24 PM | 8 | Failed
SSISApp1 | 4/26/2012 11:07:20 AM | 64 | Success
SSISApp1 | 4/26/2012 11:04:41 AM | 8221 | Running

Figure A-25. *Application Instance—in Color!*

By cleaning up the report by removing ID columns (which mean little to the user), resetting font sizes, changing text alignment, and adjusting column widths, our report appears as shown in Figure A-25.

We call this Operational Intelligence. An enterprise operations person can look at this report and glean lots of information about the current state of enterprise data integration processes.

The Package Instance report is remarkably similar. Let's begin by adding the stored procedure to the database, as shown in Listing A-23.

```
/* rpt.ReturnPkgInstanceHeader stored procedure */
If Exists(Select s.name + '.' + p.name
          From sys.procedures p
          Join sys.schemas s
            On s.schema_id = p.schema_id
          Where s.name = 'rpt'
            And p.name = 'ReturnPkgInstanceHeader')
 begin
  print 'Dropping rpt.ReturnPkgInstanceHeader stored procedure'
  Drop Procedure rpt.ReturnPkgInstanceHeader
  print 'Rpt.ReturnPkgInstanceHeader stored procedure dropped'
 end
print 'Creating rpt.ReturnPkgInstanceHeader stored procedure'
go

Create Procedure rpt.ReturnPkgInstanceHeader
 @AppInstanceID int
As

            SELECT a.ApplicationName
                   ,p.PackageFolder + p.PackageName As PackagePath
                   ,cp.StartDateTime
                   ,DateDiff(ss,cp.StartDateTime,Coalesce(cp.EndDateTime,GetDate())) As
RunSeconds
                   ,cp.Status
                   ,ai.AppInstanceID
                   ,cp.PkgInstanceID
                   ,p.PackageID
                   ,p.PackageName
            FROM log.SSISPkgInstance cp
            Join cfg.AppPackages ap
                on ap.PackageID = cp.AppPackageID
            Join cfg.Packages p
                on p.PackageID = ap.AppPackageID
            Join log.SSISAppInstance ai
                on ai.AppInstanceID = cp.AppInstanceID
            Join cfg.Applications a
                on a.ApplicationID = ap.ApplicationID
            WHERE ai.AppInstanceID = Coalesce(@AppInstanceID,ai.AppInstanceID)
             And a.ApplicationID > 0
            Order By cp.PkgInstanceID desc
go
print 'Rpt.ReturnPkgInstanceHeader stored procedure created.'
print ''
```

Listing A-23. Adding the Rpt.ReturnPkgInstanceHeader Stored Procedure

413

In SSDT, add a new report named "Package Instance" just like you added the "Application Instance" report. Make sure you use the "rpt.ReturnPkgInstanceHeader" stored procedure. To get the Report Wizard to recognize a query that expects parameters, you need to add default parameter values on the "Design the Query" page. My Query String textbox reads as follows:

```
exec rpt.ReturnPkgInstanceHeader NULL
```

This allows the query builder to locate the columns list returned from the stored procedure (which is what the Report Wizard needs to continue). Once the report is built, remember to first update the Dataset, then the Report Parameter as you did for the Application Instance report. One cool thing about this particular design is that we can reuse the expression for BackgroundColor on the data rows. Once complete, the Package Instance report appears, as shown in Figure A-26.

Package Instance

Application	Package	Start Time	Run Time	Status
SSISApp1	ErrorTest.dtsx	4/26/2012 1:21:29 PM	3	Failed
SSISApp1	Child2.dtsx	4/26/2012 1:21:26 PM	3	Success
SSISApp1	Child1.dtsx	4/26/2012 1:21:24 PM	2	Success
SSISApp1	ErrorTest.dtsx	4/26/2012 11:08:21 AM	3	Success
SSISApp1	Child2.dtsx	4/26/2012 11:08:18 AM	3	Success
SSISApp1	Child1.dtsx	4/26/2012 11:07:20 AM	57	Success
SSISApp1	Child1.dtsx	4/26/2012 11:04:42 AM	14738	Running

Figure A-26. *The Package Instance Report*

Package Instances are "children" of Application Instances. To reflect that relationship, return to the Application Instance report and add a column to the table to contain "Packages" links. Enter "Packages" in the column header and as text in the data cell. Right-click the data cell and click "Text Box Properties . . . ". On the Font page, change the font color to Blue and set the Effects property to Underline. On the Action page, select the "Go to report" option for the "Enable as an action" property and set the "Specify a report" property to "Package Instance." In the "Use these parameters to run the report" grid, click the "Add" button and map the AppInstanceID parameter to the "[AppinstanceID]" value. Click the "OK" button to close the Text Box Properties editor.

Click the Preview tab to display the Application Instance report. Select one of the "Packages" links to navigate to the Package Instance report that will contain only the Package Instances related to that particular Application Instance. Your Package Instance report should appear similar to the Package Instance report displayed in Figure A-27.

Package Instance

Application	Package	Start Time	Run Time	Status
SSISApp1	ErrorTest.dtsx	4/26/2012 11:08:21 AM	3	Success
SSISApp1	Child2.dtsx	4/26/2012 11:08:18 AM	3	Success
SSISApp1	Child1.dtsx	4/26/2012 11:07:20 AM	57	Success

Figure A-27. *Package Instances for a Single Application Instance*

Building the reports in this fashion makes sense. The Application Instance report becomes a "gateway" for the Package Instance report; a "dashboard," if you will. More in a bit . . .

Let's turn our attention to the Error log data. To retrieve it, let's use the T-SQL script shown in Listing A-24.

```
/* rpt.ReturnErrors stored procedure */
If Exists(Select s.name + '.' + p.name
          From sys.procedures p
          Join sys.schemas s
            On s.schema_id = p.schema_id
          Where s.name = 'rpt'
            And p.name = 'ReturnErrors')
 begin
  print 'Dropping rpt.ReturnErrors stored procedure'
  Drop Procedure rpt.ReturnErrors
  print 'Rpt.ReturnErrors stored procedure dropped'
 end
print 'Creating rpt.ReturnErrors stored procedure'
go

Create Procedure rpt.ReturnErrors
  @AppInstanceID int
 ,@PkgInstanceID int = NULL
As

  Select
     a.ApplicationName
    ,p.PackageName
    ,er.SourceName
    ,er.ErrorDateTime
    ,er.ErrorDescription
  From log.SSISErrors er
  Join log.SSISAppInstance ai
    On ai.AppInstanceID = er.AppInstanceID
  Join cfg.Applications a
    On a.ApplicationID = ai.ApplicationID
  Join log.SSISPkgInstance cp
    On cp.PkgInstanceID = er.PkgInstanceID
       And cp.AppInstanceID = er.AppInstanceID
  Join cfg.AppPackages ap
    On ap.AppPackageID = cp.AppPackageID
  Join cfg.Packages p
    On p.PackageID = ap.PackageID
  Where er.AppInstanceID = Coalesce(@AppInstanceID, er.AppInstanceID)
    And er.PkgInstanceID = Coalesce(@PkgInstanceID, er.PkgInstanceID)
  Order By ErrorDateTime Desc
go
print 'Rpt.ReturnErrors stored procedure created.'
print ''
```

Listing A-24. Building the Rpt.ReturnErrors Stored Procedure

The T-SQL in Listing A-24 constructs the "rpt.ReturnErrors" stored procedure, which will supply data to a new report. Let's build that report now in SSDT.

Add a new report named "Errors" to the SSISConfig2012Reports solution. Use the "rpt.ReturnErrors" stored procedure as the source. Remember to update the Dataset and both report parameters: AppinstanceID and PkgInstanceID.

On the table's data row, edit the BackgroundColor property, adding the following expression:

```
=Iif(RowNumber(Nothing) Mod 2 = 0,"White","WhiteSmoke")
```

We are not coloring the background of each cell here to reflect Status; the report would be filled with LightCoral if we did so. But we do need to break up these rows visually, so we use subtle shading to help keep the eyes moving across the row at 2:15 AM some dark and dreary morning.

Open the Application Instance report. Right-click on the "Status" data field and click "Text Box Properties." Navigate to the Font page and click the f(x) button beside the Color property dropdown. In the "Set expression for: Color" textbox, enter the following expression:

```
=Iif(Fields!Status.Value = "Failed", "Blue", "Black")
```

If the Status is "Failed," then this expression will change the color of the Status text blue. Click the f(x) button beside the Effects property dropdown. In the "Set expression for: TextDecoration" textbox, add the following expressiocv n:

```
=Iif(Fields!Status.Value = "Failed", "Underline", "Default")
```

This expression will decorate a "Failed" status with an underline. This and the previous property combine to make "Failed" status appear as a hyperlink. Where does the hyperlink take us? Let's configure that property now. Navigate to the Action page and select the "Go to report" option for the "Enable as an action" property. Click the f(x) button beside the "Specify a report" dropdown and add the following expression to the "Set expression for: ReportName" textbox:

```
=Iif(Fields!Status.Value = "Failed", "Errors", Nothing)
```

Click the "Add" button and map the "AppInstanceID" parameter Name to the "[AppInstanceID]" parameter Value. Click the f(x) button in the "Omit" column of the parameter mapping and add the following expression to the "Set expression for: Omit" textbox:

```
=Iif(Fields!Status.Value = "Failed", False, True)
```

The two previous property settings configure the Action property of the Status value. If the Status is "Failed," clicking the word "Failed," which will appear to be a hyperlink, will cause the Errors report to display. When it displays, it will only show those error rows associated with the Application Instance displayed in that row of data.

Let's test it! When we run the Application Instance report, it now appears as shown in Figure A-28.

Application Instance

Application	Start Time	Run Time	Status	Packages
SSISApp1	4/26/2012 5:14:18 PM	7	Failed	Packages
SSISApp1	4/26/2012 5:14:01 PM	8	Failed	Packages
SSISApp1	4/26/2012 1:21:24 PM	8	Failed	Packages
SSISApp1	4/26/2012 11:07:20 AM	64	Success	Packages
SSISApp1	4/26/2012 11:04:41 AM	24386	Running	Packages

Figure A-28. The Application Instance Report, Including Status, and Packages Decoration

Clicking one of the "Failed" hyperlinks takes me to the Errors report for that Application Instance. Your report should appear similar to that shown in Figure A-29.

Errors

Application	Package	Source	Error Time	Description
SSISApp1	ErrorTest.dtsx	Succeed or Fail?	4/26/2012 1:21:32 PM	The script returned a failure result.

Figure A-29. *Displaying an Error*

Quickly isolating the source of an error in an SSIS package is one way to improve overall operational efficiency. These reports, working in tandem, facilitate efficient root cause analysis.

The Events report is very similar to the Errors report. The T-SQL script for creating the "rpt.ReturnEvents" stored procedure is shown in Listing A-25.

```
/* rpt.ReturnEvents stored procedure */
If Exists(Select s.name + '.' + p.name
          From sys.procedures p
          Join sys.schemas s
            On s.schema_id = p.schema_id
          Where s.name = 'rpt'
            And p.name = 'ReturnEvents')
 begin
  print 'Dropping rpt.ReturnEvents stored procedure'
  Drop Procedure rpt.ReturnEvents
  print 'Rpt.ReturnEvents stored procedure dropped'
 end
print 'Creating rpt.ReturnEvents stored procedure'
go

Create Procedure rpt.ReturnEvents
  @AppInstanceID int
 ,@PkgInstanceID int = NULL
As

  Select
     a.ApplicationName
    ,p.PackageName
    ,ev.SourceName
    ,ev.EventDateTime
    ,ev.EventDescription
  From log.SSISEvents ev
  Join log.SSISAppInstance ai
    On ai.AppInstanceID = ev.AppInstanceID
  Join cfg.Applications a
    On a.ApplicationID = ai.ApplicationID
  Join log.SSISPkgInstance cp
    On cp.PkgInstanceID = ev.PkgInstanceID
       And cp.AppInstanceID = ev.AppInstanceID
  Join cfg.AppPackages ap
    On ap.AppPackageID = cp.AppPackageID
  Join cfg.Packages p
    On p.PackageID = ap.PackageID
```

```
    Where ev.AppInstanceID = Coalesce(@AppInstanceID, ev.AppInstanceID)
     And ev.PkgInstanceID = Coalesce(@PkgInstanceID, ev.PkgInstanceID)
    Order By EventDateTime Desc
go
print 'Rpt.ReturnEvents stored procedure created.'
print ''
```

Listing A-25. Building the Rpt.ReturnEvents Stored Procedure

Add a new report named "Events," use the "rpt.ReturnEvents" stored procedure, and remember to configure the Dataset and report parameters. Add the alternating row shading we demonstrated in the Errors report. The same expression will work in the Events report:

```
=Iif(RowNumber(Nothing) Mod 2 = 0,"White","WhiteSmoke")
```

Return to the Application Instance Report and add another column to the data table. Label it "Events" and set the data grid value to "Events" as well. Open the Text Box Properties for the Events data field and navigate to the Font page. Change the Color property to "Blue" and the Effects property to "Underline." On the Actions page, change the "Enable as an action" property to "Go to report" and the "Specify a report" dropdown to "Events." Add a parameter mapping and map the "AppInstanceID" parameter Name to the "[AppinstanceID]" parameter Value. Click the "OK" button to close the Text Box Properties Editor. Let's test it!

The Application Instance report now appears, as shown in Figure A-30.

Application Instance

Application	Start Time	Run Time	Status	Packages	Events
SSISApp1	4/26/2012 5:14:18 PM	7	Failed	Packages	Events
SSISApp1	4/26/2012 5:14:01 PM	8	Failed	Packages	Events
SSISApp1	4/26/2012 1:21:24 PM	8	Failed	Packages	Events
SSISApp1	4/26/2012 11:07:20 AM	64	Success	Packages	Events
SSISApp1	4/26/2012 11:04:41 AM	25016	Running	Packages	Events

Figure A-30. *The New and Improved Application Instance Report*

Clicking the Events hyperlink takes us to the Events report, which should be to similar the report shown in Figure A-31.

Events

Application	Package	Source	Event Time	Description
SSISApp1	ErrorTest.dtsx	Log Package Variables	4/26/2012 11:08:21 AM	ChildPackagePath: F:\SSIS 2012 Design Patterns \SSISConfig2012\SSISConfig2012\ErrorTest.dtsx AppPackageID: 3 PkgInstanceID: 4
SSISApp1	Child2.dtsx	Log Package Variables	4/26/2012 11:08:18 AM	ChildPackagePath: F:\SSIS 2012 Design Patterns \SSISConfig2012\SSISConfig2012\Child2.dtsx AppPackageID: 2 PkgInstanceID: 3
SSISApp1	Child1.dtsx	Log Package Variables	4/26/2012 11:07:20 AM	ChildPackagePath: F:\SSIS 2012 Design Patterns \SSISConfig2012\SSISConfig2012\Child1.dtsx AppPackageID: 1 PkgInstanceID: 2

Figure A-31. *The Events Report for an Application Instance*

This latest round of reports and updates to the Application Instance report reinforce its status as the Operational Intelligence Dashboard. Similar changes can be made to the Package Instance report. Let's add the "Failed" link functionality and the "Events" column now.

On the Package Instance report, open the Text Box Properties for the "Status" data field. As we did for the "Status" data field in the Application Instance report, navigate to the Font page and click the f(x) button beside the Color property dropdown. In the "Set expression for: Color" textbox, enter the following expression:

```
=Iif(Fields!Status.Value = "Failed", "Blue", "Black")
```

This expression will change the color of the Status text blue if the Status is "Failed." Click the f(x) button beside the Effects property dropdown. In the "Set expression for: TextDecoration" textbox, add the following expression:

```
=Iif(Fields!Status.Value = "Failed", "Underline", "Default")
```

As with the Application Instance report, this expression will decorate a "Failed" status with an underline. This and the previous property combine to make "Failed" status appear as a hyperlink. Where does the hyperlink take us? Let's configure that property now. Navigate to the Action page and select the "Go to report" option for the "Enable as an action" property. Click the f(x) button beside the "Specify a report" dropdown and add the following expression to the "Set expression for: ReportName" textbox:

```
=Iif(Fields!Status.Value = "Failed", "Errors", Nothing)
```

Click the "Add" button and map the "AppInstanceID" parameter Name to the "[AppInstanceID]" parameter Value. Click the "Add" button again and map the "PkgInstanceID" parameter Name to the "[PkgInstanceID]" parameter Value. Click the f(x) button in the "Omit" column of each parameter mapping and add the following expression to each "Set expression for: Omit" textbox:

```
=Iif(Fields!Status.Value = "Failed", False, True)
```

As with the Application Instance report, the two previous property settings configure the Action property of the Status value. If the Status is "Failed," clicking the word "Failed," which will appear to be a hyperlink, will cause the Errors report to display. When it displays, it will only show those error rows associated with the Application Instance displayed in that row of data.

Let's test it! When we run the Package Instance report, it now appears as shown in Figure A-32.

Package Instance

Application	Package	Start Time	Run Time	Status
SSISApp1	ErrorTest.dtsx	4/26/2012 5:14:23 PM	2	Failed
SSISApp1	Child2.dtsx	4/26/2012 5:14:19 PM	4	Success
SSISApp1	Child1.dtsx	4/26/2012 5:14:18 PM	1	Success
SSISApp1	ErrorTest.dtsx	4/26/2012 5:14:06 PM	3	Failed
SSISApp1	Child2.dtsx	4/26/2012 5:14:03 PM	3	Success
SSISApp1	Child1.dtsx	4/26/2012 5:14:02 PM	1	Success
SSISApp1	ErrorTest.dtsx	4/26/2012 1:21:29 PM	3	Failed
SSISApp1	Child2.dtsx	4/26/2012 1:21:26 PM	3	Success
SSISApp1	Child1.dtsx	4/26/2012 1:21:24 PM	2	Success
SSISApp1	ErrorTest.dtsx	4/26/2012 11:08:21 AM	3	Success
SSISApp1	Child2.dtsx	4/26/2012 11:08:18 AM	3	Success
SSISApp1	Child1.dtsx	4/26/2012 11:07:20 AM	57	Success
SSISApp1	Child1.dtsx	4/26/2012 11:04:42 AM	26417	Running

Figure A-32. *Failed "Hyperlinks" for the Package Instance Report*

Clicking a "Failed" "link" takes us to the Errors report for that Package Instance. Cool. Now let's add the "Events" column to the Package Instance report. Add a column with the header and data field hard-coded "Events." Open the Text Box Properties for the "Events" data field and navigate to the Font page. Set the Color property to "Blue" and the Effects property to "Underline." Navigate to the Action page and set the "Enable as an action" property to "Go to report." Select the Events report from the "Specify a report" dropdown and click the "Add" button twice to map two parameters. Map the "AppInstanceID" parameter Name to the "[AppInstanceID]" parameter Value and the "PkgInstanceID" parameter Name to the "[PkgInstanceID]" parameter Value. Close the Text Box Properties window and click the Preview tab to test. Your Package Instance report should appear as shown in Figure A-33.

Package Instance

Application	Package	Start Time	Run Time	Status	Events
SSISApp1	ErrorTest.dtsx	4/26/2012 5:14:23 PM	2	Failed	Events
SSISApp1	Child2.dtsx	4/26/2012 5:14:19 PM	4	Success	Events
SSISApp1	Child1.dtsx	4/26/2012 5:14:18 PM	1	Success	Events
SSISApp1	ErrorTest.dtsx	4/26/2012 5:14:06 PM	3	Failed	Events
SSISApp1	Child2.dtsx	4/26/2012 5:14:03 PM	3	Success	Events
SSISApp1	Child1.dtsx	4/26/2012 5:14:02 PM	1	Success	Events
SSISApp1	ErrorTest.dtsx	4/26/2012 1:21:29 PM	3	Failed	Events
SSISApp1	Child2.dtsx	4/26/2012 1:21:26 PM	3	Success	Events
SSISApp1	Child1.dtsx	4/26/2012 1:21:24 PM	2	Success	Events
SSISApp1	ErrorTest.dtsx	4/26/2012 11:08:21 AM	3	Success	Events
SSISApp1	Child2.dtsx	4/26/2012 11:08:18 AM	3	Success	Events
SSISApp1	Child1.dtsx	4/26/2012 11:07:20 AM	57	Success	Events
SSISApp1	Child1.dtsx	4/26/2012 11:04:42 AM	26417	Running	Events

Figure A-33. *The finished Package Instance Report*

Clicking the "Events" link will take us to the Events report and display only the events for the Package Instance on the referenced row.

To wrap it up, you can start at the Application Instance report; it is on the dashboard. You can click the Packages "link" to view all the SSIS Child Packages that executed as part of the selected SSIS Application Instance. From there, you can drill into the Errors report and observe the errors that caused a Package to fail, or you can view all of the events recorded by the OnInformation event handler for the selected Package Instance on the Events report. You can reach all errors and events for an SSIS Application Instance from the Application Instance report, as well.

Summary

This isn't an exhaustive example of an SSIS Framework, but it does demonstrate the utility of patterns-based data integration development using SSIS. This framework provides repeatable, metadata-driven SSIS execution without leaving the SSIS and SQL Server database realms. Monitoring is provided by a set of SQL Server Reporting Services reports driven by stored procedures that read metadata automatically captured by the Framework's Parent.dtsx SSIS package. Zero lines of code are required in child packages to capture error and event information, and this information is logged centrally in a consistent format, which makes it perfect for reporting.

Index

■ F, G

■ H

CPSIA information can be obtained at www.ICGtesting.com
Printed in the USA
LVOW03s0240300114

371597LV00004B/79/P